INTERNATIONAL HUMAN RIGHTS

IN A NUTSHELL®

FIFTH EDITION

THOMAS BUERGENTHAL
Former Judge, International Court of Justice
Former President, Inter-American Court of Human Rights
Lobingier Professor Emeritus of Comparative Law and Jurisprudence
The George Washington University

DINAH SHELTON
Manatt/Ahn Professor Emeritus of International Law
The George Washington University Law School
Former Member, Inter-American Commission on Human Rights

DAVID P. STEWART
Professor from Practice
Director, Center on Transnational Business and the Law
Georgetown University Law Center
Former Member, Inter-American Juridical Committee

CARLOS M. VÁZQUEZ
Professor of Law
Georgetown University Law Center
Former Member, UN Committee for the Elimination
of Racial Discrimination
Former Member, Inter-American Juridical Committee

WEST
ACADEMIC
PUBLISHING

Nutshell Series, In a Nutshell and the Nutshell Logo are trademarks registered in the U.S. Patent and Trademark Office.

COPYRIGHT © 1988, 1995 WEST PUBLISHING CO.
© West, a Thomson business, 2002
© 2009 Thomson Reuters
© 2017 LEG, Inc. d/b/a West Academic
    444 Cedar Street, Suite 700
    St. Paul, MN 55101
    1-877-888-1330

West, West Academic Publishing, and West Academic are trademarks of West Publishing Corporation, used under license.

Printed in the United States of America

ISBN: 978-1-63460-598-4

PREFACE

The fifth edition of this book follows the basic format of the previous editions. The purpose of the book remains the same: both to serve as a self-contained introduction to the international law of human rights and to complement other course materials by providing the reader with a concise overview of human rights norms and the institutional context within which they evolve. The book continues to grow in size, however, to take account of many new developments in the field.

The fourth edition was published in 2009. While the geo-political changes that have occurred in the past seven years have been less dramatic than those that took place during the interval between the first and second editions (which saw the collapse of the Soviet empire, the end of the Cold War, and the abolition of apartheid in South Africa), they are nonetheless important in the evolution of international human rights law. As was the case for the interval between the third and fourth editions, continuing internal and international armed conflicts have brought increased attention to the interaction of humanitarian law and international human rights law. In particular, the disastrous civil war in Syria and other conflicts in the Mid-East, Africa and Central Asia) have created humanitarian crises unparalleled since the end of World War II. Human rights and fundamental freedoms remain under threat in every corner of the globe, and the international community continues to struggle to hold individuals accountable for wartime and peacetime atrocities.

At the same time, the international community continues its efforts to strengthen the normative and institutional framework for dealing with human rights problems. The United Nations adopted new agreements addressing forced disappearances and protecting the rights of migrant workers and the disabled. At the regional level, the Council of Europe adopted a Convention against Trafficking in Human Beings, while the African system concluded agreements on the rights of women and the rights and welfare of children. The revised Arab Charter on Human Rights entered into force, while the Association of South-East Asian Nations (ASEAN) adopted a basic treaty containing human rights provisions and also adopted a convention on migrant workers. Institutionally, the United Nations human right treaty bodies have continued to strengthen their monitoring functions while the Office of the UN High Commissioner for Human Rights has further promoted the world-wide enjoyment of human rights through the creation of numerous field offices. The most extensive institutional change came with the replacement of the UN Commission on Human Rights and abolition of its Sub-Commission on the Promotion and Protection of Human Rights. The new UN Human Rights Council, which reports directly to the General Assembly, was elected and began functioning in 2006. At the regional level, the African Court on Human Rights was elected, drafted its rules of procedure, and began hearing cases. It decided numerous matters of its jurisdiction and issued its first merits determination in 2014.

As with the fourth edition, the length of this book has unavoidably grown in order to take account of the continuing expansion of international human rights norms and institutions. Some chapters have been extensively revised, especially those on the United Nations and the regional systems. The chapter on domestic implementation of human rights law in the United States has similarly been updated. We have chosen to omit the discussion of international humanitarian law in preference to a more extensive discussion of the role of non-state actors, particularly non-governmental organizations, in the international field. In short, the revisions take account of many developments and institutions that are new or that have gained greater importance since the publication of the fourth edition.

THOMAS BUERGENTHAL
DINAH SHELTON
DAVID P. STEWART
CARLOS M. VÁZQUEZ

March 2017

ACKNOWLEDGMENTS

A book of this scope is generally the product of efforts beyond those of the authors; this volume is no exception.

Thomas Buergenthal would like to express his profound appreciation to his secretary, Danielle Okandeji-Touffet, for her important contributions to this book. He is also most grateful to the many colleagues, former research assistants and law clerks whose suggestions and helpful memoranda greatly improved the quality of various editions of this book.

Dinah Shelton would like to thank persons at the Council of Europe and the European Court of Human Rights who provided information on recent developments in the European system. Particular thanks are owed to Andrew Drzemczewski, Michael O'Boyle, Caroline Ravaud and Hans Christian Kruger. Similar gratitude must be expressed to Carlos Villan Duran of the Office of the United Nations High Commissioner for Human Rights and to Martin Oelz and Lee Swepston of the International Labour Organization.

David P. Stewart gratefully acknowledges the very able assistance of Erin Reynolds, Andrea Zumbado, and Lisa Marie Passarella for their contributions to this edition.

Carlos M. Vázquez would like to thank Yateesh Begoore Shivaswamy for excellent research assistance, as well as Marie-Joseph Ayissi of the UN Office of the High Commissioner for Human Rights and Gerald Neuman of Harvard Law School for helpful comments.

Finally we would like to thank each other for an exceptionally pleasant collaboration and the opportunity to work together.

FOREWORD

When the first edition of this book was published in 1988, only a handful of American law schools offered courses or seminars on International Human Rights Law. Today a majority do. This development is due to the recognition of the ever more pervasive impact International Human Rights Law has on contemporary international relations and the behavior of states; on the rights of individuals and non- state entities; on international treaties and international legislation as well as customary international law; on the law of international and regional organizations; on the growth and legal status of non-governmental international organizations; on the domestic implementation of international law; and on related subjects. Although International Human Rights Law once played a minor role on the international scene, it has over the years become a major branch of public international law and transformed it and international relations to an extent not previously imagined.

That is also why this edition of the book has more than doubled in size when compared to its first edition. Although I was the sole author of the first two editions of this book, the growth of the subject compelled me to invite Professors Dinah Shelton and David P. Stewart to join me as co-authors for the third, fourth and subsequent editions. This decision resulted not only in an effective scholarly collaboration; it also proved most satisfying on a personal level: we produced a better book and became even better friends. I am delighted now to be able to report that for this, the fifth and subsequent editions of the book, Professor Carlos M. Vázquez of Georgetown Law has agreed to join us as our fourth co-author. I know that his presence will further enrich the quality and scope of this book.

This edition of the book will also be my last one. I have made this decision because I have retired from teaching and because of my age which, to my surprise, has been advancing from edition to edition. This Nutshell has been the love of my academic publications because of my lifelong commitment to the promotion of international human rights through education and scholarship. I know that my co-authors will continue to produce subsequent editions of this book with the same commitment to high quality scholarship and sound educational standards. I wish them well and thank them for their friendship and kindness.

THOMAS BUERGENTHAL

March 2017

OUTLINE

TABLE OF CASES

References are to Pages

TABLE OF AUTHORS

References are to Pages

INTERNATIONAL HUMAN RIGHTS

IN A NUTSHELL®

FIFTH EDITION

CHAPTER 1

HISTORICAL ANTECEDENTS OF INTERNATIONAL HUMAN RIGHTS LAW

I. INTRODUCTION

This chapter describes the principal historical antecedents of the modern international law of human rights. As used in this book, the international law of human rights is defined as the law concerned with the protection of individuals and groups against violations of their internationally guaranteed rights, and with the promotion of these rights. This branch of the law is sometimes also referred to as the international protection of human rights or international human rights law. Although scholars might disagree over whether one or the other of these labels is more appropriate, they are used interchangeably in this book.

II. PRE-WORLD WAR II LAW

§ 1–1. INTRODUCTION

International human rights law has its historical antecedents in several international legal doctrines and institutions. *See generally* L. Henkin, *The Age of Rights* 13 (1990). The most important of these are humanitarian intervention, state responsibility for injuries to aliens, protection of minorities, the Mandates and Minorities Systems of the League of Nations, and international humanitarian law. To the extent that these doctrines and institutions survive today, they may be said to form an integral part of contemporary international human rights law. We address them in this chapter principally for the purpose of exploring the role they played in the development of that law.

§ 1–2. HUMAN RIGHTS AND TRADITIONAL INTERNATIONAL LAW

International law was defined traditionally as the law governing relations between nation-states exclusively. This meant that only states were subjects of and had legal rights and duties under international law. The classic definition was expanded somewhat after World War I to include various newly created intergovernmental organizations, which were acknowledged to have some very limited international legal personality. Human beings were not deemed to have international legal rights as such; they were said to be *objects* rather than *subjects* of international law. To the extent that states had any international legal obligations towards individuals, they were deemed to be obligations owed to the states whose nationality the individuals possessed. *See, e.g.*, Oppenheim, *International Law: A Treatise* p. 16 (9th ed. 1992) (edited by Jennings and Watts).

The traditional theories about the nature of international law compelled the conclusion that the manner in which a state treated its own nationals was not regulated by international law because it did not affect the rights of other states. The entire subject-matter was deemed to fall within the exclusive domestic jurisdiction of each state, barring other states from interceding or intervening on behalf of the nationals of any state which maltreated them.

Yet, there were some exceptions to this rule. They are addressed in the sections that follow. Additionally, it is important to recall the moral and philosophical antecedents of international human rights law in natural law theory. Even while early international law was understood to only cover state to state relations, natural law theorists posited certain limitations on the absolute nature of sovereignty. Hugo Grotius' conception of international law was based on the natural law theory. *See* Grotius, *The Rights of War and Peace (2005 ed.) vol. 1 (Book I)* [1625]. John Locke later maintained that a sovereign who violated natural law could be justifiably overthrown. *See* Locke, *Two Treatises of Government,* Chapter 13, § 149. The influence of natural law can be seen in many early documents asserting individual rights, such as the Magna Carta (1215), the French Declaration on the Rights of Man and Citizen (1789), and the American Declaration of Independence (1776), each of which rejected the absolute power of the sovereign on the basis of certain unalienable rights, the existence of which was declared to be self-evident.

§ 1–3. HUMANITARIAN INTERVENTION

The doctrine of humanitarian intervention, as expounded by some early international legal scholars, including Hugo Grotius in the 17th century, recognized as lawful the use of force by one or more states to stop the maltreatment by a state of its own nationals when that conduct was so brutal and large-scale as to shock the conscience of the community of nations. *See* E.C. Stowell, *Intervention in International Law* 53 (1921); L. Sohn & T. Buergenthal, *International Protection of Human Rights* 137 (1973). This doctrine was greatly misused and frequently served as a pretext for the occupation or invasion of weaker countries. Nevertheless, the doctrine of humanitarian intervention was the first to give expression to the proposition that there are some limits to the freedom states enjoyed under international law in the treatment of their own nationals. *See generally* F. Teson, *Humanitarian Intervention: An Inquiry into Law and Morality* (3d ed. 2005); G.P. Fletcher, *Defending Humanity: When Force is Justified and Why* (2008); E. Bruch, *Human Rights and Humanitarian Intervention: Law and Practice in the Field* (2016).

Contemporary arguments about the rights of international organizations or groups of states to use force, if necessary, to put an end to massive violations of human rights have been justified at times by reference to this doctrine. *See, e.g.*, N. Wheeler, *Saving Strangers: Humanitarian Intervention in International Society* (2000); S. Murphy, *Humanitarian Intervention* (1996); T. Franck, *Recourse to Force* (2002). The NATO military action in Kosovo in 1999 revived debates over the legality of unilateral and multilateral humanitarian intervention. *See* J.L. Holzbrefe & R.O. Keohane, eds.

Humanitarian Intervention: Ethical, Legal and Political Dilemmas (2003); M.P. Marchak, *No Easy Fix: Global Responses to Internal Wars and Crimes Against Humanity* (2008). Despite the on-going controversy, state practice in some regions supports the doctrine. For example, the Constitutive Act of the African Union, adopted July 11, 2000 (entry into force May 26, 2001), explicitly recognizes the right of the Union to intervene in a member state pursuant to a decision of the Assembly in respect of "grave circumstances, namely: war crimes, genocide and crimes against humanity." Constitutive Act of the African Union, art. 4(h).

Since the end of the Cold War, the United Nations Security Council has increasingly taken action to respond to large-scale violations of human rights by authorizing enforcement measures pursuant to its powers under Chapter VII of the UN Charter. This chapter applies to situations involving a "threat to the peace, breach of the peace, or act of aggression." UN Charter, art. 39. The Security Council has adopted decisions relating to the Kurds and other civilians in Iraq, the former Yugoslavia, Haiti, Sierra Leone, East Timor, and the Darfur region of the Sudan, as well as Libya, Côte d'Ivoire and the Central African Republic. Because the resolutions authorizing these measures are ambiguous in terms of the legal norms and factual considerations giving rise to them, it may be premature to assert that the Security Council has adopted a modern version of the doctrine of collective humanitarian intervention. Considering, however, that its recent decisions contain important characteristics traditionally associated with this doctrine, it appears that the Council has moved in that direction. *See* Brown, "Humanitarian Intervention at a Crossroads," 41 Wm. & Mary L. Rev. 1683 (2000); Delbrück, "A More Effective International Law or a New World Law?—Some Aspects of the Development of International Law in a Changing International System," 68 Ind. L. J. 705, 707 (1993). *See also* Hutchinson, "Restoring Hope: U.N. Security Council Resolutions for Somalia and an Expanded Doctrine of Humanitarian Intervention," 34 Harv. Int'l L.J. 624 (1993); R. Higgins, Problems and Progress: International Law and How We Use it 245–48 (1996). *See generally* Mohamed, "Restructuring the Debate on Unauthorized Humanitarian Intervention," 88 N.C. L. Rev. 1275, 1282–1289 (2010); C.C. Joyner, *"The Responsibility to Protect": Humanitarian Concern and the Lawfulness of Armed Intervention*, 47 Va. J. Int'l L. 693 (2007); Levitt, "Pro-Democratic Intervention in Africa," 24 Wis. Int'l L.J. 785 (2006); Young Sok Kim, "Responsibility to Protect, Humanitarian Intervention and North Korea," 5 J. Int'l Bus. & L. 74 (2006); A. Bellamy and T. Dunne, *The Oxford Handbook of the Responsibility to Protect* (2016). For more on the Responsibility to Protect, *see infra* § 2–22(2).

The establishment by the Security Council of various *ad hoc* international tribunals, including the International Tribunals for the Former Yugoslavia and for Rwanda and the mixed war crimes tribunals for Sierra Leone and Cambodia, to punish those responsible for crimes against humanity, genocide and war crimes committed in those regions may also be seen as a modern form of collective humanitarian intervention in response to massive human rights violations. *See* Weisbord, "Judging Aggression," 50 Colum. J. Transnat'l L. 82, 160 (2011); Buergenthal, "The Evolving International Human Rights System," 100 Am. J. Int'l L. (2006); Meron, "International Criminalization of Internal Atrocities," 89 Am. J. Int'l L. 554 (1995). On this subject, *see also* Article 41 of the International Law Commission's articles on state responsibility, adopted in 2001. Report of the International Law Commission, GAOR, Supp. No. 10 (A/56/10) at 277–94.

§ 1–4. EARLY HUMAN RIGHTS TREATIES

It is a well-established principle of international law that a state may limit its sovereignty by treaty and thus internationalize a subject that would otherwise not be regulated by international law. For example, if one state concludes a treaty with another state in which they agree to treat their nationals in a humane manner and to accord them certain human rights, they have, to the extent of the agreement, internationalized that particular subject. *See* Henkin, "Human Rights and 'Domestic Jurisdiction'," *in* T. Buergenthal (ed.), *Human Rights, International Law and the Helsinki Accord* 21 (1977). Neither of the two states can thenceforth lawfully assert that the treatment of its own nationals is a subject exclusively within its domestic jurisdiction. Advisory Opinion on Nationality Decrees Issued in Tunis and Morocco, P.C.I.J., Ser. B, No. 4 (1923).

This principle has been extremely important in the development of international human rights law and the gradual internationalization of human rights. Buergenthal, "Domestic Jurisdiction, Intervention and Human Rights," *in* P. Brown & D. MacLean (eds.), *Human Rights and U.S. Foreign Policy* 111 (1979). Although the internationalization process continues to this day every time a human rights treaty enters into force, it began in the 19th century with the conclusion of treaties to ban the slave trade and international agreements to protect Christian minorities in the Ottoman (Turkish) Empire. *See, e.g.,* Treaty of Paris of 30 March 1856; Treaty of Berlin of 13 July 1878. *See generally* Jenny S. Martinez, *The Slave Trade and the Origins of International Human Rights Law* (2012). The latter treaties were relied upon by the states comprising the Concert of Europe to intercede diplomatically and at times even to intervene militarily on behalf of the Christian populations in the Turkish Empire. *See* Sohn & Buergenthal, *supra*, at 143–92. The Treaty of Berlin of 1878 is of particular interest because of the special legal status it accorded to some religious groups; it also served as a model for the Minorities System that was subsequently established within the framework of the League of Nations.

§ 1–5. THE LEAGUE OF NATIONS

The Covenant of the League of Nations, the 1920 treaty that established the League and served as its constitution, contained no general provisions dealing with human rights. The notion that human rights should be internationally protected had not yet gained acceptance by the community of nations, nor was it seriously contemplated by those who drafted that treaty, despite efforts by Japan to have the principle of equality and non-discrimination included in the text. The Covenant did, however, contain two provisions (Articles 22 and 23) that bear on the development of international human rights law. The League also played an important role in helping with the implementation of post-World War I treaties for the protection of minorities.

1. The Mandates System

Article 22 of the Covenant established the Mandates System of the League. This provision applied only to the former colonies of the states that had lost the First World War. It transformed these colonies into League Mandates to be administered by the victorious powers. The latter agreed with the League to administer the territories pursuant to "the principle that the well-being and development of [the native] peoples form a sacred trust of civilization. . ." The Mandatory Powers also undertook to provide the League with annual reports bearing on the discharge of their responsibilities. These reports were reviewed by the Mandates Commission of the League.

The Mandates Commission gradually acquired more power in supervising the administration of the Mandates and the manner in which the native populations were treated. *See generally* Sohn & Buergenthal, *supra,* at 337–73. The dissolution of the League ended this development. In its stead, the United Nations established the UN Trusteeship

System, which was entrusted with supervisory power over the remaining eleven Mandates and other non-self-governing territories. Among the last of these territories to gain independence (in 1990) was Namibia. It had been administered by South Africa under the South-West Africa Mandate. South Africa had for many years refused to comply with U.N. General Assembly and Security Council resolutions calling on it to relinquish control over Namibia. The bitter dispute between the U.N. and South Africa concerning Namibia generated considerable litigation before the International Court of Justice. *See* Advisory Opinion on the International Status of South-West Africa, 1950 I.C.J. Rep. 128; Advisory Opinion on Voting Procedure, 1955 I.C.J. Rep. 67; Advisory Opinion on Hearings of Petitioners, 1956 I.C.J. Rep. 23; Ethiopia and Liberia v. South Africa (Preliminary Objections), 1962 I.C.J. Rep. 319; Ethiopia and Liberia v. South Africa (Judgment), 1966 I.C.J. Rep. 6; Advisory Opinion on the Legal Consequences for States of the Continued Presence of South Africa in Namibia, 1971 I.C.J. Rep. 16. For an analysis of these cases and the relevant resolution, *see* L. Sohn, *Rights in Conflict: The United Nations and South Africa* 24–31 and 148–49 (1994). *See also* Schwelb, "The International Court of Justice and the Human Rights Clauses of the Charter," 66 Am. J. Int'l L. 337 (1972).

By 1994, all Trust Territories had attained self-governing status or independence, either as separate States or by joining neighboring independent countries.

2. International Labor Standards

Article 23 of the League of Nations Covenant concerned human rights in that it dealt, *inter alia*, with questions relating to the "fair and humane conditions of labour for men, women, and children." It also envisaged the establishment of an international organization to promote this objective. That function was assumed by the International Labor Organization, which came into being at about the same time as the League. The ILO survived the League and is now one of the Specialized Agencies of the United Nations. *See* § 2–29, *infra*. The legislative activities and the supervisory machinery established by the ILO to promote and monitor compliance with international labor standards have made important contributions over the years to the improvement of conditions of work and the development of international human rights law. *See* C.W. Jenks, *Human Rights and International Labour Standards* (1960); V. Leary, *International Labour Conventions and National Law* (1981); H.J. Bartolomei de la Cruz et al., *The International Labour Organization: The International Standards System & Basic Human Rights* (1996); Ho, "The International Labour Organization's Role in Nationalizing the International Movement to Abolish Child Labor," 7 Chi. J. Int'l L. 337 (2006); L.R. Helfer, *Understanding Change in International Organizations: Globalization and Innovation in the ILO* (2006); S. Kott and J. Droux (eds.), *Globalizing Social Rights: The International Labour Organization and Beyond* (2013).

For a discussion of the increasing relevance of international labor standards for contemporary trade agreements, including the North American Free Trade Agreement (NAFTA) and the World Trade Organization (WTO), *see* Summers, "The Battle in Seattle: Free Trade, Labor Rights, and Societal Values," 22 U. Pa. J. Int'l Econ. L. 61 (Spring 2001); Mansoor, "Laughter and Tears of Developing Countries: The WTO and the Protection of International Labor Standards," 14-SUM Currents: Int'l Trade L.J 60 (2004); Manley, "International Labor Standards in Free Trade Agreements of the Americas," 18 Emory Int'l L. Rev. 85 (2004).

3. The Minorities System

The League of Nations also played a very important role in developing an international system for the protection of minorities. *See generally* Sohn & Buergenthal, *supra,* at 213. This subject was not regulated by the Covenant. Instead, the League derived its powers in this field from a series of treaties concluded after World War I. One consequence of that war was a substantial redrawing of the political map of Europe and the Middle East. A number of new states came into being and others regained their independence. Some of these countries, notably Poland, Czechoslovakia, Hungary, Yugoslavia, Bulgaria, Albania and Romania, included pockets of ethnic, linguistic and religious minorities. These minorities had good historical reasons for fearing that the new political order would threaten their cultural survival. The governments of the victor nations—the so-called Principal Allied and

Associated Powers—insisted therefore that the new states conclude special treaties for the protection of their ethnic, linguistic and religious minorities. *See generally* H. Hannum, *Autonomy, Sovereignty and Self-Determination* 52 (rev. ed. 1996).

The first treaty to establish this protective regime was the Treaty between the Principal Allied and Associated Powers and Poland, signed at Versailles on June 29, 1919. It served as a model for the other treaties. In these treaties, the states to which the minorities system applied undertook not to discriminate against members of the protected minorities and to grant them the rights necessary for the preservation of their ethnic, religious or linguistic integrity, including the right to the official use of their languages, the right to maintain their schools, and the right to practice their religions. To ensure compliance, the treaties contained provisions similar to Article 12 of the Polish treaty, which declared that "Poland agrees that the stipulations in the foregoing Articles, so far as they affect persons belonging to racial, religious or linguistic minorities, constitute obligations of international concern and shall be placed under the guarantee of the League of Nations."

The League of Nations agreed to serve as guarantor of the obligations the parties assumed in these treaties. It exercised that function by developing a system for dealing with petitions by minorities charging violations of their rights. That system was relatively effective and quite advanced for its time. The petitions were reviewed by a

Committee of Three of the League Council, the states concerned were given an opportunity to present their views and, when appropriate, the Permanent Court of International Justice was asked to render advisory opinions on disputed questions of law. *See generally* J. Stone, *International Guarantees of Minority Rights* (1934). *See also* Advisory Opinion on Minority Schools in Albania, P.C.I.J., Ser. A/B, No. 64 (1935); Advisory Opinion on Access to German Minority Schools in Upper Silesia, P.C.I.J., Ser. A/B, No. 40 (1931); Advisory Opinion on Greco-Bulgarian "Communities," P.C.I.J., Ser. B, No. 17 (1930). In addition, the League served as guarantor for certain special political arrangements that also provided for the protection of the rights of minorities. *See, e.g.,* Advisory Opinion on the Consistency of Certain Danzig Legislative Decrees with the Constitution of the Free City, P.C.I.J., Ser. A/B, No. 65 (1935), an important case that examines the meaning of "law" in the context of the Nazi takeover of Danzig.

Although some isolated minorities arrangements of the League era survive to this day, the League's minorities system as such died with the League. *See generally* T. Modeen, *The International Protection of National Minorities in Europe* (1969); I.L. Claude, *National Minorities: An International Problem* (1955). It is important to recognize nevertheless that some modern international human rights institutions bear considerable resemblance to the institutions that were first developed by the League for the administration of the minorities system.

For many years after their establishment, the United Nations and other international organizations showed very little interest in the protection of minorities, focusing instead on individual rights, non-discrimination and equal protection. With the end of the Cold War and the rise of nationalism in various parts of the world, the international community began again to focus on the development of international norms and institutions designed to protect the rights of minorities. Efforts to lay the normative foundation for a system that would accomplish this objective were initiated in the United Nations with the adoption by the General Assembly of the 1992 Declaration on the Rights of Persons Belonging to National or Ethnic, Religious and Linguistic Minorities. *See generally* Thornberry, "The UN Declaration on the Rights of Persons Belonging to National or Ethnic, Religious and Linguistic Minorities: Background, Analysis and Observations," *in* A. Phillips & A. Rosas (eds.), *The UN Minority Rights Declaration* 11 (1993).

Within Europe, the Organization on Security and Cooperation in Europe pioneered in taking measures to protect minorities with the 1990 Copenhagen Concluding Document and a number of later OSCE instruments on the subject, culminating in 1992 with the establishment of the office of the OSCE High Commissioner for National Minorities. *See* Foundation on Inter-Ethnic Relations, *The Role of the High Commissioner on National Minorities in OSCE Conflict Prevention* (1997). The Council of Europe followed with the adoption in 1994 of the Framework Convention for the Protection of National Minorities.

See Klebes, "The Council of Europe's Framework Convention for the Protection of Minorities," 16 Hum. Rts. L.J. 92 (1995). Some of the actions taken in this regard within the framework of the United Nations, the Council of Europe, and the OSCE are discussed in §§ 2–13, 3–20 and 3–32, *infra.*

§ 1–6. STATE RESPONSIBILITY FOR INJURY TO ALIENS

Traditional international law recognized very early that states had an obligation to treat foreign nationals in a manner that conformed to certain minimum standards of civilization or justice. Because human beings as such were not recognized as holders of rights under international law, this obligation was deemed to be owed to the state of the individual's nationality. Hence, when individuals were subjected by a foreign government to treatment falling short of the minimum standards, the state of their nationality was considered to have a cause of action under international law against the offending state. Mavrommatis Palestine Concessions (Jurisdiction), P.C.I.J., Ser. A, No. 2 (1934). When damages were awarded, however, the successful state usually compensated its nationals for the damages they had sustained, although international law did not require such payment.

Disputes involving claims under the law of state responsibility for injuries to aliens were commonly resolved through diplomatic negotiations between the governments concerned. Sometimes the failure of the offending state to comply with demands for satisfaction, usually the payment of compensation, led to the use of force. For discussion of some of these cases, *see* Sohn & Buergenthal, *supra,* at 40. More often than not, however, the disputes were resolved by diplomatic means, international arbitration or adjudication. For the relevant legal doctrines, *see* E.M. Borchard, *The Diplomatic Protection of Citizens Abroad or the Law of International Claims* (Reprint 2003); C.F. Amerasinghe, *State Responsibility for Injuries to Aliens* (1967); R.M. Lillich, *International Law of State Responsibility for Injuries to Aliens* (1983); J. Crawford, *State Responsibility: The General Part* (Cambridge Studies in International and Comparative Law) (2014).

The principle that the injury suffered by the alien abroad was an injury to the state of the alien's nationality preserved the notion that only states were subjects of international law. It also had the negative consequence of leaving stateless persons and those who possessed the nationality of the offending state without protection. No state had standing to espouse their claims because no state could validly claim that its rights were affected when these human beings were injured.

The substantive law applicable to claims by states on behalf of their nationals was derived for the most part from so-called "general principles of law recognized by civilized nations." *See* I.C.J. Statute, art. 38 (1)(c). These principles had their source in natural law and various domestic legal doctrines applicable to the treatment of individuals. International arbitrators and tribunals drew on this body of law and doctrine to give substance to concepts such as "denial of justice" and "minimum standards of justice." When modern international law came to recognize that individuals, irrespective of their nationality, should enjoy certain basic human rights, the substantive principles of the law of state responsibility provided a reservoir of norms that could be drawn upon in codifying international human rights law. Today, because of the dramatic evolution and extensive codification of human rights law, human rights law nourishes the law of state responsibility.

It is important to remember, as the *Restatement of the Foreign Relations Law of the United States (Third)* (1987) [hereinafter cited as *Restatement (Third)*] aptly noted, that "the difference in history and in jurisprudential origins between the older law of responsibility for injury to aliens and the newer law of human rights should not conceal their essential affinity and their convergence." Introductory Note to Part VII, *id.*, vol. 2, at 145. The *Restatement* went on to point out that "as the law of human rights developed, the law of responsibility for injury to aliens, as applied to natural persons, began to refer to violations of their 'fundamental human rights,' and states began to invoke contemporary norms of human rights as the basis for claims for injury to their nationals." *Id.*, at 1058. *See generally* F.V. Garcia-Amador, L. Sohn & R. Baxter, *Recent Codification of the Law of State Responsibility for Injuries to Aliens* (1974).

The law of state responsibility for injuries to aliens continues to play an important role in contemporary diplomatic relations. In 2001, the International Law Commission adopted a set of articles on the Responsibility of States for Internationally Wrongful Acts. The UN General Assembly took note of the articles and commended them to the attention of governments. G.A. Res. 56/83, U.N. Doc. A/RES/56/83 (Dec. 12, 2001). The ILC also adopted draft articles on diplomatic protection in 2006. Report of the International Commission, GAOR, Supp. No. 10 (A/61/10) at 16 (2006).

States still espouse the claims of their nationals, be they natural persons or corporations, in some instances bringing claims to the International Court of Justice. The Case Concerning Ahmadou Sadio Diallo (Rep. of Guinea v. DRC), 2010 I.C.J. Rep. (Nov. 30), was based in part on customary international norms of state responsibility. In contrast, the Case Concerning Application of the International Convention on the Elimination of All Forms of Racial Discrimination (Georgia v. Russian Federation), 2011 I.C.J. Rep 70 (April 1), was based on one of the core UN human rights treaties. *See infra* § 2–14. Other cases of diplomatic protection have been filed with human rights bodies. *See* Nicaragua v. Costa Rica, Rep. No. 11/07, Interstate Case 01/06, Inter-Am. Comm. H.R., March 8, 2006.

Many state responsibility and diplomatic protection claims are based on the growing number of bilateral and multilateral investment treaties and on so-called treaties of friendship, commerce and navigation (FCN treaties). These treaties frequently confer jurisdiction on existing or *ad hoc* international tribunals to resolve disputes relating to the application or interpretation of these agreements and thus provide an international remedy which may in some cases be more effective than available human rights procedures. *See generally* D. Shelton, *Remedies in International Human Rights Law* (3rd ed. 2015). For a modern case involving a bilateral treaty between the United States and Italy, *see* Case Concerning Elettronica Sicula S.p.A. (Elsi), 1989 I.C.J. Rep. 15. Sometimes special *ad hoc* tribunals are created to deal with a host of similar disputes. One notable example is the Iran-United States Claims Tribunal, which was established in 1981. *See generally* G. Aldrich, *The Jurisprudence of the Iran-United States Claims Tribunal* (1996); C. Brower & J. Brueschke, *The Iran-United States Claims Tribunal* (1998); R. Lillich & D. Magraw (eds.), *The Iran-United States Claims Tribunal: Its Contribution to the Law of State Responsibility* (1998). Following the Iraqi invasion of Kuwait in 1991, the United Nations Security Council established the United Nations Compensation Commission to adjudicate individual and corporate claims against Iraq arising from its invasion. *See* R. Lillich (ed.), *The United Nations Compensation Commission* (1995); Bederman, "The United Nations Compensation Commission and the Tradition of International Claims Settlement," 27 N.Y.U. J. Int'l L. & Pol. 1 (1994).

§ 1–7. RESPONSIBILITY OF INDIVIDUALS AND OTHER PRIVATE ENTITIES

In the past, international efforts to protect human rights have tended to focus on holding only governments internationally responsible for violations. The gradual recognition that some governments are simply not able (or willing) to protect those within their territory from violations of human rights committed by powerful private actors has motivated the international community to seek ways of holding individual violators responsible. *See* Buergenthal, "The Evolving International Human Rights System," 100 Am. J. Int'l L. 783 (2006); A. Clapham, *Human Rights Obligations of Non-State Actors* (2006); Knox, "Horizontal Human Rights Law," 102 Am. J. Int'l L. 1 (2008); Vázquez, "Direct Vs. Indirect Obligations of Corporations Under International Law," 43 Colum. J. Transnat'l L 927 (2005).

Initial efforts sought accountability of terrorist groups, criminal organizations and, in certain countries, paramilitary groups. Individuals belonging to these groups have often been able to engage in large-scale violations of human rights while enjoying *de facto* immunity (impunity) from prosecution for what in theory at least are criminal acts under the law of the state where these acts take place. *See* N. Roht-Arriaza (ed.), *Impunity and Human Rights in International Law and Practice* (1997). While various principles of international criminal law permitted the imposition of individual responsibility for international crimes, no international tribunals with jurisdiction to apply that law existed following the dissolution of the Nuremberg and Tokyo War Crimes Tribunals. For a compilation of applicable international norms, *see* A. Cassese, *International Criminal Law* (3rd ed. 2013); D. Stewart, *International Criminal Law in a Nutshell* (2013); D. Luban, J. O'Sullivan, D. Stewart, *International and Transnational Criminal Law* (2nd ed. 2014).

This situation began to change in 1993 and 1994 with the establishment by the United Nations Security Council of the International Criminal Tribunals for the Former Yugoslavia and for Rwanda, which were granted jurisdiction over crimes against humanity, genocide, and war crimes committed in those territories. *See* J. Jones, *The Practice of the International Criminal Tribunals for the Former Yugoslavia and Rwanda* (2d. ed. 2000); T. Meron, *War Crimes Law Comes of Age* 210 (1998). In 1998, a diplomatic conference convened by the United Nations adopted the Statute of the permanent International Criminal Court. *See generally* R. Lee (ed.), *The International Criminal Court: The Making of the Rome Statute* (1999); M.C. Bassiouni (ed.), *The Statute of the International Criminal Court: A Documentary History* (1998). The Statute entered into force on July 1, 2002 and the prosecutor's office began investigating allegations of international criminal conduct in Uganda, the Democratic Republic of the Congo, the Central African Republic and Sudan. The first three situations were referred by the governments themselves, while the U.N. Security Council asked the office to investigate the situation in the Sudan. Some dozen indictments resulted, including one against the sitting Sudanese head of state. *See* Warrant of Arrest for Omar Hassan Ahmad Al Bashir, No. ICC–020–5–01/09 (Mar. 4, 2009). *See generally* Jorda, "Reflections on the First Years of the International Criminal Court," 36 Hofstra L. Rev. 239, 239 (2007). For additional background, *see* W. Schabas, *An Introduction to the International Criminal Court* (5th ed. 2017).

The question of human rights obligations of other non-state actors, especially intergovernmental organizations and business entities, has emerged in recent years as these actors have become more active and powerful. *See* Kinley & Chambers, "The UN Human Rights Norms for Corporations: The Private Implications of Public International Law," 6 Hum. Rts. L. Rev. 477 (2006); *see also* Chander, "Googling Freedom," 99 Cal. L. Rev. 1 (2011). While only states are party to human rights treaties, the obligations contained in these agreements usually require the parties to act with due diligence to protect human rights not only against state action, but also against private conduct that violates the guaranteed rights. Velásquez Rodríguez v. Honduras, 4 IA Ct.H.R. (Ser. C)(1988). In 2011, the UN Human Rights Council endorsed the "Guiding Principles on Business and Human Rights," which were developed by John Ruggie, the Special Representative of the Secretary General on the issue of human rights and transnational corporations. While recognizing that states have the primary duty to protect against human rights abuses by private parties, the Guiding

Principles also recognize that business enterprises have a responsibility to respect human rights wherever they operate, a responsibility over and above that imposed by national law, and which exists independently of the states' ability or willingness to fulfill their own human rights obligations. *See generally* Weissbrodt, "Human Rights Standards Concerning Transnational Corporations and Other Business Entities," 23 Minn. J. Int'l L. 135 (2014).

For more on the role of the non-governmental organizations and corporations, *see* Chapter 7, *infra*.

§ 1–8. HUMANITARIAN LAW

Humanitarian law, which might be understood as the human rights component of the law of armed conflict, significantly predates international human rights law. Its origins can be traced to agreements between ancient Egyptians and Sumerians concerning the treatment of prisoners, circa 1400 B.C. In 200 B.C., the Hindu Code of Manu detailed numerous rules applicable during war, such as the prohibition of use of poisoned weapons, the prohibition against killing an enemy attempting to surrender, and the prohibition against attacking those who are badly wounded. Rules governing armed conflict were also found in Sun Tzu's 6th Century B.C. teachings and in the Roman text *Strategica*. The trial of Peter Von Hagenbach in Austria, in 1474, was the first recorded international war crimes prosecution. *See generally* Gary Solis, *The Law of Armed Conflict: International Humanitarian Law in War* (2d ed. 2016).

The modern development of humanitarian law is usually traced to a series of initiatives undertaken in the 19th century by a number of Swiss individuals, who advocated the conclusion of international agreements making certain humanitarian rules applicable in the conduct of war. *See* P. Boissier, *History of the International Committee of the Red Cross: From Solferino to Tsushima* (1985). These initiatives produced the Geneva Convention of 1864, which was designed to protect medical personnel and hospital installations. It also provided that "wounded or sick combatants, to whatever nation they may belong, shall be collected and cared for." (Article 6(1).) For the text of this and other relevant instruments, *see International Red Cross Handbook*, published and periodically updated by the International Committee of the Red Cross. The Geneva Convention of 1864 was followed by the Hague Convention No. III of 1899, which established comparable humanitarian rules applicable to naval warfare. Several provisions in these treaties reflect state practice as it existed before and after their adoption. *See* Meron, "Francis Lieber's Code and Principles of Humanity," 36 Colum. J. Transnat'l L. 269 (1997).

These treaties have been revised, amplified and modernized from time to time and now comprise a vast body of law addressing almost all aspects of modern armed conflict. Much of that law is today codified in the four Geneva Conventions of 1949 and the two 1977 Protocols Additional to these Conventions. *See generally* G. Solis, *supra*; E. Crawford & A. Pert, *International Humanitarian Law* (2015); Y. Dinstein, *The Conduct of Hostilities*

Under the Law of International Armed Conflict (2d ed. 2012); F. Kalshoven, *Constraints on the Waging of War: An Introduction to International Humanitarian Law* (4th ed. 2011); T. Meron, *War Crimes Law Comes of Age* (1998); M. Bothe, K.J. Partsch & W. Solf, *New Rules for Victims of Armed Conflicts: A Commentary on the Two 1977 Protocols Additional to the Geneva Conventions of 1949* (1982); Bassiouni, "The New Wars and the Crisis of Compliance with the Law of Armed Conflict by Non-State Actors," 98 J. Crim. L. & Criminology 711 (2008); Hosni, "The ABCs of the Geneva Conventions and their Applicability to Modern Warfare," 14 New Eng. J. Int'l & Comp. L. 135 (2007).

Although humanitarian law predates the development of international human rights law and had some influence on it, *see, e.g.,* common Article 3 of the Geneva Conventions of 1949, various provisions of the most recent Protocols mirror the principles underlying modern international human rights instruments. *See generally* T. Meron, *Human Rights and Humanitarian Norms as Customary Law* (1989). It is also worth noting that the derogation clauses of the principal international human rights treaties incorporate by reference the humanitarian law treaties and obligations of the state parties thereto. *See* International Covenant on Civil and Political Rights, art. 4; European Convention of Human Rights, art. 15; American Convention on Human Rights, art. 27. In addition, the practice of existing international war crime tribunals has had a substantial impact on the development of international humanitarian law.

§ 1–9. THE PAST AND MODERN INTERNATIONAL HUMAN RIGHTS LAW

Traditional international law developed various doctrines and institutions designed to protect different groups of human beings: slaves, minorities, certain native populations, foreign nationals, victims of massive violations, combatants, etc. That law and practice provided the conceptual and institutional underpinnings for the development of contemporary international human rights law. Moreover, many of the older institutions and doctrines continue to exist side-by-side with, or form an inherent part of, the modern international law of human rights. For certain matters, that law has been profoundly influenced by its antecedents. An awareness of the historical roots of modern international law of human rights will consequently give the reader a deeper understanding of that law. *See, e.g.,* P.G. Lauren, *The Evolution of International Human Rights: Vision Seen* (3rd ed. 2011); S. Moyn, *Human Rights and the Uses of History* (2014).

As we shall see in the chapters that follow, modern international human rights law differs most significantly from its historical antecedents in today recognizing that individual human beings have internationally guaranteed rights as individuals and not as nationals of a particular state. A growing number of international institutions now have jurisdiction to protect individuals against human rights violations committed by their state of nationality as well as by any other state. Although the remedies often remain inadequate or ineffective, the vast body of international human rights law now in existence—as well as the great increase in the number of international institutions designed to implement that law—have internationalized the subject of human rights beyond all expectations. This development has in turn produced a political climate in which the protection of human rights has become one of the most important items on the agenda of contemporary international political discourse involving governments, inter-governmental organizations, and a vast international network of non-governmental organizations.

The end of the Cold War has brought widespread international political acceptance of the proposition that democracy is a precondition for the effective protection of human rights. *See* Carothers, "Democracy and Human Rights: Policy Allies or Rivals?" 17 Wash. Q. 109–20 (1994). This development has led, *inter alia*, to the emergence of "an internationally constituted right to electoral democracy that builds on the human rights canon, but seeks to extend the ambit of protected rights to ensure meaningful participation by the governed in the formal political decisions by which the quality of their lives and societies are shaped." Franck, "Legitimacy and the Democratic Entitlement," *in* G. Fox & B. Roth (eds.), *Democratic Law and International Law* 25, 26 (2000); *see also* Fox, "The Right to Political Participation in International Law," *id.* at 48–90. These rights are reflected in, *inter alia*, article 25 of the International Covenant on Civil and Political Rights, *discussed infra* § 2–7, and the

Inter-American Democratic Charter, *discussed infra* § 4–18.

In the long run, the most important developments in the international human rights field can be attributed to the fact that human beings around the world have increasingly come to believe that states and the international community have an obligation to protect their human rights, be they civil and political rights or economic, social and cultural rights. The expectations that this phenomenon creates make it politically ever more difficult for states to deny the existence of this obligation, which, in turn, facilitates efforts to promote and protect human rights on the international plane. In other words, what we have been witnessing is a human rights revolution. The gains are many, but they remain to be consolidated. Much of the needed law has been enacted, but the national and international institutions to enforce the law are still rather weak. *See* Buergenthal, "The Evolving International Human Rights System," 100 Am J. Int'l L. 783 (2006). One major task that remains is to give "teeth" to the law by strengthening international mechanisms that protect human rights and to extend their reach to all parts of the world.

It must also be kept in mind, however, that progress in the human rights area is greatly hampered in many countries by endemic poverty, illiteracy, corruption and various forms of discrimination that prevent large segments of the population from enjoying their internationally recognized human rights. These scourges cannot be eradicated by law and legal enforcement mechanisms alone. They require international cooperation and development assistance geared to the needs of individual countries, educational programs that focus on the promotion of a culture of human rights, on inter-personal and inter-group tolerance, and on the creation of national and local institutions capable of translating international human rights norms into reality. It is here that international lending and development institutions, such as the World Bank, the International Monetary Fund and regional development banks as well as bilateral governmental assistance agencies and non-governmental aid agencies can play an important role. Some of these agencies have in the past shied away from the adoption of a "human rights policy," fearing that they would be accused of politicizing their mandates. This view changed with the end of the Cold War and the gradual recognition that economic development without democracy and human rights cannot succeed in the long run. As a result, some of these agencies have begun to incorporate human rights objectives into their development programs, and the World Bank has established an Inspection Panel, an independent complaints mechanism for people who believe they have been or will be harmed by a World Bank-funded project. *See* http://ewebapps.worldbank.org/apps/ip/PanelInBrief/English.pdf.

CHAPTER 2

THE UNITED NATIONS HUMAN RIGHTS SYSTEM

I. INTRODUCTION

This chapter examines the human rights provisions of the Charter of the United Nations and provides an overview of the law and institutions that have emerged from the UN framework. These legal norms and institutions derive either from the Charter itself or the human rights treaties adopted under the auspices of the UN or its specialized agencies.

II. THE UN CHARTER

§ 2–1. INTRODUCTION

Modern international human rights law is largely a post-World War II phenomenon. Its development can be attributed to the monstrous violations of human rights committed during the Nazi era and to the belief that these violations and possibly the war itself might have been prevented had an effective international system for the protection of human rights existed in the days of the League of Nations.

President Franklin D. Roosevelt eloquently espoused the international human rights cause as early as 1941. In his famous "Four Freedoms" speech, he called for "a world founded upon four essential human freedoms." These he identified as "freedom of speech and expression," "freedom of every person to worship God in his own way," "freedom from want," and "freedom from fear." Roosevelt's vision of "the moral order," as he characterized it, became the clarion call of the nations that fought the Axis in the Second World War and founded the United Nations. *See* A. Holcombe, *Human Rights in the Modern World* 4–5 (1948); R. Normand & S. Zaidi, *Human Rights at the UN: The Political History of Universal Justice* (2008).

§ 2–2. THE SAN FRANCISCO CONFERENCE AND HUMAN RIGHTS

The human rights provisions that ultimately found their way into the Charter of the United Nations fell far short of the expectations created by Roosevelt's vision and the wartime rhetoric. *See generally* J. Robinson, *Human Rights and Fundamental Freedoms in the Charter of the United Nations: A Commentary* (1946). That was to be expected, for each of the principal victorious powers had troublesome human rights problems of its own. The Soviet Union had its *Gulag*, the United States its *de jure* racial discrimination, France and Great Britain their colonial empires. Given their own gaps in respect for human rights, it was not in the political interest of these countries to draft a Charter that established an effective international system for the protection of human rights, which is what some smaller democratic nations and non-governmental organizations advocated. Although the big powers prevailed to the extent that the San Francisco Conference produced no protective system as such, the UN Charter nevertheless established the legal and conceptual foundation for the development of contemporary international human rights law. Sohn, "The New International Law: Protection of the Rights of Individuals Rather than States," 32 Am. U. L. Rev. 1 (1982). *But cf.* Samuel Moyn, *The Last Utopia* (2010) (tracing the origins of the contemporary human rights movement to events in 1977).

§ 2–3. HUMAN RIGHTS IN THE UN CHARTER

Article 1(3) of the Charter of the United Nations proclaims the following goal as one of the three "purposes" of the UN:

> To achieve international co-operation in solving international problems of an economic, social, cultural, or humanitarian character, and in promoting and encouraging respect for human rights and for fundamental freedoms for all without distinction as to race, sex, language, or religion.

The basic obligations of the United Nations Organization and its Member States in achieving this goal are set out in Articles 55 and 56 of the Charter. These provisions read as follows:

ARTICLE 55

> With a view to the creation of conditions of stability and well-being which are necessary for peaceful and friendly relations among nations based on respect for the principle of equal rights and self-determination of peoples, the United Nations shall promote:

(a) higher standards of living, full employment, and conditions of economic and social progress and development;

(b) solutions of international economic, social, health, and related problems; and international cultural and educational cooperation; and

(c) universal respect for, and observance of, human rights and fundamental freedoms for all without distinction as to race, sex, language, or religion.

ARTICLE 56

All Members pledge themselves to take joint and separate action in co-operation with the Organization for the achievement of the purposes set forth in Article 55.

Although the subject matter mandate spelled out in Article 55 is broad, it confers only limited powers on the Organization. The charge is to "promote" human rights, and that responsibility is assigned to the UN General Assembly and the Economic and Social Council, organs whose resolutions on this subject are not legally binding. The "pledge" of the Member States under Article 56 is limited to the promotion of the "achievement of the purposes set forth in Article 55," that is, "to promote . . . universal respect for, and observance of, human rights and fundamental freedoms. . . ." (Art. 55(c).) Moreover, the UN Charter does not define what is meant by "human rights and fundamental freedoms." Article

55(c) does, however, contain a very unambiguous non-discrimination clause which, when read together with Article 56, makes clear that the Member States and the Organization have an obligation to promote human rights and fundamental freedoms "without distinction as to race, sex, language, or religion."

Article 56 requires Member States "to take joint and separate action in co-operation with the Organization" to accomplish the objectives spelled out in Article 55. To facilitate this cooperation, Article 13(1) of the Charter provides that the General Assembly "shall initiate studies and make recommendations for the purpose of: ... (b) ... assisting in the realization of human rights and fundamental freedoms for all without distinction as to race, sex, language, or religion." The Charter confers similar power on the UN Economic and Social Council (ECOSOC). It authorizes the ECOSOC to "make recommendations for the purpose of promoting respect for, and observance of, human rights and fundamental freedoms for all" and requires it to "set up commissions in economic and social fields and for the promotion of human rights. . . ." (Arts. 62(2) and 68.) The General Assembly, in particular, has been active throughout its history in standard-setting and raising issues of human rights violations taking place in Member States. For its part, the UN Security Council is authorized to take up any dispute or matter that could lead to a threat to peace or a breach of peace (Chapter VI) and to take action whenever it determines the existence of such threat or breach, or an act of aggression (Chapter VII).

Despite their vagueness, the human rights provisions of the UN Charter have had a number of important consequences. First, the UN Charter "internationalized" human rights. That is to say, by adhering to the Charter, which is a multilateral treaty, the States Parties recognized that the "human rights" referred to in it are a subject of international concern and, to that extent, are no longer within their exclusive domestic jurisdiction. *See* § 1–4, *supra.* Although the validity of this proposition was frequently challenged by some states in the early years of the United Nations, the issue is today no longer open to doubt. *See* L. Henkin, *The Age of Rights* 51 (1990).

The fact that a state that has ratified the Charter cannot assert that human rights as a subject falls within its exclusive domestic jurisdiction does not necessarily mean that every infringement of human rights by a Member State of the UN is a matter of international concern. What it does mean is that even in the absence of any other treaty obligations, a state today can no longer assert that the maltreatment of its own nationals, regardless of how massive or systematic, is a matter within its exclusive domestic jurisdiction. For the practice of the UN on this subject, *see* R. Higgins, *The Development of International Law through the Political Organs of the United Nations* 58 (1963); L. Sohn & T. Buergenthal, *International Protection of Human Rights* 556 (1973); L. Sohn, *Rights in Conflict: The United Nations and South Africa* 48 and 63 (1994). *See also* Cassese, "The General Assembly: Historical Perspective 1945–1989," *in* P. Alston (ed.), *The United Nations and*

Human Rights: A Critical Appraisal 25 (1992); Shelton, International Human Rights Law: Principled, Double, or Absent Standards?, 25 Law & Ineq. 467, 470 (2007). *See generally* B. Simma, D.-E. Khan, G. Nolte and A. Paulus, *The United Nations Charter: A Commentary* (3d ed. 2012).

Second, the obligation of the Member States of the UN to cooperate with the Organization in the promotion of human rights and fundamental freedoms has provided the UN with the requisite legal authority to undertake a massive effort to define and codify these rights. That effort is reflected in the adoption of the International Bill of Human Rights, § 2–4, *infra*, and the other core human rights instruments in force today. This vast body of legal norms constitutes a veritable human rights code that gives meaning to the phrase "human rights and fundamental freedoms" and clarifies the obligations imposed by Articles 55 and 56 of the Charter. Buergenthal, "The Normative and Institutional Evolution of International Human Rights Law," 19 Hum. Rts. Q. 703 (1997). *See also* Simma & Alston, "The Sources of Human Rights Law: Custom, Jus Cogens and General Principles," 12 Australian Y.B. Int'l L. 82 (1992). The UN texts are reproduced in a two-volume United Nations publication, entitled *Human Rights: A Compilation of International Instruments* (2006), which is periodically updated.

Third, the Organization has over the years succeeded in clarifying the scope of the Member States' obligation to "promote" human rights and creating UN Charter-based institutions designed to ensure compliance by governments with this obligation. Today it is generally recognized, for example, that a UN Member State that engages in practices amounting to a "consistent pattern of gross violations" of internationally guaranteed human rights is not in compliance with its obligation to "promote . . . universal respect for, and observance of . . . " these rights and that, consequently, it is in violation of the UN Charter. *See* § 2–23 and § 2–25, *infra. See also Restatement (Third)* § 701 and § 702, and the accompanying notes. The UN has sought to enforce this obligation with resolutions calling on specific states to stop such violations and by empowering its human rights bodies to establish procedures to review allegations of violations. *See* Sohn, "Human Rights: Their Implementation and Supervision by the United Nations," *in* T. Meron (ed.), *Human Rights in International Law: Legal and Policy Issues* 368, 384–89 (1984); Rodley & Weissbrodt, "United Nations Non-Treaty Procedures for Dealing with Human Rights," *in* H. Hannum (ed.), *Guide to International Human Rights Practice* 65 (4th. ed. 2004).

III. THE INTERNATIONAL BILL OF HUMAN RIGHTS

§ 2–4. INTRODUCTION

The International Bill of Human Rights consists of the human rights provisions of the UN Charter, the Universal Declaration of Human Rights, and the two International Covenants on Human Rights. *See generally*, Henkin, "The International Bill of Rights:

The Universal Declaration and the Covenants," *in* R. Bernhardt & J.A. Jolowicz (eds.), *International Enforcement of Human Rights* 1 (1987). These instruments will be analyzed in the sections that follow.

Proposals to append a "Bill of Rights" or "Declaration of the Essential Rights of Man" to the Charter were made but not acted upon at the San Francisco Conference. These efforts were revived at the very first meeting of the United Nations. Shortly thereafter, its newly created Commission on Human Rights was charged with drafting "an international bill of human rights." The Commission soon recognized that it would be relatively easy to adopt the text of a hortatory declaration, but that it would prove much more difficult to reach agreement on the wording of a legally binding treaty. The Commission decided, therefore, to work first on a declaration and to take up immediately afterwards the preparation of one or more draft treaties. This approach produced the Universal Declaration of Human Rights, which was adopted by the UN General Assembly on December 10, 1948. UN Gen.Ass.Res. 217A (III). *See generally* N. Robinson, *The Universal Declaration of Human Rights: Its Origin, Significance, and Interpretation* (1958); J. Morsink, *The Universal Declaration of Human Rights: Origins, Drafting, and Intent* (2000); M. Glendon, *A World Made New: Eleanor Roosevelt and the Universal Declaration of Human Rights* (2001). It took 18 more years before the treaties—the two Covenants and the (First) Optional Protocol—were adopted by the Assembly and opened for signature. For the drafting history of these documents, *see* Sohn, "A Short History of United Nations Documents on Human Rights," *in The United Nations and Human Rights* 101 (18th Report of the Commission to Study the Organization of Peace, 1968). Another ten years elapsed before the two Covenants entered into force in 1976.

§ 2–5. THE UNIVERSAL DECLARATION OF HUMAN RIGHTS

The Universal Declaration of Human Rights (UDHR) is the first comprehensive human rights instrument to be proclaimed by a global international organization. *See generally* A. Eide *et al.* (eds.), *The Universal Declaration of Human Rights: A Commentary* (1992); W. Schabas (ed.), *The Universal Declaration of Human Rights: The Travaux Préparatoires* (2013). Because of the moral status and the legal and political importance it has acquired over the years, the Declaration ranks with the Magna Carta, the French Declaration of the Rights of Man and the American Declaration of Independence as a milestone in mankind's struggle for freedom and human dignity. Its debt to these great historic documents is unmistakable. "All human beings are born free and equal in dignity and rights," proclaims Article 1 of the Universal Declaration, and Article 28 adds "everyone is entitled to a social and international order in which the rights and freedoms set forth in this Declaration can be fully realized."

1. The Rights and Freedoms

The Universal Declaration proclaims civil, political, economic, social and cultural rights. Its catalog of civil and political rights includes the right to life, liberty, and security of the person; the prohibition of slavery, torture, and cruel, inhuman or degrading treatment; the right not to be subjected to arbitrary arrest, detention or exile; the right to a fair trial in both civil and criminal matters, the presumption of innocence and the prohibition against the application of *ex post facto* laws and penalties. The Declaration recognizes the right to privacy and the right to own property. It proclaims freedom of speech, religion, assembly and freedom of movement, which embraces the right of everyone "to leave any country, including his own, and to return to his country." Also guaranteed are the right "to seek and to enjoy in other countries asylum from persecution" and the right to a nationality. Important political rights are proclaimed in Article 21 of the Declaration, including the individual's right "to take part in the government of his country, directly or through freely chosen representatives." That provision also declares that the "will of the people shall be the basis of the authority of government" and recognizes the right to "periodic and genuine elections" by universal suffrage.

The catalog of economic, social and cultural rights proclaimed in the Declaration starts with the proposition, expressed in Article 22, that:

> Everyone, as a member of society ... is entitled to realization, through national effort

and international co-operation and in accordance with the organization and resources of each State, of the economic, social and cultural rights indispensable for his dignity and the free development of his personality.

The Declaration then proclaims the individual's right to social security, to work, and to "protection against unemployment," to "equal pay for equal work," and to "just and favourable remuneration ensuring for himself and his family an existence worthy of human dignity, and supplemented, if necessary, by other means of social protection." Article 24 recognizes the right "to rest and leisure, including reasonable limitation of working hours and periodic holidays with pay." Article 25 states that everyone has the right "to a standard of living adequate for the health and well-being of himself and of his family." It also recognizes the individual's right "to security in the event of unemployment, sickness, disability, widowhood, old age or other lack of livelihood in circumstances beyond his control."

The right to education is addressed in Article 26 of the Declaration, which provides, among other things, that education shall be free "at least in the elementary and fundamental stages." Article 26 also declares that:

Education shall be directed to the full development of the human personality and to the strengthening of respect for human rights and fundamental freedoms. It shall promote understanding, tolerance, and friendship among all nations, racial or religious groups, and shall further the activities of the United Nations for the maintenance of peace.

Article 27 of the Declaration specifies cultural rights and states, *inter alia,* that every human being has "the right freely to participate in the cultural life of the community, to enjoy the arts and to share in scientific advancement and its benefits."

The Declaration recognizes that the rights it proclaims are not absolute. It permits a state to enact laws limiting the exercise of these rights, provided their sole purpose is to secure "due recognition and respect for the rights and freedoms of others and of meeting the just requirements of morality, public order and the general welfare in a democratic society." Art. 29(2). A government's authority to impose such restrictions is further limited by Article 30, which provides that "nothing in this Declaration may be interpreted as implying for any State, group or person any right to engage in any activity or to perform any act aimed at the destruction of any of the rights and freedoms" proclaimed in the Declaration. This means, inter alia, that a government would violate its obligations if its reliance on the power to impose lawful restrictions or limitations on the exercise of certain human rights was a mere pretext for denying these rights.

2. Legal Effect and Political Importance

The Universal Declaration is not a treaty. It was adopted by the UN General Assembly by means of a non-binding resolution. Its purpose, according to its preamble, is to provide "a common understanding" of the human rights and fundamental freedoms referred to in the UN Charter and to serve "as a common standard of achievement for all peoples and all nations. . . ."

In the decades that have elapsed since its adoption in 1948, the Declaration has undergone a dramatic transformation. Today few international lawyers would deny that the Declaration is a normative instrument that creates or at least reflects some legal obligations of the Member States of the UN. The dispute about its legal character concerns not so much claims that it lacks all legal force. The disagreement focuses instead on questions about whether all the rights it proclaims are binding and under what circumstances, and on whether its obligatory character derives from its status as an authoritative interpretation of the human rights obligations contained in the UN Charter, its status as customary international law, or its status as reflecting general principles of law. *See Restatement (Third)* § 701, Reporters' Notes 4–6; Sohn, "The New International Law: Protection of the Rights of Individuals Rather than States," 32 Am. U. L. Rev. 1, 16–17 (1982); L. Henkin, *The Age of Rights* 19 (1990); Simma & Alston, "The Source of Human Rights Law: Custom, Jus Cogens, and General Principles," 12 Australian Y.B. Int'l L. 82 (1992).

The process that transformed the Universal Declaration from a non-binding recommendation to an instrument having a normative character came about, in part at least, because the effort to draft and adopt the Covenants remained stalled in the UN for almost two decades. During that time the need for authoritative standards defining the human rights obligations of UN Member States became ever more urgent. As time went on, the Declaration came to be utilized with ever greater frequency for that purpose. Whenever governments, the UN or other international organizations wished to invoke human rights norms or condemn their violations, they would refer to and draw on the Declaration as the applicable standard. Thus the Declaration came to symbolize what the international community means by "human rights," reinforcing the conviction that all governments have an "obligation" to ensure the enjoyment of the rights the Declaration proclaims. *See* Humphrey, "The Universal Declaration of Human Rights: Its History, Impact and Juridical Character," *in* B. Ramcharan (ed.), *Human Rights: Thirty Years After the Universal Declaration* 21, at 28–37 (1979).

The legal significance of this process has been analyzed in at least three ways. Some international lawyers and governments have contended that the UN's consistent reliance on the Universal Declaration when applying the human rights provisions of the UN Charter compels the conclusion that the Declaration has come to be accepted as an authoritative interpretation of these provisions. According to this view, the Member States of the UN have agreed that they have an obligation under the Charter to promote "universal respect for, and observance of" the rights which the Declaration proclaims. Waldock, "Human Rights in Contemporary International Law and the

Significance of the European Convention," in *The European Convention of Human Rights* 1, at 14 (Int'l & Comp. L. Supp. Publ. No. 11, 1965); Buergenthal, "International Human Rights Law and Institutions: Accomplishments and Prospects," 63 Wash. L. Rev. 1, at 9 (1988). Whether a state will be deemed to have violated this obligation when it denies all, some or even only one of these rights will then depend upon the interpretation given to the undertaking contained in Article 55(c) of the Charter read together with Article 56.

Another view with considerable support sees in the repeated reliance on and resort to the Universal Declaration by governments and intergovernmental organizations the requisite state practice which is capable of giving rise to customary international law. This theory leads to the conclusion that the Declaration or, at least, some of its provisions, have become customary international law. A careful analysis of the relevant state practice suggests, however, that not all the rights proclaimed in the Declaration have acquired this status to date. That is why the *Restatement (Third)* characterizes only some rights proclaimed in the Universal Declaration as customary international law. Without claiming to be exhaustive, it lists the following governmental practices as violating customary international law: genocide, slavery, murder or causing the disappearance of individuals, torture or other cruel, inhuman or degrading treatment or punishment, prolonged arbitrary detention, systematic racial discrimination, and consistent patterns of gross violations of internationally recognized human rights. *Restatement (Third)* § 702. *See also* T. Meron, *Human Rights and Humanitarian Norms as Customary Law* 92–95 (1989) (containing a useful analysis of the process for reaching conclusions of this type).

One distinguished commentator combined the two aforementioned theories by advancing the following view:

> The Declaration . . . is now considered to be an authoritative interpretation of the U.N. Charter, spelling out in considerable detail the meaning of the phrase "human rights and fundamental freedoms," which Member States agreed in the Charter to promote and observe. The Universal Declaration has joined the Charter . . . as part of the constitutional structure of the world community. The Declaration, as an authoritative listing of human rights, has become a basic component of international customary law, binding all states, not only members of the United Nations.

Sohn, "The New International Law: Protection of the Rights of Individuals Rather than States," 32 Am. U. L. Rev. 1, at 16–17 (1982).

Some commentators are now putting forth a third theory, which characterizes the international human rights norms contained in the Universal Declaration as being reflective of a dynamic modern aspect of general principles of law. Simma & Alston, "The Source of Human Rights Law: Custom, Jus Cogens, and General Principles," 12 Australian Y.B. Int'l L.

82 (1992). *See also* Charney, "Universal International Law," 87 Am. J. Int'l L. 529, 549 (1993). This theory is supported by the adoption of the Universal Declaration verbatim or by reference into the constitutions of many states throughout the world. Hannum, "The UDHR in National and International Law," 25 Ga. J. Int'l & Comp. L. 287 (1995/96). The Declaration is also referred to in all regional human rights treaties. Whatever the theory, it is clear that the international community today attributes a very special moral and normative status to the Universal Declaration that no other instrument of its kind has acquired. *See* B. van der Heijden & B. Tahzib-Lie, *Reflections on the Universal Declaration of Human Rights* (1998).

§ 2–6. THE INTERNATIONAL COVENANTS ON HUMAN RIGHTS: INTRODUCTION

The International Covenant on Economic, Social and Cultural Rights (ICESCR) and the International Covenant on Civil and Political Rights (ICCPR) were adopted by the UN General Assembly and opened for signature in December 1966. Another decade passed before thirty-five states—the number required to bring the Covenants into force—ratified both instruments. This number has increased steadily in recent years and by 2016 had grown to 168 States Parties to the Covenant on Civil and Political Rights and 164 to the Covenant on Economic, Social, and Cultural Rights. As treaties, the Covenants create binding legal obligations for the States Parties. Therefore, as between them, issues relating to compliance with and the enjoyment of the rights guaranteed by the Covenants are matters of international concern and not exclusively within the domestic jurisdiction of the States Parties. *See* Henkin, "Human Rights and 'Domestic Jurisdiction'," *in* T. Buergenthal, *Human Rights, International Law and the Helsinki Accord* at 29–33 (1977).

The Covenants have a number of common substantive provisions. Two of these address what might be described as "peoples" or "collective" rights. Article 1(1) of both Covenants proclaims that "all peoples have the right of self-determination." *See* Hannum, "Rethinking Self-Determination," 34 Va. J. Int'l L. 1, 17–18 (1993). Both instruments recognize in Article 1(2) that "all peoples" have the right to freely dispose of their natural resources and that "in no case may a people be deprived of its own means of subsistence." *See generally* Morphet, "The Development of Article 1 of the Human Rights Covenants," *in* D.M. Hill (ed.), *Human Rights and Foreign Policy—Principles and Practice* 67 (1989). They also bar discrimination based on race, color, sex, language, religion, political or other opinion, national or social origin, property or birth. *See* ICCPR, art. 2(1); ICESR, art. 2(2). *See generally* Ramcharan, "Equality and Nondiscrimination," *in* L. Henkin (ed.), *The International Bill of Human Rights* 246 (1981).

As will be seen below, each Covenant establishes a distinct international enforcement system designed to ensure that the States Parties comply with their obligations. These monitoring mechanisms are amplified by Optional Protocols permitting individuals to file petitions charging violations of their rights under the Covenants. All of the core U.N. human rights treaties include self-reporting by States Parties, as well as inter-state and individual communications procedures, among their monitoring mechanisms.

§ 2–7. COVENANT ON CIVIL AND POLITICAL RIGHTS (ICCPR)

The catalog of civil and political rights enumerated in this Covenant is drafted with greater juridical specificity and lists more rights than the Universal Declaration. For the drafting history of the Covenant, *see* M. Bossuyt, *Guide to the "Travaux Préparatoires" of the International Covenant on Civil and Political Rights* (1987). The text of the Covenant is reprinted in 6 ILM 368 (1967). One important addition is the undertaking by states not to deny members of ethnic, religious or linguistic minorities the right, "in community with other members of their group, to enjoy their own culture, to profess and practice their own religion, or to use their own language." ICCPR, art. 27. For an analysis of this provision, *see* P. Thornberry, *International Law and the Rights of Minorities* 141 (1991). Article 27 inspired the Declaration on the Rights of Persons Belonging to National or Ethnic Religious and Linguistic Minorities, adopted by the United Nations in 1992. *See* A. Phillips & A. Rosas (eds.), *The UN Minority Rights Declaration* (1993). *See also* Human Rights Committee, General Comment No. 23 (art. 27), Doc. CCPR/C/21/Rev. 1/Add. 5 (1994).

Other rights in the ICCPR that are not expressly mentioned in the Universal Declaration include freedom from imprisonment for debt, the right of all persons deprived of their liberty to be treated with humanity and with respect for the inherent dignity of the human person, and the right of every child "to acquire a nationality" and to be accorded "such measures of protection as are required by his status as a minor."

Some important rights proclaimed in the Universal Declaration do not appear in the ICCPR, including the right to own property, the right to seek and enjoy asylum, and the right to a nationality. The right to own property was not included in the Covenant because the various ideological and political blocs represented in the UN at the time could not agree on its scope and definition. For an overall analysis of the rights and their legislative history, *see* L. Henkin (ed.), *The International Bill of Human Rights: The Covenant on Civil and Political Rights* (1981); Lillich, "Civil Rights," *in* T. Meron (ed.), *Human Rights in International Law: Legal and Policy Issues* 115 (1984); M. Nowak, *UN Covenant on Civil and political Rights: CCPR Commentary* (2d ed. 2005); J. Bair, *The International Covenant on Civil and Political Rights and its (First) Optional Protocol: a Short Commentary Based on Views, General Comments and Concluding Observations by the Human Rights Committee* (2005); A. Conte & R. Burchill, *Defining Civil and Political Rights: The Jurisprudence of the United Nations Human Rights Committee* (2009); S. Joseph & M. Castan, *The*

International Covenant on Civil and Political Rights: Cases, Materials & Commentary (3d ed. 2013).

The ICCPR contains a "derogation clause," which permits the States Parties "in time of public emergency that threatens the life of the nation" to suspend their obligations under the Covenant "to the extent strictly required by the exigencies of the situation." ICCPR, art. 4. However, the clause goes on to list seven specific rights that are non-derogable, and the Human Rights Committee has made clear that, in its opinion, this list is not exhaustive. *See* General Comment 29, para. 13, UN Doc. CCPR/CR/21/Add. 11 (2001). *See also* Buergenthal, "To Respect and to Ensure: State Obligations and Permissible Derogations," *in* Henkin, *supra,* at 72, 78–86; J. Fitzpatrick, *The International System for Protecting Rights During States of Emergency* 82 (1994); Hughes, "Entrenched Emergencies and the War on Terror: Time to Reform the Derogation Procedure in International Law?," 20 N.Y. Int'l L. Rev. 1, 10–12 (2007).

The Covenant permits States Parties to limit and restrict the exercise of some of the rights it proclaims, but these "limitations clauses" are themselves subject to limitations. A good example is found in Article 18, which guarantees freedom of religion and declares in paragraph 3 that "freedom to manifest one's religion or beliefs may be subject . . . to . . . limitations" but goes on to specify that such limitations must be "prescribed by law" and "necessary to protect public safety, order, health, or morals or the fundamental rights and freedoms of others." For an interpretation of this provision by the Human Rights Committee, *see* General Comment No. 22, Doc. A/48/40, Annex IV (1993). Another example is found in Article 19, which provides that freedom of expression (though not freedom of opinion) "may . . . be subject to certain restrictions," but goes on the specify that such restrictions must be "provided by law" and "necessary . . . [f]or respect of the rights and reputation of others" or "[f]or the protection of national security or of public order (ordre public), or of public health or morals." For the Human Rights Committee's interpretation of these provisions, *see* General Comment 34, CCPR/C/GC/34 (2011). *See also* Higgins, "Derogations under Human Rights Treaties," 48 Brit. Y. B. Int'l L. 281, 283–86 (1975–76); Kiss, "Permissible Limitations on Rights," *in* Henkin, *supra,* at 290.

These types of provisions are additionally qualified by Article 5(1), which prohibits the imposition of restrictions or limitations aimed at the destruction of the rights or "their limitation to a greater extent than is provided for in the present Covenant." In practice, particularly in states that lack a strong and independent judiciary, the provisions that permit derogations and other restrictions are frequently invoked to justify non-compliance by governments violating their human rights obligations. *See generally* D. McGoldrick, *The Human Rights Committee: Its Role in the Development of the International Covenant on Civil and Political Rights* 300 (1994).

The obligations that the States Parties assume by ratifying the ICCPR are set out in Article 2. Paragraph 1 of that provision reads as follows:

> Each State Party to the present Covenant undertakes to respect and to ensure to all individuals within its territory and subject to its jurisdiction the rights recognized in the present Covenant, without distinction of any kind, such as race, colour, sex, language, religion, political or other opinion, national or social origin, property, birth or other status.

This provision is supplemented by Article 2(2), which requires the States Parties "to adopt such legislative or other measures as may be necessary to give effect to the rights" guaranteed in the Covenant whenever such provisions do not already exist in its domestic law. Unlike the Covenant on Economic, Social and Cultural Rights, which calls for progressive implementation tied to available resources, the ICCPR imposes an immediate obligation "to respect and to ensure" the rights it proclaims and to take whatever other measures are necessary to bring about that result. *See generally* General Comment 31, "The Nature of the Legal Obligation Imposed on States Parties to the Covenant," CCPR/C/21/Rev.1/ Add.13 (2004). *Cf.* Schachter, "The Obligation to Implement the Covenant in Domestic Law," *in* Henkin, *supra* at 311. *But see* Buergenthal, "To Respect and To Ensure," in Henkin, *supra* at 72–78. For a discussion of the extraterritorial reach of the Covenant (and other human rights treaties), *see* Marko Milanovic, *Extraterritorial Application of*

Human Rights Treaties: Law Principles, and Policy (2013); Meron, "Extraterritoriality of Human Rights Treaties," 89 Am. J. Int'l L. 78 (1995); Kamchibekova, "State Responsibility for Extraterritorial Human Rights Violations," 13 Buff. Hum. Rts. L. Rev. 87, 133–40 (2007).

§ 2–8. THE HUMAN RIGHTS COMMITTEE

The ICCPR establishes a Human Rights Committee and confers on it various functions designed to ensure that the States Parties comply with the obligations they assume by ratifying the treaty. These functions concern the administration of the reporting system and the inter-state complaint mechanism provided for in the Covenant. Additional functions are exercised by the Committee under the (First) Optional Protocol to the ICCPR, which established a right of individual petition. *See* § 2–9, *infra*.

The Committee consists of 18 members. They are nominated and elected by the States Parties, but serve in their individual capacities and not as government representatives. ICCPR, art. 28. On the practice of the Committee, *see generally* Buergenthal, "The U.N. Human Rights Committee," 5 Max Planck UNYB 341 (2001); Y. Tyagi, *The UN Human Rights Committee: Practice and Procedure* (2011). *See also* McGoldrick, *supra*.

The Committee's principal function is to examine the reports all States Parties are required to submit "on the measures they have adopted which give effect to the rights recognized . . . [in the Covenant] and on

the progress made in the enjoyment of these rights."
ICCPR, art. 40(1). The evolution of the reporting
system has accelerated in recent years, transforming
it into an increasingly more effective instrument for
the implementation of the Covenant. For an
historical overview of this evolution, *see* Opsahl, "The
Human Rights Committee," *in* P. Alston, *The United
Nations and Human Rights: A Critical Appraisal*
369, 397–419 (1991); Pocar, "Current Developments
and Approaches in the Practice of the Human Rights
Committee in Consideration of State Reports," *in* A.
Eide & J. Helgesen (eds.), *The Future of Human
Rights Protection in a Changing World* 51 (1991); W.
Kaelin, "Examination of States Reports," *in* H. Keller
and G. Ulfstein (eds.), *UN Human Rights Treaty
Bodies: Law and Legitimacy* 32 (2012).

The Covenant does not expressly confer on the
Committee the power to verify the state reports by
undertaking its own investigations. Committee
members may, however, draw on their own
knowledge as human rights experts. In addition,
although this power was once disputed, the
Committee may consider information from other
sources—including other UN treaty bodies, special
rapporteurs, field offices, and specialized agencies, as
well as non-governmental human rights
organizations (NGOs), national human rights
institutions (NHRIs), and other stakeholders, such as
trade unions—in questioning the state
representatives who, under the Committee's rules of
procedure, are to be present when their reports are
examined. By requiring the state representatives to
explain the contents of the reports and by asking for

supplemental information, the Committee is able to identify serious compliance problems and to call them to the attention of the UN General Assembly. ICCPR, art. 40(4). *See* T. Meron, *Human Rights Law-Making in the United Nations* 123 (1986).

Furthermore, building on its practice in dealing with individual petitions and in examining state reports, the Committee has adopted an increasing number of so-called General Comments that spell out the meaning of various provisions of the Covenant. The General Comments resemble advisory opinions which interpret the Covenant.

The Committee meets in three annual sessions of three or four weeks each and generally examines five to six State reports per session in addition to its work on individual communications.

1. The Reporting Procedure

Article 40(1) of the Covenant requires States Parties "to submit reports on the measures they have adopted which give effect to the rights recognized [in the Covenant] and on the progress made in the enjoyment of those rights." The Covenant specifies that the reports are to indicate any factors or difficulties affecting their ability to implement the Covenant. The Covenant requires all States Parties to submit their initial report within one year of the entry into force of the Covenant for them and thereafter whenever the Committee so requests. In practice, the Committee requests the submission of periodic reports every four to seven years.

Over the years, the Human Rights Committee has developed a comprehensive set of reporting guidelines and procedures for dealing with these reports. *See* "Guidelines for the treaty-specific document to be submitted by States Parties under article 40 of the International Covenant on Civil and Political Rights," CCPR/C/2009/1 (2010), and supplemental information available on the Committee's web site, http://www.ohchr.org/EN/HR Bodies/CCPR/Pages/CCPRIndex.aspx. *See generally,* Boerefijn, "Towards a Strong System of Supervision. The Human Rights Committee's Role in Reforming the Reporting Procedure under Article 40 of the Covenant," 17 Hum. Rts. Q. 766 (1995). These guidelines are designed to prod the States Parties into compliance with their treaty obligations and to assist them in overcoming difficulties in doing so.

After a report has been received by the Committee, it is studied by a country rapporteur and a Country Report Task Force of four to six members. The country rapporteur presents the draft list of issues for discussion to the Country Report Task Force, which makes observations and adopts the final list of issues. The list of issues is then transmitted to the State Party, which is expected to provide written responses. The Task Force allocates to each of its members principal responsibility for a certain number of questions included in the list of issues, based in part on the areas of particular expertise or interest of the member concerned. The list of issues is adopted one or more sessions prior to the Committee's public examination of the State report, thereby allowing a significant period for States

Parties to prepare for the discussion with the Committee.

In 2009, the Committee adopted an optional "simplified reporting" procedure. *See* "Focused Reports Based on Replies to List of Issues Prior To Reporting (LOIPR)," UN Doc. CCPR/C/99/4 (2010). Under this new procedure, the Committee transmits a list of issues to States Parties *before* submission of a periodic report. This list is drafted by the Country Task Force on the basis of information provided by the Secretariat, including the State Party's previous reports to the Committee, the summary record of the previous consideration of the State Party, the Committee's previous observations and recommendations, the observations and recommendations of other treaty bodies, reports of special procedures, Universal Periodic Review documents, and any information provided by NHRIs and NGOs. The State Party provides written responses to the issues raised by the Committee *in lieu* of its periodic report. The simplified reporting procedure eases the burden on States parties by eliminating the need to provide both a periodic report and written responses to the list of issues. The process is also speedier, as the focused reports drafted on the basis of an LOIPR are given priority for consideration over other periodic reports, so as to ensure that they are considered within a maximum time frame of one year after submission.

In examining State reports, the Committee can draw on information from specialized agencies of the UN, studies by other UN bodies including reports of

UN country and thematic rapporteurs. In addition, the Committee invites NGOs and other stakeholders to submit "alternative" or "shadow" reports. NGOs and other stakeholders are also given the opportunity to address the Committee in public session before the Committee reviews the State Party. The State Party's NHRI is also invited to address the Committee.

The Committee examines the States Parties' periodic reports (or the focused reports drafted on the basis of the LOIPR) in public session. Following the oral presentation by the State's representative, the country rapporteur and members of the Country Task Force pose questions to the delegation, after which other members may pose additional questions and comments. Two three-hour sessions, held on successive days, are usually devoted to the public examination of each country's report. These sessions are normally webcast live, and the webcasts are archived and available on line. *See* http://www.treaty bodywebcast.org/category/webcast-archives/hrcttee/.

Once the public hearing is complete, the Committee meets in private and adopts its "Concluding Observations." The Concluding Observations consist of an assessment of the State's human rights situation in light of the information provided in the State report, the answers the Committee received to the questions posed by its members during the examination of the report, and information available to the members from other sources, all analyzed in terms of the country's obligations under the Covenant.

The Committee transmits its Concluding Observations to the State Party shortly before the end of the session, and they are soon thereafter published on the Committee's web site. Concluding Observations are adopted by the Committee as a whole in closed meetings after a thorough paragraph-by-paragraph discussion of a draft text prepared by a country rapporteur, working alone or with the Country Report Task Force. For discussion of the contribution of Concluding Observations towards the Committee's "jurisprudence" interpreting the obligations of the States Parties under the Covenant, *see* Joseph, "New Procedures Concerning the Human Rights Committee's Examination of State Reports," 13 Neth. Q. Hum. Rts. 5, at 8–12 (1995); J. Blair, *The ICCPR and its (First) Optional Protocol: A Short Commentary Based on Views, General Comments and Concluding Observations by the Human Rights Committee* (2005); K. Young, *The Law and Process of the U.N. Human Rights Committee* (2002).

Among the recommendations included in the Concluding Observations, between two and four are designated for the Committee's "follow-up" procedure. The State Party is requested to submit a follow-up report within one year regarding its implementation of these recommendations. NGOs and other stakeholders are invited to submit "alternative" follow-up reports, either before or within one month after the posting of the State Party's follow-up report. Based on the State Party's follow-up report and any alternative reports received, the Committee's Special Rapporteur for Follow-Up on Concluding Observations prepares a follow-up progress report, which is presented to and discussed by the Committee at its following session. The Committee then gives the State Party a grade of A, B, C, D, or E (with A being the best) for its compliance with the Committee's recommendations. After the adoption of the follow-up progress report, the Special Rapporteur sends letters to the State Party, usually requesting additional action or further information. For a discussion of the follow-up procedures of the Committee and other treaty bodies, *see* Schmidt, "Follow-up Activities by UN Human Rights Treaty Bodies and Special Procedures Mechanisms of the Human Rights Council—Recent Developments," in G. Alfredsson et al. (eds.), *International Human Rights Monitoring Mechanisms: Essays in Honour of Jacob Th. Möller*, at 25–34 (2d ed. 2009).

A significant challenge to the reporting system has been the failure of some States to submit their reports to the Committee in a timely fashion. Some of these States have been motivated by a desire to avoid public scrutiny of their failure to comply with the Covenant; others lack the necessary resources or professional staff to prepare their reports within a reasonable period of time. Occasionally civil wars or internal turmoil have played a role, as has bureaucratic inertia. *See generally* Schmidt, "Follow-up Mechanisms Before UN Human Rights Treaty Bodies and the UN Mechanisms Beyond," *in* A. Bayefsky (ed.), *The UN Human Rights Treaty System in the 21st Century* 233 at 244 (2000). Public and private reminders, designed to shame States into complying with their reporting obligations, have eventually produced the desired result in most, but not all, cases. *See, e.g.,* Report of the Human Rights Committee, UN Doc. A/63/40 (2 Vols.), pp. 16–19 (GAOR, 63d sess., Suppl. No. 40 (2008)).

Recognizing that reporting by States Parties is the fundamental mechanism by which the Committee discharges its obligation to monitor the observance of obligations under the Convention, the Committee has adopted special procedures for considering the situation of States Parties that fail to report, beginning with the most overdue reports. The Committee notifies the State Party of the date on which the Committee proposes to examine the measures taken by the State Party to implement the rights guaranteed under the Covenant, providing it with a list of issues for review in the absence of a report. Some States Parties have answered the list of issues but not appeared for the review; others have both answered the list of issues and appeared. The Committee may proceed whether or not representatives of the State Party appear at the meeting. If the consideration goes forward, the Committee prepares Concluding Observations and transmits them to the State Party.

To address the problem of late or absent reports, the General Assembly in 2014 encouraged all treaty bodies to adopt the simplified reporting procedure employing LOIPR. *See* GA Res. 68/268, Strengthening and enhancing the effective functioning of the human rights treaty body system, UN Doc. A/68/268 (April 9, 2014), paras. 1, 2. In addition, in order to assist States Parties to build their capacity to meet their reporting and other obligations, the General Assembly called for the Office of the High Commissioner for Human Rights to provide technical assistance to States Parties in need of such assistance. *See id.*, para. 17. For a discussion of this and other reforms and recommendations growing out of the "treaty body strengthening" discussions that took place between 2009 and 2014, including increased meeting time for all treaty bodies, *see* C. Broecker & M. O'Flaherty, *The Outcome of the General Assembly's Treaty Body Strengthening Process: An Important Milestone on a Longer Journey* (2014).

2. General Comments

Over the years, the Committee has adopted nearly three dozen so-called General Comments. General Comments are addressed to the States Parties as a whole and are designed to provide guidance to them in discharging their obligations under the Covenant. Although not legally binding, General Comments can be considered "secondary soft law instruments," that is, sources of nonbinding norms in which the Committee spells out its interpretation of different provisions of the Covenant. *See* D. Shelton, *Commitment and Compliance* 449–64 (2000); Keller & Grover, "General Comments of the Human Rights Committee and Their Legitimacy," *in* H. Keller & G. Ulfstein, *UN Human Rights Treaty Bodies: Law and Legitimacy* at 129 (2012). The General Comments are largely derived from the Committee's prior decisions on individual communications and its Concluding Observations, and the General Comments are in turn relied upon by the Committee in evaluating compliance by States with their obligations under the Covenant, be it in examining State reports or considering individual communications under the Optional Protocol.

The first few General Comments adopted by the Committee were terse and hesitant in their interpretation of the Covenant. They became more exhaustive in the late 1980's, in large measure because the end of the Cold War made it easier for the Committee to reach the desired consensus. General Comments are now, as a rule, longer and more analytical, and frequently address difficult issues of interpretation and policy. Over time, General Comments have become important guideposts for the interpretation and application of the Covenant. The Committee's General Comments are collected on the web site of the Office of the High Commissioner for Human Rights, at http://tbinternet. ohchr.org/_layouts/treatybodyexternal/TBSearch.asp x?Lang=en&TreatyID=8&DocTypeID=11.

The Committee's procedure for adopting General Comments is not described in its Rules of Procedure, and it has evolved over the years. Under the current procedure, once the Committee has decided to elaborate a General Comment, it designates one or more Committee members as rapporteurs. The Committee then holds a half day of general discussion on the topic, after which the rapporteur presents a draft of the General Comment to the Committee for paragraph-by-paragraph discussion at a public session. The revised draft that emerges from this first reading is then posted on the

Committee's web site, and States Parties and non-state actors are invited to submit written comments. The rapporteur takes these comments into account in further revising the draft General Comment. For example, with respect to General Comment 33, the Committee received comments from 21 States Parties and six NGOs, which resulted in significant revisions. *See* General Comment No. 33, Obligations of States Parties under the Optional Protocol to the Civil and Political Covenant, CCPR/C/GC/33, Nov.5, 2008. At a subsequent session, the revised draft is presented to the Committee for a second reading before being finally adopted by consensus.

In addition to commenting on the draft after the first reading, States Parties have the right under Article 40(5) to submit to the Committee observations on any General Comments after they have been adopted. States Parties have not as a rule availed themselves of this opportunity, yet General Comment 24, which sets out the Committee's position on reservations to the Covenant, elicited a number of highly critical observations challenging the Committee's position. The United States and United Kingdom observations are reprinted in [1994–95] HRC Report, GAOR, Supp. No.40 (A/50/40), Vol. I, at 131 and 135, respectively (1995). For the observations of the French Government, *see* [1995–96] HRC Report, GAOR, Supp. No. 40 (A/51/40) (1996). *See* Buergenthal, "The U.N. Human Rights Committee," *supra*, at 381–84.

3. Inter-State Communications

The Covenant also provides for an inter-state complaint procedure that enables one State Party to charge another with a violation of the treaty. ICCPR, arts. 41 and 42. *See generally* M. Nowak, *U.N. Covenant on Civil and Political Rights: CCPR Commentary* 753, 777 (2d ed. 2005). This procedure can be resorted to only by and against States Parties that have made a separate declaration recognizing the Committee's jurisdiction to receive such complaints. ICCPR, art. 41(2). Although the provision of the Covenant permitting this action entered into force after ten states accepted the requisite jurisdiction, no inter-state complaints have as yet been submitted.

The system for dealing with inter-state complaints provides neither for adjudication nor quasi-adjudication. Instead, it establishes little more than a formal conciliation machinery. *See generally,* Robertson, "The Implementation System: International Measures," *in* Henkin, *supra,* at 332, 351–56.

Given the weak nature of the inter-state complaint system, and the fact that it has never been invoked, it is important to note that Article 44 of the Covenant expressly permits the States Parties thereto to have "recourse to other procedures for settling a dispute in accordance with general or special international agreements in force between them." ICCPR, art. 44. This provision would enable States Parties, for example, to take disputes relating to the interpretation or application of the Covenant to the

·International Court of Justice, provided they have accepted the Court's jurisdiction. For example, the Congo alleged violations of the ICCPR in its ICJ litigation against Rwanda, Burundi and Uganda. *See Armed Activities on the Territory of the Congo (DRC v. Uganda)*, 2005 I.C.J. Rep. 168 (Dec. 19). And in *Case Concerning Ahmadou Sadio Diallo* (Rep. of Guinea v. DRC), 2010 I.C.J. Rep. 639 (Nov. 30), Guinea alleged violations of the ICCPR by the Congo, and the Court found that the Congo had committed violations of Articles 13 (recognizing the right of lawfully admitted aliens not to be arbitrarily expelled) and Article 9 (recognizing the right of persons not to be arbitrarily arrested or detained).

§ 2–9. THE (FIRST) OPTIONAL PROTOCOL TO THE COVENANT ON CIVIL AND POLITICAL RIGHTS

This treaty, adopted as a separate instrument, supplements the measures of implementation of the ICCPR. It enables private parties, claiming to be victims of a violation of the Covenant, to file individual complaints, known as "communications," with the Human Rights Committee. The complaints may be filed only against States Parties to the Covenant that have ratified the Protocol. Protocol, arts. 1 and 2. *See* Buergenthal, "The U.N. Human Rights Committee," 5 Max Planck UNYB 341, 364–81 (2001). Of the 168 countries that have become parties to the Covenant, 115 have ratified the Optional Protocol.

This individual petition system resembles a quasi-judicial system, allowing victims to file a communication with the Committee if they have exhausted available and effective domestic remedies. To be admissible, the communications must not be anonymous, abusive of the "right of submission" or "incompatible with any provision of the Covenant." Optional Protocol, art. 3. The Committee may not consider a communication if "the same matter is . . . being examined under another procedure of international investigation or settlement." Optional Protocol, art. 5(2)(a). Higgins, "Admissibility under the Optional Protocol to the International Covenant on Civil and Political Rights," [1991–1992] Canadian Human Rights Yearbook 58 (1992).

The Committee examines all communications in private sessions on the basis of the written information submitted to it by the individual claimant and the State concerned. *See* Optional Protocol, arts. 5(1), 5(3). *See generally* Buergenthal, "U.N. Human Rights Committee," 5 Max Planck UNYB 341 at 364 (2001). On receipt of a communication by the Committee, the State Party is given six months within which to submit its arguments on the merits of the case. *See* Rules of Procedure, Rule 91. Where the State Party concerned has an objection relating to admissibility alone, it has two months within which to submit an application for rejection of the communication on those grounds. The individual then has an opportunity to reply within a time period fixed by the Committee.

Individual communications are initially reviewed by the Committee's Special Rapporteur on New Communications, a position established by the Committee in 1989. The Special Rapporteur determines whether a new communication needs to be amplified for admissibility purposes and whether it should be referred to the State Party concerned for its observations on issues of admissibility and merits. The Special Rapporteur may also issue interim measures to "avoid irreparable damage to the victim of the alleged violation" in appropriate cases falling within the scope of his/her mandate. *See* Rules of Procedure, Rule 86. The Special Rapporteur may recommend to the Committee that a communication be declared inadmissible, but the power to decide the issue is vested in the Committee. Ordinarily, the question of admissibility is considered at the same time as the merits. A pre-sessional Working Group makes recommendations to the Committee; the Committee then analyzes these recommendations and in due course adopts its decision in the case. Decisions on the merits are designated as "Views." Individual members of the Committee are free to append dissenting and concurring opinions, and frequently do so. *See generally* Y. Tyagi, *The UN Human Rights Committee: Practice and Procedure* (2011).

The Optional Protocol is silent on the issue of the Committee's role in ensuring that States Parties comply with its Views. The Committee filled this gap by establishing the position of Special Rapporteur for the Follow-up of Views. *See* Schmidt, "Follow-up Activities by UN Human Rights Treaty Bodies and

Special Procedures Mechanisms of the Human Rights Council—Recent Developments," in G. Alfredsson et al. (eds.), *International Human Rights Monitoring Mechanisms: Essays in Honour of Jacob Th. Möller*, at 25–34 (2d ed. 2009). In addition, the Committee's list of issues routinely ask about unimplemented Views on communications so that the matter can be discussed in the Committee's dialogue with the State Party.

If the Committee finds that the State Party has violated the Covenant, it will request that the State Party provide it, within 180 days, with information on measures taken to comply with the Committee's recommendations. The information provided is routinely sent to the victim for comments. If the State Party fails to provide the follow-up information, the Special Rapporteur for Follow-up of Views may send a reminder and, if necessary, organize follow-up meetings with State representatives. The Committee may also organize follow-up missions to States parties, although this has happened only once. The Special Rapporteur's activities also include meetings in Geneva or New York with the heads of diplomatic missions to the United Nations of States Parties whose governments have failed to comply with Committee Views to encourage the governments to give effect to those Views. For the mandate of the Special Rapporteur on Follow-up, *see* Rules of Procedure, Rule 101. The Committee includes information on follow-up activities in its annual report to the General Assembly. For additional information, *see* Schmidt, *supra*.

Since the entry into force of the Protocol in 1976, the Human Rights Committee has dealt with an ever-increasing number of individual communications. Many of these were found inadmissible, in large part because domestic remedies had not been exhausted or because they involved "the same matter" that was "being examined under another procedure of international investigation or settlement." Protocol, art. 5(2). In recent years, the number of admissible communications has grown significantly.

In dealing with communications, the Committee has been able to develop a valuable body of decisional precedent interpreting and applying the Covenant and Protocol. The Committee has asserted that its views under the Optional Protocol "represent an authoritative determination by the organ established under the Covenant itself charged with the interpretation of that instrument," General Comment 33, CCPR/C/GC/33, para. 13. That position has been disputed by some States parties. *See* Comments of the United States of America on the Human Rights Committee's "Draft General Comment 33," para. 8 (Oct. 17, 2008). It is, in any event, clear that the Committee's decisions on individual communications, because of their increasingly more thorough and sound legal analysis, have contributed importantly to the corpus of contemporary human rights law. The decisions are available on line at http://www.ohchr.org/EN/HR Bodies/CCPR/Pages/Jurisprudence.aspx.

The jurisprudence of the Human Rights Committee (as of the other UN treaty bodies) is extensive and rich. Space constraints preclude a discussion of this jurisprudence here. Interested readers may consult, *inter alia*, J. Möller & A. de Zayas, *United Nations Human Rights Committee Case Law 1977–2008: A Handbook* (2009); A. Conte & R. Burchill, *Defining Civil and Political Rights: The Jurisprudence of the United Nations Human Rights Committee* (2009); S. Joseph & M. Castan, *The International Covenant on Civil and Political Rights: Cases, Materials & Commentary* (3d ed. 2013).

§ 2–10. SECOND OPTIONAL PROTOCOL TO THE INTERNATIONAL COVENANT ON CIVIL AND POLITICAL RIGHTS

The objective of the Second Optional Protocol is the abolition of the death penalty. To this end it provides, first, that once a state has ratified the Protocol, "no one within [its] jurisdiction . . . shall be executed," and, second, that each State Party must take whatever measures are necessary to abolish the death penalty within its jurisdiction. Second Optional Protocol, art. 1. The only reservation that may be made to the Protocol would allow "for the application of the death penalty in time of war pursuant to a conviction for a most serious crime of a military nature committed during wartime." *Id.*, art. 2. The Protocol also makes the right it guarantees non-derogable under Article 4 of the Covenant. *Id.*, art. 6(2).

The Protocol extends the jurisdiction of the Human Rights Committee under Article 40 of the Covenant regarding State Party reporting. It also does so for inter-state complaints with regard to states that have recognized the Committee's jurisdiction under Article 41 of the Covenant and for individual complaints in cases involving States Parties to the First Optional Protocol. Second Optional Protocol, arts. 3–5.

The Second Optional Protocol was opened for signature on December 15, 1989 and entered into force on July 11, 1991. The text is reprinted in 6 ILM 360 (1966). As of 2016, 82 of the 168 States Parties to the Covenant had accepted the Protocol. Pursuant to its terms, it is deemed to be an additional provision of the Covenant.

§ 2–11. COVENANT ON ECONOMIC, SOCIAL AND CULTURAL RIGHTS

This Covenant contains a longer and much more comprehensive catalog of economic, social and cultural rights than the Universal Declaration. *See generally* Eide, "Economic and Social Rights" *in* J. Symonides, *Human Rights: Concepts and Standards*, 109 at 119 (2000); M. Baderin & R. McCorquodale (eds.), *Economic, Social and Cultural Rights in Action* (2007); B. Saul, D. Kinley, & J. Mowbray, *The International Covenant on Economic, Social and Cultural Rights: Commentary, Cases, and Materials* (2014). It recognizes the following rights: the right to work; the right to the enjoyment of just and favorable conditions of work; the right to form and join trade unions; the right to social security, including social insurance; the right to the protection of the family; the right to an adequate standard of living; the right to the enjoyment of the highest attainable standard of physical and mental health; the right of everyone to education; and the right to take part in cultural life.

The Covenant does not merely list these rights; it describes and defines them in considerable detail and frequently sets out the steps that should be taken to achieve their realization. Typical of this approach is Article 7, which reads as follows:

The States Parties to the present Covenant recognize the right of everyone to the enjoyment of just and favourable conditions of work, which ensure, in particular:

(a) Remuneration which provides all workers as a minimum with:

> (i) Fair wages and equal remuneration for work of equal value without distinction of any kind, in particular women being guaranteed conditions of work not inferior to those enjoyed by men, with equal pay for equal work;

> (ii) A decent living for themselves and their families in accordance with the provisions of the present Covenant;

(b) Safe and healthy working conditions;

(c) Equal opportunity for everyone to be promoted in his employment to an appropriate higher level, subject to no considerations other than those of seniority and competence;

(d)   Rest, leisure and reasonable limitation of working hours and periodic holidays with pay, as well as remuneration for public holidays.

1. Nature of the Obligations

By ratifying this Covenant, a State Party does not undertake to give immediate effect to all of the rights it enumerates, as is the case with the ICCPR. The ICESCR adopts a different approach, which finds expression in Article 2(1):

> Each State Party to the present Covenant undertakes to take steps, individually and through international assistance and co-operation, especially economic and technical, to the maximum of its available resources, with a view to achieving progressively the full realization of the rights recognized in the present Covenant by all appropriate means, including particularly the adoption of legislative measures.

As this language indicates, the state obligates itself to take steps "to the maximum of its available resources" in order to achieve "progressively the full realization" of these rights. Also unlike the ICCPR, the ICESCR includes a transnational dimension in its reference to international assistance and co-operation.

The different approaches taken in the two Covenants towards implementation stems from the understanding that, as a general matter, the protection of most civil and political rights vis-à-vis the state requires few, if any, economic resources. With some exceptions, such as the requirement of an independent judiciary and access to justice, little more is required of a government than legislation and a decision not to engage in certain illegal practices—not to torture people, not to imprison them arbitrarily, etc. The burden tends to be heavier and the task more complicated when economic, social or cultural rights are involved. In general, their enjoyment cannot be fully ensured without economic and technical resources, education and planning, the gradual reordering of social priorities and, in many cases, international cooperation.

These differences between the two categories of rights are more a matter of degree than of kind, however. As discussed below, the Committee on Economic, Social and Cultural Rights (CESCR) (the body established to supervise the implementation of this Covenant) has recognized that some E.S.C. rights are of an immediate and absolute nature. For its part, the Human Rights Committee (which interprets the ICCPR) has come to recognize an obligation of states to use due diligence to protect individuals from violations of their rights by non-state actors, *see, e.g.,* Jimenez-Vaca v. Colombia, CCPR/C/74/D/859/1999 (Mar. 25, 2002), thus recognizing that the ICCPR does impose some affirmative (not just negative) obligations on States Parties. Moreover, it is widely accepted and oft-repeated that "all human rights are . . . indivisible and interdependent and interrelated." *See, e.g.,* Vienna Declaration and Program of Action, para 5 (June 25, 1993).

Nevertheless, the affirmative character of most economic social and cultural rights underlies the "progressive" or "programmatic" nature of most of the obligations assumed by States Parties to the ICESCR. It would be unrealistic to require immediate compliance with all of these rights, given the nature of these rights and the specific problems each state must deal with to ensure their full enjoyment. *See* Trubek, "Economic, Social and Cultural Rights in the Third World: Human Rights and Human Needs," *in* T. Meron, *Human Rights in International Law,* 205, 213–22 (1984); A.G. Mower, *International Cooperation for Social Justice: Global and Regional Protection of Economic/Social Rights* (1985); M. Magdalena & S. Carmona, *The Nature of the Obligations Under the International Covenant on Economic Social and Cultural Rights* (2003); Khaliq & Churchill, "The Protection of Economic and Social Rights: A Particular Challenge?," *in* H. Keller & G. Ulfstein, *UN Human Rights Treaty Bodies: Law and Legitimacy* 199–260 (2012).

These considerations also explain why, as a practical matter, the standards by which to measure compliance under the ICESCR will differ from those that apply to treaties dealing with civil and political rights. Different criteria will have to be applied to different states in determining whether they are living up to their treaty obligations, because each state will invariably face different problems and no two states are likely to have the same "available resources."

This is not to say, however, that no rights guaranteed in this Covenant can be enforced by legislation or that judicial remedies will always be inappropriate. Indeed, the constitutional courts of some states have recognized such rights to be justiciable. *See, e.g.,* Gov't of South Africa v. Grootboom, Case CCT 11/00, 4 Oct. 2000) (South Africa); Olga Tellis v. Bombay Municipal Corp., AIR 1986 SC 18 (India). The assumption that the E.S.C. Covenant creates no immediate obligations for the States Parties was rejected by the ICESCR in its General Comment No. 3 (1990). Report of the Committee on Economic, Social and Cultural Rights, Fifth Session, U.N. Doc. E/199/23, E/C.12/1990/8, at 83 (1991). In its thorough analysis of Article 2(1), the Committee points out that "while the Covenant provides for progressive realization and acknowledges the constraints due to limits of available resources, it also imposes various obligations, which are of immediate effect." Among these, the Committee singles out two in particular: the undertaking of the States Parties to guarantee that the rights set out in the Covenant will be exercised without discrimination; and the undertaking in Article 2(1) "to take steps."

Regarding the undertaking of non-discrimination, the Committee notes that legislation and the provision of judicial remedies can often appropriately promote compliance with this obligation. As for the undertaking to take steps, the Committee insists that although "the full realization of the relevant rights may be achieved progressively, steps towards that goal must be taken within a reasonably short time after the Covenant's entry into force for the States concerned." The Committee also emphasizes "that a minimum core obligation to ensure the satisfaction of, at the very least, minimum essential levels of each of the rights is incumbent upon every State Party." *Id.*, at 86. *See generally* Andreassen *et al.*, "Compliance with Economic and Social Human Rights: Realistic Evaluations and Monitoring in the Light of Immediate Obligations," *in* A. Eide & B. Hagtret (eds.), *Human Rights in Perspective: A Global Assessment* 252 (1992).

2. Overseeing Implementation

The ICESCR does not itself establish any inter-state or individual complaints system. It only requires the States Parties to submit "reports on the measures which they have adopted and the progress made in achieving the observance of the rights recognized herein." ICESCR, art. 16(1). The Covenant itself does not, moreover, establish a special committee to review the reports; it stipulates merely that they are to be submitted to the UN Economic and Social Council.

Starting in 1976, ECOSOC adopted a series of resolutions that culminated in the establishment of a Committee on Economic, Social and Cultural Rights (CESCR), composed of 18 experts who are elected by the States Parties but serve in their personal capacities. ECOSOC Resolution 1985/17 of May 22, 1985. The Committee held its first meeting in March 1987. Alston & Simma, "First Session of the UN Committee on Economic, Social and Cultural Rights,"

81 Am. J. Int'l L. 747 (1987). Prior thereto ECOSOC had delegated the task of reviewing the state reports to a working group of its members, known as the Sessional Working Group on the Implementation of the International Covenant on Economic, Social and Cultural Rights. That body reported its general findings to ECOSOC, the UN Commission on Human Rights and to the Specialized Agencies of the UN concerned with economic, social and cultural rights. *See* Alston, "The United Nations Specialized Agencies and Implementation of the International Covenant on Economic, Social and Cultural Rights," 18 Colum. J. Transn. L. 79 (1979). These early efforts to promote the implementation of the ICESCR were not very effective.

The situation changed with the establishment of the permanent Committee. Despite numerous obstacles, some bureaucratic and others inherent in the nature of the ICESCR, this body has gradually devised a sound and creative approach for pressing states to live up to their treaty obligations. It has also used its General Comments and analyses of state reports to clarify the meaning of the many ambiguous provisions of the Covenant, thus providing the international community with an analytically helpful interpretative gloss on the normative character of economic, social and cultural rights. *See* Alston, "The Committee on Economic, Social and Cultural Rights," *in* P. Alston (ed.), *The United Nations and Human Rights: A Critical Appraisal* 473 (1992). *See also* M.C.R. Craven, *The International Covenant on Economic, Social and Cultural Rights: A Perspective on its Development* (1995); Chapman, "A New

Approach to Monitoring the International Covenant on Economic, Social and Cultural Rights," 55 Int'l Comm'n Jurists Rev. 23 (1995). For a list of relevant publications, see P. Alston, Economic and Social Rights: A Bibliography (2008).

As early as 1990, the CESCR began discussing the advisability of an optional protocol to create an individual complaints mechanism for the ICESCR. The proposal was controversial but after more than a decade of work by the Committee, the Commission on Human Rights and an open-ended Working Group, the protocol was adopted on December 10, 2008. The Protocol entered into force in May of 2013 and has been ratified by 22 States Parties. The Committee issued its first views under the Protocol in 2016. On the merits of the protocol, see Dennis & Stewart, "Justiciability of Economic, Social, and Cultural Rights," 98 Am. J. Int'l. L. 462 (2004); Alston, "Establishing a Right to Petition under the Covenant on Economic, Social and Cultural Rights," 4/2 Coll. Courses of the Academy of European Law 107 (1995).

Some of the procedures set forth in the Protocol are innovative, reflecting the distinct character of some economic, social and cultural rights. Article 2 of the Optional Protocol provides that communications may be submitted by or on behalf of individuals or groups of individuals, under the jurisdiction of a State Party, claiming to be victims of a violation of any of the rights set forth in Parts II and III of the Covenant by that State Party. Where a communication is submitted on behalf of individuals or groups of individuals, this shall be with their consent unless the author can justify acting on their behalf without such consent. Article 8 authorizes the Committee to consult, in addition to the parties' submissions, "relevant documentation emanating from other United Nations bodies, specialized agencies, funds, programmes and mechanisms, and other international organizations, including from regional human rights systems." Although NGOs are not mentioned in the article, the Committee has issued a "Guidance on Third-Party Interventions," setting forth guidelines for "individuals or entities seeking to submit interventions as a third party."

The Protocol provides in art. 4 that the Committee "may, if necessary, decline to consider a communication where it does not reveal that the author has suffered a clear disadvantage, unless the Committee considers that the communication raises a serious issue of general importance." Article 5 gives the Committee express authority to issue interim measures to avoid irreparable harm to victims, and article 6 requires the Committee to transmit all admissible communications confidentially to the State Party concerned, which shall provide a reply within six months. Article 7 instructs the Committee to "make available its good offices . . . with a view to reaching a friendly settlement" of the matter. The Committee's Rules of Procedure provide that any of the parties may request the initiation of this procedure at any time after the receipt of the communication and before a decision is reached. *See* Provisional rules of procedure under the Optional Protocol to the International Covenant on Economic, Social and Cultural Rights (Jan. 12, 2013), rule 15. If a friendly settlement is reached, the Committee is to adopt a statement of the facts and solution reached, which is to be published in the Committee's annual report. *Id.*

The Committee's consideration of communications is to take place in closed session. Unusually, the Protocol gives guidance on the standard to be applied by the Committee in judging whether or not a violation has been shown:

> When examining communications under the present Protocol, the Committee shall consider the reasonableness of the steps taken by the State Party in accordance with Part II of the Covenant. In doing so, the Committee shall bear in mind that the State Party may adopt a range of possible policy measures for the implementation of the rights set forth in the Covenant.

Art. 8(4), Optional Protocol. The State Party concerned is to report within six months on the measures it takes in response to the views of the Committee (art. 6(2)). The Protocol also establishes an optional inter-state procedure (art. 10) and an optional inquiry procedure to respond to allegations of grave and systematic violations (art. 11). To date, only five States Parties have declared their acceptance of these procedures. Article 14 contains measures designed to provide technical and financial assistance when appropriate, including through the establishment of a United Nations trust fund to aid in the further implementation of the E.S.C. rights.

IV. OTHER CORE UN HUMAN RIGHTS TREATIES

§ 2–12. INTRODUCTION

In addition to the International Bill of Human Rights, the UN has over the years adopted a large number of treaties addressing specific types of human rights violations, including genocide, racial discrimination, apartheid, discrimination against women, and torture. Many of the treaties define terms, such as "torture" and "racial discrimination," that are not clearly defined in the more general treaties, thereby providing more precise legal norms. Each of the core human rights treaties provides for the establishment of a committee of independent experts to monitor implementation of the treaty provisions by States Parties. Each treaty body is directed to consider periodic state reports containing information on steps taken to implement the provisions of the relevant treaty (and in the case of the Committee on the Rights of the Child (CRC) its substantive protocols). Most of the treaties establish a timetable for the submission of initial and periodic reports, although the Covenants discussed above do not do so. All the committees have adopted guidelines on the form and content of reports. Meetings of the chairpersons of the various treaty bodies in 2006 resulted in the adoption of harmonized guidelines on reporting, including guidelines for a common core document and treaty-specific documents. All states were notified of the new harmonized guidelines and asked to use them starting in 2007. Once the report has been submitted, most treaty bodies will prepare lists of issues to give the States Parties the opportunity to supplement the information initially provided, although the Committee for the Elimination of Racial Discrimination (CERD) instead prepares a "list of themes" intended to guide the constructive dialogue but requiring no written responses. As noted above, the General Assembly has encouraged the treaty bodies to adopt the simplified reporting procedure described in § 2–8, and most have begun employing that procedure.

The treaties do not give details about how the various treaty bodies are to proceed with consideration of the state reports, but all treaties empower the committees to adopt their own rules of procedure. Over time, the committees have adopted the same basic framework for review and for the adoption of Concluding Observations based on the report. The main feature of the procedure is the "constructive dialogue" in which the committees engage with representatives from the State Party whose report is under consideration. All treaty bodies may consider reports in the absence of a delegation, but this rarely happens, as the Committees use every means at their disposal to ensure that the State Party sends a delegation. When a report is submitted and a list of issues conveyed to the State Party, the Secretariat organizes a briefing with representatives of the State Party. The State Party is then requested to provide a list of the members of the delegation.

In addition, all committees follow the practice initiated by CERD in 1991 of undertaking a "review procedure" in the absence of a report to examine

implementation of the relevant treaty by a State
Party whose report is at least five years overdue. The
notification that a treaty body plans to do so has been
sufficient in many instances to encourage the state to
submit the missing report. In a number of cases,
however, States Parties have been considered under
the review procedure in the absence of a report. For
further discussion, *see* Report on the Working
Methods of the Human Rights Treaty Bodies relating
to the State Party Reporting Process, HRI/MC/2010/2,
May 10, 2010; W. Vandenhole, *The Procedures before
the UN Human Rights Treaty Bodies: Divergence or
Convergence?* (2004); H. Keller & G. Ulfstein, *UN
Human Rights Treaty Bodies: Law and Legitimacy*
(2012).

Many of the committees appoint one or two
members to serve as country rapporteurs with
respect to the report under consideration. Country
rapporteurs undertake a thorough study of the report
and assume the task of drafting the list of issues (or
LOIPR) presented to the state. The rapporteur
initiates the interactive dialogue by presenting his or
her analysis of the State Party's implementation of
the treaty. At the end of the dialogue, the rapporteur
sums up the discussion and presents his or her
preliminary conclusions. After the dialogue, the
rapporteur takes primary responsibility for drafting
Concluding Observations for adoption by the
Committee. The Concluding Observations typically
acknowledge progress made and set forth
recommendations in areas in which further action is
required. All the treaties allow States Parties to
respond to the treaty body's comments,

recommendations or suggestions with their own observations. The treaty bodies now all request States Parties to provide information on implementation of the recommendations contained in the concluding observations. Some committees have more formal follow-up procedures. *See* M. O'Flaherty, *Human Rights and the UN: Practice before the Treaty Bodies* (2002); Schmidt, *supra.*

To assist the treaty bodies with their work, the Office of the UN High Commissioner for Human Rights, in response to a request from the inter-committee meeting of treaty bodies in June 2006 prepared a report on indicators for monitoring the implementation of human rights. HRI/MC/2008/3, June 6, 2008. The report sets forth a conceptual and methodological framework for identifying quantitative indicators and making use of statistics provided by states in their periodic reports.

All of the treaty bodies except the Committee on Migrant Workers (CMW) have the authority to consider individual communications with respect to States Parties that have accepted this procedure. In addition, the Committee Against Torture (CAT), the Committee for the Elimination of Discrimination Against Women (CEDAW), the Committee on the Rights of the Child (CRC), the Committee on the Rights of Persons with Disabilities (CRPD), and the Committee on Enforced Disappearances (CED) (as well as the CESCR, as discussed above) may conduct inquiries into alleged violations if this procedure has been accepted by the State Party in question. The CED also has the authority to consider requests for "urgent action" on behalf of disappeared persons at the behest of the person's relative or another person having a legitimate interest. *See* Convention for the Protection of All Persons from Enforced Disappearance, art. 30. Although not provided for in the Convention, CERD has established an early warning and urgent action procedure for the prevention of serious violations of its Convention.

All of the treaty bodies also adopt General Comments clarifying the States parties' obligations under their respective Conventions and otherwise elaborating the Committees' interpretations of the Conventions. CERD and CEDAW denominate these "General Recommendations," in line with the terminology employed in those Conventions.

The treaties designated by the United Nations as "core" agreements are discussed in the sections that follow, along with the first human rights treaty adopted by the United Nations, the Convention against Genocide. *See* U.N. High Commissioner for Human Rights, *The Core International Human Rights Treaties* (2006); *The New Core International Human Rights Treaties* (2007). The rules of procedure for the human rights treaty bodies have been published together as *Compilation of Rules of Procedure adopted by Human Rights Treaty Bodies*, HRI/GEN/3/Rev.3, May 28, 2008.

§ 2–13. THE CONVENTION ON THE PREVENTION AND PUNISHMENT OF THE CRIME OF GENOCIDE

The Genocide Convention was adopted by the UN General Assembly on December 9, 1948 and entered into force on January 12, 1951. The extermination of millions of Jews and members of other national, ethnic and religious groups during the Nazi Holocaust prompted the adoption of the Genocide Convention, which outlaws this crime. *See* Lemkin, "Genocide as a Crime under International Law," 41 Am. J. Int'l L. 145 (1947); W. Schabas, *Genocide in International Law* (2nd ed. 2009).

The Convention declares that genocide, whether committed in time of peace or time of war, is a crime under international law. A "crime under international law" is a grave offense against the law of nations for which the individual perpetrator is punishable. It differs from a mere violation of international law, which makes a government liable for the resulting damages without imposing criminal responsibility on individuals. Article IV of the Genocide Convention accordingly provides that "persons committing genocide . . . shall be punished, whether they are constitutionally responsible rulers, public officials or private individuals."

The Convention defines "genocide" as the commission of certain enumerated acts "with intent to destroy, in whole or in part, a national, ethnic, racial or religious group, as such." (Art. II.) Other groups, *e.g.,* political or economic ones, are not included, nor is widespread killing of persons because of their gender, although such deliberate attacks would be considered a crime against humanity. The acts constituting genocide are: (a) killing members of the group; (b) causing serious bodily or mental harm to members of the group; (c) deliberately inflicting on the group conditions of life calculated to bring about its physical destruction in whole or in part; (d) imposing measures intended to prevent births within the group; and (e) forcibly transferring children of the group to another group. To be guilty of the crime of genocide, an individual must have committed one of the foregoing acts with the specific intent of destroying, in whole or in part, a national, ethnic, racial or religious group. The killing of some members of a group could consequently amount to genocide if carried out with the intent of destroying the group or a substantial part thereof. *See* Application of the Convention on the Prevention and Punishment of the Crime of Genocide (Bosnia and Herzegovina v. Serbia and Montenegro, 2007 ICJ Rep. 43 (26 Feb.).

It is worth noting that by outlawing the destruction of national, ethnic, racial and religious groups, the Genocide Convention formally recognizes the right of these groups to exist as groups. Viewed in this light, the Convention must be considered the centerpiece of the international law that applies to the protection of the rights of groups, be they minorities or majorities. Dinstein, "Collective Human Rights of Peoples and Minorities," 25 Int'l & Comp. L.Q. 102, 105 (1976).

The Genocide Convention takes account of the possibility that those charged with genocide might be tried by an international criminal court, but it does not establish such a tribunal. The Statutes of the *ad hoc* Tribunals for the former Yugoslavia and Rwanda adopt the definition contained in the Genocide Convention as a basis in conferring jurisdiction over genocide on these tribunals. The same is true of the Statute of the International Criminal Court. For some of the relevant case law, *see* A. Cassese, *International Law* 444 (2nd ed. 2005).

Disputes between two or more States Parties relating to the interpretation of the Convention may be submitted by either of them to the International Court of Justice. Genocide Convention, art. IX. The armed conflict in the Former Yugoslavia produced the first such cases in the ICJ. *See, e.g.,* Application of the Convention on the Prevention and Punishment of the Crime of Genocide (Bosnia and Herzegovina v. Yugoslavia), Order of 17 December 1997, 1997 ICJ Rep. 243 and the subsequent 2007 judgment, *supra. See* Ben-Naftali & Sharon, "What the ICJ Did Not Say About the Duty to Punish Genocide," 5 J. Int'l Crim. Just. 859, 868–70 (2007). National prosecutions for genocide are also contemplated. Article VI of the Genocide Convention speaks of "a competent tribunal of the State in the territory of which the act [of genocide] was committed." It is clear that the courts of other states, particularly those of the perpetrator's nationality, would also have jurisdiction under international law generally.

Today universal jurisdiction appears to be increasingly accepted with respect to the crime of genocide and a number of states have adopted legislation asserting jurisdiction over the offense no matter where it is committed or by whom. *See* T. Meron, *War Crimes Law Comes of Age* 249–50 (1998); Attorney General of Israel v. Eichmann, 36 Int'l L. Rep. 5 (1968); *Restatement (Third)* § 404. On the drafting history of the Convention, *see* N. Robinson, *The Genocide Convention: A Commentary* (1960); Lippman, "The Drafting of the 1948 Convention on the Prevention and Punishment of the Crime of Genocide," 3 B. U. Int'l L.J. 1 (1984).

§ 2–14. INTERNATIONAL CONVENTION ON THE ELIMINATION OF ALL FORMS OF RACIAL DISCRIMINATION

The UN General Assembly adopted this treaty in 1965 and it entered into force in 1969 (before either of the Covenants). It has been ratified by 177 states. The text is reprinted in 5 ILM 352 (1966). The Convention has been described as "the most comprehensive and unambiguous codification in treaty form of the idea of the equality of races." Schwelb, "The International Convention on the Elimination of Racial Discrimination," 15 Int'l & Comp. L.Q. 996, at 1057 (1966).

The Convention prohibits "racial discrimination," which it defines as "any distinction, exclusion, restriction or preference based on race, colour, descent, or national or ethnic origin" having the purpose or effect of "nullifying or impairing the recognition, enjoyment or exercise, on an equal footing, of human rights and fundamental freedoms in the political, economic, social, cultural or any other field of public life." (Art. 1(1).) The International Court of Justice has accepted this definition of racial discrimination as an authoritative interpretation of the meaning and scope of the non-discrimination clause of the UN Charter. Advisory Opinion on Legal Consequences for States of the Continued Presence of South Africa in Namibia, I.C.J. Rep., 1971, p. 16, at 57; Schwelb, "The International Court of Justice and the Human Rights Clauses of the Charter," 66 Am. J. Int'l L. 337, 350–51 (1972).

The States Parties to the Convention have the legal obligation to eliminate racial discrimination and to enact whatever laws are necessary to ensure non-discrimination in the exercise and enjoyment of various human rights. The Convention enumerates a long but non-exhaustive list of basic civil, political, economic, social and cultural rights to which this obligation applies. The list includes the rights set out in the Universal Declaration and the two Covenants. *See* Racial Convention, art. 5.

Besides prohibiting racial discrimination by governmental authorities, the Convention requires each State Party to "prohibit and bring to an end, by all appropriate means, including legislation as required by circumstances, racial discrimination by any person, group or organization." Art. 2(1)(d). The Convention also declares, in art. 1(4), that:

Special measures . . . for the sole purpose of securing adequate advancement of certain racial or ethnic groups or individuals requiring such protection as may be necessary in order to ensure such groups or individuals equal enjoyment or exercise of human rights and fundamental freedoms shall not be deemed racial discrimination, provided, however, that such measures do not, as a consequence, lead to the maintenance of separate rights for different racial groups and that they shall not be continued after the objectives for which they were taken have been achieved.

Furthermore, article 2(2) provides that the States Parties "shall . . . take" such special measures "when the circumstances so warrant." In light of these provisions, CERD has concluded that affirmative action and similar programs designed to improve the situation of disfavored minority groups are lawful, and in certain circumstances are required by the Convention. *See* General Recommendation 32, The Meaning and Scope of Special Measures in the International Convention for the Elimination of Racial Discrimination, CERD/C/GC/32 (2009).

Article 4 of the Convention requires States Parties to "declare an offence punishable by law all dissemination of ideas based on racial superiority or hatred, incitement to racial discrimination, as well as all acts of violence or incitement to such acts against any race or group of persons of another colour or ethnic origin." The latter obligation is subject to the proviso that any such legislation is to be drafted and enforced "with due regard to the principles embodied in the Universal Declaration of Human Rights and the rights expressly set forth in article 5 of this Convention," including notably the rights to freedom of expression and association. On the relationship between the obligation to combat hate speech and the right to freedom of expression, *see* General Recommendation 35, Combatting Racial Hate Speech, CERD/C/GC/35 (2013). For an analysis of the Convention, *see* Patrick Thornberry, *The International Convention on the Elimination of All Forms of Racial Discrimination: A Commentary* (2016); T. Meron, *Human Rights Law-Making in the United Nations* 7 (1986); N. Lerner, *The UN Convention on Elimination of All Forms of Racial Discrimination* (Reprint Rev. 2015). *See also* N. Lerner, *Group Rights and Discrimination in International Law* (2nd ed. 2003).

The monitoring of the Convention is conducted by the Committee on the Elimination of Racial Discrimination (CERD), which is composed of 18 members who are elected by the States Parties but serve in their individual capacities. CERD was the first UN human rights treaty body to be established and has been functioning since 1970. *See generally* Wolfrum, "The Committee on the Elimination of Racial Discrimination," 3 Max Planck UNYB 489 (1999); UN Centre for Human Rights, *The First Twenty Years: Progress Report of the Committee on the Elimination of Racial Discrimination* (1991); Partsch, "The Committee on the Elimination of Racial Discrimination," *in* P. Alston, *The United Nations and Human Rights* 339 (1992).

The Convention confers a number of functions on CERD. These include the review of the periodic reports the States Parties have an obligation to prepare "on the legislative, judicial, administrative or other measures which they have adopted to give effect to the provisions" of the Convention. Racial Convention, art. 9. CERD also has the power to deal with inter-state and individual communications. *Id.*, arts. 11 and 14.

CERD initially developed a number of promising approaches designed to transform the review of state reports into a dynamic monitoring mechanism. Its practice served as the model for subsequently-created treaty bodies, such as the Human Rights Committee. *See* Buergenthal, "Implementing the UN Racial Convention," 12 Tex. Int'l L.J. 187 (1977); Gomez del Prado, "United Nations Conventions on Human Rights: The Practice of the Human Rights Committee and the Committee on the Elimination of Racial Discrimination in Dealing with Reporting Obligations of States Parties," 7 Hum. Rts. Q. 492 (1985). After other human rights bodies began to innovate in significant ways, CERD also moved to strengthen its monitoring procedures. Wolfrum, *supra*, at 505–511. It now conducts general and thematic debates on issues within its mandate and may establish working groups on implementation of its decisions and recommendations, as well as for consideration of early warning and urgent measures. The Committee pays particular attention to States Parties who fail to comply with the reporting obligation, reminding them of their obligations under article 9 of the Convention and making recommendations with a view to ensuring the implementation of the Convention.

By ratifying the Racial Convention, a state automatically submits itself to the jurisdiction of the Committee to deal with inter-state communications directed against it by any other State Party. Thus, unlike in the case of the ICCPR, the inter-state complaint system under the Racial Convention is not optional. Racial Convention, art. 11. The procedure for dealing with these communications envisages a two-stage process. First, the Committee passes on the admissibility of the complaint and gathers all relevant information thereon. Thereafter, an *ad hoc* Conciliation Commission is established and charged with the task of preparing a report on the dispute and making appropriate recommendations to the states concerned. Racial Convention, arts. 12 and 13. The inter-state complaint mechanism has not as yet been utilized. Instead, as discussed further at the end of this section, inter-state disputes arising under the Convention have been submitted directly to the ICJ.

The individual petition system established by the Racial Convention is optional, requiring a separate declaration recognizing the jurisdiction of the Committee to receive such communications. Racial Convention, art. 14. *See generally* Wolfrum, *supra*, at 511; Lerner, "Individual Petitions Under the International Convention on the Elimination of all Forms of Racial Discrimination," *in* I. Cotler & F.P. Eliadis (eds.), *International Human Rights Law: Theory and Practice* 435 (1992). CERD's process for handling individual communications, and for following up on States Parties' compliance with its decisions, is similar to that of the Human Rights Committee, as described above, § 2–8.

Although the Racial Convention entered into force in 1969, the number of ten states necessary to bring the individual petition system into effect was not reached until 1982. Despite the fact that 177 states have ratified the Convention, only 58 have thus far accepted the right of individual petition. Here it is interesting to note that a much larger number of states (115) have ratified the Optional Protocol to the Covenant on Civil and Political Rights, even though fewer states (168) are parties to the Covenant. To date the CERD has dealt with fifty-eight individual petitions. *See* Report of the Committee on the Elimination of Racial Discrimination, para. 34, U.N. Doc. A/71/18 (2016).

The Racial Convention also confers jurisdiction on the International Court of Justice to deal with disputes between the States Parties. The relevant provision is Article 22, which reads as follows:

Any dispute between two or more States Parties with respect to the interpretation or application of this Convention, which is not settled by negotiation or by the procedures expressly provided for in this Convention, shall, at the request of any of the parties to the dispute, be referred to the International Court of Justice for decision, unless the disputants agree to another mode of settlement.

Thus, by ratifying the Convention a state is deemed to have accepted the jurisdiction of the Court to decide disputes arising under the treaty. The Racial Convention was invoked in an application filed by the Congo against Rwanda, held inadmissible on February 3, 2006. *See* Armed Activities on the Territory of the Congo (New Application 2002) (DRC v. Rwanda), 2006 ICJ Rep. In 2008, the Republic of Georgia filed a case alleging violations of the Racial Convention by Russian authorities in the Georgian territories of Abkhazia and South Ossetia. *See* Case Concerning Application of the International Convention on the Elimination of All Forms of Racial Discrimination (Georgia v. Russian Federation), 2011 I.C.J. Rep. 70 (April 1). The ICJ interpreted article 22 to require, as a condition of maintaining an action in the ICJ, that the parties have attempted to settle the dispute "by negotiation or by the procedures expressly provided for in this Convention." Because the parties had not invoked the conciliation procedures of article 11 or otherwise pursued settlement negotiations, the Court dismissed the case for lack of jurisdiction.

Many States Parties, including the United States, have ratified the Convention with a reservation to Article 22, requiring the consent of both parties to the dispute before it may be referred to the Court. They have thus effectively opted out of Article 22.

The Committee began in 1993 to include in its regular agenda the consideration of preventive measures, which include an early-warning system and an "urgent action" procedure to respond to problems requiring immediate attention. A/62/18, Annex III. Early warning is directed at preventing existing problems from escalating into a conflict. Urgent action responds to problems requiring immediate attention to prevent or limit the scale or number of serious violations of the Convention. The procedures may be invoked by the Committee itself or by interested parties, including NGOs. The Committee may proceed through written submissions or by a hearing which the state is invited to attend. The Committee has adopted decisions, statements or resolutions or taken further action under these procedures in relation to more than 20 States Parties, including conducting two field visits. It has drawn the attention of the Secretary-General, the Security Council, the Human Rights Council, and other relevant bodies, including regional bodies such as the Council of Europe and the European Union, to a variety of situations.

§ 2–15. CONVENTION ON THE ELIMINATION OF ALL FORMS OF DISCRIMINATION AGAINST WOMEN

The UN General Assembly adopted this Convention on December 18, 1979; it entered into force on September 3, 1981. The text is reprinted in 19 ILM 33 (1980). The Convention, which has been ratified by 189 states, seeks to end discrimination against women, which it defines as "any distinction, exclusion, or restriction made on the basis of sex" that impairs the enjoyment by women of "human rights and fundamental freedoms in the political, economic, social, cultural, civil or any other field."

Art. 1. In addition to the obligation to condemn discrimination against women, the States Parties undertake, *inter alia,* "to embody the principle of equality of men and women in their national constitutions or other appropriate legislation" and to adopt laws or other measures "including sanctions where appropriate, prohibiting all discrimination against women." Art. 2. The Convention also requires the States Parties to take a series of measures in the political, social, economic and cultural realm to advance the enjoyment of equal rights by women in all walks of life. Thus, for example, Article 5 of the Convention provides that:

States Parties shall take all appropriate measures:

(a) To modify the social and cultural patterns of conduct of men and women, with a view to achieving the elimination of prejudices and customary and all other practices which are based on the idea of the inferiority or the superiority of either of the sexes or on stereotyped roles for men and women.

In like manner, the Convention addresses a wide range of problems encountered by women in their struggle for equality. *See generally* N. Hevener, *International Law and the Status of Women* (1983); T. Meron, *Human Rights Law-Making in the United Nations* 53 (1986); Cook, "State Accountability Under the Convention on the Elimination of All Forms of Discrimination Against Women," *in* R.J. Cook (ed.), *Human Rights of Women* 228 (1994); Banks, "CEDAW, Compliance, and Custom: Human Rights Enforcement in Sub-Saharan Africa," 32 Fordham

Int'l L. J. 781 (2009); Jivan & Forster, "What Would Gandhi Say? Reconciling Universalism, Cultural Relativism and Feminism through Women's Use of CEDAW," 9 Singapore Y.B.I.L. 103 (2005). *See generally* M. Freeman, C. Chinkin & B. Rudolf (eds.), *The UN Convention on the Elimination of All Forms of Discrimination Against Women: A Commentary* (2013).

The effectiveness of the Convention in its first twenty-five years in promoting the protection of the rights it guarantees was undermined to a significant extent by the many reservations made by states in ratifying this treaty. For an analysis of some of these reservations, *see* Tomaševski, "Women's Rights," *in* J. Symonides (ed.), *Human Rights: Concept and Standards* 231, at 235–38 (2000); Riddle, "Making CEDAW Universal: A Critique of CEDAW's Reservation Regime under Article 28 and the Effectiveness of the Reporting Process," 34 Geo. Wash. Int'l L. Rev. 605 (2002). These reservations have sought to preserve various national or religious institutions that are in conflict with the Convention. Some of them are clearly incompatible with the object and purpose of the Convention, despite the fact that its Article 28(2) declares that "a reservation incompatible with the object and purpose of the present Convention shall not be permitted." *See* Clark, "The Vienna Convention Reservations Regime and the Convention on Discrimination Against Women," 85 Am. J. Int'l L. 281 (1991).

The effort to get states to withdraw their reservations received a boost from the 1993 Vienna

World Conference on Human Rights, which called on CEDAW to "continue its review of reservations to the Convention" and urged the states "to withdraw reservations that are contrary to the object and purpose of the Convention or which are otherwise incompatible with international treaty law." Vienna Declaration and Programme of Action, U.N. Doc. A/Conf. 157/23, Art. II, para. 39 (1993). *See* Sullivan, "Women's Human Rights and the 1993 World Conference on Human Rights," 88 Am. J. Int'l L. 152 (1994). Since the Vienna Conference, more than thirty states have withdrawn reservations that they had made at the time of ratification or accession. UN Treaty Collection, Declarations and Reservations, http://www.unhchr.ch/html/menu3/b/treaty9_asp.htm.

The measures of implementation provided for by the Convention include periodic reports by the States Parties relating to "the legislative, judicial, administrative or other measures they have adopted to give effect to the provisions of the Convention." Art. 18(1). These reports are reviewed by CEDAW. Art. 17. The Committee consists of 23 experts elected by the States Parties but serving in their personal capacities. CEDAW follows procedures similar to other treaty bodies in its consideration of State Reports, having adopted reporting guidelines. It makes use of pre-session working groups, which prepare lists of issues to discuss with representatives of the State Party whose report is under consideration. In 2015, the Committee began to offer the simplified reporting procedure as well, on a pilot basis, to those States Parties with overdue reports that wish to make use of that procedure. For a description of this procedure, *see* § 2–8, above. Following consideration of the report, CEDAW adopts Concluding Observations, which are transmitted to the State. CEDAW has adopted 34 General Recommendations elaborating its interpretation of various provisions of the Convention. It reports on its activities to the States Parties, the UN Commission on the Status of Women, and the General Assembly.

CEDAW was for a long time something of a stepchild among UN human rights treaty bodies because Article 20 (1) of the Convention provides that "the Committee shall normally meet for a period of not more than two weeks annually." This soon proved to be totally insufficient time to comply with its obligations under the Convention. In 1996, pending the entry into force of an amendment to Article 20(1), the General Assembly authorized CEDAW, on an interim basis, to hold two annual sessions of three weeks each. In 2005, General Assembly resolution 60/230 (23 December 2005) expanded the meeting time further, allowing the Committee to meet for the coming two years for three sessions. *See* Shalev, "State Reporting and the Convention on the Elimination of All Forms of Discrimination Against Women," *in* A. Bayefsky (ed.), *The UN Human Rights Treaty System in the 21st Century* 233 at 244 (2000).

The powers of the Committee expanded with the adoption on October 6, 1999 and entry into force on December 22, 2000, of the Optional Protocol to the Convention, giving the Committee the power to accept and consider communications. Of the 189

States Parties to the Convention, 108 have ratified the Protocol. The communications procedure allows either individuals or groups of individuals claiming to be victims of a violation of the Convention to submit complaints to the Committee against a State Party to the Protocol. Communications may also be submitted on behalf of individuals or groups of individuals, with the victims' consent or with a showing of justification for acting without their consent. A communication must be submitted in writing and may not be anonymous. The Committee must determine that all available domestic remedies have been exhausted, that the complaint has not been previously examined by the Committee, and that it has not been or is not being examined under another procedure of international investigation or settlement.

In addition, a communication must be compatible with the provisions of the Convention; it must not be an abuse of the right to submit a communication. Claimants' allegations must be verifiable, and the facts presented must have occurred after the State Party ratified the Protocol. The Committee may request that urgent measures be taken by the State Party to prevent irreparable harm to the petitioner. The procedure is not a public one and results in views and recommendations which are transmitted to the parties concerned. The State Party has six months to consider the views of the Committee and provide a written response, including remedial steps taken. The Committee may request further information from the State Party, including subsequent reports.

See Sokhi-Bulley, "The Optional Protocol to CEDAW: First Steps," 6 Hum. Rts. L. Rev. 143 (2006).

The Protocol broke new ground by also establishing, in Article 8, an inquiry procedure that allows the Committee to initiate a confidential investigation by one or more of its members, when it has received reliable information of grave or systematic violations by a State Party of rights established in the Convention. Where warranted, and with the consent of the State Party, the Committee may visit the territory of the State Party. Any findings, comments or recommendations will be transmitted to the State Party concerned, to which it may respond within six months. No reservations to the Optional Protocol are permitted, but Article 10 provides an opt-out clause that allows a State Party, upon ratification of the Optional Protocol, to refuse to recognize the competence of the Committee to initiate and conduct the inquiry referred to in Article 8. This declaration may be withdrawn at a later time. CEDAW completed its first Article 8 study in July 2004. *See* Report on Mexico produced by the Committee on the Elimination of Discrimination against Women under article 8 of the Optional Protocol to the Convention, and reply from the Government of Mexico, CEDAW/C/2005/OP.8/ MEXICO. The Committee has also conducted inquiries relating to Canada and the Philippines.

Under Article 29(1) of the Convention, disputes between the States Parties relating to the interpretation or application of the Convention may be submitted to the International Court of Justice by any of the parties to the dispute if the parties have previously attempted to settle the dispute by negotiation and arbitration. However, many states have availed themselves of the right, provided for in Article 29(2), to decline to accept the Court's jurisdiction under Article 29(1). No State Party has to date invoked Article 29(1).

On the CEDAW Committee generally, *see* Byrnes, "The Other Human Rights Treaty Body: The Work of the Committee on the Elimination of Discrimination against Women," 14 Yale J. Int'l L. 1 (1989); Jacobson, "The Committee on the Elimination of Discrimination against Women," *in* Alston, *supra*, at 444. *See also* Schopp-Schilling, "Treaty Body Reform: The Case of the Committee on the Elimination of Discrimination Against Women," 7 Hum. Rts. L. Rev. 201 (2007); Evatt, "Finding a Voice for Women's Rights: The Early Days of CEDAW," 34 Geo. Wash. Int'l L. Rev. 515 (2002).

§ 2–16. CONVENTION AGAINST TORTURE AND OTHER CRUEL, INHUMAN OR DEGRADING TREATMENT

This treaty was adopted by the UN General Assembly on December 10, 1984 and entered into force on June 28, 1987. *See generally* Lerner, "The U.N. Convention on Torture," 16 Israel Y.B. Hum. Rts. 126 (1986); J.H. Burgers & H. Danelius, *The United Nations Convention against Torture: A Handbook on the Convention against Torture and Other Cruel, Inhuman or Degrading Treatment or Punishment* (1988); M. Nowak & E. McArthur, *The*

United Nations Convention against Torture: A Commentary (2008). The text of the Convention is reprinted in 23 ILM 1027 (1984), as modified 24 ILM 525 (1985). It has been ratified by 160 states.

The Convention is designed to prevent and punish torture committed "by or at the instigation of or with the consent or acquiescence of a public official or other person acting in an official capacity." Art. 1(1). In other words, it covers not only torture inflicted by government officials but also by torture by private individuals or groups whose conduct such officials encourage or tolerate.

The Convention defines torture as "any act by which severe pain or suffering, whether physical or mental, is intentionally inflicted on a person" for the purpose, *inter alia,* of "obtaining from him or a third person information or a confession." Art. 1(1). The States Parties undertake to adopt "effective legislative, administrative, judicial or other measures to prevent" torture in any territory under their jurisdiction. Art. 2(1). Each State Party must ensure that all acts of torture (as defined in the treaty) are offenses under its criminal law, and its courts must have jurisdiction if the offense occurred within its territory, if the alleged offender is its national, and if the victim is its national (as each State considers appropriate). Arts. 4(1), 5. If an alleged torturer is found in the territory of a State Party which does not have jurisdiction under those provisions, it is required either to extradite him for prosecution elsewhere or to submit the case for prosecution under its own law (a principle known as *aut dedere aut judicare*). Art. 7(1). The Convention declares torture to be an extraditable offense (Art. 8) but prohibits States Parties from extraditing a person to a country where he or she "would be in danger of being subjected to torture." Art. 3(1). On this latter point, *see, e.g.,* Mutomba v. Switzerland, Communication No. 13/1993, UN Committee on Torture (CAT), Decision of April 27, 1994, 15 Hum. Rts. L.J. 164 (1994), holding that Switzerland would violate Article 3 of the Convention were it to expel or return Mr. Mutomba to Zaire, where he was in danger of being tortured, and A.S. v. Sweden, Communication No. 149/1999, Decision of November 6, 1999, Report of the Torture Committee, UN Doc. A/56/44, p. 173, making the same finding with regard to a threatened expulsion to Iran.

The Torture Convention is clear that there are "no exceptional circumstances whatsoever" to justify torture and that no orders from superior officers or a public authority may be invoked as a justification. Arts. 2(2) and 2(3). The Convention also contains a number of provisions designed to ensure that the formal prohibition of torture becomes a reality on the domestic plane. Article 11, for example, reads as follows:

> Each State Party shall keep under systematic review interrogation rules, instructions, methods and practices as well as arrangements for the custody and treatment of persons subjected to any form of arrest, detention or imprisonment in any territory under its

jurisdiction, with a view to preventing any cases of torture.

The Convention establishes the Committee Against Torture (CAT) to monitor States Parties' compliance with their obligations. *See generally* N. Rodley and M. Pollard, *The Treatment of Prisoners Under International Law* 210–219 (3rd ed. 2009); Dormenval, "UN Committee Against Torture: Practice and Perspectives," 8 Neth. Q. Hum. Rts. 26 (1990); Byrnes, "The Committee against Torture," *in* Alston, *supra*, at 509; Inglese, "The Committee Against Torture: One Step Forward, One Step Back," 18 Neth. Q. Hum. Rts. 307 (2000). The CAT is composed of ten independent experts elected by the States Parties to the Convention. The monitoring measures the Convention creates consist of an obligatory reporting system (Art. 19) as well as optional inter-state (Art. 21) and individual complaint (Art. 22) mechanisms. These two mechanisms are patterned on comparable provisions found in the Covenant on Civil and Political Rights and its Optional Protocol. As of late 2016, sixty-five States Parties have accepted the individual complaint mechanism and sixty-three have accepted the inter-state mechanism.

The Torture Convention also empowers the CAT to undertake certain investigatory actions on its own initiative. Thus, Article 20 authorizes the Committee to initiate an inquiry when it receives "reliable information" suggesting "well-founded indications that torture is being systematically practised in the territory of a State Party." Although the inquiry is to be confidential and requires the Committee to seek the cooperation of the State Party concerned, the language of Article 20 indicates that the state's failure to cooperate does not deprive the Committee *ipso facto* of the right to proceed with the investigation. However, the Committee needs the state's consent to investigate the charges in its territory. Art. 20(3). All documents and proceedings of the Committee relating to its functions under article 20 of the Convention are confidential and all the meetings concerning its proceedings under that article are closed. However, the Committee may, after consultations with the State Party concerned, include a summary account of the results of the proceedings in its annual report to the States Parties and to the General Assembly.

For an analysis of the CAT's practice under Article 20, *see* Inglese, *supra*, at 314. For action taken by CAT under Article 20, *see* "Activities of the Committee against Torture pursuant to Article 20 of the Convention against Torture and Other Cruel, Inhuman or Degrading Treatment or Punishment," UN Doc. A/48/44/Add.1 (Nov. 9, 1993), 14 Hum. Rts. L.J. 426 (1993), describing an inquiry involving torture in Turkey. For a similar inquiry involving Brazil, *see* Report of the Committee against Torture, UN Doc. A/63/44 (2008), p. 99. *See also* Joseph, "Committee Against Torture: Recent Jurisprudence," 6 Hum. Rts. L. Rev. 571 (2006).

Article 28 allows the States Parties to avoid the application of the powers that Article 20 confers on the CAT. It provides that "each State may, at the time of signature or ratification of this Convention or accession thereto, declare that it does not recognize the competence of the Committee provided for in article 20." This possibility "to contract out" of Article 20 has been utilized by the States Parties much less frequently than one might expect, despite the fact that Article 20 confers on the CAT an enforcement weapon that is potentially very powerful.

The Torture Convention also confers jurisdiction on the International Court of Justice over disputes between the States Parties relating to the interpretation or application of the treaty, although States Parties may opt out of this jurisdiction at the time of ratification or accession. Art. 30. The ICJ exercised jurisdiction under Article 30 in *Questions Relating to the Obligation to Prosecute or Extradite (Belgium v. Senegal)*, 2012 I.C.J. Rep. 422 (July 20), in which the Court found that Senegal had breached the Convention's *aut dedere aut judicare* principle by failing to prosecute the former head of state of Chad for torture while refusing to extradite him to Belgium for prosecution there.

The Optional Protocol for the Prevention of Torture (OPCAT), which entered into force in 2006 and has been ratified by 83 States, establishes an additional monitoring mechanism. The OPCAT requires States Parties to establish a domestic body empowered to visit and report on places of detention (called national preventive mechanisms) (art. 3). It also establishes a separate treaty body, the Subcommittee for the Prevention of Torture (SPT), consisting of twenty-five members serving in their individual capacities (arts. 2, 5(1), 5(6)). The OPCAT requires States Parties to give both the national preventive mechanism and the SPT unrestricted access to all places of detention under its jurisdiction and control (arts. 4, 14(1), 20). These may include police stations, prisons, immigration detention centers and juvenile justice centers. The SPT conducts visits to places of detention pursuant to a program of regular visits established by the Subcommittee (art. 13(1)). The visits are carried out by two or more members, assisted by one or more experts selected from a roster prepared on the basis of proposals by States Parties, the Office of the High Commissioner for Human Rights, and the UN Centre for International Crime Prevention (art. 13(3)). The SPT's report and recommendations are to be communicated to the State Party concerned confidentially (art. 16(1)), although the Subcommittee may make its report public if the State Party refused to cooperate with the SPT as required by the Convention (art. 16(4)).

The SPT holds three meetings annually, which are confidential. Unlike other treaty bodies, the SPT does not review reports from States Parties or consider individual or inter-state communications. On the OPCAT, *see generally* R. Murray, *The Optional Protocol to the UN Convention Against Torture* (2011).

§ 2–17. CONVENTION ON THE
RIGHTS OF THE CHILD

This treaty was adopted by the UN General Assembly on November 20, 1989 and entered into force on September 2, 1990. The treaty has 196 ratifications (including the Holy See), making it the most widely accepted of all human rights treaties. Among UN Member States, only the United States has not ratified the Convention. For useful analyses of the most important aspects of the Convention, *see* "The Rights of the Child," http://indicators.ohchr. org/.

By ratifying the Convention, the States Parties assume the obligation to accord children within their jurisdiction an extensive catalog of civil, political, economic, social and cultural rights "irrespective of the child's or his or her parent's or legal guardian's race, colour, sex, language, religion, political or other opinion, national, ethnic or social origin, property, disability, birth or other status." Art. 2(1).

The Convention defines a child as "every human being below the age of eighteen unless under the law applicable to the child, majority is attained earlier." Art. 1. The guiding principle of the Convention is spelled out in Article 3(1), which declares that "in all actions concerning children, whether undertaken by public or private social welfare institutions, courts of law, administrative authorities or legislative bodies, the best interests of the child shall be a primary consideration." *See* Alston, "The Legal Framework of the Convention on the Rights of the Child," U.N. Bulletin of Human Rights, No. 91/2, at 1 (1992).

Although many of the rights the Convention proclaims are set out in one form or another in existing international human rights treaties, the Convention is the first treaty that singles out children as subjects of international rights and protection. The Convention seeks to protect children against a large number of practices of special danger to their welfare, including economic exploitation, illicit use of drugs, all forms of sexual exploitation and abuse, and trafficking. It also bars the recruitment of children under the age of fifteen into the armed forces of the States Parties. *See generally* Lopatka, "The Importance of the Convention on the Rights of the Child," U.N. Bulletin of Human Rights, No. 91/2 at 56 (1992). *See also* Price Cohen & Miljeteig-Olssen, "Status Report: United Nations Convention on the Rights of the Child," 7 N.Y.L. Sch. J. Hum. Rts. 367 (1991).

The Convention establishes a Committee on the Rights of the Child (CRC), which is charged with the task of "examining the progress made by the States Parties in achieving the realization of the obligations undertaken in the present Convention." Art. 43(1). The Committee is composed of eighteen members who serve in their personal capacities. Its principal task is to review the reports which the States Parties are required to submit to the Committee on the measures they have taken in implementing the Convention. Art. 44. For an overview of the work of the CRC, *see* www. ohchr.org/Documents/Publications/FactSheet10rev. 1en.pdf. *See generally*, Karp, "Reporting and the Committee on the Rights of the Child," *in* A. Bayefsky (ed.), *The UN Human Rights Treaty System in the 21st*

Century 35 (2000). *See also* Sardenberg, "Committee on the Rights of the Child; Basic Process," 6 Transnat'l L. & Contemp. Probs. (1996); Lansdown, "The Reporting Process under the Convention of the Rights of the Child," *in* P. Alston & J. Crawford (eds.), *The Future of UN Human Rights Treaty Monitoring* 113 (2000).

Two optional protocols to the Convention, adopted by the General Assembly on May 25, 2000, are designed to strengthen the protections afforded children. The First Optional Protocol, concerning the involvement of children in armed conflicts, entered into force on 13 February 2002 and has been ratified by 166 States (including the United States). The text is reprinted in 8 Int'l Hum. Rts. Rep. 288 (2001). It aims to raise the minimum age of persons participating in armed conflicts to 18. States Parties are required to take all feasible measures to ensure that members of their armed forces under the age of 18 do not take a direct part in hostilities; they are also required to ensure that persons who have not attained the age of 18 are not forced to serve in their armed forces. The laws on voluntary recruitment are to include special measures to protect those under 18. In one of the rare instances of direct regulation of non-state actors by a human rights instrument, Article 4 provides that armed groups that are distinct from the armed forces of a State should not, under any circumstances, recruit or use in hostilities persons under the age of 18 years. States Parties are to take measures to prevent such recruitment and use, including the adoption of legal measures necessary to prohibit and criminalize such practices.

The Second Optional Protocol, which addresses the sale of children, child prostitution and child pornography, entered into force on 18 January 2002 and has been ratified by 173 States. The text is reprinted in 8 Int'l Hum Rts. Rep. 293 (2001). Each State Party must ensure that, at a minimum, the acts and activities specified in the Protocol are criminalized, whether or not such offences are committed within their territory, or are committed on an individual or organized basis. The Protocol establishes extensive enforcement jurisdiction based on the territory where the offense is committed, the nationality of the perpetrator, and nationality of the victim. Further, States must either prosecute or extradite offenders found on their territory. The Protocol also provides for the confiscation of material and assets involved in the specified crimes and for protective measures to be taken on behalf of child victims.

A third Optional Protocol to the Convention entered into force in 2014. This Protocol enhances the monitoring powers of the CRC by empowering it to receive and decide individual complaints (art. 5) and to conduct inquiries with respect to grave or systematic violations of the Convention or the Optional Protocols (art. 13). The Protocol also empowers the Committee to received inter-state communications as between states that have accepted the Committee's jurisdiction over such complaints (art. 12). To date, 29 states have ratified the Third Optional Protocol and, of those, nine have accepted the CRC's jurisdiction over inter-state communications.

§ 2–18. INTERNATIONAL CONVENTION ON THE PROTECTION OF THE RIGHTS OF ALL MIGRANT WORKERS AND MEMBERS OF THEIR FAMILIES

One of the three most recent core human rights conventions, the Migrant Workers Convention was adopted December 18, 1990; it entered into force July 1, 2003 but has relatively few ratifications (49 as of late 2016), none of them from major labor-receiving states. The Convention is unusual in being adopted outside the framework of the International Labor Organization, whose earlier work on the topic includes the Migrant Workers (Supplementary Provisions) Convention 1975 (No. 143). One reason for the shift may be that the ILO prohibits reservations to the treaties it adopts, *see infra* § 2–29, which is not the case in general with UN human rights agreements.

The text of the Migrant Workers Convention reflects the competing interests of sending and receiving states and the considerable concern states have about controlling entry into their territory. The Convention consists of a lengthy Preamble and 93 Articles, with the latter being subdivided into 9 different Parts. The first part defines the term "migrant worker" as "a person who is to be engaged or has been engaged in a remunerated activity in a State of which he or she is not a national". Art. 2(1) Included are "frontier workers; seasonal workers; seafarers; workers on offshore installations; itinerant workers; migrants employed for a specific project; and self-employed workers." Part II consists of a single article which provides that the rights in the Convention are to be made available to all migrants without discrimination. Parts III–V set forth the guaranteed rights.

Part III lists the rights of all migrant workers regardless of their legal status, with Articles 8–24 laying out a set of civil and political rights, many of which are already contained in other human rights instruments, including the rights to life; privacy; freedom of expression; freedom of conscience; freedom from torture, slavery, arbitrary arrest and detention; equality before the law, and consular protection. Arbitrary and collective expulsions of migrant workers, without regard to their legal status, are prohibited. Arts. 22, 56. In contrast, Article 13 of the ICCPR limits the application of procedural safeguards against expulsion to lawfully resident migrants. Articles 25 to 35, explicitly accord to all migrants a range of economic and social rights, such as the right to equal remuneration with nationals; to join trade unions; to urgent medical care; to education for their children; and to respect for their cultural identity.

Part IV provides additional rights for lawfully-resident migrants while Part V sets forth specific rights for workers in particular categories of employment. Part VI contains provisions relating to international cooperation and coordination in the management of legal migration and in the prevention or reduction of irregular movements.

Among the key provisions, Article 25(1) calls for national treatment of migrant workers, establishing that they shall enjoy "treatment not less favorable than that which applies to nationals of the State of employment" in respect of terms and conditions of work. Article 33 requires States Parties to take the measures they deem appropriate to ensure that migrant workers and members of their families are informed of their rights under the Convention upon request without charge and, as far as possible, in a language they are able to understand.

The Convention establishes a Committee on Migrant Workers (CMW), initially composed of 10 independent experts of high moral character, impartiality and recognized competence in subject matter. Under Article 72(1)(b), membership increased to fourteen experts once the Convention reached forty-one States Parties. Members are elected for a term of four years by States Parties in accordance with article 72 of the Convention. Members serve in their personal capacity and may be re-elected if nominated. In common with the other core international human rights instruments, Article 73 requires that all States Parties report to the Committee on the measures taken to implement the Convention one year after ratification, and periodically thereafter; the Committee reviews the States Parties' reports and provides comments and recommendations in the form of Concluding Observations. Article 76 also establishes, once ten states agree, an inter-state complaints procedure. Similarly, Article 77 establishes an individual complaint procedure, to come into effect once ten states have declared their consent. To date, two States Parties have accepted the inter-state complaint mechanism and four have accepted the individual complaint mechanism. Like the other treaty bodies, the CMW adopts General Comments to provide guidance on the implementation of the Convention.

§ 2–19. CONVENTION ON THE RIGHTS OF PERSONS WITH DISABILITIES

Adopted December 13, 2006, this Convention (and its Optional Protocol, which establishes an individual complaint mechanism) entered into force May 3, 2008. As of late 2016, there were 168 States Parties to the Convention, of which 92 have also ratified the Protocol. The Convention aims to combat discrimination against persons with disabilities and to guarantee them the exercise of human rights. States Parties commit to develop and carry out policies, laws and administrative measures for securing the rights recognized in the Convention and abolish laws, regulations, customs and practices that constitute discrimination. Art. 4. They also agree to combat stereotypes and prejudices and promote awareness of the capabilities of persons with disabilities (Art. 8).

The Convention requires States Parties to ensure persons with disabilities their right to enjoy the inherent right to life on an equal basis with others. Art. 10. Children with disabilities shall have equal rights, shall not be separated from their parents against their will, except when the authorities determine that this is in the child's best interests, and in no case shall be separated from their parents

on the basis of a disability of either the child or the
parents. Art. 23. States Parties are to recognize that
all persons are equal before the law, to prohibit
discrimination on the basis of disability and
guarantee equal legal protection. Art. 5. Economic
rights (Art. 12), the right of access to justice (Art. 13),
the right to liberty and security (Art. 14), the right to
physical and mental integrity (Art. 17), freedom from
torture and from cruel, inhuman or degrading
treatment or punishment, and from nonconsensual
medical or scientific experiments (Art. 15) are also
guaranteed.

Laws and administrative measures must
guarantee freedom from exploitation, violence and
abuse and promote the recovery, rehabilitation and
reintegration of those who do suffer from abuse. Art.
16. Persons with disabilities are not to be subjected
to arbitrary or illegal interference with their privacy,
family, home, correspondence or communication. Art.
22. The Convention also takes into account the
special needs that disabled persons may have. Article
9 requires States Parties to identify and eliminate
obstacles and barriers and ensure that persons with
disabilities can access their environment,
transportation, public facilities and services, and
information and communications technologies.
Persons with disabilities have the right to live
independently, to be included in the community, to
choose where and with whom to live and to have
access to in-home, residential and community
support services. Art. 19. Personal mobility and
independence are to be fostered by facilitating
affordable personal mobility, training in mobility

skills and access to mobility aids, devices, assistive technologies and live assistance. Art. 20.

The Convention sets forth the right to an adequate standard of living and social protection, including public housing, services and assistance for disability-related needs, as well as assistance with disability-related expenses in case of poverty (Art. 28). States Parties are to promote access to information by providing information intended for the general public in accessible formats and technologies, by facilitating the use of Braille, sign language and other forms of communication and by encouraging the media and Internet providers to make on-line information available in accessible formats. Art. 21.

Civil rights include those relating to marriage, family and personal relations, ensuring that persons with disabilities have the equal opportunity to experience parenthood, to marry and to found a family, to decide on the number and spacing of children, to have access to reproductive and family planning education, and to enjoy equal rights and responsibilities regarding guardianship, wardship, trusteeship and adoption of children (Art. 23). Rights relating to education (Art. 24) and health (Art. 25) are also included. To enable persons with disabilities to attain maximum independence and ability, States Parties are to provide comprehensive habilitation and rehabilitation services in the areas of health, employment and education (Art. 26), prohibiting discrimination in job-related matters and promoting self-employment, entrepreneurship and employment in the private sector, with reasonable accommodation at work (Art. 27). Political (Art. 29) and cultural rights (Art. 30) are also specified. A unique provision requires States Parties to provide development assistance to developing countries to facilitate their compliance with the Convention (Art. 32).

To ensure implementation and monitoring of the Convention, countries are to designate a focal point in the government and create a national mechanism to promote and monitor implementation. Article 33. The Convention also creates a Committee on the Rights of Persons with Disabilities (CRPD), made up of independent experts who serve in their individual capacities. All States Parties are obliged to submit reports to the Committee within two years of becoming party to the Convention and periodically thereafter. The Committee normally holds two sessions per year. Like other treaty bodies, the CRPD reviews State Party reports and adopts comments and recommendations in the form of Concluding Observations. It also adopts General Comments to guide States Parties in their implementation of the Convention. The CRPD also examines individual communications lodged pursuant to the Optional Protocol. *See* Rosemary Kayess & Phillip French, "Out of Darkness into Light? Introducing the Convention on the Rights of Persons with Disabilities," 8 Hum.Rts L.Rev. 1 (2008).

§ 2–20. INTERNATIONAL CONVENTION FOR THE PROTECTION OF ALL PERSONS FROM ENFORCED DISAPPEARANCE

The most recent of the nine UN core human rights instruments, the Disappearances Convention, was adopted December 20, 2006. The Convention entered into force in 2010 and has been ratified by 53 states. Like the Genocide and Torture Conventions, the Disappearances Convention is not only a human rights instrument, but also one concerned with criminal law, most notably in Article 5, which declares the widespread or systematic use of enforced disappearances to be a crime against humanity.

The Convention recognizes the non-derogable right of any person not to be subjected to enforced disappearance. "Enforced disappearance" is defined in Article 2 of the Convention as

the arrest, detention, abduction or any other form of deprivation of liberty by agents of the State or by persons or groups of persons acting with the authorization, support or acquiescence of the State, followed by a refusal to acknowledge the deprivation of liberty or by concealment of the fate or whereabouts of the disappeared person, which place such a person outside the protection of the law.

States Parties are obligated to investigate any act defined in Article 2 committed by persons or groups of persons acting without the authorization, support or acquiescence of the State and to bring those responsible to justice. Art. 3. They must also make such acts crimes in domestic law and take measures to enforce the law through prosecution and punishment when they have jurisdiction to do so. Arts. 4, 6. The new rights guaranteed by the Convention include the prohibition of secret detentions (Art. 17) and the right of "any person with a legitimate interest" to obtain information about a detained person (Art. 18). Article 24 sets forth a variety of remedies that a State Party shall ensure. The Convention establishes grounds for extradition for the crime of enforced disappearance even in the absence of an extradition treaty between two States Parties (Art. 13(4)).

The Convention establishes a 10 member independent expert Committee on Enforced Disappearances (CED). Each State Party must submit periodic reports to the Committee. The Committee reviews the States Parties' reports and adopts comments and recommendations in the form of Concluding Observations. It also adopts General Comments to provide guidance to States Parties on the implementation of the Convention. The Convention provides for both an individual and an inter-state communications procedure with respect to States Parties that have declared that they accept such procedures (Arts. 31, 32). As of late 2016, twenty States Parties have accepted the inter-state communications mechanism and nineteen have accepted the individual communications mechanism. The Convention also authorizes the CED to conduct inquiries if it receives well-founded information that enforced disappearances are occurring on a widespread or systematic basis in the territory of a

State Party (Art. 34), and it has the authority to conduct *in situ* visits, after consultation with the State Party concerned, if it receives reliable information that serious violations of the Convention are occurring (Art. 33). Article 30 of the Convention establishes an innovative "urgent action" procedure.

V. UN CHARTER-BASED INSTITUTIONS

§ 2–21. INTRODUCTION

In addition to the supervisory bodies that have been established under UN human rights treaties, there also exist within the UN framework various institutions and procedures which have their constitutional basis in the Charter of the United Nations itself. This is true of such major human rights organs as the UN Human Rights Council, the Commission on the Status of Women, and the Office of the UN High Commissioner for Human Rights. Indeed, it is true of all the main organs of the United Nations, which over time have expanded their consideration of human rights issues. This section describes the institutions and the procedures for addressing human rights under the Charter, especially in regard to so-called gross violations of human rights. For a more comprehensive overview, *see* P. Alston (ed.), *The United Nations and Human Rights: A Critical Appraisal* (2002).

§ 2–22.   THE PRINCIPAL ORGANS OF THE UN

All U.N. organs deal with human rights matters today in accordance with the mandates conferred on them by the Charter.

1. The General Assembly

As the plenary UN body, the General Assembly discusses, often modifies, and adopts human rights treaties and declarations drafted by subsidiary organs. On September 13, 2007, for example, it approved the Declaration on the Rights of Indigenous Peoples, a text negotiated over more than two decades by the Sub-Commission on Promotion and Protection of Human Rights and the Commission on Human Rights, in consultation with indigenous peoples. *See* UN Declaration on the Rights of Indigenous Peoples, GA Res. 61/295, UN Doc. A/61/295 (2 Oct. 2007). The General Assembly also receives the annual reports of human rights treaty bodies and Charter-based institutions, and it generally provides support for the treaty body system. As discussed in § 2–8, in 2014 the General Assembly adopted a resolution on "Strengthening and enhancing the effective functioning of the human rights treaty body system," GA Res. 68/268, UN Doc. A/68/268 (April 9, 2014). In addition, from the General Assembly's first session, it has taken up and discussed allegations of human rights violations by Member States and adopted resolutions and recommendations on human rights matters. *See, e.g.,* G.A. Res. 44(I), at 69, U.N. Doc. A/64/Add.1 (Dec. 8, 1946).

2. The Security Council

Article 24 of the UN Charter entrusts the Security Council with primary responsibility for the maintenance of international peace and security. Article 34 of the Charter stipulates that the Security Council "may investigate any dispute, or any situation which might lead to international friction or give rise to a dispute, in order to determine whether the continuance of the dispute or situation is likely to endanger the maintenance of international peace and security". Such "situations" often emerge from, or lead to, gross and systematic human rights violations. The Council thus may need to address human rights problems. If the Council determines that a situation characterized by particularly serious human rights violations constitutes a "threat to the peace" under Article 39 of the Charter, the Council may adopt binding measures to address the situation. The Council's first such actions concerned the apartheid regime in South Africa and the white minority government which declared independence in the former Rhodesia. Since then, the Council has addressed human rights violations in numerous crises, including East Timor, Rwanda, the former Yugoslavia, the Darfur region of the Sudan, and the Democratic Republic of the Congo (formerly Zaire).

In recent years, there has been increased discussion of the appropriate role of the Security Council in humanitarian crises and situations of massive violations of human rights. In 2001, an International Commission on Intervention and State

Sovereignty, formed by the Canadian Government, issued a report entitled "Responsibility to Protect." *See* Responsibility to Protect: Report of the International Commission on Intervention and State Sovereignty (2001). The Report emphasized the duties of governments to protect all persons from genocide, massive human rights abuses and other humanitarian crises. This responsibility rests primarily on each individual state, but the Report concludes that when states "manifestly fail" to protect their populations, the international community shares a collective responsibility to respond through the United Nations, especially through the Security Council. A UN Summit Outcome Document, issued by governments at the conclusion of the 2005 High-level Plenary Meeting of the General Assembly, endorsed the "Responsibility to Protect" and made commitments to strengthen international institutions. One new institution, appointed by the Secretary-General in 2004, is the Special Adviser for the Prevention of Genocide (SAPG) who reports directly to the Security Council. The mandate, set forth in Security Council Resolution 1366, is to collect existing information, particularly from within the UN system, act as an early warning mechanism, and make recommendations to the Security Council through the Secretary-General about situations where there is evidence of tensions that could lead to genocide. More broadly, in December 2007, the UN Security Council approved the creation of a position of Special Advisor on the Responsibility to Protect.

On April 28, 2006, the Security Council made its first explicit reference to the Responsibility to Protect in Resolution 1674 on the Protection of Civilians in Armed Conflict, which "reaffirm[ed] the provisions of paragraphs 138 and 139 of the World Summit Outcome Document regarding the responsibility to protect populations from genocide, war crimes, ethnic cleansing and crimes against humanity." On August 31, 2006, the Security Council again referred to the Responsibility to Protect in its resolution 1706 calling for the rapid deployment of peacekeepers to the Sudan. Since 2006, the Security Council has referenced the Responsibility to Protect in over fifty resolutions and numerous presidential statements. *See* http://www.globalr2p.org/media/files/unsc-resolu tions-and-statements-with-r2p-table-as-of-august-2016.pdf. Nevertheless, the content and criteria for applying the Responsibility to Protect remain controversial with some governments, who are hesitant to accept this new version of humanitarian intervention. It remains an evolving concept. *See* S.C. Breau, *Humanitarian Intervention: The United Nations and Collective Responsibility* (2005); A. Orford, *International Authority and the Responsibility to Protect* (2011); N. Oman, *The Responsibility to Protect in International Law* (2017).

3. The Office of the High Commissioner for Human Rights

The Office of the High Commissioner for Human Rights (OHCHR) is the part of the UN Secretariat responsible for human rights matters. The position of High Commissioner for Human Rights was established pursuant to UN General Assembly Resolution 48/141 of January 7, 1994. Earlier efforts to create the position, dating back to the 1950's and 1960's, failed largely for reasons related to the Cold War and superpower opposition. The subject was also considered at the 1993 Vienna World Conference on Human Rights. There, a group of Asian countries blocked the adoption of a consensus recommendation calling for the establishment of the office of the UN High Commissioner for Human Rights. The conference did recommend, however, that the subject be considered by the General Assembly "as a matter of priority." UN World Conference on Human Rights, Vienna Declaration and Programme of Action, UN Doc. A/Conf.157/23, part II, para. 18 (1993). The General Assembly complied and, after weeks of negotiations, adopted the resolution creating the position of High Commissioner for Human Rights. *See* G.A. Res. 48/141 (1993). *See* B.G. Ramcharan, *The United Nations High Commissioner for Human Rights: The Challenges of International Protection* (2002).

As stipulated by the General Assembly, the High Commissioner for Human Rights is the "United Nations official with principal responsibility for United Nations human rights activities under the direction and responsibility of the Secretary-General." U.N. G.A. Res. 48/148(4). In discharging these responsibilities, the High Commissioner operates "within the framework of the overall competence, authority and decisions of the General Assembly, the Economic and Social Council and the Commission on Human Rights." *Id*. Among the various functions assigned to the High Commissioner, the most important one is spelled out in paragraph 4(f) of the resolution, which empowers him or her "to play an active role in removing the current obstacles and in meeting the challenges to the full realization of all human rights and in preventing the continuation of human rights violations throughout the world." *Id*. This language is broad enough to permit the Commissioner to take on any contemporary human rights problem and to be actively engaged in efforts to prevent human rights violations around the world. For a description of relevant activities *see* the Annual Report of the United Nations High Commissioner for Human Rights, "OHCHR Report 2015," available at http://www2.ohchr.org/english/OHCHRreport2015/index.html. The Office maintains a very useful web site at http://www.unhchr.org.

The High Commissioner has the rank of an Under Secretary-General of the United Nations. Appointed by the Secretary-General with the approval of the General Assembly for a four-year term, the incumbent is charged with providing advisory services, technical and financial assistance to States in the field of human rights and with coordinating the UN's promotional and protective activities. His Office provides substantive and technical support to the UN human rights bodies and mechanisms, such as the Human Rights Council and its subsidiary bodies, the Special Procedures and the treaty bodies. It also provides technical assistance and advisory services to UN Member States. The OHCHR now has field operations in more than 20 States.

In short, the High Commissioner is the UN's human rights "Czar." The effectiveness of a given incumbent will depend on many factors, including his or her diplomatic skill, commitment and creativity, the political will of the Member States of the UN, the resources placed at the Office's disposal and the support he or she receives from the Secretary-General. While the individual performances have varied, the creation of the Office of High Commissioner for Human Rights marked an important step forward in the struggle to strengthen the ability of the UN to deal with human rights violations. *See generally* F. Gaer & C. Broecker (eds.), *The Office of the High Commissioner for Human Rights: A Conscience for the World* (2014).

4. The International Court of Justice

The International Court of Justice consists of 15 independent judges elected by the General Assembly and the Security Council. The Court is the principal judicial organ of the United Nations, established by the Charter and governed by a Statute, which is annexed to the Charter. Only States may be parties to cases before the Court (Art. 34(1) of the Statute). This means that individuals, juridical persons and international or non-governmental organizations may not litigate matters at the Court. The Court also has jurisdiction to issue advisory opinions at the request of the UN and its specialized agencies.

On occasion, the Court has taken decisions, either within its adjudicatory or advisory jurisdiction, on human rights issues. One of its influential early advisory opinions, Reservations to the Convention on the Prevention and Punishment of the Crime of Genocide, 1951 ICJ Rep. 15 (May 28), pronounced the impermissibility of States attaching reservations contrary to the object and purpose of a universal, humanitarian treaty like the Genocide Convention. Questions concerning apartheid in South Africa generated several advisory opinions and judgments. *See* International Status of South West Africa, 1950 ICJ Rep. (Advisory Opinion of July 11); South West Africa (Eth. v. S. Afr.), 1966 I.C.J. 16 (July 18); Legal Consequences for States of the Continued Presence of South Africa in Namibia (South West Africa) notwithstanding Security Council Resolution 276, 1971 ICJ Rep. (Advisory Opinion of June 21). A pair of advisory opinions affirmed that UN Special Rapporteurs with human rights mandates are entitled to the privileges and immunities of U.N. Experts on Mission under the U.N. Convention on Privileges and Immunities. They also confirmed that Special Rapporteurs are entitled to assert those privileges and immunities against their own governments. *See* Applicability of Article VI, Section 22, of the Convention on the Privileges and Immunities of the United Nations, 1998 I.C.J. 177, 200 (Dec. 15); Difference Relating to Immunity from Legal Process of a Special Rapporteur of the Commission on Human Rights, 1999 I.C.J. 62 (Apr. 26).

The Court has also addressed the relationship between international human rights law and humanitarian law. In its advisory opinion on the Legality of the Threat or Use of Nuclear Weapons,

1996 ICJ Rep. 226, the court determined that the ICCPR does not cease to apply in wartime, with the exception of provisions that may be derogated from in times of national emergency. However, international humanitarian law constitutes *lex specialis* applicable during wartime. A more recent advisory opinion elaborated on this topic. In Legal Consequences of the Construction of a Wall in the Occupied Palestinian Territory, Advisory Opinion of 9 July 2004, 2004 ICJ Rep. 136, the ICJ explained that (1) some rights may be wholly regulated by international humanitarian law; (2) some rights may be governed entirely by international human rights law; (3) still other rights may be regulated by both humanitarian law and human rights law. *Id.* at para. 106. In the last circumstance, humanitarian law would be the *lex specialis* applicable in wartime. In the Nuclear Weapons opinion, the Court also asserted that "a great many rules of international humanitarian law are so fundamental to the respect of the human person" that they are to be observed by all states whether or not they have ratified the conventions that contain them, because they constitute intransgressible principles of international customary law. Nuclear Weapons, para. 79.

States appear increasingly willing to take disputes over human rights matters to the Court. Recent cases asserting human rights and humanitarian law violations include: Questions Relating to the Obligation to Prosecute or Extradite (Belgium v. Senegal), 2012 I.C.J. Rep. 422 (July 20), discussed *supra* § 2–16; Application of the International

Convention on the Elimination of All Forms of Racial Discrimination (Georgia v. Russian Federation), 2011 I.C.J. Rep. 70 (April 1), discussed *supra* § 2–14; Ahmadou Sadio Diallo (Guinea v. DRC) 2007 ICJ Rep. (May 24); Application of the Convention on the Prevention and Punishment of the Crime of Genocide (Bosn. & Herz. v. Serbia and Montenegro), 2007 ICJ Rep. 43 (Feb. 26); Application of the Convention on the Prevention and Punishment of the Crime of Genocide (Croatia v. Serbia), Preliminary Objections, 2008 ICJ Rep. 412 (Nov. 18)); Armed Activities on the Territory of the Congo (DRC v. Uganda), 2005 ICJ Rep. 168 (Dec. 19). In addition, at the request of the General Assembly, the Court addressed the right to self-determination in its advisory opinion on whether the unilateral declaration of independence by the Provisional Institutions of Self-Government of Kosovo was compatible with international law. Accordance with International Law of the Unilateral Declaration of Independence in Respect of Kosovo, 2010 I.C.J. Rep. 403 (July 22).

For analyses of the Court's pronouncements on human rights, *see* Higgins, "Human Rights in the International Court of Justice," 20 Leiden J. Int'l L. 745 (2007); Stephen M. Schwebel, "The Seminal Contributions of the World Court to the Law of Human Rights," Address to the International Bioethics Committee of UNESCO, Fifth Sess., Proceedings (Dec. 1998); Shiv R.S. Bedi, *The Development of Human Rights Law by the Judges of the International Court of Justice* (2007).

5. ECOSOC and the Former Commission and Sub-Commission on Human Rights

Article 68 of the UN Charter mandates the Economic and Social Council (ECOSOC) to establish "commissions in economic and social fields and for the promotion of human rights." ECOSOC complied with this mandate in 1946 by creating a Commission on Human Rights of 18 Member States. As membership in the UN increased over time, the size of the Commission grew as well, reaching 53 Member States by the time it was abolished in 2006. ECOSOC elected the Commission's Member States for three-year terms based on equitable geographical distribution among the different regions of the world. The states named their own representatives, who served as instructed government delegates and not in their personal capacities. *See generally* H. Tolley, *The U.N. Commission on Human Rights* (1987); Alston, "The Commission on Human Rights," in P. Alston, *The United Nations and Human Rights: A Critical Appraisal,*(1992), at 126. In the first decades of its existence, the Commission devoted itself principally to promotional activities and the preparation of draft international human rights instruments. In those years, the Commission considered that it was barred from taking any action on specific situations or charges that a UN Member State engaged in human rights violations, a view supported by ECOSOC.

Much of the innovative work of the Commission originated in a Sub-Commission established in 1947. Initially titled the Sub-Commission on the Prevention of Discrimination and Protection of

Minorities, later more simply called the Sub-Commission on Promotion and Protection of Human Rights, it was the UN institution that was usually the most sympathetic to the cause of human rights. This receptiveness was due in large part to the fact that its 26 members, unlike those of the Commission, served in their personal capacities. While members were not always free agents—much depended upon the policies or form of government of the expert's home state—many independent-minded individuals served on this body. *See generally* Tolley, *supra*, at 163; Eide, "The Sub-Commission on Prevention of Discrimination and Protection of Minorities," *in* P. Alston, *supra,* at 211; Weissbrodt, "Highlights of the Fiftieth Session of the United Nations Sub-Commission on Prevention of Discrimination and Protection of Minorities," 17 Law & Ineq. 445 (1999).

The Sub-Commission's mandate was to undertake studies and to make recommendations to the Commission "concerning the prevention of discrimination of any kind relating to human rights and fundamental freedoms and the protection of racial, national, religious and linguistic minorities." It was also empowered "to perform any other functions which may be entrusted to it by the Economic and Social Council or the Commission on Human Rights." ECOSOC Res. 9 (II) of June 21, 1946. In practice, the Sub-Commission dealt with the whole range of human rights issues arising in the UN context and in doing so it made substantial contributions to the human rights work of the United Nations. *See generally* Haver, "The Mandate of the UN Sub-Commission on the Prevention of

Discrimination and Protection of Minorities," 21 Colum. J. Transnat'l L. 103 (1982); Eide, *supra*, at 213.

Although the Commission deserves credit for establishing many useful programs to promote human rights (*e.g.*, UN human rights advisory services), it came to focus its efforts on dealing with human rights violations. It discharged the latter function through an ever-expanding network of working groups and rapporteurs with thematic or country mandates, beginning with the Working Group on Enforced or Involuntary Disappearances (1980) and the Special Rapporteurs on Extrajudicial, Summary or Arbitrary Executions (1982), Torture (1985) and Religious Intolerance (1986). It added Special Rapporteurs on the Right to Food (2000), Adequate Housing (2000) and Indigenous Peoples (2001) among others. Generally, the mandates were for three years. For background, *see* "List of Special Procedures of the UN Commission on Human Rights," 14 Hum. Rts. L.J. 131 (1993). *See also* Rodley & Weissbrodt, "United Nations Non-Treaty Procedures for Dealing with Human Rights Violations," *in* H. Hannum (ed.), *Guide to International Human Rights Practice* 61, 70 (4th ed. 2004). The rapporteur system grew out of and is the logical consequence of special procedures established under ECOSOC Resolutions 1235 and 1503, which empowered the Commission to deal with gross violations of human rights. These procedures are discussed in § 2–25, *infra*.

The Commission initially gave most of its attention to issues of civil and political rights, including torture and detention, disappearances and summary executions, freedom of opinion and expression, religious intolerance, the independence of the judiciary, states of emergency, and the rights of particular vulnerable groups. As membership in the U.N. grew to include many newly-independent developing countries, however, the Commission gave increased attention to economic, social and cultural rights such as the rights to food, education, and an adequate standard of living including housing, as well as the human rights dimensions of such issues as bioethics, science and the environment, extreme poverty and foreign debt, child labor, HIV/AIDS, terrorism, development and the promotion of democracy. *See* Report of the Human Rights Commission on its Sixty-Second Session, UN doc. E/2006/23 (13–27 March 2006).

The Commission was frequently criticized for ineffectiveness and for being politically motivated or selective in responding to charges of human rights violations. *See* Jack Donnelly, "Human Rights at the United Nations, 1955–1985: The Question of Bias," 32 Int'l Stud. Q. 275, 277–96 (1988); *but see* Shelton, International Human Rights Law: Principled, Double, or Absent Standards?, 25 Law & Ineq. 467, 470 (2007). It was also noted that, over time, states engaged in violations of human rights increasingly sought membership on the Commission in order to deflect efforts to investigate their abuses. Concerns were also expressed that the Commission focused on a progressive expansion in the scope of human rights rather than on effective implementation of existing norms. Although some of the criticism was justified, it overlooked the fact that the Commission could do no more than the states comprising it—and those electing them—wanted it to do. *See* Tolley, *supra,* at 187. Moreover, since the Commission was a political body, it should surprise no one that it tended to politicize the issues before it; the work of its replacement, the Human Rights Council, makes this clear. Yet it would be a mistake not to recognize that the Commission played an important role in setting and broadening the human rights agenda of the UN and in developing new international techniques for preventing and responding to human rights violations. It deserves much of the credit for transforming human rights into a major item on the agenda of the international community and for broadening the legal scope and application of the human rights provisions of the UN Charter.

§ 2–23.   THE HUMAN RIGHTS COUNCIL

The UN General Assembly created the 47-member inter-governmental Human Rights Council on March 15, 2006, replacing the Human Rights Commission and abolishing the Sub-Commission. *See* GA Res. 60/251, UN Doc A/RES/60/251 (March 15, 2006). In so doing, the General Assembly attempted to address some of the widespread criticisms of the Commission and of the UN's human rights program in general.

First, the General Assembly signaled an elevated status for the Council by having it report directly to the General Assembly and not to ECOSOC, as was the case with the former Commission. Second, the General Assembly introduced criteria, although hardly stringent requirements, for selection and service on the Council. It called on Member States to take into account, in choosing members of the Council, "the contribution of candidates to the promotion and protection of human rights and their voluntary pledges and commitments made thereto." Those elected to the Council are required to "uphold the highest standards in the promotion and protection of human rights, . . . fully cooperate with the Council and be reviewed under the universal periodic review mechanism during their term of membership." Should a Council member instead engage in gross and systematic violations of human rights, the General Assembly, by a two-thirds majority of the members present and voting, may suspend the rights of membership in the Council.

Third, the Council has an open-ended time period to meet; it is given a minimum of ten weeks a year in three regular sessions (compared to the former Commission's single session) but it is also allowed to hold special sessions if one-third of the members find a need. In its first two years, it held seven special sessions, which created controversy because six of them were directed to discussing a single country, with four of them devoted to Israeli practices, and one each concerned with Darfur and Myanmar. To date, the Human Rights Council has held 26 special sessions, including on the human rights situations in Syria, Libya, the Central African Republic, and Burundi. Most of the special sessions relating to country situations have resulted in the creation and the establishment of UN Commissions of Inquiry or Fact-Finding Missions, including for each of the countries just listed. Some special sessions have been devoted to thematic issues. For example the 7th special session, held in May 2008, concerned "the negative impact on the realization of the right to food of the worsening of the world food crisis, caused inter alia by the soaring food prices." Human Rights Council, *Report of the Human Rights Council*, G.A. Official Records, 63d session, Supplement No. 53 (A/63/53) (2008).

According to its creating resolution, the Council is "responsible for promoting universal respect for the protection of all human rights and fundamental freedoms for all, without distinction of any kind and in a fair and equal manner." Its mandate also includes addressing and making recommendations on situations of violations of human rights, including gross and systematic violations, as well as promoting the effective coordination and the mainstreaming of human rights within the United Nations system. The General Assembly alluded to criticisms of the former Commission in calling on the new Council to "be guided by the principles of universality, impartiality, objectivity and non-selectivity, constructive international dialogue and cooperation, with a view to enhancing the promotion and protection of all human rights, civil, political, economic, social and cultural rights, including the right to development." It also specified that the Council should act in a "fair, transparent and impartial manner." Relations with non-governmental organizations are maintained under the ECOSOC procedures adopted in 1996. *See* Chapter 7, *infra.*

The specific functions of the Council detailed in the GA resolution include to: (*a*) promote human rights education and advisory services, technical assistance and capacity-building; (*b*) discuss thematic issues on all human rights; (*c*) make recommendations to the General Assembly for the further development of international law in the field of human rights; (*d*) promote the implementation by States of their human rights obligations and commitments made at United Nations conferences and summits; (*e*) undertake a universal periodic review of each State's implementation of its human rights obligations and commitments; (*f*) act to prevent human rights violations and respond promptly to human rights emergencies; and (*g*) make recommendations with regard to the promotion and protection of human rights. One year after holding its first meeting, on 18 June 2007, the Council adopted its "Institution-building package" providing elements to guide it in its future work.

In fulfilling its mandate, the Council has taken over the special procedures and complaints mechanisms created by the former Commission. *See supra* § 2–22(5). The Council's unique new procedure is the Universal Periodic Review, a reporting system applicable to all UN Member States, which assesses their performance with respect to all categories of human rights (civil and political, economic, social and cultural rights). On June 18, 2007, the Council adopted Resolution 5.1, outlining its procedures and method of work for Universal Periodic Review, including the basis of the review, principles and objectives to be followed, the periodicity and order of review of countries, procedures, and the outcome and the follow-up to the review. The Council also adopted general Guidelines for the national reports, which are reviewed by all 47 Member States of the Council. The legal standards used for the review consist of the UN Charter, the Universal Declaration on Human Rights, human rights treaties to which the state under review is a party, its voluntary commitments, and applicable norms of humanitarian law.

In its review, the Council takes into account, in addition to the 20-page national reports that States are required to submit, a range of information from other sources. The OHCHR prepares a 10-page compilation of information contained in the reports of the treaty bodies, special procedures, and other relevant official United Nations documents. *See, e.g., Compilation prepared by the Office of the High Commissioner for Human Rights, In Accordance with Paragraph 15(B) of the Annex to Human Rights Council Resolution 5/1: Barbados*, A/HRC/WG.6/3/ BRB/2, Sept. 25, 2008. Civil society actors, NHRIs, and regional mechanisms are also invited to submit written information about the countries being examined; based on these submissions, the OHCHR prepares a ten-page summary of "credible and reliable information" provided by NGOs and other civil society groups. Even with these page limitations, the Council could not review all 192 Member States in the contemplated four-year cycle if it met in plenary meetings only. Instead, the Council appoints a group of three rapporteurs (*troika*), selected by the drawing of lots among the members of the Council and from different Regional Groups, to facilitate each review, including the preparation of the report of the working group.

The OHCHR provides assistance and expertise to the rapporteurs. The Council devotes three hours to the review by the working group for each country, with an additional hour allocated for the consideration of the outcome by the plenary of the Council. The outcome of the review is a report consisting of a summary of the proceedings of the review process; conclusions and/or recommendations; and the responses of the reviewed states to the recommendations as well the voluntary commitments of the state concerned. *See, e.g.,* Report of the Working Group on the Universal Periodic Review: United Kingdom of Great Britain and Northern Ireland. Addendum: Views on conclusions and/or recommendations, voluntary commitments and replies presented by the State under review, A/HRC/8/25/Add.1, Aug. 25, 2008. The Council has also established a follow-up procedure under which states previously reviewed submit interim reports on steps taken to implement previous recommendations, resulting in significant voluntary commitments by reviewed states. The Council completed its second cycle of reviews in November of 2016 and the third cycle is scheduled to take place between 2017 and 2021.

A new 18 member Advisory Committee, whose mandate and powers are substantially less than those of the former Sub-Commission, was created to provide the Council with expertise and advice on thematic human rights issues and the revised Complaints Procedure. The Advisory Committee has no power to act on its own, but can only respond to requests coming from the Council. It functions as a think-tank for the Council and works at its direction. Its initial membership included long-serving members of the former Sub-Commission, and its membership has included former government officials, academics, and individuals with experience in non-governmental organizations. The Advisory Committee has completed 17 sessions and has addressed such topics as human rights education and training, the right to food, and the human rights of women; promotion of a democratic and equitable international order; missing persons; elimination of discrimination against persons affected by leprosy and their family, unaccompanied migrant children and adolescents; the negative impact of the non-repatriation of funds of illicit origin on the enjoyment of human rights; and regional arrangements for the promotion and protection of human rights. *See* Report of the Advisory Committee on its Seventeenth Session, A/HRC/AC/17/2 (Sept. 7, 2016).

Overall, the Council has proven to be neither as much of an improvement as its proponents hoped nor as dismal as its detractors feared. Like the former Commission, it has continued to engage in standard-setting, completing the two-decade long process of negotiating the Declaration on the Rights of Indigenous Peoples, which the General Assembly adopted. The Council also adopted a Declaration on

Human Rights Education and Training, A/HRC/RES/ 13/15, based on a draft submitted by its Advisory Committee, A/HRC/AC/4/4. This Declaration was likewise endorsed by the General Assembly. *See* A/ RES/66/137. The Council has also taken up new and often controversial issues, such as defamation of religion and "Islamophobia," climate change and human rights, human rights and extreme poverty, foreign debt, and solidarity. Contrary to fears expressed by many human rights activists, the Council has not eliminated the investigation of human rights violations by specific countries, although it ended some of the country mandates created by the Commission. For more on the Human Rights Council, *see generally* R. Freedman, *United Nations Human Rights Council: A Critique and Early Assessment* (2013); B. Ramcharan; *UN Human Rights Council* (2011).

§ 2–24. COMMISSION ON THE STATUS OF WOMEN

This Commission was established in 1946. It consists of 45 members elected as state representatives along geographic lines similar to those applicable to the former Commission on Human Rights. The Commission's mandate charges it with the preparation of studies, reports and recommendations on human rights and related issues affecting women. It has played an important role in initiating UN programs designed to eradicate *de jure* and *de facto* discrimination against women, including the drafting of the principal contemporary treaties dealing with women's rights. *See* Galey,

"Promoting Non-Discrimination Against Women: The UN Commission on the Status of Women," 23 Int'l Studies Q. 273 (1979); Reanda, "Human Rights and Women's Rights: The United Nations Approach," 3 Hum. Rts. Q. 11 (1981).

The first few decades of the Commission's existence were devoted to these normative activities. In recent years the Commission has been able to focus more on issues relating to the role and needs of women in contemporary societies and on improving their political, economic, and social status. By serving as the preparatory committee for increasingly more important UN world conferences on the subject, the Commission has gradually gained the political influence it needed but lacked in the past to make a significant impact. On the evolution of the Commission's role, *see* Reanda, "The Commission on the Status of Women," *in* Alston, *supra,* at 265.

Following the 1995 Fourth World Conference on Women, the General Assembly asked the Commission to integrate into its program a follow-up process to the Conference, regularly review the critical areas of concern in the Beijing Platform for Action, and help mainstream a gender perspective in United Nations activities. ECOSOC further modified the Commission's terms of reference in resolution 1996/6 to include identifying emerging issues, trends and new approaches to issues affecting equality between women and men.

Thus far, it has proved much easier for the Commission to engage in promotional activities than to act on specific violations of women's rights. The

Commission has had to struggle for a long time to acquire the authority to deal with complaints alleging such violations. In the early 1980's ECOSOC empowered the Commission to undertake a limited review of communications charging specific violations of women's rights. The Commission used these communications principally as a source of information for its studies rather than as an instrument designed to prod governments to address the specific complaints. For a telling historical review of the early efforts, *see* Galey, "International Enforcement of Women's Rights," 6 Hum. Rts. Q. 463 (1984). *See also* Guggenheim, "The Implementation of Human Rights by the UN Commission on the Status of Women: A Brief Comment," 12 Tex. Int'l L.J. 239 (1977). The culmination of this work was the adoption of the Optional Protocol to the Convention on the Elimination of All Forms of Discrimination Against Women in 1999, discussed at § 2–15 *supra*. *See* UN General Assembly Res. 54/4 (Oct. 15, 1999). The Optional Protocol is reprinted at 38 ILM 763 (1999).

§ 2–25.   PROCEDURES FOR DEALING WITH GROSS VIOLATIONS OF HUMAN RIGHTS

The establishment of the UN created great expectations and gave hope to millions of oppressed peoples the world over who believed that the Organization would bring them the freedom and justice for which they had been waiting so long. It is not surprising, therefore, that almost as soon as the UN came into being, it began to receive a large number of petitions from individuals and non-governmental organizations alleging violations of human rights and seeking UN intervention. From 1947 to 1957, for example, some 65,000 such communications were received by the UN. Buergenthal, "The United Nations and the Development of Rules Relating to Human Rights," Proc. Am. Soc. Int'l L. 132, 135 n.7 (1965). These numbers increased even more in later years. Tardu, "United Nations Response to Gross Violations of Human Rights: the 1503 Procedure," 20 Santa Clara L. Rev. 559 (1980). But the UN Commission on Human Rights, logically the most appropriate body within the Organization to deal with these petitions, decided in 1947 that it had "no power to take any action in regard to any complaints concerning human rights." L. Sohn & T. Buergenthal, *International Protection of Human Rights* 747 (1973). This decision was confirmed by ECOSOC in Resolution 75(V) of August 5, 1947, which nevertheless established a method for classifying the petitions and provided that they be included in a confidential list. Access to that list was so severely restricted that the information contained in it could not even be used by members of the Commission to initiate any action in specific cases. *Id.* at 748–50.

Between 1947 and 1959, various efforts were made to persuade ECOSOC to reverse its 1947 decision and empower the Commission to act on communications alleging violations of human rights. Although these efforts were unsuccessful, they led to the adoption of ECOSOC Resolution 728F (XXVIII) of July 30, 1959, which consolidated existing UN procedures for classifying communications while at the same time reaffirming the decision of the Commission that "it has no power to take any action in regard to any complaints concerning human rights." Subsequent resolutions empowered the Commission to deal with and act on certain very serious human rights violations. *See* Sohn, "Human Rights: Their Implementation and Supervision by the United Nations," *in* T. Meron (ed.), *Human Rights in International Law: Legal and Policy Issues* 369, 385 (1984); Rodley, "United Nations Non-Treaty Procedures for Dealing with Human Rights Violations," *in* H. Hannum (ed.), *Guide to International Human Rights Practice* 65 (4th ed. 2004).

Changes were ushered in by two ECOSOC resolutions: Resolution 1235 (XLII) of June 6, 1967, and Resolution 1503 (XLVIII) of May 27, 1970. *See generally* Alston, "The Commission on Human Rights," *in* P. Alston, *supra*, at 138. Resolution 1235 permitted the Commission to examine publicly certain gross violations of human rights that came to its attention, whereas Resolution 1503 established a limited confidential petition system for dealing with communications that "reveal a consistent pattern" of such violations. In establishing "standards and criteria" for the admissibility of human rights complaints, Sub-Commission Resolution 1 (XXIV) of August 13, 1971, referred to "the relevant principles of the Charter, of the Universal Declaration of Human Rights and of other applicable instruments in the field of human rights." Res. 1 (XXIV) at para. 1(a). The General Assembly resolution creating the Human Rights Council expressly authorized it to continue examining gross violations of human rights. Human Rights Council Resolution 5/1, establishing the HRC's new complaints procedure, is modeled on Resolution 1503.

The various resolutions and the vast human rights practice of UN organs implementing them, and subsequent resolutions, have established an important legal principle applicable to the interpretation of the UN Charter. That principle holds that a state which engages in gross violations of the human rights proclaimed by the Universal Declaration and other relevant human rights instruments violates the UN Charter obligations spelled out in Articles 55 and 56. It is therefore not illegal for the UN under Article 2(7) of the Charter, which bars intervention in matters essentially within a Member State's domestic jurisdiction, to take appropriate measures designed to compel that state not to engage in gross violations of human rights.

The internationalization of human rights and the nature of the obligations the Charter imposes on UN Member States are thus closely linked to the concept of gross violations. That concept is by no means static. Although it is today identified with massive and systematic violations of some of the most fundamental rights proclaimed in the Universal Declaration, *see* § 2–3, *supra,* many other rights may in time come to be viewed as equally fundamental. Their massive and systematic violation by a government would then also have to be considered a breach of its UN Charter obligations. The required magnitude of the concept of "massive" or "gross" violations may also gradually require a lower threshold of severity as the international community becomes less tolerant of what is unlawful behavior under the Charter. Viewed in this light, the human rights provisions of the Charter are "elastic clauses" whose expansion is tied to the evolving standards of international legality and decency.

1. Resolution 1235

ECOSOC Resolution 1235 originally authorized the Commission and its Sub-Commission

> to examine information relevant to gross violations of human rights and fundamental freedoms, as exemplified by the policy of *apartheid* as practised in the Republic of South Africa ... and to racial discrimination as practised notably in Southern Rhodesia, contained in the communications listed ... pursuant to ... resolution 728F (XXVIII) of 30 July 1959. (Paragraph 2).

When this examination disclosed the existence of "situations which reveal a consistent pattern of violations of human rights, as exemplified by the policy of *apartheid* . . . and racial discrimination," the Commission could undertake a "thorough study" and report its conclusions to the Economic and Social Council. (Paragraph 3).

While some countries sought to limit the application of the 1235 procedure to *apartheid* and related policies, these efforts did not succeed. The Commission created working groups and appointed special rapporteurs to report on these types of violations. Sometimes the mandates were limited to a single country; in other instances, when the violations appeared to be common in several countries, the Commission called for a thematic study of the problem. *See, e.g.*, the resolutions adopted by the Commission under agenda item 9 ("Question of the violations of human rights and fundamental freedoms in any part of the world", Commission on Human Rights, Report of the Fifty-Seventh Session, E/2001/23, E/CN.4/2001/167, at 381 (2001).

2. Resolution 1503

Resolution 1503 established a procedure for the examination of communications received from individuals and other private groups with a view to identifying those that "appear to reveal a consistent pattern of gross and reliably attested violations of human rights and fundamental freedoms." The 1503 procedure was not intended to establish an individual petition system as that concept is usually understood. Although individuals and non-governmental groups had standing to file petitions, the petitions had to be based on a showing of "a consistent pattern of gross and reliably attested violations." The Office of the UN High Commissioner for Human Rights screened complaints to eliminate those presenting "manifestly ill-founded claims," and referred the rest to the appropriate government for a response. The communication and response (if any) could then be examined by a Working Group of the Sub-Commission.

If a majority of the Working Group believed that the communication concerned a situation which "appears to reveal a consistent pattern of gross and reliably attested violations of human rights and fundamental freedoms," the communication, together with the Working Group's report and recommendations, could be submitted to the Commission's Working Group on Situations. On the basis of its own examination, the Working Group on Situations then made its own determination whether a particular country situation should be considered by the full Commission. Resolution 1503 empowered the Commission to decide whether to undertake a "thorough study" thereof in accordance with the provisions of paragraph 3 of Resolution 1235, *supra,* or to make it the "subject of an investigation by an *ad hoc* Committee to be appointed by the Commission which shall be undertaken only with the consent of the State concerned. . . ." Over time, the Commission adopted several alternative responses, including (among others) submitting a request for additional information from the concerned government, naming an independent expert or special rapporteur to investigate the conditions in question, taking the matter up under its public procedures, dropping the case or keeping it under consideration.

3. The Human Rights Council's Procedures

The Human Rights Council has continued nearly all of the mandates established by the Commission to investigate specific country situations or thematic issues (described *supra* § 2–22(5)). These mandates are known collectively as the Human Rights

Council's system of Special Procedures. Some of the mandates are held by individuals, called variously "Special Rapporteurs" or "Independent Experts." Some mandates are exercised by multi-member working groups, such as the Working Group on the Issue of Human Rights and Transnational Corporations and Other Business Enterprises. For a directory of Special Procedures mandate holders, *see* www.ohchr.org/Documents/HRBodies/SP/Visual DirectoryDecemberJune2016_en.pdf.

Mandate-holders serve in their personal capacities, for up to six years, and do not receive salaries or any other financial compensation for their work. The Office of the High Commissioner for Human Rights provides support to the special procedures. Country mandate-holders normally are conferred authority to examine, monitor, give advice and publicly report on human rights situations in specific countries or territories. Thematic mandates examine major phenomena of human rights violations worldwide, such as torture, summary executions and disappearances. Mandate holders may also conduct studies on issues related to their mandates.

The mandates of the special procedures are established and defined by the resolutions creating them. Some mandates allow the mandate holder to receive and respond to individual complaints; other may make urgent appeals to governments when violations are threatened or imminent. Mandate holders, with the permission of the government, also carry out country visits to investigate the situation of human rights *in situ*. After their visits, the mandate-holders issue reports setting forth their findings and recommendations. *See, e.g.,* Report of the Special Rapporteur on extrajudicial, summary or arbitrary executions, Philip Alston: Addendum: Summary of cases transmitted to Governments and replies received, A/HRC/8/3/Add.1, May 30, 2008.

The Human Rights Council began a review of the special procedures in 2006. As of September 2008, all thematic mandates had been reviewed and were extended. Some new thematic mandates were established, including those on contemporary forms of slavery, the use of mercenaries, and access to safe drinking water and sanitation. *See* Hannum, "Reforming the Special Procedures and Mechanisms of the Commission on Human Rights," 7 Hum. Rts. L. Rev. 73 (2007). As of 2016, the Council had approved 43 thematic mandates and 14 country mandates, *see* www.ohchr.org/EN/HRBodies/SP/Pages/Welcomepage.aspx. *See generally* J. Gutter, *Thematic Procedures of the United Nations Commission on Human Rights and International Law* (2006). For a (generally positive) evaluation of the Human Rights Council's Special Procedures, *see* T. Piccone, *Catalysts For Rights: The Unique Contribution of the UN's Independent Experts on Human Rights, Final Report of the Brookings Research Project on Strengthening UN Special Procedures* (2010). In June 2007, the Council adopted Resolution 5/2, containing a Code of Conduct for special procedures' mandate holders.

The Commission's 1503 complaints procedure was also reviewed and maintained with some modifications. Council Resolution 5/1 called for establishing a new Complaint Procedure to address consistent patterns of gross and reliably attested violations of human rights, based on General Assembly resolution 60/251 of 15 March 2006. A Council Working Group met in 2006 and 2007 to adopt the new procedure. Summaries of the discussions held in the Working Group on the Complaint Procedure are contained in documents A/HRC/3/CRP.3, A/HRC/4/CRP.6 and A/HRC/5/CRP.6.

Pursuant to Council resolution 5/1, the Complaint Procedure addresses consistent patterns of gross and reliably attested violations of all human rights and all fundamental freedoms occurring in any part of the world and under any circumstances. It retains its confidential nature, but new standards require that it be victim-oriented and conducted in a timely manner. The Council has created two working groups—the Working Group on Communications (WGC) and the Working Group on Situations (WGS) —to examine communications and decide which ones should be forwarded to the Council on the basis that they reveal consistent patterns of gross and reliably attested violations of human rights and fundamental freedoms. As with the earlier 1503 procedure, the WGC screens out manifestly ill-founded and anonymous communications, based on the admissibility criteria. Communications not rejected in the initial screening are transmitted to the State concerned to obtain its views on the allegations of violations.

The WGC is part of the Council's Advisory Committee. It consists of five independent experts, representative of the five regional groups. The Working Group meets twice a year for a period of five working days to assess the admissibility and the merits of a communication, including whether the communication alone or in combination with other communications, appears to reveal a consistent pattern of gross and reliably attested violations of human rights and fundamental freedoms. All admissible communications and recommendations thereon are transmitted to the WGS.

The WGS comprises five members appointed by the regional groups from among the States Members of the Council for the period of one year, renewable once. It meets twice a year for a period of five working days in order to examine the communications transferred to it by the WGC, including the replies of States thereon, as well as the situations of which the Council is already seized under the complaint procedure. On the basis of the information and recommendations provided by the WGC, the WGS presents the Council with a report on consistent patterns of gross and reliably attested violations of human rights and fundamental freedoms and makes recommendations to the Council on the course of action to take.

A communication related to a violation of human rights and fundamental freedoms is admissible unless it has manifestly political motivations and its object is not consistent with the UN Charter, the Universal Declaration of Human Rights and other applicable instruments in the field of human rights law; or it does not contain a factual description of the alleged violations, including the rights which are alleged to be violated; or its language is abusive (although the communication may be considered after deletion of the abusive language). Standing to file complaints is broad: communications may be submitted by a person or a group of persons claiming to be the victim of violations of human rights and fundamental freedoms or by any person or group of persons, including NGOs acting in good faith in accordance with the principles of human rights, not resorting to politically motivated stands contrary to the provisions of the UN Charter and claiming to have direct and reliable knowledge of those violations. Communications need not be based on personal knowledge of the individual author, provided they are accompanied by clear evidence and not exclusively based on reports disseminated by mass media. Communications also may be excluded if they refer to a case already being dealt with by a special procedure, a treaty body or other United Nations or similar regional complaints procedure in the field of human rights. As with other human rights complaints procedures, domestic remedies must be exhausted, unless it appears that such remedies would be ineffective or unreasonably prolonged.

If the WGS transmits the situation to the Human Rights Council, the Council examines it in a confidential manner and may pursue one of the following courses of action: (a) decide that further action is not warranted; (b) request the State concerned to provide further information; (c) appoint an Independent Expert to monitor the matter and report back to the Council; (d) discontinue reviewing the situation under its confidential complaint procedure and take up public consideration of the matter; or (e) recommend provision of technical, advisory, or capacity-building assistance by the OHCHR. *See generally* www.ohchr.org/EN/HRBodies /HRC/ComplaintProcedure/Pages/HRCComplaint ProcedureIndex.aspx.

§ 2–26.   FIELD OFFICES

In recent years, international human rights bodies have sought to decentralize some of their operations by opening field offices where they can provide technical assistance and more quickly respond to emerging problems. The Office of the UN High Commissioner for Human Rights established its first field office in Cambodia in the early 1990's. As of 2016, the OHCHR had fourteen national offices (*see* www.ohchr.org/EN/Countries/Pages/CountryOffices Index.aspx) and 13 regional offices or centers (*see* www.ohchr.org/EN/Countries/Pages/RegionalOffices Index.aspx) operating in places facing serious human rights problems.

The field missions conduct monitoring, provide technical cooperation, and encourage a rights-based approach to local problems. Initially, the OHCHR acted in response to emergency situations, such as in Rwanda; to action by an intergovernmental body (the Commission on Human Rights, the Security Council or the General Assembly) such as in the case of the countries of the former Yugoslavia; or following an agreement between the Office and the government concerned, as in Colombia. Recently, requests for technical cooperation programs aimed at strengthening national human rights capacities and infrastructures have been made by numerous countries. Field work is implemented in close cooperation with regional and sub-regional organizations, UN agencies and programs, in particular the United Nations Development Programme, as well as NHRIs and NGOs. The ILO similarly stations "multi-disciplinary advisory teams" in various locations in the developing world. *See infra* § 2–29. They advise governments and non-state bodies, assist on the ratification and application of ILO standards, and provide technical, even financial assistance.

§ 2–27. UN HUMAN RIGHTS CONFERENCES

United Nations global conferences on human rights have become an important means of reaffirming and strengthening aspects of international human rights law. Although the results of such conferences are usually in the form of non-binding instruments, they have often played an important role in shaping the law and the programs of the United Nations in the field of human rights. The first such conference was held in 1968 in Teheran and was marked by the affirmation of the indivisibility and interdependence of all human rights. In 1993, the United Nations held its second World Conference on Human Rights, in which some 7000 persons representing 171 states and more than 800 non-governmental organizations participated.

On June 25, 1993, representatives of the participating states adopted by consensus the Vienna Declaration and Programme of Action of the World Conference on Human Rights, presenting a common plan for strengthening human rights throughout the world. Other important UN human rights conferences include the International Conference on Population Development (Cairo, 1994), the World Conference on Women (Beijing, 1995), the World Summit on Social Development (Copenhagen, 1995) and the World Conference against Racism, Racial Discrimination, Xenophobia and Related Intolerance (Durban South Africa, 2001).

VI. SPECIALIZED AGENCIES

§ 2–28.   INTRODUCTION

The Specialized Agencies of the United Nations are functional intergovernmental organizations affiliated with the UN. *See* T. Buergenthal & Murphy, *Public International Law in a Nutshell* 162 (5th ed. 2013). Although they are autonomous entities in the sense that they have their own constitutions and policy-making structure, they have a special institutional relationship with the UN and cooperate with it in areas of mutual concern, according to the specific mandate of each agency. This is particularly true as far as the promotion of human rights is concerned. *See* Alston, "The United Nations Specialized Agencies and the Implementation of the International Covenant on Economic, Social and Cultural Rights," 18 Colum. J. Transnat'l L. 79 (1979). The International Labor

Organization (ILO) and the United Nations Educational, Scientific and Cultural Organization (UNESCO) are among the specialized agencies that have the most developed human rights systems. The World Health Organization (WHO) and the Food and Agriculture Organization (FAO) also engage in important human rights activities. The interaction of these organizations with the UN in the promotion of human rights is described in considerable detail in U.N. Centre for Human Rights, *United Nations Action in the Field of Human Rights* (1994). *See also* Marks, "Human Rights, Activities of Universal Organizations," in *Encyclopedia of Public International Law,* Vol. II, at 893 (1995).

§ 2–29.   THE INTERNATIONAL LABOR ORGANIZATION

The International Labor Organization, established in 1919 by the Treaty of Versailles, focuses on those human rights related to the right to work and working conditions, including the right to form trade unions, the right to strike, the right to be free from slavery and forced labor, equal employment and training opportunities, the right to safe and healthy working conditions, and the right to social security. The ILO also provides protections for vulnerable groups, having adopted standards on child labor, employment of women, migrant workers, and indigenous and tribal peoples. It seeks to guarantee these rights through the adoption of conventions (now more than 180) and recommendations containing core minimum standards, and additional flexible provisions that enhance the likelihood of ratification by states. These latter provisions are of particular importance because the ILO does not allow reservations to its conventions.

Member States of the ILO are required to submit all conventions to the appropriate national authorities for possible ratification and to report on the results. They also must regularly report on all ratified conventions. Monitoring is carried out in the first place by the Committee of Experts, composed of twenty independent experts. The Committee meets annually to examine reports and may follow up with "Direct Requests" to governments and to organizations of workers and employers in the state concerned. If the Committee discovers more serious or persistent problems, it may make "Observations" to the government. Observations also are published in the Committee's annual report to the Conference. The second supervisory body is the Committee on the Application of Conventions and Recommendations, established each year by the Conference with representatives of government, employers, and workers. On the basis of the Committee of Experts' Report, the Conference Committee selects specific important or persistent cases and asks the government to appear to discuss the situation. The Conference Committee then reports to the full Conference. *See generally* Samson, "The Standard-Setting and Supervising System of the International Labor Organization," *in* R. Hanski & M. Suksi (eds.), *An Introduction to the International Protection of Human Rights: A Textbook* 149 (1997).

The ILO also has developed complaint procedures, two of which are based on provisions of the ILO Constitution and concern ratified conventions. A third procedure, which is restricted to complaints about freedom of association, applies whether or not the state has ratified any ILO conventions on the subject. *See* Swepston, "Human Rights Complaint Procedures of the International Labor Organization," in H. Hannum (ed.), *Guide to International Human Rights Practice* 89 (4th ed. 2004). The freedom of association procedure, created in the early 1950s by agreement between the ILO and the UN Economic and Social Council, is the most widely used petition process, having considered over 2000 cases. The ILO Committee on Freedom of Association receives complaints directly from workers' or employers' associations, considers them and, if it finds a violation, may ask the government concerned to continue reporting to it. It may also refer the case to either the Committee of Experts, if it concerns a ratified Convention, or recommend referral to the Fact-Finding and Conciliation Commission on Freedom of Association (FFCC). The latter body, made up of independent experts, also may examine complaints referred to it by ECOSOC against non-member states of the ILO, an example of strong inter-agency cooperation. For the ILO case-law and comments on compliance, *see* ILOLEX, available at http://www.ilo.org.

In 1998, the ILO responded to increasing concerns about the impact of globalization on workers' rights by adopting a Declaration of Fundamental Rights and Principles at Work, together with a follow-up procedure. The Declaration declares that all ILO Member States, by virtue of joining the organization, have an obligation to ensure the protection of four areas of human rights or core labor standards: freedom of association and the right to collectively bargain; freedom from child labor; freedom from forced or compulsory labor; and non-discrimination in employment. All Member States must report annually if they have not ratified the relevant ILO conventions on these subjects, and indicate the obstacles to ratification.

There is a vast literature on the highly advanced system developed by the ILO for the protection of labor and related human rights. In addition to the sources cited above, *see, e.g.*, Valticos, "The International Labour Organisation," in K. Vasak & P. Alston (eds.), *The International Dimensions of Human Rights,* vol. 1, at 363 (1982); Leary, "Lessons from the Experience of the International Labour Organization," *in* P. Alston (ed.), *The United Nations and Human Rights: A Critical Appraisal* 580 (1992); Maupin, *The Future of the International Labour Organization in the Global Economy* (2013). *See also* V. Leary, *International Labour Conventions and National Law* (1981).

§ 2–30.   UNESCO AND OTHER SPECIALIZED AGENCIES

The United Nations Educational, Scientific and Cultural Organization, created in 1945, includes human rights within its mandate to promote education, science and culture. *See generally* Partsch

& Hufner, "UNESCO Procedures for the Protection of Human Rights," *in* J. Symonides (ed.) *Human Rights: International Protection: Monitoring Enforcement* (2003). It promotes teaching and research on human rights and adopts conventions and recommendations on human rights related to its subject areas. It has also established a complaints procedure available to individuals and NGOs. UNESCO's best known conventions are the 1960 Convention against Discrimination in Education, Dec. 14, 1960, 429 U.N.T.S. 93, and the 1954 Convention for the Protection of Cultural Property in the Event of Armed Conflict, May 14, 1954, S. TREATY DOC. No. 106–1, 249 U.N.T.S. 215; Second Protocol to the Convention for the Protection of Cultural Property in the Event of Armed Conflict, Mar. 6, 1999, 38 I.L.M. 769. It also adopted a 1997 Universal Declaration on the Human Genome and Human Rights, the first international instruments to address human rights and modern biotechnology and to reject the cloning of human beings. Universal Declaration on the Human Genome and Human Rights, UNESCO Gen. Conf. Res. 29, at 41 (Nov. 11, 1997). The U.N. General Assembly endorsed the Declaration. G.A. Res. 53/152, U.N. Doc. A/RES/53/152 (Dec. 9, 1998).

UNESCO has a non-judicial communications procedure that was established in 1978. The procedure allows a victim or anyone with reliable knowledge about a human rights violation concerned with education, science or culture to submit a petition to UNESCO. The communication is brought to the notice of the Committee on Conventions and

Recommendations (C.C.R.) and transmitted to the government concerned, which may submit a reply. In addition, all parties may appear before the Committee. Several actions may be taken on communications. First, the Director-General of UNESCO may initiate consultations, if the circumstances warrant humanitarian intercession. This action may be taken even before a communication has been declared admissible. Second, the C.C.R. Committee, after it has considered a complaint, may propose that specific measures be taken by the State concerned. The Committee reports its work on communications to each session of the Executive Board. Despite the fact that the UNESCO procedure, which emphasizes friendly settlement, is confidential and non-judicial in character, it nevertheless appears to have been relatively successful. Thus, UNESCO has reported that in its first twenty years, the C.C.R. handled some 545 communications and that 344 of them have been settled. *See* UNESCO Doc. 179 EX/CR/2, *Summary of the Results of the Application of the Procedures Laid Down by 104 EX/Decision 3.3* (2008).

The human rights activities of UNESCO are considered by Saba, "UNESCO and Human Rights," *in* Vasak & Alston, *supra* at 401; Marks, "The Complaint Procedure of the United Nations Educational, Scientific and Cultural Organization," *in* H. Hannum, *A Guide to International Human Rights Practice* 107 (4th ed. 2004).

The human rights work of the World Health Organization is based on its Constitution, which specifies that "the enjoyment of the highest attainable standard of health is one of the fundamental rights of every human being ... " Constitution of the World Health Organization pmbl., July 22, 1946, 62 Stat. 6279, 14 U.N.T.S. 145. WHO's Health and Human Rights Team works on capacity-building, and advancing the right to health in international law and development processes. The main issues on which it has worked in recent years are combating discrimination against those with HIV/AIDS, the right to safe drinking water and sanitation, and child and adolescent health rights. In respect to the last-mentioned, WHO's Child and Adolescent Health and Development department has prepared and presented to the Committee on the Rights of the Child more than 30 health commentaries over the past decade.

In 2003, in furtherance of the right of all people to the highest standard of health, the WHO adopted the Framework Convention on Tobacco Control (FCTC). According to Article 3, the objective of the Convention is "to protect present and future generations from the devastating health, social, environmental and economic consequences of tobacco consumption and exposure to tobacco smoke." The FCTC entered into force in 2005, and now has 180 States Parties, making it one of the most widely ratified of all human rights treaties. For an overview of the Convention, see http://www.who.int/fctc/en/.

CHAPTER 3

THE EUROPEAN SYSTEM FOR THE PROTECTION OF HUMAN RIGHTS

I. INTRODUCTION

The European system for the protection of human rights is a major component and *raison d'être* of the Council of Europe, a regional intergovernmental organization created in 1949 by ten Western European nations. Article 3 of its Statute provides that "every Member of the Council of Europe must accept the principles of the rule of law and of the enjoyment by all persons within its jurisdiction of human rights and fundamental freedoms. . . ." The end of the Cold War enabled Central and Eastern European nations to join the Council of Europe after declaring their acceptance of the principles spelled out in Article 3.

Today the COE comprises 47 Member States, 28 of which are also members of the European Union. *See generally*, http://www.coe.int/en. For a criticism of the rapid expansion, *see* Leuprecht, Innovations in the European System of Human Rights Protection: Is Enlargement Compatible with Reinforcement? 8 Transnational Law and Contemporary Problems 313–36 (1998). States granted observer status at the Council of Europe also must accept these principles and adhere to the same human rights standards as Member States. Statutory Resolution (93) 26.

The Council's human rights system began with the adoption of the Convention for the Protection of

Human Rights and Fundamental Freedoms on November 4, 1950 guaranteeing some core civil and political rights and creating monitoring institutions. Commonly referred to as the European Convention on Human Rights, this Convention remains the centerpiece of the European human rights system. Fourteen protocols to the Convention have lengthened the list of guaranteed rights and strengthened the institutional framework to supervise implementation and compliance by the Contracting Parties; two further protocols, adopted in 2013, are not yet in force. The Council proclaimed economic and social rights in the 1961 European Social Charter and later protocols.

Other specific human rights issues are dealt with in the European Convention for the Prevention of Torture and Inhuman or Degrading Treatment or Punishment (1987), the European Charter for Regional or Minority Languages (1992), the Framework Convention for the Protection of National Minorities (1995), the Convention for the Protection of Human Rights and Biomedicine (1997) and its Additional Protocol on the Prohibition of Cloning Human Beings (1998), and the Convention on Action against Trafficking in Human Beings (2005). *See generally* Bates, *The Evolution of the European Convention on Human Rights* (2010).

The Council also has promoted human rights through activities undertaken without the need to conclude additional treaties. It created the post of Commissioner for Human Rights on May 7, 1999. The Commissioner is elected by the Parliamentary

Assembly from a list of candidates drawn up by the Committee of Ministers and serves a non-renewable six-year term. The Commissioner serves independently and impartially as "a non-judicial institution to promote education in, awareness of and respect for human rights, as embodied in the human rights instruments of the Council of Europe." The functions of the Commissioner are thus primarily promotional and preventive; she cannot accept communications from individuals or groups. *See* Committee of Ministers Resolution (99) 50 on the Council of Europe Commissioner for Human Rights. The successive Commissioners have undertaken fact-finding missions, *e.g.,* on the situation in Chechnya, the treatment of migrant workers and the Roma in Italy, and the situation of human rights in Cyprus. *See* Drzemczewski, "The Prevention of Human Rights Violations: Monitoring Mechanisms of the Council of Europe," in L.-A. Sicilianos (eds.), *The Prevention of Human Rights Violations* 139 (2001); L. Glas, *The Theory, Potential and Practice of Procedural Dialogue in the European Convention on Human Rights System* (2010).

Another extra-conventional organ is the European Commission against Racism and Intolerance (ECRI), established pursuant to the Vienna Declaration of the first Summit of the Heads of State and Government of the Member States of the Council of Europe, signed October 9, 1993. A second Summit held in Strasbourg in October 1997 strengthened ECRI's mandate and on June 13, 2002 the Committee of Ministers granted ECRI its own Statute, consolidating its role as an independent human rights monitoring body. ECRI reviews Member States' legislation, policies and other measures to combat racism and intolerance and proposes action at local, national and European levels. ECRI addresses General Policy Recommendations to the governments of all Member States; these Recommendations provide guidelines which policy-makers are invited to use when drawing up national strategies and policies.

ECRI monitors the situation in Member States through an in-depth study of the situation in each country followed by specific proposals designed to solve problems and remedy deficiencies. A contact visit is organized for the ECRI Rapporteurs before the preparation of each country report, in order to examine on site the situation as regards racism and intolerance. Draft texts are communicated to national liaison officers to allow national authorities to respond with observations. After confidential dialogue, ECRI adopts a final report and submits it to the state concerned through the Committee of Ministers. State reports are made public two months after transmission to the government unless the government expressly objects. ECRI reports on ten to twelve countries each year. *See* http://www.coe.int/t/dghl/monitoring/ecri/default_en.asp.

The European Commission for Democracy through Law, or Venice Commission, is the Council of Europe's advisory body on constitutional matters and works to uphold democracy, human rights, and the rule of law. Among other functions, it issues advisory opinions to national institutions. For example, on 20

February 2009, the Constitutional Court of Albania requested the Commission to present an amicus curiae opinion on five specific questions concerning the Albanian lustration law adopted at the end of 2008. In its opinion CDL-AD (2009)044, the Commission determined that lustration may be applied by Albania, on condition that the constitution and rule of law are respected. The Commission found that the lustration law in question violated the Albanian Constitution.

Finally, the Secretary General of the Council of Europe set up a Human Rights Trust Fund on 28 March 2008, funded in large part by the governments of Norway, Germany, and the Netherlands, as well as the Council of Europe Development Bank. The Trust Fund has supported projects to enhance the effectiveness of the system by improving compliance with judgments of the Court.

The sections that follow review the evolution of the European human rights system. They also examine the impact of the European Convention of Human Rights on the human rights actions of the European Union and describe the human dimension component of the Organization for Security and Cooperation in Europe.

II. THE EUROPEAN CONVENTION ON HUMAN RIGHTS: AN OVERVIEW

§ 3–1. INTRODUCTION

The decision to draft the European Convention was made after the UN General Assembly adopted the

Universal Declaration of Human Rights, when it became clear that it would take the UN many years to agree on the instruments to transform the Declaration into binding treaty obligations. *See* § 2–5, *supra*. The historical relationship between the Universal Declaration and the European Convention finds expression in the latter's preamble wherein the signatories declare their resolve "as the Governments of European countries which are like-minded and have a common heritage of political traditions, ideals, freedom and the rule of law, to take the first steps for the collective enforcement of certain of the rights stated in the Universal Declaration." The human rights system established by the Convention is the oldest and the most effective of those currently in existence. On the origins and legislative history of the Convention, *see* A.H. Robertson & J.G. Merrills, *Human Rights in Europe* (4th ed. 2001) at 1; Council of Europe, *Collected Edition of the 'Travaux Préparatoires' of the European Convention on Human Rights* (8 vols., 1975–85).

The European Convention on Human Rights entered into force on September 3, 1953. Only Member States of the Council of Europe may become Contracting Parties to the European Convention. Convention, art. 59(1). Although the Statute of the Council of Europe does not require its members to ratify the Convention, all Council members had ratified the Convention by the time the Cold War was over and the Council decided that new applicant states would be required to ratify the Convention as a condition of membership. By the end of 2008, all 47 Member States had adhered to the Convention:

Albania, Andorra, Armenia, Austria, Azerbaijan, Belgium, Bosnia and Herzegovina, Bulgaria, Croatia, Cyprus, Czech Republic, Denmark, Estonia, Finland, France, Georgia, Germany, Greece, Hungary, Iceland, Ireland, Italy, Latvia, Liechtenstein, Lithuania, Luxembourg, Malta, Monaco, Montenegro, Netherlands, Norway, Poland, Portugal, Republic of Moldova, Romania, Russian Federation, San Marino, Serbia, Slovak Republic, Slovenia, Spain, Sweden, Switzerland, the Former Yugoslav Republic of Macedonia, Turkey, Ukraine, United Kingdom. Belarus has applied for Council of Europe membership but it has not been accepted due to concerns over its commitment to the requirements of the Council of Europe Statute art. 3.

§ 3–2. RIGHTS GUARANTEED

As originally adopted, the European Convention guaranteed the following rights: right to life; right not to be subjected to torture, inhuman or degrading treatment or punishment; freedom from slavery; right to liberty, security of person, and due process of law; freedom from *ex post facto* laws and punishment; right to private and family life; freedom of thought, conscience and religion; freedom of expression and of peaceful assembly; and the right to marry and found a family. A non-discrimination clause applies to the "enjoyment of the rights and freedoms" the Convention proclaims, art. 14.

Another provision requires the Contracting Parties to provide an "effective remedy before a national authority" to anyone whose rights have been violated, art. 13. The beneficiary of the rights and freedoms which the Convention guarantees is "everyone" within the "jurisdiction" of the Contracting Parties to it (art. 1), meaning the nationality of the person does not matter and in some circumstances a Contracting Party may be responsible for violations of the Convention that occur outside its national territory. *See* Issa and Others v. Turkey, Judgment of November 16, 2004; Loizidou v. Turkey, Judgment of December 18, 1996, Reports of Judgments and Decisions of the European Court of Human Rights from 1996 [hereinafter cited as Reports] 1996-VI; Case of Ilascu and Others v. Moldova and Russia, Judgment of July 8, 2004, Reports 2004-VII; Chiragov and Others v. Armenia, [GC] Judgment of June 16, 2015; Assanidze v. Georgia [GC], ECHR 2004-II; Belozorov v. Russia and Ukraine, Judgment of October 15, 2015. The Court will not hear complaints, however, about extra-territorial acts of a Contracting Party taken under the authority of a U.N. Security Council peace-keeping operation. *See* Behrami and Behrami v. France and Saramati v. France, Germany and Norway, admissibility decision of May 31, 2007.

Additional Protocols have expanded the catalogue of rights guaranteed by the Convention for those states that have ratified the later instruments. The first Protocol added a right to property, a right to education and an undertaking to hold free and secret elections at reasonable intervals. Protocol No. 4 enlarged the list further by prohibiting deprivation of liberty for failure to comply with contractual obligations and by guaranteeing the right to liberty of movement. It also barred forced exile of nationals and the collective expulsion of aliens. Protocol No. 6 abolished the death penalty during peacetime, while Protocol No. 13 removed the exception to Protocol No. 6 that permitted executions during war, making the death penalty now illegal under all circumstances.

Protocol No. 7 requires states to accord aliens various due process safeguards before they may be expelled from a country where they reside. Protocol No. 7 also provides for a right of appeal in criminal proceedings, for compensation in cases of miscarriage of justice, for the right not to be subjected to double jeopardy, as well as for equality of rights and responsibilities between spouses. Protocol No. 12 augments the non-discrimination guarantee in Convention Art. 14 by providing that "the enjoyment of any right set forth by law shall be secured without discrimination on any ground . . . " and that no one shall be discriminated against by any public authority.

See generally D. Harris, M. O'Boyle and C. Warbrick, *Law of the European Convention on Human Rights* (3rd ed. 2014); E. Bates, *The Evolution of the European Convention on Human Rights* (2011); P. van Dijk et al., *Theory and Practice of the European Convention on Human Rights* (4th ed. 2006); R. Blackburn and J. Polakiewicz (eds.), *Fundamental rights in Europe: The European Convention on Human Rights 1950–2000* (2001); Jean-François Renucci, *Introduction to the European Convention on Human Rights: The Rights Guaranteed and the Protection Mechanism* (2005);

Steven Greer, *The European Convention On Human Rights* (2006); Jacobs, White and Ovey, *The European Convention on Human Rights* (6th ed. 2014). *See also* William A. Schabas, *The European Convention on Human Rights: A Commentary* (2015) which contains a thorough analysis of the rights guaranteed in the Convention in the light of the relevant caselaw. Other Protocols have made institutional changes relating to the Convention organs and procedures, as discussed in the following section.

§ 3–3. CONVENTION INSTITUTIONS

The Convention established two institutions "to ensure the observance of the engagements undertaken by the High Contracting Parties": the European Commission of Human Rights and the European Court of Human Rights. Art. 19. The former Commission and Court were replaced on November 1, 1998, with the entry into force of Protocol No. 11 and the inauguration of a permanent, full time Court. *See* N. Bratza and M. O'Boyle, "The Legacy of the Commission to the New Court under the Eleventh Protocol" in M. de Salvia and M. Villiger (eds.), *The Birth of European Human Rights Law: Essays in Honour of Carl Aage Norgaard* (1998), at 388; A. Drzemczewski, "The European Human Rights Convention: Protocol No. 11—Entry into Force and First Year of Application," 21 Hum.Rts.L.J. 1 (2000).

The Convention also confers some supervisory functions relating to the enforcement of the rights it guarantees on the Committee of Ministers of the Council of Europe. Convention, arts. 46(2) and 54. The Committee of Ministers may suspend or terminate a State's membership, and it has the critically important function of supervising the execution of judgments of the European Court of Human Rights. In addition to this supervisory role, the Committee of Ministers undertakes thematic monitoring of human rights matters, pursuant to a 1994 declaration on compliance with commitments made by new Member States. A third major function of the Committee of Ministers is to approve protocols to the Convention and other human rights treaties, which are then submitted to the Member States for ratification. *See* Convention, arts. 15(3), 22(1), 30(1), 52 and 58.

The Parliamentary Assembly, composed of national parliamentarians from Member States of the Council of Europe, also exercises important functions in verifying compliance by Members States with their human rights commitments and in selecting judges for the European Court. *See* § 3–13 *infra*.

The European Court of Human Rights is composed "of a number of judges equal to that of the High Contracting Parties" to the Convention. Convention, art. 20. They are elected for a non-renewable nine-year term by the Parliamentary Assembly from a list of three nominees submitted by each Member State. *See* Drzemczewski, "The Parliamentary Assembly's Committee on the Election of Judges to the European Court of Human Rights, Council of Europe," 35

Human Rights Law Journal 269 (2015). The judges serve in their individual capacities and must be persons of "high moral character," who "possess the qualifications required for appointment to high judicial office or be jurisconsults of recognized competence." Convention, art. 21(1). The judges do not have to be nationals of the Member States of the Council of Europe. For many years a Canadian national, Professor R. St. J. Macdonald, served as a judge after being nominated by Liechtenstein. Upon entry into force of Protocol 15, Member States will no longer be able to propose candidates for the Court who are over 65 years of age. Judges serve full-time during their term and may not undertake any activity incompatible with their judicial functions. The permanent Court has its seat in Strasbourg, which is the seat of the Council of Europe.

Before the entry into force of Protocol No. 11, which abolished the European Commission of Human Rights and created the permanent Court, all cases were first dealt with by the Commission, which established the facts, decided on admissibility and, in admissible cases, invited the applicant and the respondent states to reach a friendly settlement. For a description of the former system, *see* F. Jacobs and R.C.A. White, *The European Convention on Human Rights* (1996), ch. 1; R. Beddard, *Human Rights and Europe* (1993), ch. 3. Now the Court has sole compulsory jurisdiction over determinations of admissibility, fact-finding and the merits of cases. The Committee of Ministers continues to supervise compliance with the Court's judgments, assisted by the Council of Europe secretariat, which has established a Department for the Execution of Judgments within its Directorate of Monitoring, part of the Directorate General for Human Rights and Legal Affairs.

Although the Convention entered into force in 1953, the original Court was not established until 1959, after eight states filed the acceptances that were required under Convention art. 56. The first case to reach the Court was the "Lawless" Case, Judgment of July 1, 1961 (Merits), 4 Yearbook of the European Convention of Human Rights [hereinafter cited as Y.B.] 438 (1961), which was referred to it by the Commission in 1960. That same year the Commission also filed the "De Becker" Case, Judgment of March 27, 1962, 5 Y.B. 321 (1962). Five years elapsed before another case reached the Court. *See* Case Relating to Certain Aspects of the Laws on the Use of Languages in Education in Belgium, Judgment of July 23, 1968 (Merits), 11 Y.B. 833 (1968). Thereafter the Court's business doubled roughly every five years.

In the early 1980's, the caseload began to climb significantly, eventually leading to the restructuring provided by Protocol No. 11. However, the reforms did not significantly slow the number of applications received: during 2015, the Court delivered 2,441 judgments, more than double the number issued a decade earlier. The Court also adopted 43,135 decisions striking out or declaring applications inadmissible. The Court does not report statistics on the number of communications it receives annually, but only counts applications allocated to a decision body, because the remaining files frequently never go forward for adjudication due to lack of completeness or jurisdictional barriers.

The caseload reported in 2014 and 2015 declined as a result of measures taken by the States Parties and the Court to strengthen admissibility and filing requirements, in effect restricting access to the Court. Protocol No. 14 instituted some of these changes, making a single judge competent to declare inadmissible or strike out an individual application. The single judge's decision-making is assisted by non-judicial rapporteurs from the registry. Second, the Protocol added a new admissibility criterion, empowering the Court to declare inadmissible applications where the applicant has not suffered a "significant disadvantage," provided respect for human rights does not otherwise require an examination on the merits by the Court. The Protocol also provides for three judge committees to decide both on admissibility and the merits of cases that are deemed repetitive, that is, those that raise no new issues of law different from those decided in prior cases.

Protocol No. 15 will add further restrictions, shortening from six to four months the time limit within which an application must be made to the Court and amending the 'significant disadvantage' admissibility criterion to remove the second safeguard preventing rejection of an application that has not been duly considered by a domestic tribunal. The Protocol will also remove the right of the parties to a case to object to relinquishment of jurisdiction over it by a Chamber in favor of the Grand Chamber. Protocol No. 16 further provides for the highest national court of Member States to request an advisory opinion of a Grand Chamber in pending cases "on questions of principle relating to the interpretation or application of the rights and freedoms defined in the Convention or the protocols thereto." Art. 1(1). The aim is to have more cases disposed of at the national level and further reduce the need to have recourse to the European Court.

In addition to the requirements added by Protocols, the Court has amended its rules of procedure within the strictures of the Convention to improve its case management and reduce the number of applications it receives. *See* Eaton & Schokkenbroek, "Reforming the Human Rights Protection System Established by the European Convention on Human Rights," 26 HRLJ 1 (2005); Hioureas, "Behind the Scenes of Protocol No. 14: Politics in Reforming the European court of Human Rights," 24 Berkeley J. Int'l L. 718 (2006).

First, the Court has instituted the procedure of taking up "pilot" cases to address the existence of structural problems in countries that lead to numerous repetitive applications being filed. *See* Broniowski v. Poland, Judgment of June 22, 2004, Reports 2004-V; Garlicki, "Broniowski and After: The Dual Nature of 'Pilot' Judgments," in *Human Rights—Strasbourg Views: Liber Amicorum Luzius Wildhaber* 177 (2007). The Committee of Ministers invited this innovation, asking the Court to identify underlying systemic problems and their source, in particularly when they are likely to give rise to numerous applications. *See* Committee of Ministers Res. CM(2004)3 on Judgments Revealing an Underlying Systemic Problem (May 12, 2004). Despite this innovation, in 2016, the Court reported that 30,500 of the pending 64,850 cases were repetitive ones—that is, nearly half of all cases stem from failing to cure a problem previously identified and judged against the state. Most of these cases concerned Russia, Turkey and Ukraine.

Second, in June 2009 the Court amended its Rules of Court to change what had been a largely chronological order to process cases. The Court became concerned that with its increasing case-load certain serious allegations of human rights violations were taking too long to be examined, especially with regard to applications coming from countries with the highest volume of complaints. Amended Rule 41 now establishes a policy listing the order of priority as follows: (1) urgent applications, in particular those involving a particular risk to the life or health of the applicant, or other circumstances linked to the personal or family situation of the applicant, particularly where the well-being of a child is at issue; (2) structural or endemic situations that the Court has not yet examined; those suitable for the pilot-judgment procedure; applications raising an important question of general interest, and inter-state cases; (3) applications which on their face raise as main complaints issues under Articles 2, 3, 4 or 5 § 1 of the Convention ("core rights"), and which have given rise to direct threats to the physical integrity and dignity of human being. The remaining categories in order are (4) the potentially well-founded applications based on other Articles, (5) applications raising issues already dealt with in a pilot/leading judgment (repetitive cases), (6) applications identified as giving rise to a problem of admissibility, and (7) applications which are manifestly inadmissible.

III. THE ENFORCEMENT MECHANISM OF THE CONVENTION

§ 3–4. INTRODUCTION

The rights guaranteed in the European Convention are enforced on the national and international level. In a substantial number of the Contracting Parties, the Convention enjoys the status of domestic law. *See generally*, Keller and Stone Sweet, Assessing the Impact of the ECHR on National Legal Systems, in H. Keller and A. Stone Sweet, eds., *A Europe of Rights: The Impact of the ECHR on National Legal Systems* (2008) 677–712; Anagnostou and Mungiu-Pippidi, "Domestic Implementation of Human Rights Judgments in Europe: Legal Infrastructure and Government Effectiveness Matter," 25 Eur. J. Int'l L. 205 (2014); T. Barkhuysen, M. van Emmerijk, and P. van Kempen, *The Execution of Strasbourg and Geneva Human Rights Decisions in the National Legal Order* (1999). In these countries the Convention may be invoked as law in the national courts and creates rights directly enforceable by individuals.

In Contracting Parties where the Convention as such does not enjoy domestic law status, implementing legislation may be required to enforce the rights it guarantees unless existing national law already ensures the protection of comparable rights. *See* J.P. Gardner (ed.), *Aspects of Incorporation of the European Convention of Human Rights into Domestic Law* (1993). Even in these countries the national courts frequently look to the Convention when interpreting and applying domestic law in order to avoid, if at all possible, violating this treaty. *See* Buergenthal, "Self-Executing and Non-Self-Executing Treaties in National and International Law," 234 Recueil des Cours 303, 359 (1992); Frowein, "The Transformation of Constitutional Law Through the European Convention on Human Rights," 35 Human Rights Law Journal 1 (2015).

Only when domestic law does not provide relief capable of remedying a violation of the Convention may recourse be had to the European Court. This rule has its basis in the requirement found in all human rights treaties, including the Convention, that before international remedies may be invoked, available and effective domestic remedies must be exhausted. Convention, art. 35(1). In a broader sense, it can also be said to derive from the principle of subsidiarity. *See* Petzold, "The Convention and the Principle of Subsidiarity," in Macdonald *et al.*, *supra*, at 41; Shelton, "Subsidiarity, Democracy and Human Rights," in *Broadening the Frontiers of Human Rights* (D. Gomien ed. 1993).

§ 3–5. JURISDICTION OF
THE EUROPEAN COURT

Initially the Convention conferred only contentious jurisdiction on the Court. Protocol No. 2 added limited advisory jurisdiction, which was extended by the Convention on Human Rights and Biomedicine, and will be further expanded when Protocol No. 16 enters into force. The Court's contentious jurisdiction extends to all cases brought by a Contracting Party against another Party for breach of the Convention and to cases brought by victims alleging a violation by a Contracting Party of the rights guaranteed by the Convention or a Protocol. Convention, arts. 33 and 34. Complaints concerning other rights, such as those in the European Social Charter, fall outside the jurisdiction of the Court. Zechnalova & Zehnal v. The Czech Republic, Reports 2002-V (13 May 2002). All matters concerning the interpretation and application of the Convention and its protocols fall within the Court's jurisdiction. *See* § 3.7 *et seq.*, *infra*. Judgments of the Court are available at www.echr. coe.int.

Advisory opinions are given by a Grand Chamber of the Court and adopted by a majority vote. For the history of the Court's advisory power, *see* Council of Europe, *Explanatory Reports on the Second to Fifth Protocols to the European Convention for the Protection of Human Rights and Fundamental Freedoms*, Doc. H (71) 11, at 3–18 (1971). Article 47 empowers only the Committee of Ministers to request advisory opinions. The power is limited, moreover, to "legal questions concerning the interpretation of the

Convention and the protocols thereto." Convention, art. 47(1). In exercising its advisory jurisdiction, the Court may not interpret "the content or scope of the rights or freedoms" that are guaranteed by the Convention and its Protocols. It may not deal with "any other question which the Court or the Committee of Ministers might have to consider in consequence of any such proceedings as could be instituted in accordance with the Convention." Convention, art. 47(2).

Given this narrow jurisdiction, it is not surprising that the Court has received only three requests for advisory opinions. The first request, submitted on January 9, 2002, asked the court to rule on the compatibility with the Convention of a human rights instrument adopted by the Commonwealth of Independent States. On June 2, 2004, the Court decided that the request was outside the scope of its competence because it concerned an issue that might come before the Court in a contentious case. Although styled as a "decision," it was effectively the first advisory opinion. *See* Decision on the Competence of the Court to Give an Advisory Opinion, June 2, 2004, available at http://www. echr.coe.int.

On February 12, 2008, the Court issued its first formally-designated advisory opinion, "on certain legal questions concerning the lists of candidates submitted with a view to the election of judges to the European Court of Human Rights." The requested opinion arose of out a dispute between the Maltese government and the Parliamentary Assembly concerning the composition of the Maltese list of candidates for the post of judge at the Court. Malta's list failed to include a woman, contrary to the stated policy of the Assembly. The Court's opinion was that the Assembly could not add additional criteria for candidates to those set forth in the Convention.

In January 2010, the Court issued its second formal Advisory Opinion "on certain legal questions concerning the lists of candidates submitted with a view to the election of judges to the European Court of Human Rights." The issue concerned the fact that Ukraine had withdrawn its list of three Court candidates, after one of the three indicated no further interest in being presented. The withdrawal of the entire list took place after the deadline set for submission of candidate names by the Parliamentary Assembly. The Court's opinion was that such a withdrawal could take place only if the deadline set by the Parliamentary Assembly had not yet passed and once passed, as in this instance, Ukraine could only submit a new candidate to replace the person that had withdrawn, but could not remove the other two names on the original list. The Court's Opinion supported the stance taken by the Parliamentary Assembly on this issue.

§ 3–6. INTER-STATE COMPLAINTS

By ratifying the European Convention, a state is deemed to have accepted the jurisdiction of the Court to receive complaints from other States Parties alleging a violation of the treaty. Convention, art. 33. The Applicant State does not have to demonstrate any special interest in or relationship to the victim of the violation or its subject matter. Austria v. Italy, Application No. 78/8/60, 4 Y.B. 116 (1961). The European Court has said: " . . . the Convention allows Contracting States to require the observance of these obligations [contained in the Convention] without having to justify an interest deriving, for example, from the fact that a measure they complain of has prejudiced one of their nationals." Ireland v. United Kingdom, Judgment of January 18, 1978, 25 Publ. Eur. Court H.R. 1, at 91 (1978).

Inter-state complaints are not subject to the same admissibility requirements prescribed for individual petitions other than the obligation to exhaust domestic remedies. Convention, arts. 33 and 35. Nevertheless, between 1953 and 2005 fewer than two dozen inter-state cases were brought; in the past decade, however, seven cases have been filed against Russia by Georgia and Ukraine. Most of the earlier cases were filed against states that had not as yet recognized the right of individual petition and thus could be held internationally accountable for a breach of the Convention only by means of an inter-state proceeding. *See* Greece v. United Kingdom, Application No. 17/6/56, 2 Y.B. 182 (1958–59); Greece v. United Kingdom, Application No. 29/9/57, 2 Y.B. 186 (1958–59); Austria v. Italy, Application No. 78/8/60, 4 Y.B. 116 (1961); Denmark et al. v. Greece, Applications Nos. 3321–23/67 & 33–44/67, 11 Y.B. 690 (1968); Denmark et al. v. Greece, Application No. 44/48/70, 13 Y.B. 108 (1970); Cyprus v. Turkey, Application Nos. 678/0/74 and 69/50/75, 18 Y.B. 82 (1975); Cyprus v. Turkey, Application No. 8/007/77,

21 Y.B. 100 (1978); Denmark et al. v. Turkey, Application No. 99/40/82, 35 Decisions and Reports of the European Commission on Human Rights 143 (1984).

The motivations for filing inter-state cases have been political in a number of cases, but humanitarian for other complaints. The latter was true, for example, of the proceedings that were instituted against Greece and Turkey by various Scandinavian nations. For an overview of early inter-state cases, *see* Prebensen, "Inter-State Complaints under Treaty Provisions—The Experience under the European Convention on Human Rights," 20 Hum. Rts. L. J. 445 (1999). As a general rule, however, states have been reluctant to file cases against other states, fearing that this action will be interpreted as an unfriendly act and adversely affect their diplomatic relations.

§ 3–7. INDIVIDUAL PETITIONS

Any "person, non-governmental organization or group of individuals claiming to be the victim of a violation . . . of the rights set forth in the Convention or the protocols thereto" may file an application with the European Court. Convention, art. 34. The word "person" includes legal persons in cases where their rights have been violated. *See, e.g.,* The Sunday Times Case, Judgment of April 1979, 30 Publ. Eur. Court H.R. 5 (1979); Stran Greek Refineries and Stratis Andreadis v. Greece, Judgment of 9 December 1994, 301-B Publ. Eur. Court H.R. (1994),19 Eur. H.R. Rep. 293.

The notion of "victim" is interpreted autonomously and irrespective of domestic rules such as those concerning standing to sue. Gorraiz Lizarraga and Others v. Spain, Judgment of 27 April 2004, ECHR 2004-III, § 35. The requirement that the petitioner be "a victim of a violation" has been interpreted by the European Court to mean that "an individual applicant should claim to have been actually affected by the violation he alleges . . . . Article [34] does not institute for individuals a kind of *actio popularis* for the interpretation of the Convention. . . ." *Case of Klass and Others*, Judgment of September 6, 1978, 28 Publ. Eur. Court H.R. 5, at 17–18 (1979); Tănase v. Moldova, Judgment of April 27, 2010 [GC], § 104; Burden v. the United Kingdom, Judgment of April 29, 2008 [GC], § 33).

Indirect as well as direct victims may submit an application; the former generally are relatives or others with close connection to the victim. *See* Application No. 100/55, 1 Y.B. 162 and Application No. 282/57, 1 Y.B. 166. *See also* Open Door and Dublin Well Woman v. Ireland, Judgment of October 29, 1992, 246 Publ. Eur. Court H.R. 22 (1992) and generally T. Zwart, *The Admissibility of Human Rights Petitions* (1994) ch. 3. If the applicant dies while the case is pending, the Court's practice generally is to strike the application in the absence of an heir or close relative who expresses the wish to pursue the case; however, if the main issue raised by the case transcends the person and the interests of the application, the Court may decide on public policy grounds in the common interest of protecting human rights to continue its consideration. Karner v. Austria, Judgment of 24 July 2003, 38 Eur. H.R. Rep.

The acts in question must be attributable to a Contracting Party. The European Court has declared inadmissible cases against states participating in NATO and UN activities in Kosovo. The Court held that the responsibility should be attributed to the organizations and not to the individual states, because the Security Council retained ultimate authority and control, and effective command of the relevant operational matters remained with NATO. The Court expressed concern that application of the Convention to state acts undertaken in compliance with Security Council decisions could interfere with the fulfillment of the UN's collective security mission. Agim Behrami & Bekir Behrami v. France; Ruzhdi Saramati v. France, Germany & Norway, joined app. Nos. 71412/01 and 78166/01, European Court of Human Rights (Grand Chamber) May 2, 2007.

The admissibility of individual petitions is governed by the provisions of Article 35 of the Convention, which reads as follows:

1. The Court may only deal with the matter after all domestic remedies have been exhausted, according to the generally recognized rules of international law, and within a period of six months from the date on which the final decision was taken.

2. The Court shall not deal with any application submitted under Article 34 that

(a) is anonymous; or

(b) is substantially the same as a matter that has already been examined by the Court or has already been submitted to another procedure of international investigation or settlement and contains no relevant new information.

3. The Court shall declare inadmissible any individual application submitted under Article 34 if it considers that:

(a) the application is incompatible with the provisions of the Convention or the Protocols thereto, manifestly ill-founded, or an abuse of the right of individual application; or

(b) the applicant has not suffered a significant disadvantage, unless respect for human rights as defined in the Convention and the Protocols thereto requires an examination of the application on the merits and provided that no case may be rejected on this ground which has not been duly considered by a domestic tribunal.

4. The Court shall reject any application which it considers inadmissible under this Article. It may do so at any stage of the proceedings.

Rule 47 of the Rules of Court, which introduced stricter conditions for applying to the Court, came into force on 1 January 2014. The new Rule, accompanied by a Practice Direction, introduced two major changes which will determine whether an application is rejected or allocated to a judicial formation. These require, firstly, completion in full of a new simplified application form accompanied by copies of all relevant supporting documents. The application will not be examined if any elements are missing or incomplete. Secondly, if the application form or the case file is completed only after the six-month period has expired, the case will normally be rejected as having been lodged out of time.

The question whether a petition is or is not admissible is first reviewed by the Registry. Applications which are clearly inadmissible are dealt with by a single judge assisted by non-judicial rapporteurs, rather than by a three-judge committee. Other applications are referred to a Judge Rapporteur on the Committee, who may refer the petition to the three judges if the Judge Rapporteur finds a barrier to admissibility. The Committee may agree and conclude unanimously that the petition is inadmissible; this decision is final. Convention, arts. 27, 28. If the Judge Rapporteur considers that the petition is not inadmissible or the Committee decision is not unanimous on this issue, the petition is transferred to a seven judge Chamber which will normally decide all issues of admissibility, merits, and reparations. To speed up proceedings, the Court now frequently examines admissibility and merits together. Separate admissibility decisions are only adopted in more complex cases.

As Article 35 indicates, an application is inadmissible if it has already been the subject of a case before an international body, or is being examined by such a body, because the purpose of the requirement is to avoid the same case becoming the object of various international procedures. The petitioner can prevent the application being declared inadmissible by withdrawing it from the other procedure. The procedures envisaged are procedures in which a matter is submitted by way of "a petition" lodged formally or substantively by the applicant in judicial or quasi-judicial proceedings similar to those set up by the Convention. It has been held that the term "international investigation or settlement" refers to institutions and procedures set up by states, thus excluding non-governmental bodies. *See* Application No. 16358/90, Decision of October 12, 1992, unpublished, and Lukanov v. Bulgaria, Application No. 21915/93, Decision of 12 January 1995, Reports1997-II.

The assessment of similarity of the matters usually involves a comparison of the parties in the respective proceedings, the relevant legal provisions relied on by them, the scope of their claims and the types of redress sought. OAO Neftyanaya Kompaniya Yukos v. Russia, Judgment of Sept. 20, 2011, § 521; Greek Federation of Bank Employee Unions v. Greece (dec.), Nov. 12, 2010, § 39. In addition, the relevant body must be one that is "international" and not domestic. *See* Jeličić v. Bosnia and Herzegovina, Judgment of 15 Nov. 2005 (the Human Rights Chamber of Bosnia-Herzegovina was set up pursuant to the Dayton Accords, an international treaty, but the applicant's proceedings before the Chamber were not "international" within the meaning of Article 35 § 2 (b) of the Convention because the characteristics of proceedings before the Chamber indicate it should be considered a "domestic" remedy within the meaning of Article 35 § 1 of the Convention).

In another effort to avoid duplicate international procedures, some States Parties to the European Convention, in ratifying the Optional Protocol to the International Covenant on Civil and Political Rights, made reservations to prevent considerations of cases by the UN Human Rights Committee that had already been considered within the European system. On this subject, *see* Communication No. 121/1982, UN Human Rights Committee, *Selected Decisions under the Optional Protocol (Second to Sixteenth Sessions)*, at 32 (1985) (holding an application against Denmark inadmissible).

The most common grounds for the inadmissibility of individual petitions are those set out in Article 35(2) and (3). For a detailed discussion of the admissibility criteria and case law, *see Practical Guide on Admissibility Criteria* (European Court of Human Rights, 2014); Van Dijk & Van Hoof, *supra*, at 61, and Zwart, *supra*.

§ 3–8. ADMISSIBILITY: INCOMPATIBLE, ILL-FOUNDED, OR ABUSE OF THE RIGHT OF PETITION

Under Article 35(3) an application must be considered inadmissible if it is "incompatible with the provisions of the .... Convention or the protocols thereto, manifestly ill-founded, or an abuse of the right of application." The requirement that an application not be "manifestly ill-founded" calls for a determination whether the application states a *prima facie* case. *Airey Case*, Judgment of October 9, 1979, 32 Publ. Eur. Court H.R. 4, 10 (1979). Any application will be considered "manifestly ill-founded" if a preliminary examination of its substance does not disclose any appearance of a violation of the rights guaranteed by the Convention. Case of Ferrazzini v. Italy, Judgment of 12 July 2001.

This conclusion is not always evident on the face of the application. In order to conclude that an application is manifestly ill-founded, the Court sometimes invites observations from the parties and may issue a detailed reasoned decision. Mentzen v. Latvia (dec.), Dec. 7, 2004, 377. The majority of manifestly ill-founded applications are declared inadmissible by a single judge or a three-judge committee, but some cases are examined by a Chamber or exceptionally by the Grand Chamber. Gratzinger and Gratzingerova v. the Czech Republic (dec.) July 10, 2002 [GC] 2002-VII 399; Demopoulos and Others v. Turkey (dec.) March 1, 2010 [GC] 50 E.H.R.R. SE14. The term "manifestly ill-founded" may apply to the application as a whole or to a particular complaint within the broader context of an otherwise admissible case. The Court divides manifestly ill-founded complaints into four categories: "fourth instance" complaints seeking review of national judgments not presenting a human rights issue, complaints where there has clearly or apparently been no violation, unsubstantiated complaints and, finally, confused or far-fetched complaints.

"Abuse of the right of application" refers to conduct such as knowingly making false or groundless allegations, repeatedly using abusive and defamatory language about the Respondent Government, or intentionally breaching the rule of confidentiality applicable to the proceedings. *Drozd v. Poland*, Comm. Decision of March 5, 1996 (striking the application from the list). But the mere fact that an applicant may have political motives in filing the case does not constitute an abuse of the right of application, provided that the complaint otherwise states a valid cause of action. *Lawless v. Ireland*, Application No. 3/32/57, 2 Y.B. 308 (1958–59). Also, filing a petition after refusing to negotiate a friendly settlement at the national level is not construed as an abuse of the right of petition, at least when the proposed settlement contains no admission of the government's responsibility for the violation. Case of Andronicou and Constantinou v. Cyprus, Application No. 86/1996/705/897, Judgment of 9 October 1997, Reports 1997-VI, 2059.

§ 3–9. EXHAUSTION OF DOMESTIC REMEDIES AND THE SIX-MONTHS RULE

Article 35(1) of the Convention provides that "the Court may only deal with the matter after all domestic remedies have been exhausted, according to the generally recognized rules of international law, and within a period of six months from the date on which the final decision was taken." This language does not distinguish between individual and inter-state applications; to be admissible, both types of application must comply with the requirement for the exhaustion of domestic remedies. Ireland v. United Kingdom, Judgment of January 18, 1978, 25 Publ. Eu. Court H.R. 5, 64 (1978).

Article 35(1) establishes two requirements: exhaustion of domestic remedies and the so-called six months rule. The Court has explained the first requirement as follows: "the rule of exhaustion of domestic remedies ... dispenses States from answering before an international body for their acts before they have had an opportunity to put matters right through their own legal system. . . ." De Wilde, Ooms and Versyp Cases, Judgment of June 18, 1971, 12 Publ. Eur. Court H.R. 12, 29 (1971). In short, it is not permitted to make an international case out of a matter that can be resolved on the local level. The rule emphasizes the primary role of national institutions and the subsidiary functions of the European Court. Akdivar and others v. Turkey, Judgment of September 16, 1996, Reports 1996-IV, 1192 at 1210 (referring to the requirement of exhaustion of local remedies as a reflection of the subsidiary role of international institutions). An application will, therefore, be dismissed for failure to exhaust domestic remedies when it appears that issues relevant to it were not brought to the attention of national bodies which could have resolved the matter. Cardot v. France, Judgment of March 19, 1991, 200 Publ. Eur. Court H.R.1, 18–19 (1991). For the manner in which this rule is applied in practice see Castells v. Spain, Judgment of April 23, 1992, 236 Publ. Eur. Court H.R. 1, 19–20 (1992).

The Court's case-law and international law generally indicate that applicants need not have recourse to remedies which are not effective or are unduly prolonged. Akdivar and others v. Turkey, *supra* at para. 68. "The only remedies which . . . the Convention requires to be exhausted are those that relate to the breaches alleged and at the same time are available and sufficient. . . ." Van Oosterwijck Case, Judgment of November 6, 1980, 40 Publ. Eur. Court H.R. 5, at 13 (1981). A remedy is "sufficient" if it is capable of redressing the wrong allegedly committed. Stögmüller Case, Judgment of November 10, 1969, 12 Y.B. 364 (1969).

The failure of a petitioner to resort to a consistently unsuccessful domestic remedy will not result in a rejection of the petition. Neither will the failure to file an appeal against a law that prior judgments suggest will be upheld; this is so even in countries where the courts are free to depart from such precedents. Sigurjonsson v. Iceland, Application No. 16130/90, Eur. Comm. H.R., decision of July 10, 1991, 12 Hum Rts L.J. 402 (1991). The Court reached the same conclusion in a case where the national courts reversed themselves while the case was being considered by the former Commission. De Wilde, Ooms and Versyp Cases, Judgment of June 18, 1971, 12 Publ. Eur. Court H.R. 12, 34 (1971). However, if the domestic law on the subject is open to conflicting interpretations, a reasonable effort to exhaust potential remedies must be made. Van Oosterwijck Case, Judgment of November 6, 1980, 40 Publ. Eur. Court H.R. 4, 18–19 (1981).

If more than one potentially effective remedy is available, the applicant is only required to have used one of them. Moreira Barbosa v. Portugal (dec.) April 29, 2004; Jeličić v. Bosnia and Herzegovina (dec.) Oct. 31, 2006; Karakó v. Hungary, Judgment of April 28, 2009, § 14; Aquilina v. Malta [GC], Judgment of April 29, 1999, 1999-III, IHRL 3001, § 39). Indeed, when one remedy has been attempted, use of another remedy which has essentially the same purpose is not required. Riad and Idiab v. Belgium, Judgment of Jan. 24, 2008, § 84; Kozacioğlu v. Turkey [GC] Judgment of Feb. 19, 2009, §§ 40 et seq.; Micallef v. Malta [GC], Judgment of Oct. 15, 2009, § 58). It is for the applicant to select the remedy that is most appropriate in his or her case.

The domestic remedies requirement may be waived by the state because it is deemed to be procedural in nature. Bozano Case, Judgment of December 18, 1986, 111 Publ. Eur. Court H.R. 6, 19–20 (1987). According to the European Court, "there is nothing to prevent States from waiving the benefit of the rule of exhaustion of domestic remedies, the essential aim of which is to protect their national legal order." De Wilde, Ooms and Versyp Cases, *supra*, at 31. The waiver may be express, but more often than not it is inadvertent, for example, when the Respondent State fails to raise the issue in a timely manner and is thereafter estopped. Case of De Jong, Baljet and Van den Brink, Judgment of May 22, 1984, 77 Publ. Eur. Ct. H.R. 6 at 18–19; Zana v. Turkey, Judgment of 25 November 1997, Reports 1997-VII, 2546.

An important issue relating to exhaustion of domestic remedies concerns the burden of proof. Rule 47 of the Rules of Court specifies that a petitioner must include information about exhaustion of local remedies in the application to the Court. The Court undertakes a preliminary examination of admissibility based upon the allegations contained in the application and the accompanying documents. If it appears from these materials that the applicant has not exhausted available domestic remedies, the application may be rejected summarily.

After an application passes the preliminary examination, if the Respondent State pleads the non-exhaustion of domestic remedies, the State has the burden of proof to demonstrate the existence of an effective and accessible remedy capable of providing redress to the applicant. DeWeer Case, Judgment of February 27, 1980, 35 Publ. Eur. Court H.R. 4, 15 (1980). According to the Court, "such remedies must be sufficiently certain not only in theory but also in practice, failing which they will lack the requisite accessibility and effectiveness; and it falls to the respondent State, if it pleads non-exhaustion, to establish that these various conditions are satisfied. . . ." Case of Johnston and Others, Judgment of December 18, 1986, 112 Publ. Eur. Court H.R.8, 22 (1987). *See also* Case of De Jong, Baljet and Van den Brink, *supra* at 19.

Once the state has satisfied its burden of proof, it falls to the applicant to establish that the remedy indicated was in fact exhausted or was for some reason inadequate or ineffective in the particular circumstances of the case or that there existed "special circumstances" absolving the applicant from the requirement. Akdivar v. Turkey, *supra*, para. 68; Mentes and Others v. Turkey, Judgment of November 28, 1997, Reports 1997-VIII, 2689, para. 57. Such circumstances may include the inaction of national authorities in the face of serious allegations of misconduct or infliction of harm by state agents, for example where the authorities have failed to investigate or offer assistance in the face of evidence that violations occurred. *See* Akdivar v. Turkey, *supra* at 1210–11; Selçuk and Asker v. Turkey, 24 April 1998, Reports 1998-II 891.

The European Court also has indicated that the rule of exhaustion of remedies must make "due allowance" for the fact that the rule arises in the context of human rights proceedings and thus it must be applied "with some degree of flexibility and without excessive formalism." Aksoy v. Turkey, Reports 1996-VI, 2260, para. 53 (1997). For example, a general situation of violence may create obstacles to the proper functioning of the system of the administration of justice, including the securing of probative evidence, and make the pursuit of judicial remedies futile. In such circumstances, the Court will make "a realistic assessment" of the general legal and political context in which the remedies operate and the personal circumstances of the applicant.

The six-months rule spelled out in Article 35 requires that the petition be filed with the Court "within a period of six months from the date on which the final decision was taken." Its purpose is to ensure an end to litigation within a reasonable period of time or, put another way, "to prevent the past judgments being constantly called into question." DeBecker v. Belgium, Application No. 2/14/56, 2 Y.B. 214, at 244 (1958–59).

Reading the six-months rule together with the requirement for the exhaustion of domestic remedies helps to clarify what is meant by the "final decision" from which the six-month period is measured. That is, in any given case, the final decision must be determined by reference to the last domestic remedy that must be exhausted pursuant to Article 35(1). If, for example, under the applicable domestic law all available domestic remedies are exhausted with an appeal to the superior court of X, then the judgment of that tribunal is the "final decision" for purposes of the six-months rule. Blecic v. Croatia, Judgment of March 8, 2006 (GC). But a decision from an appeal to a domestic court which clearly lacks the power or jurisdiction to grant the relief sought under the Convention will not be taken into account for this purpose. *Neilson v. Denmark*, Application No. 3/43/57, 2 Y.B. 412 (1958–59);

Hence, if more than six months have passed after the "final decision," but the petitioner thereafter nevertheless appeals to a higher or special court which clearly lacks the power to affect that decision, the petition will be deemed inadmissible barring some very special circumstances. *Id. See also* Sibson v. United Kingdom, Application No. 14327/88, Europ. Comm'n H.R., Decision of April 9, 1991, 12 Hum. Rts. L.J. 351 (1991)(dealing with "special circumstances" applicable to the six-months rule). But the six-month rule is inapplicable when a violation of the Convention is continuous and there exist no domestic remedies to challenge it. In application of the six months rule, the first day of the time-limit is considered to start on the day following the final decision, whereas "months" are calculated as calendar months regardless of their actual duration. An application is considered to be introduced within the time-limit only once it has been completed pursuant to the Rules of Court. Oberschlick v. Austria, Judgment of 23 May 1991, 204 Publ. Eur.Court H.R. 21 paras. 38–40; Istituto di Vigilanza v. Italy, Judgment of 22 September 1993, 265-C Publ. Eur. Court H.R. 35 para. 14; Pollard v. the United Kingdom, Application No. 28189/95, Decision of April 12, 1996.

§ 3–10.   "SIGNIFICANT DISADVANTAGE"

Since the entry into force of Protocol No. 14 in 2010, the Court has been directed to declare inadmissible any individual application submitted under Article 34 if it considers that:

. . .

(b)   the applicant has not suffered a significant disadvantage, unless respect for human rights as defined in the Convention and the Protocols thereto requires an examination of the application on the merits and provided that no case may be rejected on this ground which has not been duly considered by a domestic tribunal.

Once it enters into force, Protocol No. 15 will remove the concluding safeguard about domestic remedies from this provision and will shorten the period of time to apply to the Court from six months to four months.

During 2013 and 2014, when single judges began evaluating cases for admissibility, the number of rejected applications grew considerably, perhaps suggesting a broad application of the new criterion, although the lack of any reporting on inadmissibility decisions by single judge makes it impossible to know the basis on which applications were excluded. The jurisprudence during a one-year transition period of reported decisions suggested that the Court considered certain violations inherently to produce a significant disadvantage to the applicant. The decisions also made clear the distinction between victim status and significant disadvantage, and elaborated the factors that should determine whether the applicant has or has not experienced the requisite level of disadvantage due to the alleged violation.

Logically, the Court should test for significant disadvantage only after reviewing potential jurisdictional problems and after examining other objections to admissibility, because it is only if an otherwise admissible case is presented that the Court should examine whether, despite having a *prima facie* case, the applicant's claim should be rejected because the alleged violation produced consequences insignificant to the victim and to human rights in general. In some cases, however, the Court has looked at the new criterion before examining other admissibility requirements. Korolev v Russia, Admissibility, 21 October 2010; Rinck v France, Admissibility, 19 October 2011; Gaftoniuc v Romania, Admissibility, 22 February 2011; Burov v Moldova, Admissibility, 14 June 2011; Shefer v Russia, Admissibility, 13 March 2012.

In Korolev v Russia, the leading early decision on significant disadvantage, the Court established that the new criterion, inspired as it was by the *de minimis* principle, hinged "on the idea that a violation of a right, however real from a purely legal point of view, should attain a minimum level of severity to warrant consideration by an international court." The Court indicated that it would make a contextual assessment based on two factors: the subjective perception of the applicant and an objective assessment of what was at stake in the case. The subjective perception should be justified on objective grounds, the Court determined, because although the applicant's feelings are relevant, those feelings, without being justified objectively in any way, are insufficient to conclude that an applicant has suffered a significant disadvantage.

In the judgment of Giusti v. Italy, the Court further indicated factors it would consider to determine significant disadvantage: the nature of the allegedly violated right, the gravity of that alleged violation, and/or the possible consequences of the alleged violation on the personal situation of the applicant. These criteria may imply that violations of certain rights, including non-derogable rights, inherently cause a significant disadvantage to applicants. Giusti v. Italy, Application No 13175/03, Merits, 18 October 2011. *See* Shelton, "Significantly Disadvantaged? Shrinking Access to the European Court of Human Rights," 16 Human Rights Law Review 305 (2016).

§ 3–11.   PROCEEDINGS ON THE MERITS

Since the reforms of Protocol No. 11, individual applicants have been able to bring complaints directly to the Court and participate in all the proceedings. Convention, art. 34. The individual must be represented by a lawyer licensed to practice law in one of the States Parties to the Convention once the communication is declared admissible and for any hearing that is held. Convention, art. 38(1) and Rules of Court, art. 36.

In examining a case, the Court must place itself at the disposal of the parties concerned with a view to securing a friendly settlement of the matter. The friendly settlement can only be realized "on the basis of respect for human rights as defined in the convention and the protocols thereto." Convention, art. 38(1)(b). If a friendly settlement is reached, the Court strikes the case from its list and issues a decision giving the facts and the solution reached. For an annual report on cases settled, *see* Eur. Court H.R., Statistical Information, available at http://www.echr.coe.int. An important consequence of issuing the settlement in the form of a decision is that it allows the Committee of Ministers to supervise the execution of the terms of the agreement. The Court also may decide to strike an application for failure to pursue the claim, if the matter has been resolved, or if "for any other reason established by the Court" it finds it is no longer justified to continue the examination of the application. Convention, art. 37. The last ground may be relevant in a case where the government offers a fair settlement of the merits and that offer is rejected by the applicant. *See* Akman v. Turkey, Judgment of June 26, 2001.

In dealing with cases on the merits, the Court may hold hearings, receive written submissions, and examine witnesses either at its seat in Strasbourg or, if necessary, by interviewing them wherever they may be. The Court may ask any person or institution of its choice to obtain information, express an opinion or make a report on any specific point. Rule 42, Rules of Court. It also may accept written or oral comments from *amicus curiae* and must allow the intervention of any state whose national is the applicant in the proceedings. Convention, art. 36. Hearings are open to the public unless the Court "in exceptional circumstances" decides otherwise, and submissions are publicly accessible unless the President of the Court closes the record.

Respecting the merits, the Court has held that applicants, both private parties and states, must prove their allegations by "proof beyond a reasonable doubt." Ireland v. the United Kingdom, judgment of 18 Jan. 1978, 25 Pub. Eur. Ct. Hum. Rts., § 161. After criticism of this high standard, normally applied in criminal prosecutions, the Court has clarified that the phrase does not have the same meaning as in domestic law and that "[s]uch proof may follow from the coexistence of sufficiently strong, clear and concordant inferences or of similar unrebutted presumptions of fact."

Moreover, when the events in issue lie wholly or in large part within the exclusive knowledge of the authorities, as in the case of persons within their control or custody, strong presumptions of fact will arise in respect of injuries occurring during such detention. Indeed, in such cases the Court shifts the burden of proof to the authorities to provide a satisfactory and convincing explanation. *Salman v. Turkey* [GC], Reports 2000-VII. In addition, where allegations are made under Articles 2 and 3 of the Convention, the Court applies "a particularly thorough scrutiny" (Ribitsch v. Austria, Judgment of 4 Dec. 1995, 336 Pub. Eur. Ct. H.R., § 32; Avsar v. Turkey, Reports 2001-VII § 283), even if certain domestic proceedings and investigations have already taken place.

§ 3–12. JUDGMENTS OF THE COURT

Most cases are decided by a seven-judge Chamber. The Convention provides a limited review procedure of Chamber decisions. Within three months of the date of the judgment, any party to the case may request that the case be referred to the Grand Chamber, which consists of 17 judges. A panel of five judges may decide to accept the request, but only "if the case raises a serious question affecting the interpretation or application of the Convention or the protocols thereto, or a serious issue of general

importance." Convention, art. 43(2). The Chamber
also may relinquish jurisdiction in favor of the Grand
Chamber prior to issuing its judgment, for any of the
same stated reasons, unless one of the parties to the
case objects. Convention, art. 30. The Grand
Chamber will then issue its own judgment, which is
final. Chamber decisions become final in any of the
three following circumstances: when the parties
declare that they will not ask for a review of the
judgment by a Grand Chamber; three months from
the date of the judgment if no request is made; or
when the Grand Chamber panel rejects a referral
request. A judgment of the Grand Chamber is final
on the date it is issued.

The Convention declares that "the High
Contracting Parties undertake to abide by the
decisions of the Court in any case to which they are
parties." Convention art. 46(1). The Committee of
Ministers supervises the execution of the Court's
judgments. Convention, art. 46(2). The fact that the
judgment of the Court is law only for the party to the
case means that the Court's decisions are not
formally binding precedent (*stare decisis*) for the
Contracting Parties generally. But the Court
normally follows its caselaw. Indeed, if a Chamber
intends not to follow the Court's prior judgments, it
is supposed to relinquish jurisdiction in favor of the
Grand Chamber, if none of the parties to the case
objects.

This reliance on prior decisions gives the
judgments important precedential value for states
parties and national courts. *See generally*

Buergenthal, "The Effect of the European Convention on Human Rights on the Internal Law of Member States," in Int'l & Comp. L.Q. Supp. Publ. No. 11, 79, 94 (1965); Sundberg, "The European Experience of Human Rights: The Precedent Value of the European Court's Decisions," 20 Akron L. Rev. 629 (1987).

Article 41 of the Convention provides that, when the Court finds a state responsible for a violation of the Convention and the internal law of the state allows only partial reparation to be made, the Court shall "afford just satisfaction to the injured party." The reference to lack of reparations in national law might be read to require a further domestic proceeding to remedy the violation, but the Court has rejected this interpretation whenever it has been advanced. De Wilde, Ooms and Versyp Cases, Judgment of March 10, 1970 (Article 50), 14 Publ. Eur. Court H.R. 1, 8 (1972); Ringeisen Case, Judgment of June 22, 1972 (Article 50), 15 Publ. Eur. Court H.R. 1, 9 (1972). On the jurisprudence of the European Court, *see* D. Shelton, *Remedies in International Human Rights Law* (3rd ed. 2015). In most cases, the Court awards "just satisfaction" in its judgment on the merits, but in complex cases it may hold separate proceedings on the subject.

Just satisfaction may consist of a finding of the violation itself, which is seen by the Court as a form of remedy for moral harm. It may also include compensation for proven pecuniary and non-pecuniary injuries, as well as costs and attorneys' fees for representation that is not covered by the

Court's legal aid program. *Campbell v. United Kingdom*, Judgment of March 25, 1992, 223 Publ. Eur. Court H.R. 1, at 23 (1992); *X v. France*, Judgment of March 31, 1992, 234C Publ. Eur. Court H.R. The Court lacks the power to reverse domestic judicial decisions or to annul national laws, but it has called for restitution of property and liberty of detained persons. Brumarescu v. Romania (Article 41), Judgment of January 23, 2001, 33 Eur.H.R. Rep. 35 (2001); Assanidze v. Georgia, Judgment of 8 April 2004 (GC), Reports 2004-II.

In addition to affording remedies under Article 41, the Court has begun to indicate those general measures that may help prevent repetitious cases. Scozzari and Giunta v. Italy, para. 249, ECHR 2000-VIII. The Court calls these "exceptional cases," but now frequently indicates the type of measure that might be taken in order to put an end to a situation it has found to exist, including legislative reforms. Manole and Others v. Moldova (2009); Lukenda v. Slovenia (2005); Volkov v. Ukraine (2013); Aslakhanova and Others v. Russia (2012), para. 238; Dimitrov and Hamanov v. Bulgaria (2011); Gulmez v. Turkey (2008).

§ 3–13.   ENFORCEMENT OF JUDGMENTS BY THE COMMITTEE OF MINISTERS

Article 46(2) of the Convention empowers the Committee of Minsters to ensure the enforcement of judgments of the European Court of Human Rights. The provision reads as follows: "The final judgment of the Court shall be transmitted to the Committee of

Ministers, which shall supervise its execution." In order to discharge this obligation, the Committee has adopted "Rules Concerning the Application of Article [46] of the European Convention on Human Rights." They provide that as soon as a judgment of the Court has been transmitted, it shall be inscribed on the Committee's agenda (Rule 1). The state concerned must then inform the Committee of the steps it has taken to comply with the judgment. If the state has not taken the requisite action, the case is automatically placed on the Committee's agenda for consideration by it within the next six months. (Rule 2). *See* Resolution DH (2000) 105 concerning the judgments of the European Court of Human Rights of 18 December 1996 and 28 July 1998 in the case of *Loizidou v. Turkey.*

When the just satisfaction awarded consists of money damages, it is usually easy for the state to pay the injured party and to inform the Committee. The Committee will then pass a resolution that might, in part, read as follows:

> Having satisfied itself that the Government of Belgium has awarded the just satisfaction provided for in the judgment of the Court of 24 October 1983,

> Declares, after taking note of the information supplied by the Government of Belgium, that it has exercised its functions under Article 54 of the Convention in this case.

Committee of Ministers, Resolution D.H. (85) 14, 28 June 1985 concerning the judgments of the European

Court of Human Rights of 10 February 1983 and 24 October 1983 in the Albert and Le Compte Cases, Council of Europe, *Collection of Resolutions Adopted by the Committee of Ministers in Application of Articles 32 and 54 of the European Convention on Human Rights 1984–85* [hereinafter cited as *Committee of Minsters Resolutions*], 38–39 (1986).

Sometimes the Court's judgment may declare that certain national laws or practices are in conflict with the Convention and that appropriate legislation needs to be adopted. Compliance with this type of judgment is harder to monitor. Often the state will require more time, since the domestic legislative process moves at its own pace. *See, e.g.*, Committee of Ministers, Final Resolution D.H. (89) 31 (concerning the judgments of the European Court of Human Rights of 21 February 1984 and 23 October 1984 in the Öztürk Case, Committee of Ministers Resolutions, at 86–87 (Supp. 1988–89)).

It is also not always easy for the Committee, which is not a judicial body, to determine whether the legislative measures do in fact fully comply with the Court's mandate. On this subject, *see* Robertson & Merrills, *supra*, at 340–41; Committee of Ministers Resolution D.H. (82) 2, 24 June 1982, concerning the judgment of the European Court of Human Rights of 24 October 1979 in the Winterwerp Case, Committee of Minsters Resolutions 1959–1983, 128–29 (1984). It remains to be decided whether a case can come back to the Court on that issue.

The execution of judgments is a priority concern in the system. Given the increased number and

complexity of the execution problems posed, the
Committee is facing difficulties in ensuring states'
rapid compliance with judgments. Moreover, in
recent years some states have challenged the
authority of the Court's judgments with regard either
to just satisfaction or to specific measures required
by the judgments. In such cases, the Chairman of the
Committee can make direct, usually confidential
contacts with the Minister of Foreign Affairs of the
respondent state. Public interim resolutions may be
adopted to convey concern to interested states,
organizations and parties and to make suggestions to
the government in question. Given these problems,
and the increased caseload of the Court, the
Committee is also facing a growing backlog. As a
result, not all cases are receiving the necessary
attention.

To take further action to ensure compliance, the
Parliamentary Assembly has created a monitoring
mechanism to verify compliance with human rights
obligations and commitments of all Council of Europe
Member States. Parliamentary Assembly Resolution
1115 (1997). An Assembly Monitoring Committee is
responsible for verifying the fulfillment of obligations
assumed by Member States under the terms of the
Council of Europe Statute, the European Convention
and all other Council of European human rights
conventions, as well as the honoring of commitments
entered into by the national authorities upon
accession to the Council of Europe. The procedure
permits the Assembly to sanction persistent non-
compliance by adopting resolutions and
recommendations, by non-approval of the credentials

of a national parliamentary delegation, or ultimately by recommending action to the Committee of Ministers. For its part, the Committee of Ministers adopted a 1994 Declaration on compliance with commitments and a follow-up procedure for thematic monitoring. In each instance, the Secretary General's Monitoring Union submitted a report to the Committee of Ministers which drew up conclusions and recommended follow-up action.

§ 3–14. INTERPRETATION OF THE RIGHTS GUARANTEED

The European Court of Human Rights has today for all practical purposes become the constitutional court for civil and political rights of Europe. By the end of 2015, it had issued 18,577 judgments of which 15,570 found at least one violation. As a result, it has now had an opportunity to interpret most of the rights guaranteed by the Convention. *See* Frowein, "The European Convention on Human Rights as the Public Order of Europe," 1 Collected Courses of the Academy of European Law (Book 2), at 267 (1992). In doing so, the Court has developed and applied doctrines such as "margin of appreciation" which affords a varying degree of discretion to national decisions. *See* Y. Arai-Takahashi, *The Margin of Appreciation Doctrine and the Principle of Proportionality in the Jurisprudence of the ECHR* (2002); Kratochvil, "The Inflation of the Margin of Appreciation by the European Court of Human Rights," 29 Netherlands Quarterly of Human Rights, 324 (2011); G. Letsas, "Two Concepts of the Margin of Appreciation," 26 Oxford J. Legal Studies 705 (2006).

The Court often invokes general methods of treaty interpretation such as those expressed in the Vienna Convention on the Law of Treaties, but also has stressed that human rights treaties have a distinct character, establishing objective norms for the protection of individuals rather than reciprocal obligations benefiting states. Wemhoff v. Germany, (1969) ECHR (Ser. A) no. 7 para. 8. The most prevalent doctrines that have emerged are the *pro homine* principle, the notion of the *effet utile*, and the evolutionary approach or rule of dynamic interpretation. Tyrer v. United Kingdom (1978), Series A, No. 26. The European Court will apply general principles of law as it finds them in texts of universal and regional scope (not only human rights treaties), in the jurisprudence of international and domestic courts that apply these instruments, and in intrinsically non-binding instruments of Council of Europe organs, in particular recommendations and resolutions of the Committee of Ministers and the Parliamentary Assembly. Demir and Bayakara, Judgment of Nov. 12, 2008 [GC] [2008] ECHR 1345, para. 77. *See* Dzehtsiarou, "Does Consensus Matter? Legitimacy of European Consensus in the Case Law of the European Court of Human Rights," 2011 Pub. L. 534.

A sampling of the matters the Court examined in 2015 indicates the range of issues presented by applicants, including the absence of an adequate legal framework to ensure the accountability of members of the security forces guilty of torture and other ill-treatment (Cestaro v. Italy, Judgment of April 7, 2015); the point in time when applications for conditional release had to be considered by a judge (Magee and Others v. the United Kingdom, Judgment of May 12, 2015); a parent's right to contact with his child (Kuppinger v. Germany, Judgment of January 15, 2015); and the conditions imposed on an applicant seeking gender reassignment surgery (Y.Y. v. Turkey, Judgment of March 10, 2015).

Other such issues have included the protection of medical data on the admission of an HIV-positive patient to hospital (Y.Y. v. Turkey, Judgment of March 10, 2015), the refusal to recognize marriage to a minor (Z.H. and R.H. v. Switzerland, Judgment of Dec. 8, 2015); protection against domestic violence (M. and M. v. Croatia, Judgment of Sept. 3, 2015); the prevention of terrorism (Sher and Others v. the United Kingdom, Judgment of October 20, 2015); the right to receive and impart information (Delfi AS, Guseva and Cengiz and Others v. Estonia [GC], Judgment of June 16, 2015); the right to strike (Junta Rectora Del Ertzainen Nazional Elkartasuna (ER.N.E.)); and the expulsion of aliens (Z.H. and R.H. v. Switzerland, *supra*).

Other important cases concerned the armed forces (Mustafa Tunç and Fecire Tunç, Lyalyakin and Chitos), prisons (Khoroshenko and Szafrański); religion (Karaahmed and Ebrahimian); nationality (Petropavlovskis); and various social sectors and activities including the banking (Adorisio and Others and M.N. and Others v. San Marino), social welfare (Fazia Ali), medical (Lambert and Others, Parrillo, Bataliny, Elberte, Constancia and Y v. Turkey), education (Memlika) and the electoral (Dicle and Sadak and Riza and Others) sectors. The Court also examined cases involving a lack of legal recognition for homosexual couples (Oliari and Others) and the limits of freedom of artistic expression (M'Bala M'Bala). The cases are all summarized in the Court's 2015 Annual Report (Council of Europe 2016).

The largest number of cases the Court has considered thus far have raised due process issues, that is, the cases have dealt with the interpretation and application of Article 5 (right to liberty and security of person) and Article 6 (right to a fair hearing). *See, e.g.,* Stögmüller Case, Judgment of 10 November 1969, Publ. Eur. Court H.R.4 (1969); Golder Case, Judgment of 21 February 1975, 18 Publ. Eur. Court H.R. 5 (1975); Case of Engel and Others, Judgment of 8 June 1977, 22 Publ. Eur. Court H.R. 4 (1977); Sramele Case, Judgment of 22 October 1984, 84 Publ. Eur. Court H.R. 6 (1984); Sanchez-Reisse Case, Judgment of 21 October 1986, 107 Publ. Eur. Court H.R. 1 (1990); Mats Jacobson Case, Judgment of June 28, 1990, 180 Publ. Eur. Court H.R. 1 (1990); Letellier v. France, Judgment of June 27, 1991, 207 Publ. Eur. Court H.R. 1 (1991); Kraska Case, Judgment of April 19, 1993, 254 Publ. Eur. Court H.R. 42 (1993). *See generally* S. Stavros, *The Guarantees for Accused Persons under Article 6 of the European Convention on Human Rights* (1993).

The Court has been presented with major political and cultural matters debated throughout Europe, including such issues as state measures to ban the wearing of headscarves in public schools and employment, Refah Partisi (The Welfare Party) and Others v. Turkey, Judgment of 13 Feb. 2003, Reports 2003-II and Leyla Sehin v. Turkey, Judgment of Nov. 10, 2005; ownership and disposal of human embryos, Evans v. The United Kingdom, Judgment of 7 March 2006; and the deprivation of voting rights of convicted felons, Hirst v. The United Kingdom (No. 2), Judgment of 6 October 2005, Reports 2005-IX. In 2015, for the first time, the Court examined the prohibition of the donation of embryos to scientific research following in vitro fertilization (Parrillo). Also the first time, it considered the duties and responsibilities of an Internet news portal providing, for financial gain, a platform for user comments, made anonymously and without preregistration (Delfi AS, *supra*).

The Court has rendered a number of important decisions bearing on questions of freedom of expression, which is guaranteed in Article 10 of the Convention. *See, e.g.,* Handyside v. United Kingdom, Judgment of 4 Nov. 1976, 24 Publ. Eur. Court H.R. 1 (1976); The Sunday Times Case, Judgment of 8 July 1986, 30 Publ. Eur. Court H.R.5 (1979); Barthold Case, Judgment of 25 March 1985, 90 Publ. Eur. Court H.R.1 (1985); Lingens Case, Judgment of 8 July 1986, 103 Publ. Eur. Court H.R. 11 (1986); Otto-Preminger-Institut v. Austria, Judgment of September 20, 1994, 15 Hum Rts. L.J. 371 (1994);

Jersild v. Denmark, Judgment of 22 August 1994, 19 Eur. H.R.Rep. 1 (1994).

Freedom of association, proclaimed by Article 11, has been considered by the Court in, *inter alia,* Case of Young, James and Webster, Judgment of 13 August 1981, 44 Publ. Eur. Court H.R. 5 (1981); Case of Le Compte, Van Leuven and De Meyere, Judgment of 23 June 1981, 43 Publ. Eur. Court H.R. 5 (1981); Ezelin v. France, Judgment of April 26, 1991, 202 Publ. Eur. Court H.R. 1 (1991); United Communist Party of Turkey v. Turkey, Publ. Eur. Court H.R., www.echr.int/eng/Judgments.htm. The Court has also addressed difficult issues involving the right to privacy and interference with the right to a family life, which is protected by Article 8 of the Convention. *See, e.g.,* Dudgeon Case, Judgment of 22 October 1981, 45 Publ. Eur. Court H.R. 5 (1982); Malone Case, Judgment of 2 August 1984, 82 Publ. Eur. Court H.R. 7 (1984); Case of Johnston and Others, Judgment of 18 December 1986, 112 Publ. Eur. Court H.R. 8 (1987); Niemitz v. Germany, Judgment of December 16, 1992, 251 Publ. Eur. Court H.R. 25 (1993). The Court has accepted that environmental degradation can amount to an infringement of Article 8 and when it results in death can constitute a violation of Article 2. *See* Lopez-Ostra v. Spain, Judgment of 24 Nov. 1994, 303 Publ. Eur. Court H.R. (1994), 20 Eur.H.R.Rep. 277; Oneryildiz v. Turkey, Judgment of 30 Nov. 2004, Reports 2004-XII.

Article 3 of the Convention provides that "no one shall be subjected to torture or degrading treatment or punishment." The leading cases on this subject are

Ireland v. United Kingdom, Judgment of January 18, 1978, 25 Publ. Eur. Court H.R. 1 (1978), and Selmouni v. France, Judgment of 28 July 1999, 29 Eur. H.R.Rep. 403 (1999). For a thorough analysis of the case law relating to this provision, *see* Cassese, "Prohibition of Torture and Inhuman or Degrading Treatment of Punishment," *in* Macdonald *et al., supra*, at 225; Van Dijk & Van Hoof, *supra*, at 226.

In an important decision involving the application of Article 3, the Court determined that the United Kingdom would violate this provision were it to extradite a West German national, Jens Soering, to Virginia, where he had been charged with capital murder and thus would be subject to the death penalty. Soering Case, Judgment of July 7, 1989, 161 Publ. Eur. Court H.R. 8 (1989). The Court did not hold that the death penalty as such violated Article 3, but that the "death row phenomenon" to which Soering would be exposed once a sentence of capital punishment was pronounced would violate that provision given his youth and mental state.

Soering was subsequently extradited to Virginia, but only after an undertaking by the State of Virginia that he would not be charged with a capital crime. Steinhardt, "Recent Developments in the Soering Litigation," 11 Hum. Rts. L.J. 453 (1990). For a critical analysis of the case, *see* Lillich, "The Soering Case," 85 Am. J. Int'l L. 128 (1990). It may be noted, in this connection, that Article 2 of the Convention, which addresses the right to life, permits the imposition of the death penalty. Protocol No. 6 subsequently outlawed the death penalty, but the

United Kingdom was not a party to the Protocol at the time of the Soering litigation. Had it been, the Court could have relied on the Protocol rather than Article 3 of the Convention to bar the extradition.

The Court has increasingly recognized that many articles, including Articles 2 and 3, impose positive obligations on the state to protect rights, including ensuring that custodial conditions do not fall below the standards of humane treatment. In respect to Article 2, the right to life imposes a duty to undertake an effective official investigation when individuals have been killed, McCann v. United Kingdom, 21 Eur.H.R.Rep. 97 (1997), para. 161; Kaya v. Turkey, 28 Eur.H.R.Rep. 1 (1998), para. 86, and to take appropriate measures to protect against life-threatening circumstances (Pretty v. the United Kingdom, no. 2346/02, ECHR 2002-III), including life-threatening natural disasters. Budayeva and Others v. Russia, Judgment of March 20, 2008; Murillo Saldias and Others v. Spain, Judgment of Nov. 28, 2006, and M. Özel and Others v. Turkey, Judgment of November 17, 2015 In Scialacqua v. Italy, 26 Eur.H.R.Rep. 164 (1998), the former Commission suggested that Article 2 could be interpreted as imposing on states the obligation to cover the costs of medical treatments or medicines essential to save life. In Peers v. Greece, Judgment of 19 April 2001, 33 Eur. H.R.Rep. 9, and Valasinas v. Lithuania, Judgment of 24 July 2001, the Court examined prison conditions and the positive obligations of states to afford adequate conditions of confinement. *See generally* A.R. Mowbray, *The Development of Positive Obligations under the*

European Convention on Human Rights by the European Court of Human Rights (2004).

Over the years, the Court has had to rule on a number of questions concerning the right to property, which is guaranteed by Article 1 of Protocol No. 1 to the Convention. Thus, for example, in Case of Lithgow and Others, Judgment of 8 July 1986, 102 Publ. Eur. Court H.R. 9 (1987), the Court dealt with issues arising out of the nationalization of the British shipbuilding industries. In *Case of James and Others*, Judgment of 21 February 1986, 98 Publ. Eur. Court H.R. 14 (1986), the Court determined that the British Leasehold Reform Act of 1967, which affected the property interests of the Duke of Westminster, among others, did not violate Article 1 of Protocol No. 1 to the Convention. *See also* Pine Valley Development Ltd. v. Ireland, Judgement of November 29, 1991, 222 Publ. Eur. Court H.R. 1 (1992) (involving a discriminatory taking of property); Papamichaelopoulos v. Greece, Judgment of 330 Publ. Eur. Court Hum. Rts (1995); Stran Greek Refineries and Stratis Andreadis v. Greece, 301B Publ. Eur. Court Hum. Rts (1994).

In the first case to reach the Court, the Lawless Case (Merits), Judgment of 1 July 1961, Publ. Eur. Court H.R. (Series A: Judgments and Decisions 1960–61), at 24 (1961), the Court had to interpret and apply Article 15, which permits the States Parties to derogate, in time of war or other national emergency, from some of their obligations under the Convention. This provision and its implications were the subject of a much more extensive analysis in Ireland v.

United Kingdom, Judgment of 18 January 1978, 25 Publ. Eur. Court H.R. 5 (1978), which remains the leading case on the subject. Here the Court made clear that, although the States Parties have "a margin of appreciation" in assessing the facts bearing on the existence of a public emergency and the need for suspending certain rights which the Convention guarantees,

> the States do not enjoy an unlimited power in this respect. The Court, which . . . is responsible for ensuring the observance of the States' engagements (Article 19), is empowered to rule on whether the States have gone beyond the 'extent strictly required by the exigencies' of the crisis. . . . The domestic margin of appreciation is thus accompanied by a European supervision.

Id., at 79. In a 1993 case, the Court reiterated this principle almost *verbatim* while emphasizing that "in exercising its supervision the Court must give appropriate weight to such relevant factors as the nature of the rights affected by the derogation, the circumstances leading to, and the duration of, the emergency situation." Brannigan and McBride v. United Kingdom, Judgment of May 26, 1993, 14 Hum. Rts. L.J. 184, 186 (1993).

Article 64 of the Convention permits the States Parties to attach reservations when adhering to the Convention, subject to a number of conditions. Article 64(1) specifies that such reservations may be made only with regard to any provision of the Convention that is incompatible with any laws "then in force" within the reserving state; it also prohibits "reservations of a general character." Article 64(2) requires the reserving state to accompany the reservation with "a brief statement of the law" motivating the reservation.

In Belilos v. Switzerland, Judgment of April 29, 1988, 132 Publ. Eur. Court H.R. 1 (1988), the Court was called upon to apply Article 64 to an "interpretative declaration," which the Swiss Government made in adhering to the Convention. The Court concluded that the declaration was in fact a reservation and that, as such, it was invalid because it met neither the requirements of paragraphs 1 nor 2 of Article 64. Addressing the question of the effect of the invalidity of the reservation on Switzerland's continued membership in the Convention, the Court declared that " . . . it is beyond doubt that Switzerland is, and regards itself as, bound by the Convention irrespective of the validity of the declaration." *Id.*, at 28. This language leaves open the question whether Switzerland would have been bound by the Convention even if it had considered the validity of the reservation an indispensable condition of its adherence to the treaty. On this subject, *see* Bourguignon, "The Belilos Case: New Light on Reservations to Multilateral Treaties," 29 Va. J. Int'l L. 347 (1989); Van Dijk & Van Hoof, *supra*, at 606. In the case of Loizidou v. Turkey, Judgment of 28 Nov. 1996, Reports 1996-VI, 2216, the former Commission and Court examined the scope of Turkey's declaration accepting the right of individual petition. *See* Tomuschat, "Turkey's Declaration under Article 25 of the European

Convention on Human Rights," *in* Nowak *et al.*, *supra*, at 119.

Not all judgments of the Court have been received positively by Member States and there has been some backlash against controversial decisions. This, coupled with concern over the high caseload, led the Member States to convene four high-level conferences on the future of the European Court between 2010 and 2015. In addition, parliamentary debates have been held in the British Parliament and the Netherlands Senate.

The third conference, convened by the United Kingdom in the context of its Chairmanship of the Committee of Ministers of the Council of Europe, was held in Brighton on April 19–20, 2012 with the aim of obtaining a political declaration on reforms of the Court. The British government has been among the strongest critics of what it views as 'judicial activism' on the part of the Court. Authorities reacted negatively in particular to the Court decisions condemning the law depriving convicted felons of the right to vote. The Court's decisions on asylum-seekers have also produced intense and widespread criticisms, particularly when coupled with extension of economic and social rights to those seeking entry. Critics complain that the decisions interfere with national immigration policies, especially in the light of anti-terrorism efforts. *See* Muylle "Prisoners' Right to Vote: The Hirst Case Law of the European Court of Human Rights and its Application by the Belgian Constitutional Court," in *Liberae Cogitationes: Liber amicorum Marc Bossuyt* (2013), 403.

The outcome of the Brighton Conference was a Declaration and the subsequent adoption of Protocol No. 15, which inserts a reference to the principle of subsidiarity and the doctrine of the margin of appreciation into the Convention's preamble. The Declaration reaffirms the commitment of Member States to the Convention and the right of individual application to the Court, but also refers to "the fundamental principle of subsidiarity" that should apply to the Court, a reference that indicates the desire of some Member States for greater deference to domestic laws, practices, and judicial decisions. The Court itself has been divided over its role in looking towards the future. *See* Wildhaber "Rethinking the European Court of Human Rights," in Jonas Christoffersen and Mikael Rask Madsen, eds., *The European Court of Human Rights between Law and Politics* (2011) 204–29.

Concern has also been raised about the actions of some Member States with respect to the nomination and election of judges, where the domestic processes do not comply with the principles of transparency, fairness and consistency. Some observers claim that the processes have resulted in the nomination and election of candidates that are lacking in the qualifications necessary for the position. *See, e.g.,* Dzehtsiarou and Coffey, Legitimacy and Independence of International Tribunals: An Analysis of the European Court of Human Rights, 37 Hastings Int'l & Comp. L. Rev. 271 (2014); Engel, "More Transparency and Governmental Loyalty for Maintaining Professional Quality in the Election of

Judges to the European Court of Human Rights," 32 HRLJ 448 (2012).

IV. THE EUROPEAN SOCIAL CHARTER

§ 3–15.　INTRODUCTION

The European Social Charter (ESC), like the European Convention of Human Rights, was drafted under the auspices of the Council of Europe. It complements the Convention by establishing a system for the protection of economic and social rights. The Charter was opened for signature on October 18, 1961 and entered into force on February 26, 1965. All of the forty-seven Member States of the Member States of the Council of Europe have signed the original Charter or the Charter as it has been revised. An Additional Protocol to the Charter, expanding its catalog of rights, was concluded on May 5, 1988.

Two further instruments have continued the evolution of the Social Charter. On November 9, 1995, an Additional Protocol was concluded that provides for a system of collective complaints; it entered into force on July 1, 1998 and has fourteen States Parties. Finally, in 1996, a revised Social Charter, bringing up to date the earlier documents and adding some new rights, was opened for signature. It entered into force on July 1, 1999; it is progressively replacing the original Charter and as the consolidated text is the instrument described in the following sections. *See generally* Andrzej Swiatkowski, *Charter of Social Rights of the Council of Europe* (2007); *Social Rights in Europe* (Gráinne de Búrca & Bruno de Witte, eds. 2005); John Darcy & David Harris, *The European Social Charter* (2d ed. 2001); M. Bell, "Combating Discrimination through Collective Complaints under the European Social Charter" 3 Eur. Anti-Discrim. L. Rev. (2006); "The Collective Complaints Mechanism within the European Social Charter: Making Economic and Social Human Rights Really Matter," in *Human Rights at the Center* 103 (Samantha Besson et al, eds. 2006); H. Cullen, "The Collective Complaints Mechanism under the European Social Charter," 2000 Eur. L. Rev. 18 (2000); J. Darcy, "Forced Labour in Greece," in 27 Eur. L. Rev. 218 (2002); "The European Social Charter—Instruments and Procedures," 25 Nordic J. Hum. Rts. 58 (2007).

§ 3–16. THE CATALOG OF RIGHTS

The Revised Charter proclaims a list of 31 categories of "rights and principles," including the right to work, to just conditions of work, to safe working conditions, to fair remuneration, to organize, and to bargain collectively. It proclaims the right of children, of young people, and of employed women to protection. Also recognized are the right of the family to social, legal and economic protection, the right of mothers and children to social and economic protection, and the right of migrant workers and their families to protection and assistance. Additional rights listed in the Charter are the right to vocational guidance and training, to protection of health, to social security, to social and medical assistance, and to benefit from social welfare services.

The Revised Charter also establishes the right of disabled persons to training and rehabilitation, and the equal right to engage in gainful occupations in the territory of other Contracting Parties. The right of workers to equal treatment and non-discrimination on the grounds of sex, the right to be informed and consulted, and the right to take part in the determination and improvement of the working conditions and environment in their place of employment, are also included. It provides that "every elderly person has the right to social protection" and contains guarantees in case of termination of employment or employer insolvency. Protections also are afforded for dignity at work, against discrimination due to family responsibilities, and against poverty. Finally, it contains the right of everyone to housing.

These rights are proclaimed in general terms in Part I of the Revised Charter, where the High Contracting Parties declare that they " . . . accept as the aim of their policy, to be pursued by all appropriate means both national and international in character, the attainment of conditions in which . . . [these] rights and principles may be effectively realised." Hence, despite the fact that the catalog enumerated in Part I of these instruments speaks of "rights and principles," these are policy objectives. The purpose of the Charter is to transform them into enforceable rights.

Part II of the Revised Charter defines the meaning and elaborates on the "rights and principles" proclaimed in general terms in Part I. Thus, the right to safe and healthy working conditions, which is identified in paragraph 3 of Part I of the Charter, finds expression in the following undertaking contained in Article 3 of Part II:

1. to formulate, implement and periodically review a coherent national policy on occupational safety, occupational health and the working environment. The primary aim of this policy shall be to improve occupational safety and health and to prevent accidents and injury to health arising out of, linked with or occurring in the course of work, particularly by minimising the causes of hazards inherent in the working environment;

2. to issue safety and health regulations;

3. provide for the enforcement of such regulations by measures of supervision;

4. to promote the progressive development of occupational health services for all workers with essentially preventive and advisory functions.

As we shall see in § 3–17, *infra,* this bifurcated drafting approach was devised to establish various types of obligations and to give states different compliance options.

§ 3–17.   LEGAL OBLIGATIONS ASSUMED BY THE CONTRACTING PARTIES

Article A (Part III) of the Revised Charter specifies the obligations the States Parties assume by ratifying the Charter. The instrument gives the states a set of options. First, by becoming a party to the Charter, a state undertakes "to consider Part I of this Charter as a declaration of the aims which it will pursue by all appropriate means. . . ." Charter, art. A(1)(a). Second, the state must accept as binding upon it the undertakings contained in at least six out of nine articles found in Part II. The nine provisions are Article 1 (right to work), Article 5 (right to organize), Article 6 (right to bargain collectively), Article 7 (the right of children and young persons to protection), Article 12 (right to social security), Article 13 (right to social and medical assistance), Article 16 (right of the family to social, legal and economic protection), Article 19 (right of migrant workers and their families to protection and assistance), and Article 20 (right to equal opportunities and equal treatment in matters of employment and occupation without discrimination on the grounds of sex). Third, each State Party has a further obligation to select another specified number of rights or sub-categories of rights with which it agrees to comply. *See* Revised Charter, art. A(1)(c).

This flexible system encourages states to ratify the Charter without forcing them either to accept all the rights it proclaims or to make complex reservations. It is also drafted so as to ensure that all States Parties will at the very least be bound to guarantee

some of the most basic rights. Very few states have
accepted all the rights the Charter proclaims.

§ 3–18.   INTERNATIONAL MEASURES FOR
ENFORCEMENT OF CHARTER RIGHTS

The Charter establishes a reporting system to
monitor the compliance by states with their
obligations and a system of collective complaints.
Under the reporting system established by the
Committee of Ministers on 31 October 2007, the
provisions of the 1961 Charter and the Revised
Charter have been divided into four thematic groups.
States present a report on part of the provisions
annually, with the result that each provision of the
Charter will be reported on once every four years.

The state reports are examined by the European
Committee of Social Rights (ECSR), which consists of
15 experts "of the highest integrity and recognized
competence in international social questions," elected
by the Committee of Ministers for a term of six years,
renewable once. Art. 25. The Committee assesses
whether the states have respected their
undertakings and publishes its conclusions and
decisions in an annual report. If a state takes no
action on a Committee decision of non-compliance,
the Committee of Ministers may address a
recommendation to that state, asking it to change the
situation in law and/or in practice. A Governmental
Committee comprising representatives of the
governments of the States Parties to the Charter,
assisted by observers representing European

employers' organizations and trade unions, prepares the work of the Committee of Ministers.

The Additional Protocol providing for a system of collective complaints allows complaints of "unsatisfactory application of the Charter" (art. 1) to originate with one of several types of groups: international organizations of employers and trade unions which participate in the work of the Governmental Committee according to Article 27(2); other international non-governmental organizations having consultative status with the Council of Europe and appearing on a special list drawn up by the Governmental Committee; and national organizations of employers and trade unions from the Contracting Party concerned. Each state also may declare that it accepts the right of its national non-governmental organizations to lodge complaints against it. Organizations may submit complaints only in respect of those matters regarding which they have been recognized as having particular competence. Additional Protocol art. 3.

Collective complaints are examined by the ESCR. It determines admissibility first and then examines admissible complaints on the basis of written submissions and hearings, if necessary. The Committee prepares a report on its examination of the complaint and the conclusions reached. The report is transmitted to the Committee of Ministers, the complaining organization, and the States Parties. On the basis of the report, the Committee of Ministers adopts a resolution on the matter, which may contain recommendations to the state concerned. At the time the resolution is adopted, or four months after the Committee of Ministers receives the report, the Parliamentary Assembly also receives the report which is then made public. The state must submit information on its measures to comply with the recommendations made. Art. 10.

The ESC complaint procedure is being increasingly utilized and has made the European Committee on Social Rights an increasingly judicialized body. The adversarial process received more than 65 complaints in the first decade after the entry into force of the Additional Protocol of the ESC in 1998, and the ECSR has addressed many of the rights in the ESC, including the right to housing (European Roma Rights Centre v. Italy, Merits) (2005), freedom from child and forced labor (Complaint 1/1998, International Commission of Jurists v. Portugal, Merits (1999), Complaint 7/2000, International Federation of Human Rights v. Greece, Merits (2000); access to medical treatment (Complaint No 14/2003, International Federation of Human Rights Leagues (FIDH) v. France), and the right to education (Association internationale Autisme-Europe (AIAE) v. France, Complaint No 13/2002, Merits, ECSR, 4 November 2003), often in connection with allegations of discrimination.

Many of the discrimination cases concern the Roma. *See, e.g.,* European Roma Rights Centre (ERRC) v. Greece, Complaint No 15/2003, Merits, ECSR, 8 December 2004; European Roma Rights Centre (ERRC) v. Italy, Complaint No 27/2004, Merits, ECSR, 21 December 2005; European Roma

Rights Centre (ERRC) v. Bulgaria, Complaint No 31/2005, Merits, ECSR, 18 October 2006; International Helsinki Federation for Human Rights (IHF) v. Bulgaria, Complaint No 44/2007, Merits, ECSR, 14 September 2007; European Roma Rights Centre (ERRC) v. Bulgaria, Complaint No 46/2007, Merits, ECSR, 3 December 2008; European Roma Rights Centre (ERRC) v. Bulgaria, Complaint No 48/2008, Decision on admissibility, ECSR, 2 June 2008; European Roma Rights Centre (ERRC) v. France, Complaint No 51/2008, Merits, ECSR, 19 October 2009; Centre on Housing Rights and Evictions (COHRE) v. Italy, Complaint No 58/2009, Merits, ECSR, 25 June 2009.

Many other collective complaints have concerned trade union freedoms, including collective bargaining rights. For a summary of all the complaints, *see* ECSR, Collective Complaints Procedures: Summaries of Decisions on the Merits 1998–2012 (30 May 2013).

The ECSR looks to the object and purpose of each right in determining the scope of the guarantee. The right to housing, for example, is seen as directed to the prevention of homelessness with its adverse consequences on individuals' personal security and well-being. The right to housing secures social inclusion and integration of individuals into society and contributes to the abolishment of socio-economic inequalities. Given this, adequate housing "means a dwelling which is structurally secure; safe from a sanitary and health point, i.e. it possesses all basic amenities, such as water, heating, waste disposal, sanitation facilities, electricity; not overcrowded and with secure tenure supported by law. . . . The temporary supply of shelter cannot be considered as adequate and individuals should be provided with adequate housing within a reasonable period." European Roma Rights Centre v. Italy, *supra,* para. 35.

More generally, the Committee has insisted that one of the underlying purposes of the social rights protected by the Social Charter "is to express solidarity and promote social inclusion. It follows that States must respect difference and ensure that social arrangements are not such as would effectively lead to or reinforce social exclusion." European Roma Rights Centre v. Greece, *supra.* This means the Committee strictly scrutinizes complaints alleging discrimination.

V. OTHER COUNCIL OF EUROPE HUMAN RIGHTS TREATIES

§ 3–19. THE EUROPEAN CONVENTION AGAINST TORTURE

On November 26, 1987, the Council of Europe adopted the European Convention for the Prevention of Torture and Inhuman or Degrading Treatment or Punishment. It has been ratified by all Council of Europe Member States. By the terms of Protocol No. 1 to the Torture Convention it is open to other states by invitation. (A Second Protocol makes certain technical amendments to the election process for members to the Committee for the Prevention of

Torture). While the Torture Convention Preamble refers to the Article 3 of the European Convention of Human Rights, the Convention makes no attempt to define its subject matter and contains no substantive provisions concerning torture and inhuman or degrading treatment or punishment. Those aspects, as well as the consideration of individual complaints, are left to the European Convention and Court. In its case law, the Court has adopted the definition of torture contained in the U.N. Convention Against Torture. *See* Selmouni v. France, *supra*, paras. 97–101. The aim of the Convention Against Torture is to strengthen the protection of persons deprived of their liberty by establishing non-judicial machinery of a preventive character.

The Convention creates a Committee for the Prevention of Torture (CPT), composed of independent and impartial experts whose number is equal to that of the Member States, "to examine the treatment of persons deprived of their liberty with a view to strengthening, if necessary, the protection of such persons from torture and from inhuman or degrading treatment or punishment." Art. 1. The CPT thus has the power to visit places of detention of any kind, such as prisons, police cells, military barracks, and mental hospitals; to examine the treatment of detainees; and, if appropriate, to make recommendations to the state concerned with a view to strengthening the protection of the detainees. A principle of "cooperation" governs relations between the Committee and the competent national authorities, leading the Committee to exercise its functions in strict confidentiality. The Committee will go public only if a state fails to cooperate with it or refuses to make improvements following the Committee's recommendations. The state itself may request publication of the Committee's report, together with its comments. Some 84 reports have been published in this way. In addition, the Committee's annual report to the Committee of Ministers is made available as a public document.

The Committee carries out periodic visits to all Contracting Parties and may organize such *ad hoc* visits "as appear to it to be required in the circumstances". The Committee is obliged to notify the state concerned of its intention to carry out such a visit, but no specific period of notice is required. Exceptionally, a visit may take place immediately after the notification. Government objections to the time or place of a visit can only be justified on grounds of national defense, public safety, serious disorder, the medical condition of a person or if an urgent interrogation relating to a serious crime is in progress. In such cases the state must immediately take steps to allow the Committee to visit as soon as possible. As of mid-2008, the CPT had made 252 visits (156 periodic visits and 96 *ad hoc* visits) and published 200 reports. *See* R. Morgan and M. Evans, *Combating Torture in Europe: The Work and Standards of the European Committee for the Prevention of Torture and Inhuman or Degrading Treatment or Punishment* (2002); J. Murdock, *The Treatment of Prisoners: European Standards* (2006); *Yearbook of the European Convention for the Prevention of Torture* (D. Harris, ed.).

§ 3–20. PROTECTION OF NATIONAL MINORITIES

The issue of national minorities became increasingly important in the Council of Europe in the 1980s as ethnic conflicts re-emerged in the region. The European Charter for Regional or Minority Languages was a first effort by the Council of Europe to afford protection to such groups. Adopted on November 5, 1992 and in force as of March 1, 1998, the Languages Convention has been accepted by about half the Council of Europe Member States (23 as of July 2008). The aims of the agreement are to protect and promote the historical regional or minority languages of Europe and to respect the right to use a regional or minority language in private and public life.

The Languages Charter is structured like the European Social Charter, *see* § 3–15, *supra*. It first enunciates the objectives and principles that Parties undertake to apply: respect for the geographical area of each language and promotion, facilitation and/or encouragement of the use of regional or minority languages in speech and writing, in public and private life. In Part III, the Charter sets out a number of specific measures to promote the use of regional or minority languages in public life. Each Party undertakes to apply a minimum of thirty-five paragraphs or sub-paragraphs chosen from among these measures. The measures selected must include three paragraphs or sub-paragraphs chosen from each of Articles 8 (education) and 12 (cultural activities and facilities) and one from each of Articles

9   (judicial   authorities),   10   (administrative
authorities and public services), 11 (media) and 13
(economic and social life).

Moreover, each Party has to specify in its
instrument of ratification, acceptance or approval,
each regional or minority language, or official
language which is less widely used in the whole or
part of its territory, to which the paragraphs chosen
shall apply. States Parties must submit periodic
reports that are examined by a committee of experts
(arts. 15–16). Groups or associations within a state
may submit information or comments to the
committee relating to the undertakings of the state
in respect to Part III of the Charter. On the basis of
the state report and the information received, the
committee prepares a report for the Committee of
Ministers which may make recommendations. The
Committee of Ministers also appoints the committee
of experts, one for each Member State.

On November 10, 1994 the Council of Europe
adopted   the   Framework   Convention   for   the
Protection of National Minorities. Council of Europe,
Doc. H (94) 10. The Convention entered into force of
February 1, 1998, and has thirty-nine States Parties.
The title of the Framework Convention indicates its
programmatic and largely discretionary nature, a
consequence of the political controversy surrounding
the issue. Although the instrument is legally binding,
the principles contained in it are not directly
applicable in domestic law but require the adoption
of national laws and policies by States Parties.

Section I of the Framework Convention sets out general principles on the protection of national minorities, a term not defined in the text. Section II lays down more specific principles: non-discrimination; promotion of effective equality; promotion of conditions to preserve and develop culture and religion, language, and traditions; freedom of assembly, association, expression, thought, conscience and religion; access to and use of media; language rights; education; transfrontier contacts; international and transfrontier cooperation; participation in economic, cultural and social life; participation in public life; and prohibition of forced assimilation. Section IV concerns monitoring of state compliance and confers supervisory authority on the Committee of Ministers, assisted by an Advisory Committee, a body of between twelve and eighteen persons appointed by the Committee of Ministers. States must file periodic reports on the legislative and other measures they take to give effect to the principles of the Framework Convention. The reports are examined by the Advisory Committee, which prepares an opinion on the measures taken. The Committee of Ministers then issues its conclusions concerning the adequacy of the measures taken by the State Party and may make recommendations to the state. The opinion of the Advisory Committee, any comments on it by the State Party, and the conclusions and recommendations of the Committee of Ministers are made public.

§ 3–21.   HUMAN RIGHTS AND BIOMEDICINE

The Convention on Human Rights and Biomedicine, adopted April 4, 1997, in force December 1, 1999, is the first legally-binding international text adopted to preserve human rights through a series of principles and prohibitions concerning bioethics, medical research, prior informed consent, rights to private life and information, organ transplantation, and public debate on all these issues. The Convention declares that "the interests and welfare of the human being shall prevail over the sole interest of society or science" (art. 2). It bans all forms of discrimination based on the grounds of a person's genetic make-up (art. 11) and allows the carrying out of predictive genetic tests only for medical purposes (art. 12).

The treaty allows genetic engineering, but only for preventive, diagnostic or therapeutic reasons and only where it does not aim to change the genetic make-up of a person's descendants (art. 13). It prohibits the use of techniques of medically assisted procreation to help choose the sex of a child, except where it would avoid a serious hereditary condition (art. 14). The Convention sets out rules related to medical research by including detailed and precise conditions, especially for people who cannot give their consent. It prohibits the creation of human embryos for research purposes and requires an adequate protection of embryos where countries allow in-vitro research.

The Convention states the principle of prior informed consent for treatment, except in emergencies (art. 5). Consent may be freely withdrawn at any time. The treatment of persons unable to give their consent, such as children and people with mental illnesses, may be carried out only if it could produce real and direct benefit to the individual's health (art. 6). The Convention stipulates that all patients have a right to be informed about their health, including the results of predictive genetic tests, but also recognizes the patient's right not to know (art. 11). The Convention prohibits the removal of organs and other tissues which cannot be regenerated from people not able to give consent (art. 19). The only exception is, under certain conditions, for regenerative tissue (especially marrow) between siblings (art. 20).

The human body and body parts may not be utilized for financial gain (art. 21). States Parties to the Convention are to take national measures to provide judicial protection, compensation and sanctions with respect to the rights contained in the Convention. The Steering Committee on Bioethics (CDBI), or any other committee designated by the Committee of Ministers or the States Parties may request the European Court of Human Rights to give advisory opinions on legal questions concerning the interpretation of the Convention. *See* Riedel, "Global Responsibilities and Bioethics: Reflections on the Council of Europe's Bioethics Convention," 5 Ind. J. Global Leg. Stud. 179 (1997).

An Additional Protocol on the Prohibition of Cloning Human Beings was adopted January 12, 1998 and entered into force March 1, 2001. The

Protocol prohibits "any intervention seeking to create a human being genetically identical to another human being, whether living or dead" (art. 1). It rules out any exception to this ban, even in the case of a completely sterile couple and bars States Parties from derogating to the provisions of the Protocol (art. 2).

§ 3–22. CONVENTION ON ACTION AGAINST TRAFFICKING IN HUMAN BEINGS

The Council of Europe Convention on Action against Trafficking in Human Beings focuses on the protection of victims of trafficking in human beings and also aims to prevent trafficking and to prosecute traffickers. Concluded in 2005, the Convention entered into force on February 1, 2008, E.T.S. 197. It applies to all victims of trafficking (women, men and children alike), to all forms of exploitation (including sexual exploitation, forced labour, servitude, and removal of organs) and it covers all forms of trafficking: national and transnational, related or not to organized crime.

The obligations of States Parties include raising awareness of persons vulnerable to trafficking and actions aimed at discouraging "consumers." States are to prevent trafficking in human beings and recognize victims of trafficking as such rather than treating them as illegal migrants or criminals. Victims of trafficking are to be granted physical and psychological assistance and support for their reintegration into society. Medical treatment, counseling and information as well as appropriate accommodation are all among the measures provided. Victims are also entitled to receive compensation. Victims are entitled to a minimum of 30 days to recover and escape from the influence of the traffickers and to take a decision regarding their possible cooperation with the authorities. A renewable residence permit may be granted if the personal situation of victims so requires or if they need to stay in order to cooperate in a criminal investigation.

Trafficking is to be considered a criminal offence and traffickers and their accomplices are to be prosecuted. The private life and the safety of victims of trafficking must be protected throughout the course of judicial proceedings. The Convention also recognizes the possibility of punishing those who use the services of a victim if they aware that the person is a victim of trafficking in human beings. *See* Amiel, "Integrating a Human Rights Perspective into the European Approach to Combating the Trafficking of Women For Sexual Exploitation," 12 Buff. Hum. Rts. L. Rev. 5 (2006).

VI. THE EUROPEAN UNION

§ 3–23.   ABSORBING THE EUROPEAN CONVENTION ON HUMAN RIGHTS

The treaties establishing the European Communities, later the European Community and now the European Union (EU), a supranational organization distinct from the Council of Europe, created various institutions, including a European

Court of Justice (ECJ). This Court was given the function of ensuring the observance of law in the interpretation and application of the foundational treaties. The treaties contained few human rights guarantees. As the role and powers of the European Communities, in particular in the European Economic Community (EEC) expanded, legislative and administrative activities increasingly affected the rights of individuals and companies. While the domestic constitutional law of the EEC Member States and the European Convention on Human Rights provided for the protection of these rights against state action, the treaties creating the European Communities not establish a parallel protective system against their violation by Community institutions. The risk therefore existed that they might deprive individuals and companies of human rights guaranteed them under their own domestic law and under the European Convention, without there being a remedy against such action.

In 1964 the ECJ enunciated the principle of the supremacy of Community law over the domestic law of the Member States in Costa v. ENEL, Case 6/64, 1964 ECR 585. The Supremacy Doctrine was resisted by some states on human rights grounds. Following challenges by various domestic courts, the ECJ held in a series of cases that fundamental rights of individuals are enshrined in the general principles of Community law protected by the Court and form part of Community law, inspired by the constitutional traditions of Member States. Stauder v Ulm, Case 29/69, 1969 ECR 419 and Handelsgesellschaft v. Einfuhr-und Vorratsstelle fur Getreide und

Futtermittel, Case 11/70, 1070 ECR 1125. The Single European Act of 1987, O.J. L. 169/1 (1987) adopted this view and explicitly referred to the ECHR.

The 1992 Treaty of European Union made human rights an obligation of the Union, Consolidated Version of the Treaty on the European Union, O.J. C 321 E/1 (2006). The 1999 Treaty of Amsterdam formally incorporated human rights by requiring that the "union shall respect fundamental rights, as guaranteed by the European Convention. . .as general principles of Community law." Treaty of Amsterdam, O.J. C 340/1 (1997), art. 6. In addition, human rights clauses are included in over fifty community trade or aid agreements with foreign states.

The ECJ has decided cases addressing non-discrimination and freedom of religion, association and expression. The main impact of ECJ jurisprudence has been in the area of equality and non-discrimination, which is treaty based. It has stated that the principle of non-discrimination on the grounds of age must be regarded as "a general principle of Community law." Mangold v. Helm, Case C-144/04, 2005 ECR I-998, para. 75. In the French Farmers case, the European Court of Justice decided that national authorities and courts have a duty to protect rights given by Community law against interference from other private parties as well as against interference from state authorities. Commission v. France, Case C-265/95, 1997 E.C.R. I-6959. *See also* Defrene v. Sabena, Case 43/75, 1976 E.C.R. 455; Prais v. Council, Case 130/75 1976 ECR

1589; Union Syndicale-Amalgamated European Pub. Serv. Union v. Council, Case 175/73, 1974 ECR 917; VBBB & VBVB v. Commission, Joined Cases 43 and 63/82, 1984 ECR 19.

See generally Defeis, "Human Rights and the European Court of Justice: An Appraisal," 31 Fordham Int'l L. J. 1104 (2008). For a discussion of the relevant case law, *see* Weiler, "Protection of Fundamental Human Rights within the Legal Order of the Communities," *in* R. Bernhardt & J.A. Jolowicz (eds.), *International Enforcement of Human Rights* 113 (1987); F.G. Jacobs, "Protection of Human Rights in the Member States of the European Community: Impact of the Case Law of the Court of Justice," *in* J. O'Reilly, *Human Rights and Constitutional Law (Essays in Honor of Brian Walsh)* 243 (1992). *See generally* L. Betten and D. MacDevitt (eds.), *The Protection of Fundamental Social Rights in the European Union* (1996); Besson, "The European Union And Human Rights: Towards A Post-National Human Rights Institution?," 6 Hum. Rts. L. Rev. 323 (2006).

This interactive process has been greatly facilitated by the fact that all Member States of the European Union have ratified the European Convention of Human Rights and accepted the jurisdiction of the European Court of Human Rights. (Note, however, that not all parties to the European Convention are members of the European Union.)

Attempts have been made over the years to work out some form of association agreement between the European Union and the Council of Europe, which would enable the former to join the European Convention of Human Rights. The preamble to the Maastricht Treaty, which transformed the European Community into the European Union, declared that "the Union shall respect fundamental rights, as guaranteed by the European Convention [of] . . . Human Rights . . . and as they result from the constitutional traditions common to the Member States, as general principles of Community law." Treaty on European Union, Preamble, para. F(2). 36 Int'l Legal Mat. 253, at 256 (1992). Moreover, the treaty establishes a procedure that can be used to suspend certain membership rights if a "serious and persistent" breach of human rights occurs in a Member State (art. 7). *See generally* H. Schermers & D. Waelbroeck, *Judicial Protection in the European Communities* 37 (5th ed. 1992); N. Neuwahl and A. Rosas (eds.), *The European Union and Human Rights* (1995); P. Alston (ed.), *The EU and Human Rights* (1999); Flaherty & Lally-Green, "Fundamental Rights in the European Union," 36 Duquesne L. Rev. 249 (1998); Lenaerts, "Respect for Fundamental Rights as a Constitutional Principle of the European Union," 6 Colum. J. Eur. L. 1 (2000).

§ 3–24.   THE CHARTER OF FUNDAMENTAL RIGHTS OF THE EUROPEAN UNION

In June 1999, the EU decided that a European Charter of Fundamental Rights should be drafted to recognize all rights that pertain to the Union's citizens, in effect combining the guarantees of the European Convention on Human Rights, the European Social Charter, and other human rights instruments. The Charter was proclaimed at the meeting of the Council of the European Union in Nice on December 18, 2000, but was not adopted as a treaty, due to lack of agreement among the Member States. The Charter was subsequently incorporated into the Treaty of Lisbon, which entered into force on 1 December 2009, making it binding on all EU Member States pursuant to Article 6. Treaty of Lisbon, amending the Treaty on the European Union, entry into force 13 Dec. 2007, OJ C 306/01.

The Preamble of the Charter expresses that its aim is "to strengthen the protection of fundamental rights in the light of changes in society, social progress and scientific and technological developments by making those rights more visible in a Charter" and by reaffirming those rights deriving "from the constitutional traditions and international obligations common to the Member States, the Treaty on European Union, the Community Treaties, the European Convention for the Protection of Human Rights and Fundamental Freedoms, the Social Charters adopted by the Community and by the Council of Europe and the case-law of the Court of Justice of the European Communities and of the European Court of Human Rights."

The rights guaranteed in the Charter are divided into six categories or chapters: dignity, freedoms, equality, solidarity, citizens' rights, and justice. Chapters I–III and VI basically restate the rights found in the European Convention, but in some instances the Charter goes beyond the Convention guarantees, as is the case, for example, with Charter

Article 10(2), which guarantees a right to conscientious objection to military service. Other rights expressly mentioned in these chapters of the Charter but not found in the Convention are: a prohibition on trafficking in human beings (art. 5(3)); protection of personal data (art. 8); respect for academic freedom (art. 13); freedom to conduct a business (art. 16); and rights of the child, elderly and disabled (arts. 24–26). Article 3 (right to integrity of the person) includes a restatement of the main provisions of the Convention on Biomedicine and its Protocol against Human Cloning. Chapter IV (Solidarity) encompasses the rights contained in the European Social Charter.

The most innovative aspect of the Charter is found in Chapter V. Entitled "Citizens Rights" it is a catalogue of political rights and principles of democratic governance: the rights to vote and to stand for office in internal and European Parliament elections (arts. 39–40); the right to good administration (art. 41); the right of access to documents (art. 42); the right to petition (arts. 43–44); and the right to diplomatic and consular protection (art. 45). A final chapter, entitled "General Provisions" declares in Article 51 that the Charter "is addressed to the institutions and leaders of the Union with due regard to the principle of subsidiarity and to the Member States only when they are implementing Union law."

The Treaty of Lisbon also provided that the European Union 'shall' accede to the European Convention on Human Rights. Negotiations on a draft agreement were concluded between the EU and the Council of Europe's 20 non-EU signatories in April 2013, and the Commission then asked the ECJ for its advice on the compatibility of the agreement with the EU treaties (under Article 218(11) TFEU). In Opinion 2/13 delivered on 18 December, the European Court of Justice ruled that the draft accession agreement between the European Union and the Council of Europe breaches EU law, placing in doubt the future adherence of the EU to the European Convention.

§ 3–25.   NON-JUDICIAL EU HUMAN RIGHTS BODIES

The European Union Agency for Fundamental Rights (FRA) is a body of the European Union (EU), established through Council Regulation (EC) No. 168/2007 of 15 February 2007, OJ L 53, 22.2.2007, p. 1. It is based in Vienna and is built on the foundation of the European Monitoring Centre on Racism and Xenophobia (EUMC). FRA is an independent body that cooperates with national and international bodies and organizations, in particular with the Council of Europe. It also works closely with civil society organizations. The objective of the Agency is to provide the relevant institutions and authorities of the Community and its Member States, when implementing Community law, with assistance and expertise relating to fundamental rights in order to support them to fully respect fundamental rights. (Article 2 of the Regulation). The Agency has no regulatory powers and cannot receive individual complaints. It publishes an annual report on fundamental rights in the EU, and thematic reports based on research and surveys, highlighting examples of good practice regarding fundamental rights.

The European Parliament has a subcommittee on human rights and decided in 2001 to begin drafting annual reports on fundamental rights in the European Union. Each report analyzes the degree of respect for each of the rights laid down in the Charter, making use of the work of the United Nations, Council of Europe, EU institutions, case law of the European Court of Human Rights and the Court of Justice of the European Communities, legislation, case law and practices in the Member States, and contributions by relevant NGOs. The annual reports facilitate the EP's role in triggering the warning system introduced by Article 7 (1) of the EU Treaty in the case of a serious risk of violation of fundamental rights by a Member State. Also, since 1998, the EP has issued annual reports on human rights in the world. These reports help determine the EU's bilateral and multilateral policies and dialogues with non-member states. Respect for human rights is also one of the preconditions for any candidate country's accession to the Union.

A third institution within the EU is the European Ombudsman, established in 1995 pursuant to the Maastricht Treaty to deal with complaints about maladministration by the institutions and bodies of the European Community. Any citizen of a Member State of the European Union or person living in a Member State can complain to the Ombudsman.

Businesses, associations or other bodies with a registered office in the Union can also complain. A complaint must be made within two years of the date when the complainant became aware of the facts on which the complaint is based and the person must already have contacted the institution or body concerned about the problem.

Some of the most common problems submitted to the Ombudsman concern unnecessary delay, refusal of information, discrimination and abuse of power. The Ombudsman transmits the complaint to the relevant institution, which can take steps to resolve the problem. If maladministration is found and the case is not settled during the inquiry, the Ombudsman seeks a friendly settlement. If this fails, he or she can make a draft recommendation to the relevant institution, calling on it to take the necessary steps to remedy the situation. If the institution does not accept his recommendation, he or she can make a special report to the European Parliament.

VII. ORGANIZATION FOR SECURITY AND COOPERATION IN EUROPE (OSCE)

§ 3–26.   INTRODUCTION

The Conference on Security and Cooperation in Europe (CSCE), which in 1994 became the Organization for Security and Cooperation in Europe (OSCE), is not strictly a European organization. Although its members now include all European nations, the United States and Canada are also members and were so from its very inception. One could therefore examine the OSCE in this book either in a separate chapter or include it here. We have chosen the latter approach because the OSCE works closely with the Council of Europe when it comes to the promotion of human rights.

The CSCE was created by the Helsinki Final Act (HFA), which was signed in 1975 by 33 European nations, including the Soviet Union, plus the United States and Canada. At the time only Albania refused to join. With the end of the Cold War, the membership of the OSCE has grown to 56 nations, spanning much of the Northern Hemisphere. Conceived as a compromise instrument to bridge the ideological chasm that divided East from West in the 1970's, the HFA ushered in a negotiating process that established a highly imaginative linkage between human rights and security concerns. *See generally* J. Maresca, *To Helsinki: The Conference on Security and Cooperation in Europe*, 1973–1975 (1987); W. Korey, *The Promise to Keep: Human Rights, the Helsinki Process and American Foreign Policy* (1993). This linkage, which gave human rights an important place on the political agenda of East-West relations, has not lost its significance with the end of the Cold War. It has enabled the OSCE to continue to play a major role in today's Europe and to influence the human rights policies of many of its nations.

§ 3–27. THE HELSINKI FINAL ACT

The OSCE's human rights system as we know it today comprises an ever expanding catalog of human rights and related guarantees and multifaceted supervisory institutions that have evolved over time. This evolution was possible because of the manner in which the HFA was drafted, the follow-up mechanism it established, and its character as a political rather than legally binding instrument. *See generally* A. Bloed & P. van Dijk (eds.), *Essays on Human Rights in the Helsinki Process* (1985); Buergenthal, "The CSCE Rights System," 25 Geo. Wash. J. Int'l & Econ. L. 333 (1993) [hereinafter cited as Buergenthal, "CSCE Rights System"].

The HFA is a massive document, consisting of four chapters or so-called "baskets." Basket I, entitled "Questions Relating to Security in Europe," consists of two sections ("Principles Guiding Relations Between Participating States," and "Confidence-Building Measures and Certain Aspects of Security and Disarmament"). Basket II deals with "Cooperation in the Field of Economics, of Science and Technology and of the Environment." The subject of Basket III is "Cooperation in Humanitarian and Other Fields." Basket IV, the final chapter of the instrument, spells out the so-called "follow-up" process. *See* Russell, "The Helsinki Declaration: Brobdingnag or Lilliput," 70 Am. J. Int'l L. 242 (1976).

Human rights issues are addressed primarily in the Guiding Principles proclaimed in Basket I and to some extent in Basket III, although over time the latter has become less important because the subjects it deals with—human contacts, family reunification, etc.—no longer have the importance they had during the Cold War. Of the ten Guiding Principles set out in the HFA, two relate to human rights. One is Principle VII ("Respect for human rights and fundamental freedoms, including the freedom of thought, conscience, religion or belief") and Principle VIII ("Equal rights and self-determination of peoples"). The remaining principles concern sovereignty, the use of force, inviolability of frontiers, territorial integrity, peaceful settlement of disputes, non-intervention in internal affairs, cooperation of states, and fulfillment in good faith of international legal obligations.

Principle VII consists of eight unnumbered paragraphs. In the first two the participating States undertake to "respect human rights and fundamental freedoms" and to "promote and encourage the effective exercise of civil, political, economic, social, cultural and other rights and freedoms. . . ." This principle also addresses freedom of religion, rights of individuals belonging to national minorities, and the "right of the individual to know and act upon his rights and duties in this field." The last paragraph of Principle VII reads as follows:

In the field of human rights and fundamental freedoms, the participating States will act in conformity with the purposes and principles of the Charter of the United Nations and with the Universal Declaration of Human Rights. They will also fulfil their obligations as set forth in the international declarations and agreements in this field, including inter alia the International Covenants on Human Rights, by which they may be bound.

The significance of this paragraph, at the time it was adopted, lay in the fact that until then some of the participating States, including the Soviet Union, had never formally acknowledged an obligation to conform their conduct to the Universal Declaration of Human Rights. (The Soviet Union had abstained when the UN General Assembly adopted the Universal Declaration, and its adherence to Principle VII appears to have been its first unambiguous recognition of the "normative" character of this instrument.)

Principle VIII devotes four paragraphs to the subject of "equal rights and self-determination of peoples." After undertaking to respect the equal rights of peoples and their right to self-determination, the participating States recognize that "all peoples always have the right, in full freedom, to determine, when and as they wish, their internal and external political status, without external interference. . . ." *See generally* H. Hannum, *Autonomy, Sovereignty, and Self-Determination: Accommodation of Conflicting Rights* (1990); C. Tomuschat (ed.), *The Modern Law of Self-Determination* (1993); R. Steinhardt, *International Law and Self-Determination* (The Atlantic Council, 1994).

It took quite a while before the Soviet Union and its allies fully acknowledged that these two Guiding

Principles had in fact placed human rights issues on the agenda of the on-going East-West political dialogue. Their efforts to silence that debate by the invocation of the doctrine of non-intervention in internal affairs, enshrined in Principle VI, at times threatened to break up the CSCE. They relented gradually and by the latter part of the 1980's the discussion of specific human rights violations had become routine during CSCE follow-up meetings. Moreover, as we shall see, these meetings also dramatically expanded the human rights catalog of the HFA. *See* § 3–30, *infra*.

§ 3–28.   THE OSCE PROCESS

The important impact the CSCE has had in the human rights area is partially attributable to the follow-up process provided for by Basket IV of the HFA, which has come to be known as the OSCE process. It consists of the convening by the participating States of periodic intergovernmental conferences for the purpose of achieving "a thorough exchange of views both on the implementation of the provisions of the Final Act . . . as well as . . . on the deepening of their mutual relations, the improvement of security and the development of co-operation in Europe, and the development of the process of détente in the future." These follow-up conferences have been used for the dual purpose of providing a conference forum to review compliance with human rights commitments and a mechanism for the expansion of the human rights catalog.

The existence of this negotiating process has permitted the HFA to be amplified, reinterpreted, and extensively revised at successive conferences. These meetings have of course also been used to focus public attention on the failure of certain states to live up to their human rights commitments. *See* Helgesen, "Between Helsinkis—and Beyond? Human Rights in the CSCE Process," in A. Rosas & J. Helgesen (eds.), *Human Rights in a Changing East/West Perspective* 241 (1987).

The aforementioned normative evolution is accomplished by the so-called "concluding documents" that are adopted by consensus at these conferences. *See* Schlager, "The Procedural Framework of the CSCE: From the Helsinki Consultation to the Paris Charter, 1972–1990," 12 Hum. Rts. L.J. 221 (1991). These documents are used to proclaim new OSCE commitments or to expand, modify or interpret the scope and meaning of existing ones. What we have here is a dynamic and creative process that has produced a growing body of OSCE human rights commitments. To understand their nature and evolution, it is necessary to examine the concluding documents of each OSCE follow-up conference at which human rights issues were taken up. Buergenthal, "CSCE Rights System," *supra*, at 344.

§ 3–29.   THE NON-BINDING CHARACTER OF OSCE COMMITMENTS

The HFA is not a treaty nor was it intended by the participating States to create binding legal obligations. Instead, they conceived it as a non-binding instrument proclaiming political commitments. A state's failure to comply with any of these commitments will therefore have political but not legal consequences. Put another way, non-compliance will not give rise to a cause of action under international law, but it could have very serious political repercussions. Subsequent OSCE concluding documents are also not intended to be legally binding unless the contrary intent is stated expressly. *See generally* Van Dijk, "The Implementation of the Helsinki Final Act: The Creation of New Structures or the Involvement of Existing Ones," 10 Mich. J. Int'l 110, 113–15 (1989); Schlager, "A Hard Look at Compliance with 'Soft' Law: The Case of the OSCE," in D. Shelton (ed.), *Commitment and Compliance: The Role of Non-Binding Norms in the International Legal System*; Buergenthal, "CSCE Rights System," *supra,* at 375.

The history of the HFA and of the instruments it has spawned suggests that their non-binding character has not proved detrimental to the objectives they were designed to achieve. In the past, they frequently proved useful as standards that could be invoked on the international and national planes to prod states to remedy human rights violations. National governments and legislatures, domestic courts and administrative bodies have looked to them in making, interpreting and applying national laws and regulations. They have also proved to be a useful tool for national and international non-governmental organizations seeking to promote the observance of human rights.

§ 3–30.   THE OSCE CATALOG OF RIGHTS

What distinguishes the OSCE's rights catalog from that of traditional human rights treaties—the European Convention of Human Rights or the International Covenants, for example—is that in addition to proclaiming basic individual human rights, it also addresses the rights of minorities, rule of law issues, democratic values, elections, etc. The OSCE in fact pioneered a holistic approach to human rights, which proceeds on the assumption that individual rights are best protected in states which adhere to the rule of law and democratic values and are so constituted as to permit these concepts to flourish. With the end of the Cold War, this notion has gained support elsewhere in the world. *See* Franck, "The Emerging Right to Democratic Governance," 86 Am. J. Int'l L. 46 (1992). *See also* Steiner, "Political Participation as a Human Right," 1 Harv. Hum. Rts. Y.B. 77 (1988).

The breakthrough came with the adoption of the Copenhagen Concluding Document in 1990. This instrument contains chapters dealing with human rights, the rule of law, free elections and democratic values. It also enlarged upon prior OSCE commitments on the rights of minorities. Subsequent OSCE documents, from the Charter of Paris for a New Europe (1990), the Moscow Concluding Document (1991), the 1992 Helsinki Document ("Challenges for Change"), through the 1994 Budapest Document ("Towards a Genuine Partnership in a New Era") refined, reinforced and expanded upon these commitments, which today also include commitments relating to international humanitarian law and the rights of refugees, migrant workers, and indigenous populations, among others. The essence of this expansive human rights catalogue is captured in Chapter VIII, para. 2, of the Budapest Document, which reads in part as follows:

> Human rights and fundamental freedoms, the rule of law and democratic institutions are the foundation of peace and security, representing a crucial contribution to conflict prevention. The protection of human rights, including the rights of persons belonging to national minorities, is an essential foundation of democratic civil society.

The OSCE has thus moved from traditional international human rights concerns to the articulation of those basic democratic constitutional principles and legal remedies which seek to ensure that all instrumentalities of the state exercise their powers in conformity with laws adopted by the people through their democratically elected representatives. *See OSCE Handbook* (2007).

§ 3–31.   THE HUMAN DIMENSION MECHANISM

The Vienna Concluding Document (1989) consolidated the subject of human rights, previously addressed as a Basket I item, with the human contact and related humanitarian topics set out in Basket III, and it subsumed both topics under the heading of the "Human Dimension of the CSCE." It also established the Human Dimension Mechanism for dealing with the non-observance by states with their human dimension commitments. Subsequent OSCE conferences, among them the Copenhagen (1990), Moscow (1991) and Helsinki (1992) Concluding Documents, have expanded the scope of the Mechanism in order to make it more effective. *See* Buergenthal, "CSCE Rights System," *supra,* at 369.

As a result of its long evolution, the OSCE monitors and reports on the human rights situation in each of its 56 participating States, particularly in the areas of freedom of assembly and association, the right to liberty and to a fair trial, and in the use of the death penalty. It provides training and education across the field of human rights, including for government officials, law-enforcement officers, rights defenders and students.

The Mechanism now consists of a multi-stage process of negotiations, mediation, and fact-finding, involving bilateral and multilateral negotiations, OSCE missions of experts and rapporteurs assisted by the OSCE Office for Democratic Institutions and Human Rights (ODIHR). The process usually begins with claims by one or more states that another state is not living up to its OSCE Human Dimension commitments. There follows a diplomatic exchange between the states concerned for which specific time limits are provided. If the matter is not resolved between them, the states may bring it to the attention of all OSCE states and place the matter on the agenda of OSCE follow-up or Human Dimension conferences. If this process does not produce results, OSCE expert missions or rapporteur missions may be appointed to investigate the charges. These perform the role of third-party fact-finders and mediators. As a rule, the missions are established by mutual consent of the states concerned, although such consent is not necessary in serious situations. In such cases a mission may be convoked whenever a group of states or the OSCE Senior Council considers it necessary. *See* M. Bothe, N. Ronziite and A. Rosas, *The OSCE in the Maintenance of Peace and Security* (1997); Bloed, "The Between Conflict Prevention and Implementation Review," 4 Helsinki Monitor, No. 4, at 36 (1993).

In addition to the institutions discussed in the following sections, the OSCE has taken up the issue of human trafficking as a priority matter. Permanent Council Decision 557 of July 24, 2003, adopted an Action Plan to Combat Trafficking in Human Beings based on the 2000 UN Convention on the topic. The Office of the Special Representative and Co-ordinator for Combating Trafficking in Human Beings, set up in 2006, supports the development and implementation of anti-trafficking policies in OSCE participating States. The Office of the Special Representative coordinates cooperation among relevant OSCE institutions, structures and field operations mandated to combat trafficking. The OSCE programs and policies reflect a strong regional effort to implement and enforce the global laws on the topic.

§ 3–32. THE HIGH COMMISSIONER ON NATIONAL MINORITIES

Although the HFA makes a passing reference to the rights of individuals belonging to national minorities, the subsequent Copenhagen Concluding Document (1990), the Report of the Geneva Meeting of Experts on National Minorities (1991), and the Moscow Concluding Document (1991) laid the normative foundation for a system to protect national minorities. Based on these, the OSCE in 1992 established the office of the High Commissioner on National Minorities (HCNM). *See CSCE Helsinki Document: The Challenges of Change,* ch. II, at 7 (1992) (spelling out the mandate of the HCNM). Concern with the potential for violent conflicts arising from ethnic tensions is reflected in the mandate of the HCNM, which reads in part as follows:

The High Commissioner will provide "early warning" and, as appropriate, "early action" at the earliest possible stage in regard to tensions involving national minority issues which have not yet developed beyond an early warning stage, but, in the judgement of the High Commissioner, have the potential to develop into a conflict within the CSCE area, affecting peace, stability or relations between participating States, requiring the attention of and action by the Council [of Ministers of Foreign Affairs] or the CSO [Committee of Senior Officials].

As this language indicates, the principal function of the HCNM is to address problems of minorities before they escalate into serious conflicts. In discharging this mandate, the High Commissioner is to be guided by "CSCE principles and commitments." He or she is to "work in confidence and ... act independently of all parties involved in the tensions." Chigas, "Bridging the Gap Between Theory and Practice: The CSCE High Commissioner on National Minorities," 5 Helsinki Monitor, No 3, at 26 (1994). *See also* Huber, "Preventing Ethnic Conflict in the New Europe: The CSCE High Commissioner on National Minorities," 1 CSCE Bulletin, No. 3, at 17 (ODIHR, 1993); W. Zellner, *On the Effectiveness of the OSCE Minority Regime* (1999).

By formulating a catalog of basic OSCE commitments relating to the rights of national minorities, the Copenhagen CSCE Conference (1990) tackled a subject that had attracted only sporadic interest on the part of the international community after the demise of the League of Nations minorities system. *See* § 1–5, *supra.* Shortly thereafter, the tragic events in the former Yugoslavia and elsewhere led to a renewed interest in international norms and institutions for the protection of minorities. As a result, in 1992, the United Nations adopted the "Declaration on the Rights of Persons Belonging to National or Ethnic, Religious and Linguistic Minorities," (UN General Assembly Res. 47/135 of December 18, 1992). *See generally* Thornberry, "The UN Declaration: Background, Analysis and Observations," *in* A. Phillips & A. Rosas (eds.), *The UN Minority Rights Declaration* 11 (1993). In 1994, the Council of Europe adopted and opened for signature the Framework Convention for the Protection of National Minorities, discussed *supra* § 3–20. These new United Nations and Council of Europe instruments strengthen the normative framework within which the High Commissioner on National Minorities discharges his or her mandate.

§ 3–33. REPRESENTATIVE ON FREEDOM OF THE MEDIA

The useful work of the High Commissioner on National Minorities led the OSCE to establish a similar post of Representative on Freedom of the Media. Created in November 1997, the Representative "address[es] serious problems caused by, *inter alia*, obstruction of media activities and unfavorable working conditions for journalists." Mandate of the OSCE Representative on Freedom of the Media (November 5, 1997), PC Journal No. 137, Decision No. 193, para. 2.

Unlike the High Commissioner, the Media Representative is not a mediator, but acts as an advocate, observing relevant media developments in OSCE participating States and promoting compliance with OSCE principles and commitments regarding freedom of expression and free media. The Representative also aims to provide early warning on violations of freedom of expression, concentrating on rapid response to serious non-compliance with OSCE principles and commitments by participating States. Where there are serious problems, the Representative seeks direct contacts with the participating State and other parties involved, assesses the facts and seeks to resolve the issue. The Representative collects and receives information on the situation of the media from participating States, organizations or institutions, media and their representatives, and relevant NGOs including information about hate speech. The Representative reports to the Permanent Council, recommending further action where appropriate.

CHAPTER 4

THE INTER-AMERICAN HUMAN RIGHTS SYSTEM

I. INTRODUCTION

This chapter examines the law and institutions of the Organization of American States created to promote and protect human rights. The OAS is a regional inter-governmental organization, whose 35 members comprise all sovereign states of the Americas. These states are: Antigua and Barbuda, Argentina, The Bahamas, Barbados, Belize, Bolivia, Brazil, Canada, Chile, Colombia, Costa Rica, Cuba, Dominica, Dominican Republic, Ecuador, El Salvador, Grenada, Guatemala, Guyana, Haiti, Honduras, Jamaica, Mexico, Nicaragua, Panama, Paraguay, Perú, St. Kitts and Nevis, St. Lucia, St. Vincent and the Grenadines, Suriname, Trinidad and Tobago, United States, Uruguay, and Venezuela. Cuba's Castro government was suspended from participation in the Organization in 1962, by an OAS resolution whose effects were terminated by another resolution unanimously adopted in 2009, allowing the government to request resumption of its participation. The government had not made such a request as of early 2017. Despite non-participation of the government, throughout the entire period Cuba has remained a Member State subject to the OAS human rights system.

The OAS discharges its functions through its organs, including the General Assembly and

Permanent Council. The General Assembly meets once a year in regular session and in special ones as necessary. It is the supreme policy-setting organ of the Organization. Each Member State has one vote in the Assembly. The Permanent Council is composed of the permanent representatives of each Member State to the OAS. The Council serves as the Organization's decision-making organ between Assembly sessions and performs other functions bearing on the resolution of disputes and peacekeeping. Both organs have jurisdiction to deal with human rights matters. On the OAS in general, *see* B. Horowitz, *The Transformation of the Organization of American States: A Multilateral Framework for Regional Governance* (2011). *See also* B.L. Bloom, *The Organization of American States* (2008); C. Nefstead & M. Thayer, *The Organization of American States: Elements and Considerations* (2013).

The Inter-American human rights system has two distinct legal sources: in part it has evolved from the Charter of the Organization of the OAS ("Charter"), while the other part is based on the American Convention on Human Rights ("Convention") and related treaties. The Charter-based system applies to all 35 Member States of the OAS, while the Convention and other treaties are legally binding only on the States Parties. The sources overlap and interact in a variety of ways. In some instances, the legal mechanisms or norms of several instruments apply to different aspects of the same human rights situation. *See, e.g.,* Advisory Opinion OC–10/89, IA Ct.H.R., Series A: Judgments and Opinions, No. 10

(1990) (interpreting the normative effect of the American Declaration of the Rights and Duties of Man) . Hence, although this chapter presents the Charter evolution separately from the Convention and other treaties because it is conceptually clearer to do so, as a practical matter, the two systems often function as one.

For a collection of relevant treaties and related texts, reports, judicial opinions and historical documents bearing on the OAS system, *see* T. Buergenthal & R. Norris, *Human Rights: The Inter-American System* (5 Loose-leaf volumes 1982–1994). Two official publications of the Inter-American system, one entitled *Basic Documents Pertaining to Human Rights in the Inter-American System* [hereinafter cited as *Basic Documents*] (2012), available at http://www.oas.org/en/iachr/mandate/basic_documents.asp and the other, *Inter-American Yearbook on Human Rights,* are indispensable research tools on the inter-American system. *See also* D. Shelton & P. Carozza, *Regional Protection of Human Rights* (2nd ed. 2013).

II. THE OAS CHARTER-BASED SYSTEM

§ 4–1. INTRODUCTION

The Charter-based human rights norms and institutions of the inter-American system have evolved over nearly seventy years. Legal and political events contributed to its evolution. The major legal developments include the promulgation of the American Declaration of the Rights and Duties of

Man ("Declaration"), the establishment of the Inter-American Commission on Human Rights ("Commission"), the 1970 amendment of the OAS Charter, and the entry into force of the American Convention on Human Rights. *See* S. Davidson, *The Inter-American Human Rights System* (1996); D. Harris & S. Livingstone (eds.), *The Inter-American System of Human Rights* (1998); C. Medina-Quiroga & C. Nash Rojas, *Sistema interamericano de derechos humanos: introducción a sus mecanismos de protección* (2007); Goldman, "History and Action: The Inter-American Human Rights System and the Role of the Inter-American Commission of Human Rights," 31 Hum. Rts. Q. 856 (2009).

The political factors that have played an important role include the Cuban revolution and the hemispheric reaction to it. Also important has been the attitude of the U.S. Government, which initially showed little interest in, if not outright hostility to, the development of an inter-American human rights system, and then championed it at different times and for different reasons. The fall of the Latin American dictatorships that were so prevalent in the 1980s has also had a significant political impact. *See* Buergenthal, "Human Rights in the Americas: View from the Inter-American Court," 2 Conn. J. Int'l L. 303 (1987); E.L. Cleary, *Mobilizing for Human Rights in Latin America* (2007); Mendez & Cone, "Human Rights Makes A Difference: Lessons from Latin America," in *Oxford Handbook of International Human Rights Law* 955 (D. Shelton ed., 2013).

§ 4–2. THE OAS CHARTER

The Charter, a multilateral treaty that is the constitution of the OAS, was opened for signature in Bogotá, Colombia, in 1948 and entered into force in 1951. The Charter (sometimes referred to as "the Pact of San José") was amended by the Protocol of Buenos Aires, which came into effect in 1970, followed by the Protocol of Cartagena de Indias, the Protocol of Managua, and the Protocol of Washington, in force since 1988, 1996 and 1997, respectively.

The 1948 Charter made few references to human rights. One provision of importance was Article 3(j), now Article 3(l), wherein "the American States proclaim the fundamental rights of the individual without distinction as to race, nationality, creed, or sex" among the principles to which they are committed. Another important reference to human rights appears in Article 13, now Article 17. After declaring that "each State has the right to develop its cultural, political and economic life freely and naturally," this provision prescribes that "in this free development, the State shall respect the rights of the individual and the principles of universal morality." The 1948 Charter did not define "the fundamental rights of the individual" to which Article 3 referred, nor did it create any institution to promote their observance. However, the same diplomatic conference which adopted the 1948 Charter also proclaimed the American Declaration of the Rights and Duties of Man. Promulgated in the form of a conference resolution, this instrument proclaims an extensive catalog of human rights. *See* § 4–3, *infra.*

In amending the OAS Charter, the Protocol of Buenos Aires introduced some important changes bearing on human rights: it established the Inter-American Commission on Human Rights as an OAS Charter organ and prescribed that the Commission's principal function should be "to promote the observance and protection of human rights. . . ." OAS Charter, as amended, arts. 51(e) and 112, now arts. 53(e) and 106. With these amendments, the Commission acquired the constitutional legitimacy it previously lacked. *See* § 4–4, *infra.* These changes also significantly strengthened the normative character of the American Declaration. *See* § 4–3, *infra.*

§ 4–3. THE AMERICAN DECLARATION OF THE RIGHTS AND DUTIES OF MAN

The Ninth International Conference of American States proclaimed the Declaration on May 2, 1948, antedating by a few months the Universal Declaration, with which it has much in common. The preamble of the American Declaration emphasizes that "the international protection of the rights of man should be the principal guide of an evolving American law."

The American Declaration includes a list of some 27 human rights and ten duties. The catalog of rights embraces civil and political as well as economic, social and cultural rights. These include the right to life, liberty and security of person, to equality before the law, to residence and movement, to a fair trial, to protection from arbitrary arrest, to due process of law, and to nationality and asylum. Freedom of religion, expression, assembly and association are proclaimed. Protected, too, is the right to privacy, to property, to health, to education, to the benefits of culture, to work, to leisure time, and to social security. The list of duties includes a duty to society, toward children and parents, to receive instruction, to vote, to obey the law, to serve the community and the nation, to pay taxes, and to work. Also proclaimed are duties with respect to social security and welfare, as well as the duty to refrain from political activities in a foreign country.

The Declaration was adopted as a non-binding conference resolution that was deemed by those who drafted it to have no legal effect. *See* Buergenthal, "The Revised OAS Charter and the Protection of Human Rights," 69 Am. J. Int'l L. 828, at 829 (1975). Gradually, however, the legal status of the American Declaration began to change. Today it is deemed to be the normative instrument that embodies the authoritative interpretation of "the fundamental rights of the individual," which Article 3(l) of the OAS Charter proclaims.

On this subject, the Inter-American Court of Human Rights has found that "for the member states of the Organization, the Declaration is the text that defines the human rights referred to in the Charter. . . . [T]he Declaration is for these States a source of international obligations related to the Charter of the Organization." Advisory Opinion OC–

10/89, IA Ct.H.R., Series A: Judgments and Opinions,
No. 10, para. 45 (1989). As such, the Court will apply
the Declaration as appropriate to construe the
articles of the American Convention. *See* Case of
Bueno-Alves v. Argentina, Judgment of May 11,
2007, IA Ct.H.R., Series C: Judgments and Opinions
No. 164 (2007), paras. 54–60; *but see* Case of La
Cantuta, IA Ct.H.R., Series C: Judgments and
Opinions No. 162, para. 119. This conclusion finds
support in the human rights practice of the OAS and
of its Member States, which the Court reviewed in
considerable detail in that advisory opinion. *Id.*, at
par. 43. *See also* Buergenthal, "The Inter-American
System for the Protection of Human Rights," *in* T.
Meron (ed.), *Human Rights in International Law:
Legal and Policy Issues* 438, 470–79 (1984). For a
discussion of the implications of the normative
character of the Declaration, *see* Buergenthal, "The
American Human Rights Declaration: Random
Reflections," *in* K. Hailbronner, G. Ress & T. Stein
(eds.), *Staat und Völkerrechtsordnung (Festschrift
für Karl Doehring)* 133 (1989).

§ 4–4. COMMISSION AS CHARTER ORGAN: ITS INSTITUTIONAL EVOLUTION

The establishment of the Inter-American
Commission on Human Rights (IACHR) was
mandated in 1959 by the Fifth Meeting of
Consultation of Ministers of Foreign Affairs. The
OAS Council complied with that mandate in 1960 by
adopting the Statute of the Commission and electing
the first seven Commission members. Because the
1948 OAS Charter did not provide for the

establishment of the Commission, the Council designated it as an "autonomous entity" of the OAS, "the function of which it is to promote respect for human rights." 1960 Commission Statute, art. 1. These rights were defined as follows in Article 2 of the Statute (now article 1(2)): "For the purpose of this Statute, human rights are understood to be those set forth in the American Declaration of the Rights and Duties of Man." The adoption of the Statute of the Commission and the language it employed set in motion the long process that transformed the Declaration into the important normative instrument it has become.

Article 9 of the 1960 Statute gave the IACHR various powers to promote the observance and protection of human rights, including the power to prepare studies and reports and "to make recommendations to the governments of the member states in general . . . for the adoption of progressive measures in favor of human rights within the framework of their domestic legislation. . . ." The Commission, in its first session, interpreted this language to authorize it to address general recommendations to individual states. In reliance on this interpretation and on its power to prepare studies, the Commission ushered in the practice of undertaking so-called country studies, a practice it continues; it has issued at least one report on well over half of the OAS Member States. All reports undertaken by the Commission and published since 1962 are available at http://www.oas.org/en/iachr/reports/country.asp.

The Commission later began issuing thematic reports as well on problems common throughout the region. It has published numerous such thematic reports on human rights issues including access to justice, human rights defenders, rights of migrant workers, the status of women, and terrorism and human rights. Some of the reports address institutional issues, such as the friendly settlement procedure, and achieving universal ratification of the Convention. The thematic reports are available at http://www.oas.org/en/iachr/reports/thematic.asp.

The Second Special Inter-American Conference authorized the IACHR in 1965 to receive and act on individual petitions charging OAS Member States with violations of some, but not all, rights proclaimed in the American Declaration. The new powers, which the Commission incorporated into its Statute in 1966 as Article 9(*bis*), applied to the following "preferred" rights: the right to life, liberty and security of person (Article I), equality before the law (Article II), freedom of religion (Article III), freedom of expression (Article IV), freedom from arbitrary arrest (Article XXV), and the right to due process of law (Article XXVI). In this fashion, Article 9(*bis*) authorized the Commission to establish a limited individual petition system. That system had its legal source in powers implied in the OAS Charter, rather than in any specific human rights treaty.

The status of the Commission changed in 1970 with the entry into force of the Protocol of Buenos Aires. It amended the 1948 OAS Charter and transformed the IACHR into a formal organ of the

OAS, whose "principal function shall be to promote the observance and protection of human rights and to serve as a consultative organ of the Organization in these matters." OAS Charter, as amended, arts. 51 and 112(1), now arts. 53 and 106(1). The Protocol added two other provisions applicable to the new Charter organ it created. The first was Article 112(2), now 106(2), which provides that "an inter-American convention on human rights shall determine the structure, competence and procedures of this Commission. . . ." The other was Article 150, now 145, which reads as follows: "Until the inter-American convention on human rights, referred to in . . . [Article 111, now 106], enters into force, the present Inter-American Commission on Human Rights shall keep vigilance over the observance of human rights."

By becoming an OAS Charter organ, the IACHR acquired an institutional and constitutional legitimacy it had not previously enjoyed. The reference in Article 150, now 145, to "the present" Commission, read in conjunction with Article 112, now Article 106, can also be deemed to have legitimated the practices and procedures the Commission developed under Articles 9 and 9(*bis*) of its Statute. *See generally* Buergenthal "The Revised OAS Charter and the Protection of Human Rights," 69 Am. J. Int'l L. 828 (1975); Cançado Trindade, "Co-Existence and Co-Ordination of Mechanisms of International Protection of Human Rights (At Global and Regional Levels)," 202 Recueil des Cours 10, at 190 (1987); C. Medina-Quiroga, *The Battle of Human*

Rights: Gross, Systematic Violations and the Inter-American System 85 (1988).

In 1969, the OAS adopted the "inter-American convention" to which the amended OAS Charter referred; it entered into force in 1978. Those who drafted the Convention, aware of the Commission's status in the amended OAS Charter, assigned two distinct functions to it: the functions it had previously performed in relation to all Member States of the OAS, spelled out in Article 41(a)–(e) and (g) of the Convention, on the one hand, and the functions applicable only to States Parties to the Convention, on the other. Convention, arts. 41(f), 44–51. *See* Advisory Opinion OC–13, IA Ct.H.R., Series A: Judgments and Opinions, No. 13 (1993) (interpreting Articles 41–42, 46–47, and 50–51 of the Convention).

The entry into force of the Convention required the OAS General Assembly to adopt a new Statute for the Commission, incorporating these new functions. Convention, art. 39. This it did in 1979. *See* Norris, "The New Statute of the Inter-American Commission on Human Rights," 1 Hum. Rts. L.J. 379 (1980). That Statute remains in force today, despite the efforts of some States to amend it to reduce the Commission's powers. The Statute takes account of the distinct roles the IACHR performs as an OAS Charter organ and as a Convention organ. It thus spells out the Commission's powers as they apply (a) to all OAS Member States (Article 18); (b) to the States Parties to the Convention (Article 19); and (c) to OAS Member States that are not parties to the Convention (Article 20). Articles 18 and 20 of the Statute in effect preserve for the Commission the powers it had under Articles 9 and 9(*bis*) of its old Statute.

Article 1(2) of the new Statute defines "human rights" as follows:

For the purposes of the present Statute, human rights are understood to be:

(a) The rights set forth in the American Convention on Human Rights, in relation to the States Parties thereto;

(b) The rights set forth in the American Declaration of the Rights and Duties of Man, in relation to the other Member States.

This reference to the Declaration reinforces its normative character and legitimates the authority of the Commission in relation to states that are not parties to the Convention. For these states, the OAS Charter and the Declaration impose human rights obligations which the Commission has the authority to enforce under its Statute. Inter-American Commission on Human Rights, Rep. No. 31/93 (Case No. 10.573/United States), Decision of October 14, 1993, IACHR, *Annual Report 1993*, OEA/Ser.L/V/II.85, Doc. 9 rev., at 312 (1993).

§ 4–5. THE COMMISSION AS CHARTER ORGAN: ITS PRACTICE

As a Charter organ, the Commission (IACHR) performs a variety of functions, including promotional and consultative activities. It has helped draft OAS human rights instruments, including the

American Convention on Human Rights, and it is regularly consulted by the OAS Permanent Council and the General Assembly on human rights issues. It also sponsors conferences and publishes human rights documents and pamphlets. *See, e.g.,* IACHR, *Ten Years of Activities 1971–1981* (1982); IACHR, *25 Years of Struggle for Human Rights in the Americas 1959–1984* (1984).

On different occasions during its existence, the Commission has played an important role in mediating and protecting human rights during internal and international armed conflicts and hostage seizures. *See* IACHR, "Reports of the Activities of the Inter-American Commission on Human Rights in the Dominican Republic (June 1 to August 31, 1965 and September 1, 1965 to July 6, · 1966)," in *The Organization of American States and Human Rights 1960–1967* at 359 and 439 (1972) (civil war); IACHR, "Report of the Inter-American Commission on Human Rights on the Situation regarding Human Rights in El Salvador and Honduras," *in The Organization of American States and Human Rights 1969–1970,* at 291 (1976) (international armed conflict); IACHR, Report on the Situation of Human Rights in the Republic of Colombia, OEA/Ser.L/V/II.53, doc.22, at 22 (1981) (hostage seizure). However, country and thematic studies and the examination of individual petitions, including litigation at the Inter-American Court, have occupied most of its time. *See, e.g.,* IACHR, *Annual Report of the Inter-American Commission on Human Rights 2015* (2016).

1. Country Studies and On-Site Investigations

A country study is an investigation of all or some of the human rights conditions in a state. The Commission usually initiates such a study when it receives individual communications or other credible evidence, often from non-governmental human rights organizations, suggesting that a government is engaging in large-scale violations of human rights or has a serious specific problem that needs to be addressed. *See, e.g.*, IACHR, *Access to Justice and Social Inclusion: The Road towards Strengthening Democracy in Bolivia*, OEA/Ser.L/V/II, doc. 34 (2007); IACHR, *Human Rights Situation of Refugee and Migrant Families and Unaccompanied Children in the United States of America,* OAS/Ser.L/V/II. 155, doc. 16 (2015). The first country reports were prepared in the early 1960's and dealt with Cuba, Haiti and the Dominican Republic. Cuba and Haiti refused to allow the Commission to visit their countries; the Dominican Republic gave entry permission and became the first country to be the subject of an on-site investigation. The reports relating to these countries are reproduced in *The Organization of American States and Human Rights 1960–67,* Part III (1972).

In its initial country study concerning Cuba, the Commission established the precedent of hearing witnesses and receiving evidence. In that instance, it held hearings in Miami and interviewed many refugees. During its visits to the Dominican Republic, the Commission crisscrossed the country, held hearings, met with government and opposition leaders, and interviewed representatives of various church, business and union groups as well as private individuals; it also set up offices in the country for the receipt of written and oral complaints. The *modus operandi* adopted by the Commission during its visits to the Dominican Republic in the 1960's became a model which it has followed with minor variations to this day in its on-site investigations. *See, e.g.,* IACHR, *Report on the Situation of Human Rights in Argentina,* OEA/Ser.L/V/II.49, doc. 19, corr. 1 (1980); IACHR, *Report on the Human Rights Situation in the Dominican Republic,* OEA/Ser.L/V/II, doc. 45/15 (2015); IACHR, *Report on the Human Rights Situation in Guatemala,* OEA/Ser.L/V/II, Doc. 43/15 (2016). *See also* IACHR, *Annual Report* 2015.

On-site investigations are usually arranged by an exchange of letters and cables between the chairman of the Commission and the government concerned. As a rule, the Commission requests permission to visit a particular country, but some governments have extended invitations for such visits on their own initiative. *See, e.g.,* IACHR, *Report on the Situation of Human Rights in Panama,* OEA/Ser.L/V/II.44, doc. 38 rev.1, at 1–3 (1978). *See generally* Norris, Observations *In Loco:* Practice and Procedure of the Inter-American Commission on Human Rights, 1979–1983," 19 Tex. Int'l L.J. 285 (1984).

Prior to 1977, the rules governing on-site visits were negotiated on an *ad hoc* basis. Thereafter the Commission adopted a set of rules on the subject. These are now codified in Articles 53 through 57 of the IACHR's 2013 Rules of Procedure. Article 56 of the Rules requires the host government to put at the disposal of the Commission all facilities necessary for the accomplishment of its mission and to pledge that it will impose no punitive measures against individuals who cooperate with or supply information to the Commission. The right of members of the Commission and its staff to travel freely in the host country, to meet with any individuals whatsoever, and to visit prisons is provided for in Article 57 of the Rules. This provision also establishes the government's obligation to ensure the safety of the Commission and its staff, and to provide the Commission with whatever documents or other information it may request. On-site investigations are now generally carried out by a so-called "Special Commission" of the IACHR but, in particularly serious situations, the entire Commission may undertake the visit. To avoid conflict-of-interest problems, Article 54 of the Regulations provides that members of the Commission who are nationals of or reside in a country in which the investigation is to be carried out shall be ineligible to serve on the "Special Commission."

In preparing its country studies, whether or not on-site investigations are involved, the Commission proceeds in stages. Initially, after the relevant information has been gathered, it prepares a draft report. That document examines the conditions in the country by reference to the human rights standards set out in the American Declaration of the Rights and Duties of Man or of the American Convention on Human Rights, depending upon whether or not the state is a party to the Convention.

The draft report is then submitted to that country's government for its comments. The government's response is analyzed by the Commission to determine whether the report should be amended in light of the information brought to its attention by the government. After reassessing its findings, the Commission decides whether to publish the report. Its Rules require the publication of the report if the government does not respond to the request for observations (Art. 60). The Commission does not have to publish the report, however, if the government either agrees to comply with the recommendations or demonstrates that it is not committing any violations. The IACHR's Reports published in the past few years usually have reproduced in full the government's observations.

In addition to publishing the report, the IACHR may also transmit it to the OAS General Assembly. Because debates in the Assembly attract considerable public attention, reference to and discussion by the Assembly of a country report, followed by an appropriate resolution, can have a significant impact on the behavior of a government that has been charged by the Commission with human rights violations. Although OAS General Assembly resolutions are not legally binding, they are acts emanating from the highest political organ of the Organization and, consequently, carry considerable moral and political weight. Governments tend to take these considerations into account before they decide how to react to recommendations made by the Commission in its country studies. Ultimately, as in all efforts to enforce internationally guaranteed human rights, the effectiveness of the Commission's country-study practice depends on the Commission's prestige and credibility, on the public opinion pressure its recommendations are likely to generate, and on the resolutions that the OAS General Assembly is willing to adopt in support of the Commission.

The General Assembly has over the years tended to adopt "boilerplate" resolutions that fail to fully address the recommendations of the Commission based on its country reports. These resolutions are often drafted in such a way as either to disguise the names of the countries that were the subjects of these reports or to name them without taking note of the charges against them. *See, e.g.*, AG/Res. 1269 (XXIV–O/94), OAS Gen. Ass. Doc. OEA/Ser.P./XX.O.2, vol. 1, at 75 (1994); AG/Res. 1213 (XXIII–O/93), OAS Gen. Ass. Doc. OEA/Ser.P/XXIII.O.2, vol. 1, at 31 (1993). The Permanent Council, too, has engaged in critical dialogue. In 2014, for example, it debated the situations in Venezuela and the Dominican Republic following the presentation of Commission reports, and many states expressed concern over the reported violations and called on the concerned states to respect their human rights obligations.

2. Individual Petitions

Prior to the entry into force of the American Convention, the Commission examined and acted formally on only those private communications that alleged a violation of one of the "preferred" freedoms enumerated in Article 9(*bis*) of its old Statute. *See*

§ 4–4, *supra.* This practice changed with the promulgation of its current Statute. The Commission's Rules now no longer distinguish between the "preferred freedoms" and other rights proclaimed in the American Declaration. Instead they establish a procedure, based on Article 20 of the Statute that allows the IACHR to receive and act on individual petitions charging a violation of any of the rights enumerated in the Declaration. *See* the Commission's 2013 Rules, arts. 51–52.

The Commission processes these petitions in the same way as the private communications it receives under the Convention. *See* § 4–9, *infra.* The two types of petitions are treated differently only after the conclusion of the proceedings before the Commission, because petitions brought under the Charter-based system cannot be referred to the Court. The petition process applicable to states not parties to the Convention concludes with a "final report." This report usually contains findings of facts and the Commission's conclusions and recommendations. The Commission may publish the report as a separate document and/or include it in the Commission's annual report to the OAS General Assembly. *See, e.g., IACHR, Annual Report 2015* (2016) (containing 44 decisions on admissibility/ inadmissibility, 5 friendly settlements and 22 reports on the merits involving States Parties to the Convention and states, such as the United States and Canada, which are not parties).

This Charter-based individual petition system is plagued by several weaknesses. The first has to do with the multiple functions the IACHR must perform coupled with its sitting as a part-time body. As of 2016, it had over two thousand complaints filed, but was able to meet only for eight weeks during the year. Many petitions remain in the system for many years before a decision is reached on the merits. The second problem has to do with the fact that, because the petitions are directed against states which are not parties to the Convention, the Court has no contentious jurisdiction to address them. Third, although the Commission transmits its decisions in these cases to the General Assembly, this body has shown little interest in dealing with individual petitions. Non-compliance by states with the decisions of the Commission in these cases consequently attracts little notice and thus deprives the system of effectiveness.

In order to mitigate these problems, the Commission has instituted a follow-up procedure. Commission Rules, art. 48. After the Commission has adopted recommendations or achieved a friendly settlement in a case, it may adopt the follow-up measures it deems appropriate, including holding hearings, to verify compliance with the recommendations or the terms of the settlement. Reports on compliance are included in each Annual Report of the Commission.

3. Precautionary Measures

Like all other human rights bodies, the IACHR has exercised an implied power to request states to take measures to protect those threatened with imminent and irreparable harm. It has established a mechanism to decide on such precautionary measures in Article 25 of its Rules of Procedure. Article 25 provides that, in serious and urgent situations, the Commission may, on its own initiative or at the request of a party, request that a state adopt precautionary measures to prevent irreparable harm to persons or to the subject matter of the proceedings in connection with a pending petition or case, as well as to persons under the jurisdiction of the State concerned, independently of any pending petition or case. The measures may be of a collective nature to prevent irreparable harm to persons due to their association with an organization, a group, or a community with identified or identifiable members. As a result, the number of precautionary measures granted does not reflect the number of persons protected by their adoption; as can be seen below, many of the precautionary measures issued by the Commission protect more than one person and, in certain cases, groups of persons such as communities of indigenous peoples.

The Rules of Procedure establish that the granting of such measures and their adoption by the state shall not constitute a prejudgment on any alleged violation of human rights. The 2013 amendments added that "the decisions granting, extending, modifying or lifting precautionary measures shall be adopted through reasoned resolutions."

Precautionary or interim measures have proven controversial in some instances for several reasons. First, the power to request them is implied rather than expressly mentioned by the treaties. Second, such measures have sometimes extended to large groups of people in the context of an armed conflict, making compliance with them difficult; other measures have been issued to halt large development projects the state has approved and have been politically unpopular. Third, the Commission like other human rights bodies, takes the position that at least some requests are legally binding. Many states disagree and some have sought to restrict the power of the Commission to issue such measures.

For example, when the Commission in 2011 requested precautionary measures for the members of 11 indigenous communities believed to be at risk from the construction of the Belo Monte ("Kararaô") hydroelectric power project on the Xingu River in the state of Pará, Brazil called the request "precipitous and unwarranted," severed formal relations with the Commission, recalled its OAS ambassador, and froze its annual $800,000 contribution to the IACHR in protest. PM382/10—Indigenous Communities of the Xingu River Basin, Para, Brazil. However, it is noteworthy that states have acceded to the Commission's power to issue precautionary measures in some cases, such as in cases of forced disappearance. *See* IA Convention on Forced Disappearance of Persons, art. XIII. The Commission also has the express power under the Convention to request the Court to grant provisional measures. *See* § 4–13 below.

III. THE CONVENTION-BASED SYSTEM

§ 4–6. INTRODUCTION

The American Convention on Human Rights was opened for signature on November 20, 1969 at an Inter-American diplomatic conference held in San José, Costa Rica. It entered into force on July 18, 1978 and currently has 23 OAS Member States as parties: Argentina, Barbados, Bolivia, Brazil, Chile, Colombia, Costa Rica, Dominica, Dominican Republic, Ecuador, El Salvador, Grenada, Guatemala, Haiti, Honduras, Jamaica, Mexico, Nicaragua, Panama, Paraguay, Perú, Suriname, and Uruguay. Missing from the list are Canada, the United States, and most of the English-speaking Caribbean nations. Trinidad and Tobago denounced the Convention effective in 1999 and Venezuela did so in 2012. The United States has signed the Convention and President Jimmy Carter referred it to the Senate for its advice and consent to ratification, but the Senate did not act on the request and subsequent administrations have failed to renew it. *See* § 6–3, *infra.*

The ratification record of OAS Member States reveals the cultural, linguistic and juridical split that exists in the OAS between Latin America, where all countries except Venezuela and Cuba are parties to the Convention, and the English-speaking north, where few countries have adhered. This record (and the division between civil-law and common-law systems) has affected the composition of the Court and its resulting jurisprudence. It also has brought criticism of the non-party states, with some

Convention States Parties submitting proposals to move the headquarters of the Commission away from Washington, D.C., or to ban non-parties from nominating individuals for election to the Commission.

Two protocols supplement the Convention: the Additional Protocol to the American Convention on Human Rights in the Area of Economic, Social and Cultural Rights ("Protocol of San Salvador"), which entered into force in 1999, and the Protocol to the American Convention on Human Rights to Abolish the Death Penalty, which entered into force in 1993. The 16 parties to the San Salvador Protocol are: Argentina, Bolivia, Brazil, Colombia, Costa Rica, Ecuador, El Salvador, Guatemala, Honduras, Mexico, Nicaragua, Panama, Paraguay, Perú, Suriname, and Uruguay. The latter protocol has been ratified by Argentina, Brazil, Chile, Costa Rica, Ecuador, Honduras, Mexico, Nicaragua, Panama, Paraguay, Dominican Republic, Uruguay and Venezuela.

See generally Shelton, "The Inter-American Human Rights System," in H. Hannum (ed.), *Guide to International Human Rights Practice* 121 (4th ed. 2004); Cecilia Medina, *The American Convention on Human Rights* 5–7 (2nd ed. 2016).

§ 4–7. THE CONVENTION AND ITS GUARANTEES

The Convention recognizes some two dozen categories of civil and political rights. These include the following: the right to juridical personality, right to life, right to humane treatment, freedom from slavery, right to personal liberty, right to a fair trial, freedom from ex post facto laws, right to compensation for miscarriage of justice, right to privacy, freedom of conscience and religion, freedom of thought and expression, right of reply, right of assembly, freedom of association, rights of the family, right to a name, rights of the child, right to nationality, right to property, freedom of movement and residence, right to participate in government, right to equal protection of the law, and right to judicial protection.

While article 4 of the Convention permits a state to retain capital punishment for the most serious crimes, the Inter-American Court has held that a law which provides for a mandatory death penalty without a judicial determination of mitigating or aggravating circumstances is contrary to the Convention. Case of Hilaire, Constantine and Benjamin et al. v. Trinidad and Tobago, Judgment of June 21, 2002, IA Ct.H.R., Series C: Judgments and Decisions, No. 94 (2002); Case of Raxcaco Reyes v. Guatemala, Judgement of September 15, 2005, *id.* No. 133; Case of Boyce et al. v. Barbados, Judgment of November 20, 2007, *id.* No. 169 (2007). The Commission and Court both take a strict view of the guarantees afforded in sentencing and the Commission in particular has promoted abolition of the death penalty. *See* IACHR, The Death Penalty in the Inter-American Human Rights System: From Restrictions to Abolition, OEA/Ser.L/V/II, Doc. 68 (2011). As indicated above, thirteen Member States have become party to the Protocol on the abolition of the death penalty.

The Convention's protections are reinforced by a broad non-discrimination clause and by the obligation of the States Parties to adjust their domestic laws to guarantee the rights enshrined in the Convention and to make the laws effective. *See* Case of the "Juvenile Reeducation Institute," IA Ct.H.R., Series C: Judgments and Decisions, No. 112 (2004); Case of Bulacio, *ibid*, No. 100 (2003); Case of the "Five Pensioners" *ibid*, No. 98 (2003). This means repealing rules and practices that violate the Convention or hamper the exercise of the rights recognized therein, as well as developing new rules and practices to ensure effective observance of the rights. Case of "The Last Temptation of Christ" (Olmedo-Bustos et al.), *ibid*, No. 73 (2001).

The Convention also contains an undertaking by the States Parties to take progressive measures for "the full realization of the rights implicit in the economic, social, educational, scientific, and cultural standards set forth in the Charter of the Organization of American States as amended by the Protocol of Buenos Aires." (Art. 26.) This pledge is amplified by the additional catalog of rights set out in the Protocol of San Salvador, which proclaims the right to work, to unionize and to strike, the right to social security and to health, and the right to a healthy environment, to food and to education. The Protocol sets out additional rights, including the right to the benefits of culture and to the protection of the family, as well as the rights of children, the elderly and the handicapped. However, only trade union freedoms and the right to education are explicitly subject to the petition procedure.

Whether Convention art. 26 allows complaints to be brought alleging violations of economic, social and cultural rights is a matter of considerable debate, resulting from the uncertain interaction of the American Declaration, Convention arts. 26 and 29, and the Protocol on Economic and Social Rights. *See* Cavallaro & Schaffer, "Less as More: Rethinking Supranational Litigation of Economic and Social Rights in the Americas," 56 Hastings L.J. 217 (2004); Cavallaro & Schaffer, "Rejoinder: Justice Before Justiciability: Inter-American Litigation and Social Change," 39 N.Y.U. J. Int'l L. & Pol. 345 (2006); Melish, "Rethinking the 'Less as More' Thesis: Supranational Litigation of Economic, Social, and Cultural Rights in the Americas," 39 N.Y.U. J. Int'l L. & Pol. 171 (2007). The Court itself has been cautious, but has addressed social and economic rights where these have been presented in the context of cases involving discrimination, indigenous peoples, and property. *See* Acevedo Buendía v. Perú , IA Ct.H.R., Judgment of July 1, 2009, Series C No. 198 (2009), paras. 92–107 (right to social security).

Article 1(2) declares that the term "person" as used in the Convention means "human being." Corporations and other juridical persons are thus not the intended beneficiaries of the rights the Convention guarantees. The States Parties to the Convention have an obligation not only "to respect" the rights guaranteed in the Convention, but also "to ensure" their free and full exercise. Art.1(1). They consequently have both positive and negative duties, that is, they have the obligation not to violate the rights which the Convention guarantees and are required to adopt whatever measures may be necessary and reasonable under the circumstances "to ensure" their full enjoyment. For an extensive interpretation of the obligations states have under Article 1 of the Convention, *see* Velásquez Rodríguez Case, IA Ct.H.R., Judgment of July 29, 1988, Series C: Decisions and Judgments, No. 4, paras. 159 *et seq.* (1988).

Article 27 of the Convention allows the States Parties to derogate from their obligations "in time of war, public danger, or other emergency that threatens [their] independence or security." *See* Grossman, "A Framework for the Examination of States of Emergency under the American Convention on Human Rights," 1 Am. U. J. Int'l L. & Pol. 35 (1986). Derogation is not permitted, however, from the protections of the more basic human rights which the Convention guarantees. The catalog of non-derogable rights is longer than that of the European Convention of Human Rights and the International Covenant on Civil and Political Rights. Unlike these treaties, the American Convention also declares that "the judicial guarantees essential for the protection" of the non-derogable rights may not be suspended. On this subject, *see* Advisory Opinion OC–8/87, IA Ct.H.R., Series A: Judgments and Opinions, No. 8 (1987); Advisory Opinion, OC–1987, IA Ct.H.R., Series A: Judgments and Decisions, No. 9 (1987). *See generally* Hartman, "Derogation from Human Rights Treaties in Public Emergencies," 22 Harv. Int'l L.J. 1 (1981); T. Meron, *Human Rights Law-Making in the United Nations* 86 (1986); J. Fitzpatrick, *The*

International System for Protecting Rights During States of Emergency (1994).

The rights proclaimed in the Protocol of San Salvador may however be restricted "by means of laws promulgated for the purpose of preserving the general welfare in a democratic society only to the extent that they are not incompatible with the purpose and reason underlying these rights." Art. 5. The Protocol Abolishing the Death Penalty does not contain a derogation clause. It bars general reservations but provides that "at the time of ratification or accession, the States Parties to this instrument may declare that they reserve the right to apply the death penalty in wartime in accordance with international law, for extremely serious crimes of a military nature." Art. 2.3.

The Convention also contains a so-called "federal state clause," which enables a federal state to assume more limited obligations by binding itself only in relation to matters over which it "exercises legislative and judicial jurisdiction." Art. 28. This provision was included in the Convention at the urging of the U.S. delegation to the San José Conference, which argued that the clause was needed to enable the U.S. to become a party to the Convention. *See* Buergenthal, "The Inter-American System for the Protection of Human Rights," *in* T. Meron (ed.), *Human Rights in International Law: Legal and Policy Issues* 438, 445 (1984).

§ 4–8. THE CONVENTION ORGANS

The Convention provides for the establishment of the Inter-American Commission on Human Rights (IACHR) and the Inter-American Court of Human Rights (IA Ct.H.R.), and confers on them "competence with respect to matters relating to the fulfillment of the commitments made by the States Parties" thereto. Art. 33. *See generally* Shelton, "Implementation Procedures of the American Convention on Human Rights," 26 Germ. Y.B. Int'l L. 238 (1983); Buergenthal, "Implementation in the Inter-American Human Rights System," *in* R. Bernhardt & J.A. Jolowicz (eds.), *International Enforcement of Human Rights* 57, 61 (1987); Pinto, The Role of the Inter-American Commission and Court of Human Rights in the Protection of Human Rights: Achievements and Contemporary Challenges," 20 Human Rights Brief 34–38 (2013). In addition, the Protocol of San Salvador empowers the Commission to formulate observations and make recommendations on economic, social, and cultural rights in the States Parties. Art.19(7).

The Commission and the Court consist of seven members each, elected in their personal capacities. The members of the Commission are elected by all OAS Member States, but only the States Parties to the Convention may nominate the judges of the Court and vote on their election. Since the Commission, unlike the Court, is both a Convention and an OAS Charter organ, *see* § 4–4, *supra,* all OAS Member States, whether or not they have ratified the Convention, have a right to vote in the selection of the Commissioners. The Commission has its seat at the headquarters of the OAS in Washington, D.C.; the Court sits in San José, Costa Rica. Membership on the Court and Commission is not a full-time position; both institutions have small permanent professional staffs.

IV. THE INTER-AMERICAN COMMISSION ON HUMAN RIGHTS

§ 4–9. THE COMMISSION AS CONVENTION ORGAN

The functions of the Inter-American Human Rights Commission (IACHR) are spelled out in Article 41 of the Convention, which codifies the Commission's preexisting functions as an OAS organ, *see* § 4–4, *supra,* and mandates it "to take action on petitions and other communications pursuant to its authority under the provisions of Articles 44 through 51 of this Convention." (Article 41(f).) These provisions apply only to the States Parties to the Convention and relate to the petition system it establishes. It should not be confused with the petition system the Commission administers as an OAS Charter organ. *See* § 4–5, *supra.*

1. Examination of Petitions

The Convention empowers the Commission to deal with individual petitions and inter-state communications. Arts. 44 and 45. By becoming a party to the Convention, a state is deemed to have accepted the IACHR's jurisdiction to examine private complaints lodged against that state. Art. 44. The Commission may also address inter-state complaints—complaints filed by one State Party against another—but only if both states, in addition to ratifying the Convention, have also recognized the inter-state jurisdiction of the Commission. Art. 45. In adopting this approach, the American Convention departs from the more traditional scheme utilized by the European Convention, for example, which initially established an optional individual petition system and a mandatory inter-state complaint procedure. *See* Chapter 3, *supra*. Moreover, unlike some other human rights treaties, the American Convention does not limit the right to file private petitions to victims only; any person or group of persons and nongovernmental organizations may also do so. Art. 44.

The admissibility of a petition is conditioned, *inter alia*, on (1) the exhaustion of domestic remedies "in accordance with the generally recognized principles of international law;" and (2) the requirement that the petition be submitted to the Commission within a period of six months from the date on which the victim of the alleged violation was notified of the final domestic judgment in his case. Art. 46(1). These requirements do not defeat the admissibility of a petition, however, if (1) there exist no domestic remedies to protect against the violation of the rights at issue; (2) there has been a denial of access to or interference with recourse to the applicable domestic remedies; or (3) the domestic remedies have been subjected to unwarranted delay. Art. 46(2).

The Inter-American Court of Human Rights interpreted the requirement for the exhaustion of domestic remedies in a number of its early cases and advisory opinions, including *inter alia*, Godínez Cruz Case (Preliminary Exceptions), IA Ct.H.R., Series C: Judgments and Decisions, No. 3, paras. 81 et seq. (1987); Advisory Opinion OC–11/90, *id.*, Series A: Judgments and Opinions (1992); Caballero Delgado v. Colombia (Preliminary Objection), *id.*, Series C: Judgments and Decisions, No. 17, paras. 56 et seq. (1994). *See* also the more recent judgment of Juan Humberto Sánchez v. Honduras, *id.*, Series C: Judgments and Decisions No. 99 (2003). The Commission's rules of procedure provide, moreover, that the respondent government has the burden of demonstrating the non-exhaustion of domestic remedies if it invokes that objection and if the complaint alleges that compliance with that requirement was impossible. Commission Rules, art. 31(3). This proposition is consistent with the Court's case law on the subject. *See, e.g.,* Fairen Garbi Case (Preliminary Objections), IA Ct.H.R., Series C: Decisions and Judgments, No. 2, para. 87 (1987).

A complaint will also be held inadmissible if it does not state a *prima facie* case under the Convention or if it is otherwise "manifestly groundless or obviously out of order." Art. 47(b) and (c). The petition must provide an account of the fact or situation that is denounced, specifying the place and date of the alleged violations and, if possible, the name of the victim and of any public authority who has taken cognizance of the fact or situation alleged. Commission Rules, art. 28. These facts are the basis for assessment of admissibility; the petitioner does not need to characterize the consequences by specifying which provisions of the American Convention on Human Rights or other applicable instrument has been violated. The Commission and Court both determine which rights are implicated by the facts alleged, using the principle *jura novit curia*. *See* Shelton, "Jura Novit Curia in International Human Rights Tribunals," in *International Courts and the Development of International Law* (N. Boschiero et al. eds., 2013), 187–209.

Article 47(d) requires the Commission to reject a petition that "is substantially the same as one previously studied by the Commission or by another international organization." This provision complements Article 46(1)(c), which conditions admissibility on the requirement "that the subject of the petition or communication is not pending in another international proceeding of settlement." The Commission and Court interpret these last two requirements in a manner designed to ensure that a complaint will not be rejected when the other international organization, although seized of the matter in general, is or was in no position to grant petitioners the specific relief they seek from the Commission. Commission Rules, art. 32(2); Case of the Saramaka People v. Suriname, Judgment of November 28, 2007, IA Ct.H. R., Series C: Judgments and Opinions, No. 172 (2007).

For the manner in which the Court has resolved various admissibility issues, *see* Velásquez Rodríguez Case (Preliminary Objections), IA Ct.H. R., Series C:

Decisions and Judgments, No. 1 (1987); Neira Alegría Case (Preliminary Objections), IA Ct.H.R., Series C: Decisions and Judgments, No. 13 (1991); Cayara Case (Preliminary Objections), IA Ct.H.R., Series C: Decisions and Judgments, No. 14 (1993); Caballero Delgado Case (Preliminary Objections), IA Ct.H.R., Series C: Decisions and Judgments, No. 17 (1994).

When the Commission receives a petition which meets, in principle, the requirements established in the Convention, the Commission assigns a number to that petition and begins to process it as a case, without prejudice to the Commission's eventual decision on admissibility. The pertinent parts of the petition are sent to the Government with a request for relevant information. Each party submits pleadings, but the Commission also may carry out its own investigations, including conducting on-site visits, or holding a hearing in which the government and the petitioners participate.

The Commission must also offer to "place itself at the disposal of the parties concerned with a view to reaching a friendly settlement of the matter on the basis of respect for the human rights recognized" in the Convention. Art. 48(1)(f). If a friendly settlement is reached, the Commission prepares a report that describes the facts of the case and the settlement. Art. 49. For a precedent-setting friendly settlement that the Commission negotiated with the Government of Argentina, *see* Report No. 1/93, IACHR, *Annual Report 1992–93*, OAS/Ser.L.V./II.83, Doc. 14, at 35 (1993).

If the parties are unable to reach a friendly settlement, the Commission draws up a report, setting out the facts and the conclusions it has reached about the case. Art. 50. For a finding that no violation of the Convention was committed, *see* Report No. 2/92 (Case 10.289/Costa Rica), IACHR, *Annual Report 1991*, OEA/Ser.L/V/II.8 Doc. 6 rev. 1, at 73 (1992). A report containing a finding that a violation has been committed normally includes whatever recommendations the Commission wishes to make, and is transmitted to the state concerned. The state has three months within which to comply with or react to the recommendations of the Commission.

The Convention provides that during that period, the case may also be referred to the Inter-American Court of Human Rights by the Commission or the interested states. *See* § 4–11, *infra.* In the past, the Commission made that decision on a case-by-case basis, but its Rules of Procedure since 2001 have required the Commission to refer all cases of non-compliance to the Court unless the Commission decides otherwise by an absolute majority vote. Commission Rules, art. 45.

Although individuals do not have standing to refer cases to the Court, the Commission's Rules of Procedure give the petitioner the right to be heard on that subject by the Commission. Art.44(3). *See* § 4–11, *infra.* An addition to the 2013 Rules of Procedure now governs the increasingly frequent requests from states to allow more time for compliance with the Commission's recommendations before a decision is taken to refer the case to the Court. 2013 Rules art. 46. The state must show its willingness and ability to implement the recommendations included in the merits report through the adoption of concrete and adequate measures of compliance and must irrevocably waive any right to file a preliminary objection with the Court about the failure to submit the case within three months.

In dealing with a case that has not been referred to the Court or settled by the parties, "the Commission may, by the vote of an absolute majority of its members, set forth its opinion and conclusions concerning the question submitted for its consideration." Art. 51(1). If it has concluded that the Convention was violated, the Commission must set out its "recommendations," if any, and "prescribe a period within which the state is to take the measures that are incumbent upon it to remedy the situation examined." Art. 51(2). Once this period has expired it "shall decide by a vote of an absolute majority of its members whether the state has taken adequate measures and whether to publish its report." Art. 51(3). *See, e.g.,* Report No. 32/92 (Case 10.454/Colombia), IACHR, *Annual Report 1992–93*, OEA/Ser.L/V/II.83/Doc. 14, at 52 (1993). For a discussion of the relationship between Articles 50 and 51, *see* Advisory Opinion OC–13, IA Ct.H.R., Series A: Judgments and Opinions, No. 13 (1993); Caballero Delgado Case (Preliminary Objections), IA Ct.H.R., Series C: Decisions and Judgments, No. 17 (1994).

The Commission may deal with inter-state communications only if the applicant and respondent states have recognized its jurisdiction to receive such complaints. Art. 45. Jurisdiction may be accepted on an *ad hoc* basis for a specific case or in general. About one half of the States Parties to the Convention have made the requisite general declaration. The admissibility requirements and procedures for addressing inter-state applications are in all respects the same as those that are prescribed for individual petitions.

The first inter-state case that was filed was found inadmissible because the Commission deemed that the nationals of the applicant state had not exhausted local remedies and the applicant state failed to demonstrate a systematic practice of discrimination that would have made them exempt from the requirement. *See* Nicaragua v. Costa Rica, Rep. No. 11/07, Interstate Case 01/06, IA Ct.H.R., March 8, 2006. A second inter-state case, between Colombia and Ecuador, was settled by the parties after it was declared admissible by the Commission. *See* IACHR, Rep. No. 112/10, Inter-state petition IP-02 (Admissibility) (Franklin Guillernmo Aisalla Molina) (Ecuador-Colombia), OEA/Ser.L/V/II.140, doc. 10 (2010).

A ruling by the Commission that a petition is inadmissible is a quasi-judicial decision, which is final and not subject to appeal. The Convention is silent on the legal effect of an opinion of the Commission rendered pursuant to Article 51 holding that a state has violated the Convention. Although this decision is not formally binding (as is a judgment of the Court), it is a legal determination by a body to which the Convention assigns "competence . . . relating to the fulfillment" of the obligations assumed by the States Parties. The Commission's findings under Article 51 may thus be regarded by states and the OAS as an authoritative ruling that a State Party has violated its treaty obligation. *See* Shelton & Carozza, *Regional Protection of Human Rights* 418 (2013).

2. Role Before the Court

The Convention gives the Commission standing to refer cases to the Court and provides, in addition, that "the Commission shall appear in all cases before the Court." Arts. 61 and 57. The quoted language mandates the participation of the Commission in all contentious proceedings before the Court, whether or not they originated as private petitions or as actions by one state against another. The Commission is thus more than a mere party in proceedings before the Court. Even when the Commission refers a case to the Court, it is deemed to do so not on its own behalf, but on behalf of an individual or a state. The Commission need not, moreover, adopt the contentions of the victim or state whose case it has referred to the Court. When the Commission appears before the Court, it does so not as "party" but as "the 'Ministerio Público' of the inter-American system." In the Matter of Viviana Gallardo, Case No. G 101/81, Decision of Nov. 13, 1981, IA Ct.H.R., Series A: Judgments and Opinions 77, at para. 22 (1984). The Court's reference to the Latin American legal institution known as "ministerio público" was designed to make clear that the Commission appears before the Court as protector of the legal order established by the Convention. Its function before the Court, in short, is to promote the legal and institutional integrity of the Convention system.

The Commission also has standing to request advisory opinions from the Court. *See* § 4–14, *infra.* Moreover, the provisional measures that the Court has power to enter, § 4–13, *infra,* may be granted only "at the request of the Commission." Convention, art. 63(2). Thus, in addition to the multitude of promotional and protective functions the Commission performs, it also plays an important role in assisting the Court in discharging its judicial responsibilities. The Commission's Annual Reports as a rule include a chapter or subchapter entitled "Activities of the IACHR in connection with the Inter-American Court of Human Rights," which reports on pending cases, requests for provisional measures, advisory opinion requests, and the Commission's role relating thereto.

V. THE INTER-AMERICAN COURT OF HUMAN RIGHTS

§ 4–10.   JURISDICTION OF THE COURT

The Court has contentious jurisdiction, that is, jurisdiction to adjudicate cases involving charges that a State Party has violated the Convention. It also has jurisdiction to render advisory opinions interpreting the Convention and certain other human rights treaties. *See* Buergenthal, "The Inter-American Court of Human Rights," 76 Am. J. Int'l L. 231 (1982); Jo Pasqualucci, *The Practice and Procedure of the Inter-American Court of Human Rights* (2d ed. 2014). *See also* Garcia-Sayan, "The Role of the Inter-American Court of Human Rights in the Americas," 19 U.C. Davis J. Int'l L. & Pol'y 103 (2012). Although the Convention is silent on the topic of participation in cases, the Court Rules provide in article 19 that a judge may not sit on an individual case coming from the state of which the judge is a national. The Convention and Rules provide for the appointment of an *ad hoc* judge in inter-state cases if no national of a party to the case is a judge on the Court. Convention art. 45; Rules, art. 20.

§ 4–11. CONTENTIOUS JURISDICTION

Article 62 of the Convention delimits the Court's contentious jurisdiction as follows:

1. A State Party may, upon depositing its instruments of ratification or adherence to this Convention, or at any subsequent time, declare that it recognizes as binding, *ipso facto,* and not requiring special agreement, the jurisdiction of the Court on all matters relating to the interpretation or application of this Convention.

2. Such declaration may be made unconditionally, on the condition of reciprocity, for a specified period, or for specific cases. It shall be presented to the Secretary General of the Organization, who shall transmit copies

thereof to the other member states of the Organization and to the Secretary of the Court.

3. The jurisdiction of the Court shall comprise all cases concerning the interpretation and application of the provisions of this Convention that are submitted to it, provided that the States Parties to the case recognize or have recognized such jurisdiction, whether by special declaration pursuant to the preceding paragraphs, or by a special agreement.

This provision indicates that a State Party does not accept the contentious jurisdiction of the Court merely by ratifying the Convention. To do so, it must either have filed the declarations referred to in paragraphs 1 and 2 of Article 62 or have concluded the special agreement mentioned in paragraph 3. General declarations accepting the Court's jurisdiction have been made by twenty of the States Parties to the Convention: Argentina, Barbados, Bolivia, Brazil, Colombia, Chile, Costa Rica, Ecuador, Dominican Republic, El Salvador, Guatemala, Haiti, Honduras, Mexico, Nicaragua, Perú, Panama, Paraguay, Suriname, and Uruguay.

The Convention specifies in Article 61(1) that "only the States Parties and the Commission shall have the right to submit a case to the Court." Individuals consequently do not have the right to refer a case to the Court. However, the Court's Rules of Procedure give victims and their representatives standing to participate in their own right in the proceedings once the case has been submitted to the Court. Arts. 2 and 35(4). The victims or their next of kin thus can file briefs, submit arguments and evidence independently of those filed by the Commission and even present claims inconsistent with those of the Commission. They may not, however, allege new facts distinct from those presented in the application to the Court, unless they are supervening facts. Five Pensioners v. Perú, Judgment of February 28, 2003, IA Ct.H.R., Series C No. 98, para. 150–157. In 2010, the Court established a Legal Assistance Fund of the Inter-American Human Rights System to assist victims with the costs of litigation.

Before a case may be referred to the Court, the relevant Commission proceedings applicable to it must be "completed." Art. 61(2). In the Gallardo case, the first contentious case to come before the Court, the government of Costa Rica sought to waive the proceedings before the Commission and take the matter directly to the tribunal. The Court held that it lacked jurisdiction to entertain the case until the Commission had dealt with it, emphasizing that the proceedings before the Commission "have not been created for the sole benefit of the States, but also in order to allow for the exercise of important individual rights, especially those of the victims." In the Matter of Viviana Gallardo, Case No. Gl/01/81, Decision of Nov. 13, 1981, IA Ct.H.R., Series A: Judgments and Opinions, at para. 25 (1984). The Court's concern here was that individuals, unlike a State Party, had no formal standing in the Court, whereas they do in proceedings before the Commission. This consideration would give the state a significant advantage if it were to be permitted to bypass the Commission. The changes in the Court's Rules of

Procedure, which give individuals rights to participate with their own representation in proceedings before the Court, has not thus far led the Court to reverse the above ruling in the Gallardo Case. It is also unsettled whether the States Parties to an inter-state dispute may waive the Commission proceedings. The inequality between the parties to which the Court referred in the Gallardo Case would not exist in this context.

The rule set forth in Article 61(1) that "only the States Parties and the Commission shall have the right to submit a case to the Court," requires further explanation. First, Article 62(3) indicates that a case may only be taken to the Court by one state against another state if both have accepted the Court's jurisdiction. Second, Article 62(2) permits the States Parties to accept that jurisdiction "on the condition of reciprocity," and a number of states have done so. A state that has made such a declaration cannot be taken to the Court by a State Party that has not accepted the tribunal's jurisdiction. However, even if a state has accepted the Court's jurisdiction subject to reciprocity, this reservation cannot deprive the Commission of the right to take the matter to the Court if the case grew out of an individual petition rather than an inter-state complaint. This conclusion finds support in the Court's holding regarding the limited applicability of the principle of reciprocity to human rights treaties. Advisory Opinion OC–2, IA Ct.H.R., Series A: Judgments and Opinions, No. 2 (1982). For an analysis of some of these jurisdictional issues, *see* Buergenthal, "Interim Measures in the Inter-American Court of Human Rights," *in* R.

Bernhardt (ed.), *Interim Measures Indicated by International Courts* 69, 72 (1994). Finally, Article 61(1) does not say whether it permits all States Parties to refer any case to the Court or only the cases in which the applicant states were parties in the proceedings before the Commission. To date the Court has not had the opportunity to address this issue.

§ 4–12. THE COURT'S POWERS IN CONTENTIOUS CASES

Once a case has been referred to the Court, it has the power to fully review the Commission's findings of fact and law. *See, e.g.*, Velásquez Rodríguez v. Honduras (Preliminary Objections), IA Ct.H.R., Series C: Decisions and Judgments No. 1, para. 84; Ituango Massacres v. Colombia, *id.*, No. 148 (2006)(determination of victims). The Court has the power also to hear any challenges to its jurisdiction based on non-compliance by the Commission with the procedures set out in Articles 48 to 50 of the Convention and any other relevant provisions thereof. *See, e.g.*, Godínez Cruz Case (Preliminary Objections), *id.*, No. 3 (1987). This means, for example, that the Commission's finding that the petitioner has exhausted all available domestic remedies, as required by Article 46 of the Convention, may also be reviewed. Fairen Garbi Case (Preliminary Objections), *id.*, No. 2 (1987); Neira Alegría Case (Preliminary Objections), *id.*, No. 13 (1991).

The Inter-American Court liberally applies the doctrine *jura novit curia,* according to which courts have authority to find different violations from those alleged by the applicants. *See* Ituango Massacres Case, *supra,* para. 191; Case of Bueno-Alves v. Argentina, Judgment of May 11, 2007, *id.* No. 164 (2007), para. 70. Also, unlike the general practice of the European Court of Human Rights, the Inter-American will often find violations of several rights based on the same facts. *See* Ricardo Canese Case, *id.,* No. 111 (2004) (holding that restrictions on a politician's travel abroad resulting from a slander conviction violated both freedom of expression and freedom of movement). *But see* García Asto and Ramirez Rojas Cases, *id.,* No. 137 (2005).

Article 67 of the Convention provides that the judgment rendered by the Court is "final and not subject to appeal." *See* Castillo Petruzzi Case, Order of November 17, 1999 (Compliance with Judgment), IA Ct.H.R., Series C: Decisions and Judgments, No. 59 (2000). The same provision also authorizes the Court to interpret its judgments if there is a disagreement as to its "meaning or scope." As the Court's judgments and reparations orders have become more complex over time, states are increasingly filing requests for interpretation. Nearly one-third of the 50 requests submitted during the Court's history were presented between 2010 and the end of 2015. The "States Parties to the Convention undertake to comply with the judgment of the Court in any case to which they are parties." Art. 68(1). For an interpretation of this provision, *see* Castillo Petruzzi Case (Compliance with Judgment), *supra.*

The types of judgments that the Court may render and the manner in which they are to be enforced are spelled out in two provisions of the Convention. The first is Article 63(1), which reads as follows:

> If the Court finds that there has been a violation of a right or freedom protected by this Convention, the Court shall rule that the injured party be ensured the enjoyment of his right or freedom that was violated. It shall also rule, if appropriate, that the consequences of the measure or situation that constituted the breach of such right or freedom be remedied and that fair compensation be paid to the injured party.

The Court is, consequently, empowered to award money damages and render declaratory judgments. The latter may specify not only what rights have been violated, but also how the state should remedy the violation. *See* Loayza Tamayo Case (Reparations), Judgment of November 27, 1998, IA Ct.H.R., Series C: Decisions and Judgments, No.42 (2000), as well as the concurring opinion thereto by Judge Oliver Jackman. *See also* Aloeboetoe Case (Reparations), IA Ct.H.R., Series C: Decisions and Judgments, No. 15 (1993); Godínez Cruz Case (Compensatory Damages), IA Ct.H.R., Series C: Decisions and Judgments, No. 8 (1989); Velásquez Rodríguez Case (Compensatory Damages), IA Ct.H.R., Series C: Decisions and Judgments, No. 7 (1988); Suárez Rosero Case (Reparations), Judgment of January 20, 1999, IA Ct.H.R., Series C: Decisions and Judgments, No.44 (2000). *See generally* Pasqualucci, "Victim Reparations in the Inter-American Human Rights

System: A Critical Assessment of Current Practice and Procedure," 18 Mich. J. Int'l L. 1 (1996); Antkowiak, "Remedial Approaches to Human Rights Violations: The Inter-American Court of Human Rights and Beyond," 46 Colum. J. Transnational L. 351 (2008); D. Shelton, *Remedies in International Human Rights Law* (3rd ed. 2015).

Over time, the Court has moved towards ordering various structural reforms of domestic institutions in order to prevent repetition of the violations found and has insisted on the obligation of domestic courts to apply the Convention. *See* Huneeus, "Reforming the State From Afar: Structural Reform Litigation at the Human Rights Courts," 40 Yale J. Int'l L. 1 (2015); Dulitzky, "An Inter-American Constitutional Court? The Invention of the Conventionality Control by the Inter-American Court of Human Rights," 50 Tex. Int'l L.J. 45 (2015); Abramovic, "From Massive Violations to Structural Patterns: New Approaches and Classic Tensions in the Inter-American Human Rights System," 11 Sur. Int'l J. Hum. Rts. 7 (2009); Neuman, "Bi-Level Remedies for Human Rights Violations," 55 Harv. Int'l L.J. 323 (2014).

The second provision is Article 68(2), which deals with money damages. It provides that the "part of a judgment that stipulates compensatory damages may be executed in the country concerned in accordance with domestic procedures governing the execution of judgments against the state." The language of Article 68(2) suggests that the States Parties are not required to establish a mechanism for the domestic execution of the Court's money judgments; it merely permits them to do so.

By contrast, Article 27 of the headquarters agreement between the Court and the Government of Costa Rica provides that the Court's judgments shall be enforced in Costa Rica as if they were domestic judgments. For the text, IA Ct.H.R., *Annual Report 1981*, OEA/Ser.L/III.5, Doc. 13, at 16 (1981). There has been no occasion to date to apply this provision. Some OAS Member States—notably Guatemala and Colombia—have legislation on their books that provide for the domestic enforcement of money judgments rendered against them by international human rights institutions whose jurisdiction these states have accepted. It is unclear how and to what extent these laws have been given effect. *See* Hillebrecht, "The Domestic Mechanisms of Compliance with International Human Rights Law: Case Studies from the Inter-American Human Rights System," 34 Human Rts Q 959 (2012).

The Convention does not establish any specific mechanism to supervise the enforcement of the Court's judgments. The Court itself has taken on compliance monitoring as an inherent exercise of its jurisdictional powers supported by Convention arts. 33, 62(1), 62(3) and 65 as well as Article 30 of the Court's Statute. The procedure is regulated in Article 69 of the Court's Rules. Its purpose is to ensure that the reparations ordered by the Court in each specific case are implemented.

Monitoring compliance involves periodic requests for information from each state on the measures taken to comply with the judgments against it, along with the observations of the Commission and of the victims or their representatives. The Court makes an assessment of the information and may provide further guidance to the state and, if appropriate, convenes a monitoring hearing. During such hearings, the Court seeks collaboration between the parties to suggest options to resolve difficulties, calls attention to any perceived lack of willingness to comply, and promotes the establishment of timetables for compliance. The recourse to hearings has been supported by the OAS General Assembly in a resolution which recognized "that the private hearings held on the monitoring of compliance with the Court's judgments have been important and constructive and have yielded positive results." OAS General Assembly Resolution No. AG/RES.2759 (XLII-0/12). The Court has gone further in recent years and adopted the practice of holding joint hearings to monitor compliance with the judgments in several cases against the same state, when similar reparations have been ordered, or in cases in which it has verified the existence of structural difficulties or problems that could hinder implementation of reparations measures.

In 2015, the Court began holding hearings on monitoring compliance in the territory of the states and making on-site visits. On August 28, 2015, the Court held a hearing in Honduras on monitoring compliance with the judgments in the cases of Juan Humberto Sánchez, López Álvarez, Servellón García et al., Kawas Fernández, Pacheco Teruel et al., and Luna López, IA Ct.H.R., Series C: Decisions and

Judgments No. 102 (2003). Later, the Court held a hearing in Panama on monitoring compliance in the case of the Kuna Indigenous Peoples of Madungandí and the Emberá Indigenous Peoples of Bayano and their members v. Panama, IA Ct.H.R., Series C: Decisions and Judgments No. 284 (2014). In addition, the Court conducted its first on-site visit to Panamanian territory in the context of the compliance monitoring in this case

Article 65 of the Convention also has a bearing on the subject of compliance. It reads as follows:

> To each regular session of the General Assembly of the Organization of American States the Court shall submit, for the Assembly's consideration, a report on its work during the previous year. It shall specify, in particular, the cases in which a state has not complied with its judgments, making any pertinent recommendations.

This provision requires the Court to inform the OAS General Assembly of situations involving non-compliance with its decisions, thus permitting the Assembly to discuss the matter and to take whatever political measures it deems appropriate. Although the Assembly lacks the power to adopt resolutions that are legally binding on the Member States, condemnatory OAS resolutions do carry considerable political weight, which can translate into public opinion pressure.

For a decision of the Court rendered in response to Perú's failure to comply with a judgment ordering reparations for various violations of the Convention, *see* Loayza Tamayo Case (Compliance with Judgment), Order of November 17, 1999, IA Ct.H.R. Series C: Decisions and Judgments, No. 60 (2000). *See also* Baluarte, "Strategizing For Compliance: The Evolution of a Compliance Phase of Inter-American Court Litigation and the Strategic Imperative for Victims' Representatives," 27 Am. U. Int'l L. Rev. 263 (2012).

§ 4–13.   PROVISIONAL MEASURES

The American Convention is the only major human rights treaty that expressly authorizes the issuance of provisional or protective measures during or even prior to cases being submitted to it. Article 63(2) of the Convention addresses these so-called provisional measures. It provides that:

> In case of extreme gravity and urgency, and when necessary to avoid irreparable damage to persons, the Court shall adopt such provisional measures as it deems pertinent in matters it has under consideration. With respect to a case not yet submitted to the Court, it may act at the request of the Commission.

This provision permits the Court to grant temporary restraining orders in cases pending before it and in cases that have been lodged with the Commission but not yet referred to the Court.

For the Court's orders on provisional measures, *see* Inter-American Court of Human Rights, Series E: Provisional Measures, No. 1, Compendium: 1987–96

(1999); *ibid.,* No. 2, Compendium July 1996–June 2000 (2000). *See generally* Pasqualucci, "Provisional Measures in the Inter-American Human Rights System: An Innovative Development in International Law," 26 Vand. J. Transnat'l L. 803 (1993); Buergenthal, "Interim Measures in the Inter-American Court of Human Rights," *in* R. Bernhardt (ed.), *Interim Measures Indicated by International Courts* 69 (1994); Burbano-Herrera, "The Inter-American Court of Human Rights and its Role in Preventing Violations of Human Rights through Provisional Measures," *in The Inter-American Court of Human Rights: Theory and Practice, Present and Future*, at 355 (Haeck, Ruiz-Chiriboga and Burbano-Herrera, eds. 2015).

In the two types of cases that may be brought to it under Article 63(2), the Court has to determine, if only in a preliminary manner, whether it has jurisdiction over the parties. In cases that are already pending before it, this issue will as a practical matter arise only when the request for the order is made before the question of the Court's jurisdiction to hear the case has been settled. But the jurisdictional issue will always have to be examined in those cases that are still being considered by the Commission. *See* Buergenthal, *supra*, at 71.

The Court has granted some requests for provisional measures submitted by the parties. *See, e.g.,* Decisions of January 15 and January 19, 1988 in the Honduran Disappearance Cases, IA Ct.H.R., *Annual Report 1988*, OEA/Ser.L/V/III.19, Doc. 13, at 25 and 27 (1988). The Commission has also requested such measures in matters under its consideration and the Court has granted some, but not all of them. The Commission was successful, *inter alia*, in the Bustios-Rojas Case (Perú), Decision of August 8, 1990, IA Ct.H.R., *Annual Report 1990*, OEA/Ser.L/V/III.23, Doc. 12, at 31 (1991); Decision of January 17, 1991, IA Ct.H.R., *Annual Report 1991*, OEA/Ser.L/V/III.25, Doc. 7, at 15 (1992). But the Court failed to grant the Commission's request in a number of other cases. *See, e.g.*, Peruvian Prisons Case, Decision of January 27, 1993, IA Ct.H.R., *Annual Report 1993*, OEA/Ser.L/V/III.29, Doc. 4, at 21 (1994).

Three requirements—extreme gravity, urgency and the risk of irreparable harm—have to be demonstrated satisfactorily for the Court to grant these measures. Although the Convention does not expressly address the subject, the Court's practice indicates that it considers the provisional measures issued pursuant to Article 63(3) of the Convention to be binding on the States to which they are addressed. *See, e.g.,* Constitutional Court Case (Provisional Measures), Order of the Inter-American Court of Human Rights of August 14, 2000.

§ 4–14.   ADVISORY JURISDICTION

The scope of the Court's advisory jurisdiction is very broad. *See generally* Buergenthal, "The Advisory Practice of the Inter-American Human Rights Court," 79 Am. J. Int'l L. 1 (1985); Pasqualucci, "Advisory Practice and Procedure: Contributing to the Evolution of International Human Rights Law,"

38 Stan. J.Int'l. L. 241 (2002). This power is spelled out in Article 64 of the Convention, which provides:

> 1.   The member states of the Organization may consult the Court regarding the interpretation of this Convention or of other treaties concerning the protection of human rights in the American states. Within their spheres of competence, the organs listed in Chapter X [now Chapter VIII] of the Charter of the Organization of American States, as amended by the Protocol of Buenos Aires, may in like manner consult the Court.

> 2.   The Court, at the request of a member state of the Organization, may provide that state with opinions regarding the compatibility of any of its domestic laws with the aforesaid international instruments.

Thus, any OAS Member State, and not only the States Parties to the Convention, have standing to request an advisory opinion. Moreover, the Court's advisory jurisdiction is not limited to interpretations of the Convention; it extends to any other treaty "concerning the protection of human rights in the American states." All OAS organs, including the Inter-American Commission on Human Rights, have standing to request advisory opinions. Under Article 64(2) the Court is also empowered, at the request of any Member State of the OAS, to render advisory opinions determining whether the state's domestic laws are compatible with the Convention or the aforementioned human rights treaties. On the relationship between Articles 64(1) and 64(2), *see*

Advisory Opinion OC–14/94, IA Ct.H.R., Series A: Judgments and Opinions, No. 14 (1995).

Since its establishment in 1979, the Court has rendered a substantial number of advisory opinions, extensively interpreting Article 64. For example, the Court has held that,to satisfy the requirement that an advisory opinion request fall "within their spheres of competence," OAS organs must demonstrate a "legitimate institutional interest" in the subject matter of the request. Advisory Opinion OC–2/82 of Sept. 24, 1982, IA Ct.H.R., Series A: Judgments and Opinions, No. 2 (1982). The Court has also ruled that the phrase "other treaties concerning the protection of human rights in the American states" to which Article 64 refers applies not only to OAS or inter-American treaties, but to any treaty bearing on the enjoyment or enforcement of human rights in a state belonging to the Inter-American system. Advisory Opinion OC–1/82, IA Ct.H.R., Series A: Judgments and Opinions, No. 1 (1982); Advisory Opinion OC–16/99, IA Ct.H.R., Series A: Judgments and Opinions, No.16 (2000).

In interpreting Article 64(2), the Court has held that the reference to "domestic laws" may in certain circumstances be deemed to apply also to proposed or pending legislation and not only to laws already in force. Advisory Opinion OC–4/84, IA Ct.H.R., Series A: Judgments and Opinions, No. 4 (1984). The mere fact that a request for an advisory opinion concerns a matter that is or was once the subject of a contentious proceeding before the Commission will not necessarily result in its rejection by the Court. *See*

Advisory Opinion OC–3/83, IA Ct.H.R., Series A: Judgments and Opinions, No. 3 (1983); Advisory Opinion OC–5/85, IA Ct.H.R., Series A: Judgments and Opinions, No. 5 (1985); Opinion OC–14/94, IA Ct.H.R., Series A: Judgments and Opinions, No. 14 (1995); Advisory Opinion OC–15/97, IA Ct.H.R., Series A: Judgments and Opinions, No.15 (1999).

But where a state appears to have asked for an advisory opinion in order to delay pending contentious proceedings before the Commission, or otherwise to gain an unfair advantage over the private parties in such proceedings, the Court will decline to render the requested advisory opinion. Advisory Opinion OC–12/91, IA Ct.H.R., Series A: Judgments and Opinions, No. 12 (1992). The Court has also held that a state's decision to withdraw its request for an advisory opinion does not divest the Court of jurisdiction to render the opinion. Advisory Opinion, OC–15/97, *supra.*

§ 4–15. LEGAL EFFECT OF ADVISORY OPINIONS

Advisory opinions are not, as such, legally binding. That conclusion is inherent in the concept of advisory opinions. *See* Advisory Opinion OC–3/83, IA Ct.H.R., Series A: Judgments and Opinions, No. 3 (1983). Moreover, the Convention nowhere states that these opinions are binding. Nevertheless, the Court is a "judicial institution whose purpose is the application and interpretation of the American Convention on Human Rights," Statute of the Court, art. 1, and it is an organ having "competence with respect to matters relating to the fulfillment of the commitments by the States Parties to this Convention." Convention, art. 33. The Court's pronouncements, whether made in a contentious case or advisory opinion, derive their value as legal authority from the Court's character as a judicial institution empowered to interpret and apply that instrument. In short, advisory opinions are not academic exercises; they are judicial pronouncements that could be regarded as authoritative on the legal principles enunciated by them. *See* Jo Pasqualucci, *The Practice and Procedure of the Inter-American Court of Human Rights* 37 (2nd ed. 2013).

What then is the difference between an advisory opinion and a judgment in a contentious case? Since a judgment is binding on the parties to the dispute (Convention, art. 68), a state which does not comply with it in a case to which it was a party violates the specific obligation set out in Article 68. It is also in breach of whatever other provisions of the Convention the Court determined was violated by the state. An advisory opinion, on the other hand, is not binding. Consequently, the failure of a state to comply with the opinion does not constitute a breach of the Convention. But if a state engages in activities determined by the Court in an advisory opinion to be incompatible with the Convention, the state is on notice of the Court's view that its conduct violates its treaty obligations. This fact will seriously undermine the legitimacy of any legal arguments in conflict with those pronounced in the Court's advisory opinion that the states might assert to justify its position.

For the telling consequences of an advisory opinion, *see* Moyer & Padilla, "Executions in Guatemala as Decreed by the Courts of Special Jurisdiction in 1982–1983," *in* IA Ct.H.R., *Human Rights in the Americas* 280. *See also* Buergenthal, "Self-Executing and Non-Self Executing Treaties in National and International Law," 235 Recueil des Cours 303, 390–91 (1992) (discussing a decision of the Argentine Supreme Court giving effect to an advisory opinion of the Inter-American Court of Human Rights).

§ 4–16. CASE LAW

In recent years, the policy of the Commission has been to refer all contentious cases to the Court that are within its jurisdiction, unless there are compelling reasons not to forward the case. As a result, by the end of 2015, the Court had rendered more than 300 judgments. In these judgments, the Court consistently cites to its own precedents, but also often refers to the investigations and decisions of other human rights bodies, including the UN treaty bodies and special procedures, as well as the jurisprudence of the European Court of Human Rights and sometimes the African Commission on Human and Peoples' Rights.

It has supported this practice by citing the Vienna Convention on the Law of Treaties, art. 31(2) and (3), which it says calls for a treaty to be interpreted by taking into account not only agreements and instruments related to the treaty but the international system of which it is a part. Case of

Tibi, Judgment of September 7, 2004, IA Ct.H.R., Series C: Decisions and Judgments No. 114; Case of Bueno-Alves v. Argentina, *supra.*

For example, it has pronounced some human rights violations to constitute crimes against humanity and some rights to constitute part of *jus cogens.* Case of La Cantuta, Judgment of November 29, 2006, IA Ct.H.R., Series C: Decisions and Judgments, No. 162 (2006) (a systematic pattern or practice of extra-legal executions and forced disappearances a crime against humanity and violation of jus cogens); Case of Bueno-Alves v. Argentina, *supra* (prohibition of torture *jus cogens*). The Court has also articulated the "right to know the truth" as a right implicit in the right to justice, guaranteed by Article 8 of the American Convention. Bamaca Velásquez v. Guatemala, IA Ct.H.R., Series C: Decisions and Judgments, No. 70 (2000), paras. 197–202. *See generally* "The Right to the Truth," in Burgorgue-Larsen & Ubeda de Torres, *The Inter-American Court of Human Rights: Case Law and Commentary* (2011), ch. 27.

During the first decade and a half of its existence, very few contentious cases were referred to the Court. Much of its jurisprudence during that period consisted of a series of important advisory opinions bearing on the interpretation and application of the Convention and international human rights law in general. In one of its first opinions, for example, the Court declared that "modern human rights treaties, in general, and the American Convention in particular, are not multilateral treaties of the traditional type concluded to accomplish the reciprocal exchange of rights for the mutual benefit of the contracting States." Advisory Opinion, OC–2/82, IA Ct.H.R., Series A: Judgments and Opinions, No. 2, para. 29 (1982). Since the object and purpose of these treaties "is the protection of the basic rights of individual human beings, irrespective of their nationality, both against the State of their nationality and all other contracting States," *id.,* the concept of reciprocity, which plays an important role in the application of traditional treaties, loses much of its relevance in the application of human rights treaties. The Court consequently determined that a state which had ratified the Convention with a reservation did not have to await the acceptance of the reservation by other contracting parties before it could be considered to be a party to the Convention. *Id.,* at para. 40. *See also* The Right to Information on Consular Assistance in the Framework of the Guarantees of the Due Process of Law, adv. Op. OC–16/99, IA Ct.H.R., Series A, No. 16 (1999), paras. 114–115. The Court has also insisted that the terms in human rights instruments have an autonomous meaning. The Word "Laws" in Article 30 of the American Convention on Human Rights, Advisory Opinion OC–6/86, IA Ct.H.R. Series A, no. 6 (1986) paras. 19–21; Mayagna (Sumo) Awas Tingni Community v. Nicaragua, IA Ct.H.R., Series C: Decisions and Judgments, No. 79 (2001).

Article 27 of the Convention permits the States Parties, "in time of war, public danger, or other emergency that threatens the independence or security of a State Party," to derogate from some of their treaty obligations. The second paragraph of Article 27 lists the rights which may not be suspended even during such emergencies. The European Convention on Human Rights and the ICCPR have comparable derogation clauses and the Court has sometimes referred to the jurisprudence of the European Court and Human Rights Committee on the requirements for a lawful derogation and measures taken pursuant thereto. Case of Zambrano Vélez et al. v. Ecuador, Judgment of July 4, 2007, IA Ct.H.R., Series C: Judgments and Decision, No. 166 (2007). In its Advisory Opinion OC–3/83, IA Ct.H.R., Series A; Judgments and Opinions, No. 3 (1983), the Court had to interpret the scope of a reservation to Article 4 of the Convention, which addresses the right to life and is one of the non-derogable rights listed in Article 27(2). Although it eventually found that the reservation did not authorize the measures the reserving state had taken, the Court took the position that its inquiry had to start with the question whether the reservation was compatible with the object and purpose of the treaty, which is the test for the validity of reservations under Vienna Convention on the Law of Treaties. Art. 19(c).

Article 27 of the Convention allows the States Parties to suspend, in time of war, public danger, or other emergency that threatens their independence or security, the obligations they assumed by ratifying the Convention, provided that in doing so they do not suspend or derogate from certain basic or essential rights, among them the right to life guaranteed by Article 4. It would follow therefrom that a reservation designed to enable a State to suspend any of the non-derogable fundamental rights must be deemed to be incompatible with the object and purpose of the Convention and, consequently, not permitted by it. The situation would be different if the reservation sought merely to restrict certain aspects of a non-derogable right without depriving the right as a whole of its basic purpose. Since the reservation referred to by the Commission in its submission did not appear to be of a type that is designed to deny the right to life as such, the Court concluded that, to that extent, it could be considered, in principle, as not being incompatible with the object and purpose of the Convention. *Id.*, at para. 61.

Apart from its specific holding, the real importance of this opinion derives from the fact that it is the first unambiguous international judicial articulation of the principle that incompatibility and non-derogability are conceptually interrelated.

In another opinion, the Court was asked to interpret the scope of the last phrase of Article 27(2), which prohibits the suspension "of the judicial guarantees essential for the protection" of the rights that are non-derogable. Here, the Court ruled that the right to a writ of habeas corpus and related remedies may not be suspended in emergency situations, even though these rights are not defined as non-derogable rights under Article 27(2). Advisory Opinion OC–8/87, IA Ct.H.R., Series A: Judgments and Opinions, No. 8 (1987).

The Court has also rendered several important opinions dealing with the right to freedom of expression. It ruled that a Costa Rican law, which required journalists to belong to a professional association in order to be licensed to practice their profession, violated the right to freedom of expression guaranteed in Article 13 of the Convention. Advisory Opinion OC–5/85 IA Ct.H.R., Series A: Judgments and Opinions, No. 5 (1985). A second advisory opinion dealt with the scope and nature of the right of reply, which is guaranteed in Article 14 of the Convention. Here the Court explored the delicate balance between the right of reply and freedom of expression. Advisory Opinion OC–7/86, IA Ct.H.R., Series A: Judgments and Opinions, No.7, at paras. 24–25 (1986).

In these two opinions as well as in Advisory Opinion OC–6/86, IA Ct.H.R., Series A: Judgments and Opinions, No. 6 (1986), the Court analyzed the interrelationship between representative democracy, the protection of human rights, and the inter-American system. Contentious cases have upheld the Convention's unique provision prohibiting prior censorship and condemned defamation laws that unduly restrict criticism of public officials. Case of "The Last Temptation of Christ" (Olmedo-Bustos et al.), *supra*; Case of Kimel v. Argentina, Judgment of May 2, 2008, IA Ct.H.R., Series C: Judgments and Opinions, No. 177 (2007).

In an advisory opinion rendered in December 1994, the Court ruled that government officials who enforce national laws that violate the Convention themselves incur international responsibility if the execution of these laws also constitutes an international crime. Advisory Opinion OC–14, IA Ct.H.R., Series A;

Judgments and Opinions, No. 14 (1995). Since the Court has neither international criminal jurisdiction nor jurisdiction to adjudicate cases charging individuals or other non-state actors with violations of the Convention, it remains to be seen what significance the aforementioned advisory opinion will have.

Of course, there is nothing in international law as such that would prevent the States Parties to the Convention from conferring such jurisdiction on the Court by appropriate protocols to that instrument. In the meantime, the Court has made clear that each State Party to the Convention has a duty to investigate and prosecute individuals who commit human rights violations that are crimes. Any law proclaiming amnesty for perpetrators of international crimes is incompatible with the American Convention and without effect. Barrios Altos Case, IA Ct.H.R., Series C: Judgments and Opinions, No. 75 (2001); La Cantuta Case, *supra*; Almonacid Arellano et al., IA Ct.H.R., Series C: Judgments and Decisions No. 154 (2006). The Court has also concluded that the principle against double jeopardy would not preclude a second prosecution if the first was dismissed in violation of international law or if the proceeding was not conducted independently or impartially pursuant to due process of law. Case of Almonacid-Arellano et al, *supra*; Case of Gutierrez-Soler, IA Ct.H.R., *ibid* No. 132 (2005); Case of Carpio-Nicolle et al., *ibid.*, No. 117 (2004).

Another important pronouncement by the Court is to be found in its Advisory Opinion OC–16/99, IA

Ct.H.R., Series A: Judgments and Opinions, No. 16 (2000). Here the Court was asked by Mexico to interpret Article 36 of the Vienna Convention on Consular Relations, which addresses the rights of nationals of the States Parties to the Convention who are detained in the territory of another State Party. The Court ruled, *inter alia*, that the right of the detained aliens to be informed "without delay" of their rights under the Consular Convention was a human right complementing the due process provisions of international human rights treaties, including the ICCPR. The Court also concluded that the right to be informed "without delay" must be understood to mean that the information is to be provided at the time of the alien's arrest or, in any case, before the detainee is required to make a first statement to the authorities. *See also* Case of Chaparro Alvarez and Lap Iníguez v. Ecuador, IA Ct.H.R., Series C: Judgments and Opinions, No. 170 (2007).

Among the most important decisions are the so-called Honduran Disappearance Cases, which constituted the first ever international adjudication of charges implicating a state in a policy of forced disappearances. In the first two of these cases, the Court held Honduras responsible for the disappearances of two Honduran nationals after finding that in the early 1980's there existed in that country a policy of forced disappearances that was tolerated by and imputable to its Government. Velásquez Rodríguez Case (Merits), IA Ct.H.R., Series C: Decisions and Judgments, No. 4 (1988); Godínez-Cruz Case (Merits), IA Ct.H.R., Series C:

Decisions and Judgments, No. 5 (1989). In the third case, Fairen Garbi and Solis Corrales Case (Merits), IA Ct.H.R., Series C: Decisions and Judgments, No. 6 (1989), the Court found that Honduras' responsibility for the disappearance of two Costa Rican nationals had not been proved.

These cases explore the obligations assumed by the States Parties under Article 1(1) of the Convention as well as the difficult evidentiary issues that arise in disappearance cases. *See generally* Shelton, "Judicial Review of State Action by International Courts," 12 Fordham Int'l L.J. 361 (1989); Shelton, "Private Violence, Public Wrongs, and the Responsibility of States," 13 *id.* 1 (1989–90); Buergenthal, "Judicial Fact-Finding: Inter-American Court of Human Rights," *in* R. Lillich (ed.), *Fact-Finding Before International Tribunals* 361, 267 (1990); Grossman, "Disappearances in Honduras: The Need for Direct Victim Representation in Human Rights Litigation," 15 Hastings Int'l & Comp. L. Rev. 363 (1992); Kokott, "No Impunity for Human Rights Violations in the Americas," 14 Hum. Rts. L.J. 153 (1993).

The abduction, torture and murder of street children by the police and the failure of the respondent state to properly investigate these crimes was dealt with by the Court in the Villagran Morales ("Street Children") Case, Judgment of November 19, 1999, *id.*, No. 63 (2000). In this decision, the Court found the respondent state's conduct in violation not only the Convention but also of the Inter-American Convention to Prevent and Punish Torture, even though the latter treaty makes no express reference to the Court. In another case, the Court was called upon to address the legal effect of Perú's purported withdrawal of its acceptance of the Court's contentious jurisdiction. It held that Perú could not validly withdraw the acceptance without also denouncing the Convention. Constitutional Court Case (Competence), Judgment of September 24, 1999, *id.*, No. 55 (2000). For an analysis of the procedural issues that arise in the context of the Court's contentious practice, *see* Pasqualucci, "Preliminary Objections Before the Inter-American Court of Human Rights: Legitimate Issues and Illegitimate Tactics," 40 Va. J. Int'l L. 1 (1999)

The majority of contentious cases considered by the Court have involved forced disappearances, arbitrary executions, and denials of due process. *See, e.g.,* Cesti Hurtado Case, Judgment of September 29, 1999, IA Ct. H.R., Series C: Decisions and Judgments, No. 56 (2000) (military justice, failure to comply with writ of habeas corpus); Castillo Petruzzi Case, Judgment of May 1999, *id.*, No. 52 (2000), and Suárez Rosero Case, Judgment of November 12, 1997, *id.* No. 35 (1999) (numerous due process violations); Blake Case, Judgment of January 24, 1998, *id.*, No. 36 (2000) (forced disappearance and related violations); La Cantuta, *supra* (kidnapping, killings and disappearances). In such cases, states increasingly admit the facts alleged by claimants or found by the Commission, acquiescing in the claims while continuing to contest some of the legal consequences of the findings. La Cantuta, *supra*; Case of Bueno-Alves v. Argentina, *id.*, No. (2007). In many instances, it appears that the state is seeking to avoid having the court set forth the facts in detail in its judgment, which gives the findings greater credence and visibility. The Court has said that a state's acceptance of responsibility for human rights violations "constitutes an important step" towards concluding the case before it and "for the enforcement of the principles that are consecrated by the American Convention." La Cantuta, *supra*, para. 57; Vargas-Areco, para. 65; Goiburu et al., para. 25; Servellón García et al., para. 77. However, the Court generally finds that the "best protection of human rights" requires a judgment adjudicating issues of fact and all the elements of the merits of the case and the corresponding consequences thereof, as a way of contributing to the preservation of historical memory and as part of the redress of damages suffered by the victims. La Cantuta, *supra*.

A review of the Court's contentious practice indicates that the Court has increasingly had an opportunity to interpret and apply the full range of the due process guarantees the Convention proclaims, making important contributions to the law on that subject. *See, e.g.,* Case of Chaparro Álvarez & Lap Iníguez v. Ecuador, *supra*. While some of the Court's advisory opinions have in the past dealt with various political freedoms set out in the Convention, the Court only recently began to have the same opportunity to address these issues in contentious cases. Case of Yvon Neptune v. Haiti, Judgment of May 6, 2008, IA Ct.H.R. Series C: Judgments and Opinions No. 180 (2008).

A series of cases involving the rights of indigenous and tribal peoples to their lands and resources have resulted not only in recognition of collective property rights to the territories in question, but also orders that the respective states ensure the rights of indigenous and tribal peoples to be informed about and to participate in decisions about the use and benefits derived from the resources on their lands, including the right of prior informed consent about any major development project that would affect their lands and resources. The Court has reiterated in these cases that indigenous and tribal peoples, sharing similar characteristics, are entitled to special measures under international law to guarantee the full exercise of their rights. Case of the Mayagna (Sumo) Awas Tingni Community v. Nicaragua, Judgment of August 31, 2001, IA Ct.H.R., Series C: Judgments and Opinions, No. 79 (2001); Case of the Indigenous Community Sawhoyamaxa v. Paraguay, Judgment of March 29, 2006, *id.,* No. 146; Case of the Indigenous Community Yakye Axa v. Paraguay, Judgment of June 17, 2005, *id.,* No. 125; Case of the Saramaka People v. Suriname, Judgment of November 28, 2007, *id.,* No. 172.

The early focus on the positive obligations of the state to ensure human rights has led to a growing number of cases concerned with private violence, including domestic violence and gender-based violence in general. The most significant of the series of cases addressing these issues are González et al. (Cotton Field) v. Mexico, IA Ct.H.R., Series C: Judgments and Decisions No. 205 (discussion of femicide); Veliz Franco et al. v. Guatemala, IA

Ct.H.R., Series C: Judgments and Decisions No. 277 (2014) (gender discrimination in investigating killings of women and girls); and Maria da Penha Maia Fernandes v. Brazil, a Commission report on domestic violence that led to legislative reform in Brazil. IACHR, Case No. 12.051, Report No. 54/01, Maria da Penha Maia Fernandez v. Brazil (2001).

§ 4–17. OTHER INTER-AMERICAN HUMAN RIGHTS INSTRUMENTS

Like other global and regional systems, the Inter-American system has expanded its human rights protections over time. In addition to the two protocols to the Convention, it has adopted the 1985 Inter-American Convention for the Prevention and Punishment of Torture (entry into force Feb. 28, 1987); the Inter-American Convention on the Prevention, Punishment, and Eradication of Violence against Women (Belem do Para, 1994, entry into force Mar. 5, 1995); the Inter-American Convention on Forced Disappearance of Persons (1994, entry into force March 28, 1996), and the Convention on the Elimination of All Forms of Discrimination against Persons with Disabilities (1999, entry into force Sept. 14, 2001). Unlike the U.N., however, the OAS decided to confer monitoring responsibilities on the existing Commission and Court rather than create new treaty monitoring bodies. The exception is the disabilities convention, which creates a state reporting procedure and a committee to receive and review the reports.

On June 5, 2013, the OAS adopted two conventions on the topic of equality and non-discrimination: the Inter-American Convention against Racism, Racial Discrimination, and Related Forms of Intolerance, AG/RES/2805 (XLIII-O/13) and the Inter-American Convention against All Forms of Discrimination and Intolerance AG/RES/2805 (XLIII-O/13. The reason for adopting two agreements lies in the opposition of some states to including sexual orientation among the prohibited grounds of discrimination. Apart from this issue, some of the provisions of the two treaties have been criticized for inconsistency with the American Convention's provisions on freedom of expression. *See* Raoof, "The Inter-American Anti-Discrimination Conventions and the Concealed Challenges Ahead," Oxford Human Rights Hub (July 3, 2013).

Important additional texts are the Inter-American Democratic Charter and the IACHR's Declaration of Principles on Freedom of Expression and the Principles and Best Practices on the Protection of Persons Deprived of Liberty in the Americas.

§ 4–18. DEMOCRACY AND HUMAN RIGHTS IN THE INTER-AMERICAN SYSTEM

In 1991, the OAS adopted Resolution 1080, or the Santiago Commitment, instructing the Secretary General to convoke the Permanent Council or the General Assembly in the event of "a sudden or irregular interruption" of the democratic process in a Member State, and to act to resolve that conflict. *See* O.A.S. General Assembly, Representative

Democracy, Res. 1080, Doc. No. AG/RES. 1080 (XXI-O/91) (June 5, 1991). A year later, on December 14, 1992, the OAS adopted the Washington Protocol to the OAS Charter, thereby becoming the first regional organization to allow suspension of a member state in the event that its democratically elected government is overthrown by force.

Before Resolution 1080 was superseded by the Washington Protocol, the OAS invoked it in four instances in which either a military coup, self-coup by an elected president, or severe civil-military crisis occurred: Haiti (1991), Perú (1992), Guatemala (1993), and Paraguay (1996). In the case of the coup d'état in Haiti in 1991, which overthrew a president elected in an internationally monitored election, the OAS relied on Resolution 1080 to deny recognition to coup leaders and to demand immediate reinstatement of the former government. The resolution urged Member States to "isolate" those holding power by imposing diplomatic and economic sanctions. *See* O.A.S. Meeting of Foreign Ministers, Support for the Democratic Government of Haiti, Res. 1, Doc. No. MRE/RES/1/91 (Oct. 3, 1991).

Subsequently, a Meeting of Foreign Ministers urged OAS member states to freeze the bank accounts of the coup members and to embargo the country except for humanitarian aid. In July 1993, the Haitian military leaders agreed to negotiations that led to the Governors Island Agreement; failure of the military to implement the agreement led to further UN and OAS action strengthening the sanctions. *See* Shelton, "Representative Democracy and Human Rights in the Western Hemisphere," 12 Hum. Rts. L.J. 353 (1991).

On September 11, 2001, the OAS General Assembly meeting in a special session in Lima, Perú, strengthened Resolution 1080 by adopting the Inter-American Democratic Charter ("Democratic Charter"). Unlike the Washington Protocol, the Democratic Charter is a declaration, which is formally nonbinding. Nevertheless, since it was adopted unanimously, it could be considered an authoritative interpretation of the Washington Protocol. *See* Observations of the Inter-American Juridical Committee on the Draft Inter-American Democratic Charter, CJI/Doc. 76/01, paras. 35–40.

Substantively, the difference between the two is that the Washington Protocol applies when a "democratically constituted government has been overthrown by force" whereas the Democratic Charter applies "[i]n the event of an unconstitutional alteration of the constitutional regime that seriously impairs the democratic order in a member state." The difference in wording was urged by Perú to ensure that the Democratic Charter would apply in the event of an *auto-golpe* such as Fujimori's.

The Democratic Charter proclaims that "[t]he peoples of the Americas have a right to democracy and their governments have an obligation to promote and defend it." It sets forth in detail the nature of democratic governance and the responsibilities of Member States. It reaffirms "that the promotion and protection of human rights is a basic prerequisite for the existence of a democratic society, and recognize[s] the importance of the continuous development and strengthening of the inter-American human rights system for the consolidation of democracy."

Part IV of the Democratic Charter concerns the actions to be taken by the OAS in response to "an unconstitutional interruption of the democratic order or an unconstitutional alteration of the constitutional regime that seriously impairs the democratic order in a member state." Article 19 calls coups d'état and similar takeovers "an insurmountable obstacle" to a government's participation in the Organization. In the event of an extraconstitutional taking of power, any Member State or the Secretary General may request the immediate convocation of the Organization's Permanent Council to undertake a collective assessment of the situation and to take such decisions as it deems appropriate. The General Assembly may resolve, by a two-thirds vote of the Member States, to suspend the membership of the state in question. The Democratic Charter procedure has been invoked twice, once in 2002 concerning Venezuela and again in 2009 after a coup d'état in Honduras.

In the case of Honduras, a Special OAS General Assembly convened to suspend immediately the right of the government to participate following the expulsion of President José Manuel Zelaya from power. The resolution instructed the OAS Secretary General "to reinforce all diplomatic initiatives and to promote other initiatives for the restoration of democracy and the rule of law in the Republic of Honduras and the reinstatement of President José

Manuel Zelaya Rosales." "No such initiative will imply recognition of the regime that emerged from this interruption of the constitutional order." The resolution also reaffirmed that Honduras "must continue to fulfil its obligations as a member of the Organization, in particular with regard to human rights," and urged "the Inter-American Commission on Human Rights to continue to take all necessary measures to protect and defend human rights and fundamental freedoms in Honduras." O.A.S. Gen Assembly, Resolution on the Suspension of the Right of Honduras to Participate in the OAS, Res. 2, Doc. No. AG/RES. 2 (XXXVII-E/09) (July 16, 2009).

On June 1, 2011, the OAS General Assembly voted 32–1 to readmit Honduras, following actions by the government to address the problems identified by the OAS. Ecuador was the only country in opposition, expressing concern about the lack of investigation and punishment of human rights abuses committed during and after the coup. While other states agreed that more needed to be done to improve Honduras's human rights record, they also expressed the belief that they could more effectively assert pressure on Honduras and hold it accountable if Honduras were readmitted to the international community. Some fifty nongovernmental organizations wrote a letter to OAS member states to express their opposition to the readmission because of alleged human rights violations. Subsequently, Honduras continued to appear in Chapter IV of the 2011 Annual Report of the Inter-American Commission on Human Rights, a chapter where serious concerns about human rights are discussed.

CHAPTER 5

THE AFRICAN AND OTHER REGIONAL SYSTEMS

Although the law and institutions of the European and Inter-American regional systems are the most advanced, others are developing, including in sub-regional organizations. This chapter first discusses the African region, then presents the emergent mechanisms in the Arab and Asian regions.

I. OVERVIEW OF THE AFRICAN SYSTEM

The African Charter on Human and Peoples' Rights—sometimes referred to as the "Banjul Charter"—was adopted in 1981 and entered into force on October 21, 1986. It established a system for the protection and promotion of human rights that was designed to function within the institutional framework of the Organization of African Union (OAU), a regional intergovernmental organization that came into being in 1963. In particular, the Charter created the African Commission of Human and Peoples' Rights ("African Commission"), which since its inauguration in 1987 has served as the principal regional human rights mechanism. The eleven-member Commission sits in Banjul, The Gambia and has responsibility for the protection and promotion of human and people's rights and the interpretation of the Charter.

In 2001, the OAU was replaced by a successor organization, the African Union (AU). The new African Union assumed the responsibilities of the

OAU, including the protection and promotion of human and peoples' rights in accordance with the African Charter. *See* Art. 3(h), Constitutive Act of the African Union, reprinted at 12 Afr. J. Int'l & Comp. L. 629 (2000) and available at http://www.au.int and at http://www.au2002.gov.za/docs/key_oau/au_act.htm.

While the Constitutive Act makes no explicit reference to the African Commission and no provision for any new human rights bodies, it does give a more prominent place to human rights. Member States express that they are "determined to promote and protect human and peoples' rights, consolidate democratic institutions and culture and to ensure good governance and the rule of law." The AU Objectives (Article 3) and Principles (Article 4) include the need to "promote peace, security and stability on the continent" with a recognized need to "encourage international co-operation, taking due account of the Charter of the United Nations and the Universal Declaration of Human Rights" and to "promote and protect human and peoples' rights in accordance with the African Charter on Human and Peoples' Rights and other relevant human rights instruments." States should promote gender equality, have "respect for democratic principles, human rights, the rule of law and good governance, respect the sanctity of life and condemn unconstitutional changes of government." *See* Isanga, "The Constitutive Act of the African Union, African Courts and the Protection of Human Rights: New Dispensation?," 11 Santa Clara J. Int'l L. 267 (2013).

The African Commission has continued to function in the role contemplated by the African Charter. A major institutional change in the African regional human rights system came with the adoption on 8 June 1998 of an Additional Protocol to the Charter on the establishment of an African Court on Human and Peoples' Rights (ACtHPR). The AU has sought to merge this human rights court with the AU Court of Justice, adopting in July 2008 a protocol of merger for the creation of an African Court of Justice and Human Rights (ACtJHRts). The Protocol of Merger requires fifteen ratifications to enter into force; as of 2016, only five states had approved it, and the ACtHPR continues as a separate entity. These developments are discussed in more detail at § 5–10, *infra.*

All but one of the 54 AU Member States are parties to the African Charter. The South Sudan, admitted as an AU member in July 2011, has neither signed nor ratified the Charter. The only African state not a member of the AU, and also not a party to the Charter, is Morocco, which left upon admission of Western Sahara as an AU Member State.

The text of the African Charter is reprinted at 21 I.L.M. 59 (1982) and is retrievable at http://www. achpr.org/instruments/achpr/. Details concerning the African Commission's activities may be found at www.achpr.org.

For general background, *see* L. Franceschi, *The African   Human   Rights   Judicial   System: Streamlining   Structures   and   Domestication Mechanisms Viewed From the Foreign Affairs Power*

(2014); M. Ssenyonjo, *The African Regional Human Rights System: 30 Years after the African Charter on Human and Peoples Rights* (2012); M. Evans and R. Murray, *The African Charter on Human and Peoples' Rights: The System in Practice, 1986–2006* (2nd ed. 2008); F. Viljoen, *International Human Rights Law in Africa* (2d ed, 2012); Mubiala, *Le Système Régional Africain de Protection des Droits de L'Homme* (2005); F. Ouguergouz, *The African Charter on Human and Peoples' Rights* (2003). For the Charter's drafting history, *see* K.O. Kufour, *The African Human Rights System: Origin and Evolution* (2010); Mbaye, "Introduction to the African Charter on Human and Peoples' Rights," *in* International Commission of Jurists, *Human and Peoples' Rights in Africa and the African Charter* 19 (1985); Gittleman, "The African Charter on Human and Peoples' Rights: A Legal Analysis," 22 Va. J. Int'l L. 667 (1982); Ramcharan, "The Travaux Préparatoires of the African Commission on Human and Peoples' Rights," 13 Hum. Rts. L.J. 307 (1992). Useful source material may be found in Heyns and Killander, eds., *Compendium of Key Human Rights Documents of the African Union* (3rd ed. 2007) and Beattie, Christou, Raymond & Starmer, eds., *Human Rights Manual and Sourcebook for Africa* (2005). For discussion of the examination of African states by the UN system, *see* Abebe, "Of Shaming and Bargaining: African States and the Universal Periodic Review of the United Nations Human Rights Council," 9 Hum. Rts. L. Rev. 1 (2009).

II. THE RIGHTS AND DUTIES

§ 5–1. INTRODUCTION

The African Charter differs from the European and American Conventions on Human Rights in a number of respects. First, the African Charter proclaims not only rights but also duties. Second, it codifies peoples' as well as individual rights. Third, in addition to guaranteeing civil and political rights, it gives equal emphasis to economic, social and cultural rights. Fourth, the treaty is drafted in a form that could permit the States Parties to impose extensive restrictions and limitations on the exercise of the rights it proclaims. Fifth, it establishes a periodic reporting system akin to procedures of U.N. treaty bodies. *See* Flinterman & Ankumah, "The African Charter on Human and Peoples' Rights," in H. Hannum (ed.), *Guide to International Human Rights Practice* 171 (4th ed. 2004).

The provisions of the Charter reflect the influence of UN human rights instruments as well as African traditions. Thus, it bears a stronger resemblance to the International Covenants of Human Rights than to the two other regional human rights treaties. The emphasis that the Charter places on African tradition finds expression in its preamble as well as in the form in which many of its rights and duties are articulated. The preamble speaks of "the virtues of [African] historical tradition and the values of African civilization which should inspire and characterize their reflection on the concept of human and peoples' rights." Other principles that inform the

African Charter are referred to in the following provision of the preamble:

> *Convinced* that it is henceforth essential to pay particular attention to the right to development and that civil and political rights cannot be dissociated from economic, social and cultural rights in their conception as well as universality and that the satisfaction of economic, social and cultural rights is a guarantee for the enjoyment of civil and political rights.

The emphasis on the right to development, which is a peoples' right, and the linking together of different categories of individual rights has its conceptual source in the standard-setting practices of the UN.

§ 5–2. INDIVIDUAL RIGHTS

The Charter contains a broad non-discrimination clause and an equal protection clause. It guarantees the right to life and it prohibits slavery as well as torture, cruel, inhuman or degrading treatment and punishment. It bars arbitrary arrest and detention as well as *ex post facto* criminal legislation and punishment. The Charter contains provisions designed to ensure due process of law and fair hearings. It guarantees freedom of thought, conscience and religion, the right to receive information, to express one's opinions, and freedom of association and assembly. Arts. 2–8. In addition to recognizing the right to freedom of movement, the right to leave any country and to return to one's own, the Charter prohibits mass expulsions of non-nationals "aimed at national, racial, ethnic or religious groups." Arts. 12(1), (2) and (5).

The Charter also guarantees the rights to property, work, equal remuneration for equal work, the enjoyment of "the best attainable state of physical and mental health" (Art. 16(1)), and the right to education. The provision which proclaims the rights to education and to take part in the cultural life of one's community also declares that "the promotion and protection of morals and traditional values recognized by the community shall be the duty of the State." Art. 17(3). A similar concept finds expression in Article 18, which characterizes the family as "the natural unit and basis of society" and declares, *inter alia,* that "the State shall have the duty to assist the family which is the custodian of morals and traditional values recognized by the community."

Besides providing that "the aged and the disabled shall . . . have the right to special measures of protection in keeping with their physical and moral needs," Article 18(3) also contains the following provision:

> The State shall ensure the elimination of every discrimination against women and also ensure the protection of the rights of the woman and the child as stipulated in international declarations and conventions.

Very few, if any, human rights treaties resort to this extremely liberal form of incorporation by reference of other international instruments.

The AU Member States have adopted several other significant regional human rights instruments, including (1) the 2003 Protocol to the African Charter on the Rights of Women in Africa, which entered into force in 2005, (2) the 1990 African Charter on the Rights and Welfare of the Child, which entered into force in 1999, and (3) the 1969 Convention Governing the Specific Aspects of Refugee Problems in Africa, which entered into force in 1974. The Protocol on the Rights of Women has been ratified by 36 of the AU Member States, and signed by another 15, but observers have criticized the level of compliance with its provisions. *See, e.g.,* Davis, "The Emperor is Still Naked: Why the Protocol on the Rights of Women in Africa Leaves Women Exposed to More Discrimination," 42 Vand. J. Transnat'l L. 949 (2009); Banda, "Protocol to the African Charter on the Rights of Women in Africa," in Evans and Murray, *The African Charter, supra*; Murray, "A Feminist Perspective on Reform of the African Human Rights System," 1 Afr. Hum. Rts. L.J. 205 (2001).

All but eight Member States are parties to the children's convention, but some have attached problematic reservations, including Egypt's reservation to the prohibition of child marriage. For a discussion of children's rights in Africa, *see* T. Kaime, *The African Charter on the Rights and Welfare of the Child: A Socio-Legal Perspective* (2009); P. Ankut, *The African Charter on the Rights and Welfare of the Child: Linking Principles with Practice* (2008); Mezmur, "The Ninth Ordinary Session of the African Committee of Experts on the

Rights and Welfare of the Child: Looking Back to Look Ahead," 7 Afr. Hum. Rts. J. 545 (2007).

Although the aforementioned catalog of individual rights is very extensive, some of the rights contain qualifications that seem designed to deprive the guarantee of much meaning. Article 8, for example, which proclaims "freedom of conscience, the profession and free practice of religion," declares that "no one may, *subject to law and order,* be submitted to measures restricting the exercise of these freedoms." (Emphasis added.) And Article 10(1) provides that "every individual shall have the right to free association *provided that he abides by the law.*" (Emphasis added.) Similarly, Article 9(2) articulates the right to freedom of expression by declaring that "every individual shall have the right to express and disseminate his opinions *within the law.*" (Emphasis added.) It should be noted, however, that other rights, particularly those which concern the physical integrity of the individual and due process, do not authorize the restrictions that are permitted with regard to the rights applicable to the exercise of political freedoms. The Commission has interpreted these clauses restrictively against the states, as discussed *infra* at § 5–9.

Noteworthy, too, is the fact that the African Charter does not contain a general derogation clause permitting the States Parties to suspend the enjoyment of certain rights during national emergencies or other exceptional circumstances. In *Commission Nationale des Droits de l'Homme et des Libertes v. Chad*, Comm. 74/92, 9th Annual Activities

Rep. (1995), the African Commission declined to imply the right of States to derogate: "The African Charter . . . does not allow for states parties to derogate from their treaty obligations during emergency situations. Thus, even a civil war in Chad cannot be used as an excuse by the State violating or permitting violations of rights in the African Charter." It reaffirmed this view in *Article 19 v. Eritrea*, Comm. 275/2003, 22nd Annual Activities Rep. Annex II, 15 IHRR 880 (2009) (no derogations are permissible even in time of war or emergency). *See generally* Sermet, "The Absence of A Derogation Clause from the African Charter on Human and Peoples' Rights: A Critical Discussion," 7 Afr. Hum. Rts. L. J. 143 (2007).

The Charter omits mention of several rights which have assumed importance in the European and Inter-American systems, including the right to privacy, the prohibition against forced or compulsory labor, and the right to vote and be elected to public office in periodic elections, although these rights have been implied by the Court as part of the "right to political participation" (In the Consolidated Matter of Tanganyika Law Society and the Legal and Human Rights Centre v. Tanzania, App. No. 009/2011; Reverend Christopher R. Mtikila v. Tanzania, App. No. 011/2011, Judgment of June 14, 2013) and by the African Commission as part of the right of self-determination (Kevin Mgwanga Gunme v. Cameroon, Afr. Comm'n HPR, Comm No 266/2003, EX.CL/529 (XV), 45th Ordinary Sess., Annex 4 (2009).

§ 5–3. PEOPLES' RIGHTS

The African Charter is unique in the scope it affords peoples' rights (sometimes called "solidarity rights") and in distinguishing these collective rights from those accorded to individuals. Among the peoples' rights it includes is the right of peoples to self-determination and to full sovereignty over their natural resources. Also on the list are the right to development, the right to peace and security, and "the right to a general satisfactory environment favourable to their development." Arts. 20, 23, and 24.

The right to development is formulated as follows: "All peoples shall have the right to their economic, social and cultural development with due regard to their freedom and identity and in the equal enjoyment of the common heritage of mankind." Art. 22(1). This and similar language found in the African Charter reinforces the AU's political agenda by giving it treaty status. Article 22(2) emphasizes that "States shall have the duty, individually or collectively, to ensure the exercise of the right to development." The African Commission has concluded that these rights, like all others in the Charter, are justiciable. *See* Social and Economic Rights Center v. Nigeria, Afr. Comm'n HPR Comm no. 155/96 (2001) AHRLR 60 (ACHPR 2001). For a detailed discussion of the right of self-determination, *see* Gunme v Cameroon, *supra*; Shelton, "Self-Determination in Regional Human Rights Law: From Kosovo to Cameroon," 105 Am. J. In'tl L. 60 (2011). *See also* Anyangwe, "Obligations of States

Parties to the African Charter on Human and Peoples' Rights," 10 Afr. J. Int'l & Comp. L. 625, 648 (1998); Bello, "Article 22 of the African Charter on Human and People's Rights," *in* E. Bello & B. Ajibola (eds.), *Essays in Honor of Judge Taslim Olawale Elias,* vol. I, at 447 (1991); Shelton, "Environmental Rights," in P. Alston, *Peoples Rights* 185 (2001).

§ 5–4. DUTIES

A distinguished African jurist and former vice president of the International Court of Justice, who played an important role in drafting the African Charter, points out that "in Africa, laws and duties are regarded as being two facets of the same reality: two inseparable realities." Mbaye, *supra,* at 27. Mbaye suggests that it should therefore come as no surprise to anyone that the African Charter proclaims duties as well as rights. Here it is worth recalling that the American Declaration on the Rights and Duties of Man and the Universal Declaration of Human Rights adopted the same approach, but that the drafters of the OAS and UN human rights treaties did not follow that course.

The duties that the African Charter proclaims fall into two broad categories. In the first group are duties which can be characterized as correlatives of rights. The other category might be described as restrictions on the enjoyment of rights disguised as duties. Article 27(2), for example, which declares that "the rights and freedoms of each individual shall be exercised with due regard to the rights of others, collective security, morality and common interest," appears to codify both categories of duties. Here it is evident that the scope of these duties or their impact on the rights guaranteed in the Charter would differ significantly depending upon whether an individual's rights were to be limited by the rights of others or by considerations of collective security; the latter type of duties appear to be dangerously vague. The contrast between these different types of duties is even more striking in Article 29, which imposes on the individual the duty "to respect his parents at all times, to maintain them in case of need" and "to preserve and strengthen social and national solidarity, particularly when the latter is threatened." Arts. 29(1) and 29(4). The first two duties differ very considerably from the third, which is an invitation to the imposition of unlimited restrictions on the enjoyment of rights.

Other types of duties reflect the African values which the Charter seeks to advance. Article 29(7) imposes the duty "to preserve and strengthen positive African cultural values in relation with other members of the society, in the spirit of tolerance, dialogue and consultation and, in general, to contribute to the promotion of the moral well-being of society." The catalog of duties which the Charter proclaims carries with it a risk of governmental abuse. The seriousness of this risk depends, in part, on the pace and success of the process of democratization in Africa, but also on the strength and independence of the regional human rights bodies. On this subject, *see* Makau Mutua, *Human Rights: A Political and Cultural Critique* at 82–92 (2002).

III. STATE OBLIGATIONS AND MEASURES OF IMPLEMENTATION

§ 5–5. INTRODUCTION

The obligations assumed by the States Parties to the African Charter and the measures of implementation or international supervision it establishes are modeled more on the two UN Covenants than on the American or European Conventions. As we shall see in §§ 5–8 and 5–9, *infra,* unlike the international mechanisms of protection of the two other regional systems, the African system was designed to address massive denials of human rights as well as individual violations.

§ 5–6. STATE OBLIGATIONS

The basic obligation of the States Parties to the African Charter is spelled out in Article 1. It provides that they "shall recognize the rights, duties and freedoms enshrined in this Chapter and shall undertake to adopt legislative or other measures to give effect to them." This provision is supplemented by the obligations contained in Articles 25 and 26. Article 25 calls for promoting, ensuring and respecting the rights and freedoms contained in the Charter, while Article 26 requires the States Parties to guarantee the independence of the courts. These obligations have proved important in limiting the ability of states to adopt broad restrictions on rights, as has Article 27(2). The latter, although written as an individual duty to exercise rights with due regard to the rights of others, collective security, morality and common interest, has instead been read to contain an exhaustive list of legitimate reasons for limiting guaranteed rights. *See* In the Mtikila v. Tanzania, *supra*, paras. 106–07.

Article 62 provides a technique of compliance monitoring, requiring the States Parties to report biennially "on the legislative or other measures" they have adopted to give effect to the rights recognized and guaranteed by the Charter. The task of reviewing these reports was assigned to the African Commission by the OAU Assembly in 1988, which examines them at public meetings. Although states began submitting reports in 1991, *see* § 5–7, *infra,* not all AU Member States have submitted the required reports and many are overdue. Although the process has not functioned as well as intended, this has had the beneficial impact of allowing the African Commission more time to deal with individual and interstate complaints. The process has also stimulated the creation and activities of local NGOs, who are invited to present shadow reports to the Commission. Rules of Procedure 74(2). *See* T.S. Bulto, "Beyond the Promises: Resuscitating the State Reporting Procedure under the African Charter on Human and Peoples' Rights," 12 Buff. Hum. Rts. L. Rev. 57 (2006); Viljoen, "State Reporting under the African Charter on Human and Peoples' Rights: A Boost from the South," 44 J. Afr. L. 110 (2000).

§ 5–7. THE AFRICAN COMMISSION ON HUMAN AND PEOPLES' RIGHTS

As indicated above, the Charter provides for a Commission, established within the institutional framework of the OAU (now the AU), "to promote human and peoples' rights and ensure their protection in Africa." Art. 30. The Commission's 11 members are elected by the AU's Assembly of Heads of States and Governments from a list of names presented by the States Parties. They serve six-year terms in their individual capacities rather than as government representatives. As in other human rights systems, there have been concerns about ensuring the independence of commissioners, some of whom in the past held high political offices at the national level. The AU in April 2005 issued a *note verbale* to Member States prescribing guidelines for nomination of members to the Commission, calling for the exclusion of senior civil servants and diplomatic representatives. The Commission's Rules of Procedure were revised in 2010 and approved at the Commission's 47th session.

The Commission meets twice a year in "ordinary session" and occasionally in "extraordinary session." It presents an "annual activity report" to the AU's Assembly. These reports are also available on the Commission's website. Nearly 400 African and non-African NGOs now have official observer status with the Commission. The Commission is perennially short of funds and staff.

The Commission has both promotional and quasi-judicial functions. Its promotional mandate is very broad and includes the power to undertake studies, convene conferences and workshops, initiate publication programs, disseminate information, consult with governments, and collaborate with national and local institutions concerned with human and peoples' rights. As part of this promotional effort, the Commission may "give its views or make recommendation to Governments." Art. 45(1)(a). This power enables the Commission to bring to the attention of individual governments "problem areas" revealed by its studies as well as by its review of states' implementation reports.

In recent years, the Commission has adopted a number of significant reports and resolutions regarding the human rights situations in particular regions or countries as well as in specific "thematic" areas. *See*, for example, Resolution 138 on the Human Rights and Humanitarian Situation in Zimbabwe (2008); Resolution 111 on the Right to a Remedy and Reparations for Women and Girls Victims of Sexual Violence (2007), and Declaration of Principles on Freedom of Expression in Africa, 16th Ann. Act. Rep. Annex VI (2002–2003).

The Commission has increasingly used "special mechanisms" including "thematic rapporteurs" and Working Groups. Unlike in the UN system, the thematic rapporteurs are members of the Commission, while the Working Groups include commissioners, independent experts and NGO representatives. Thematic rapporteurs have been designated for such topics as summary, arbitrary and extra-judicial executions; prisons and conditions of detention; the rights of women; freedom of expression; human rights defenders; and refugees, asylum seekers, migrants and internally displaced persons. *See* Harrington, "Special Rapporteurs of the African Commission on Human and Peoples' Rights," 1 Afr. Hum. Rts. J. 247 (2001). Working Groups have been established, *inter alia,* for indigenous populations and communities; economic, social and cultural rights; and the death penalty.

The Commission has also adopted a system of "country rapporteurs" and has carried out visits to individual countries (including, among others, Nigeria, Sudan, Burundi, Rwanda and Mauritania). *See*, for example, the Report on the Fact-Finding Mission to the Republic of Sudan (Darfur), 22nd Ann. Act. Rep. Annex III (2007).

The quasi-judicial powers of the African Commission may be divided into two parts: so-called interpretative powers and powers applicable to the resolution of disputes involving allegations of human rights violations. The Commission's interpretative powers are quite extensive and resemble the advisory jurisdiction of some international courts. The Commission has jurisdiction to "interpret all the provisions of the present Charter at the request of a State Party, an institution of the OAU or an African Organization recognized by the OAU." Art. 45(3). The Commission is also empowered, in the context of its promotional activities, "to formulate and lay down, principles and rules aimed at solving legal problems relating to human and peoples' rights and fundamental freedoms upon which African

Governments may base their legislations." Art. 45(1)(b). This grant of power combines quasi-legislative and quasi-judicial aspects, for it seems to permit the Commission to prepare draft legislation, to propose legal solutions to disputes and to articulate human rights standards by means of codification and interpretation. The Commission's other quasi-judicial powers—those relating to complaints charging violations of human rights—are discussed in § 5–8 and § 5–9, *infra*.

The powers conferred by Article 45 gain special importance because of the unusual lawmaking mandate embodied in Articles 60 and 61 of the Charter. Article 60 declares that "the Commission shall draw inspiration from international law on human and peoples' rights. . . ." It then lists, by way of illustration, the normative sources of that law, making specific mention of the UN and OAU Charters, the Universal Declaration of Human Rights, African instruments on human and peoples' rights and "other instruments adopted by the United Nations and by African countries in the field of human and peoples' rights as well as from the provisions of various instruments adopted within the Specialized Agencies of the United Nations of which the parties to the present Charter are members." This provision is amplified by Article 61, which permits the Commission "to take into consideration, as subsidiary measures to determine the principles of law," various other human rights agreements to which the Member States of the OAU are parties, together with "African practices consistent with international norms on human and peoples' rights, customs generally accepted as law, general principles of law recognized by African States as well as legal precedents and doctrine."

Consequently, in interpreting and applying the African Charter, the Commission has a broad mandate to draw on a vast body of law which Articles 60 and 61 incorporate by reference into the African Charter. These provisions grant the Commission an invaluable tool capable of ensuring that the interpretation of the Charter will keep up with the growth of general international law of human and peoples' rights.

§ 5–8. INTERSTATE COMPLAINTS

The African Charter establishes an inter-state complaint mechanism that provides for two distinct methods of dispute resolution.

The first permits a State Party that believes that another State Party has violated the Charter to bring the matter to that state's attention in a formal communication which is copied to the Commission. The respondent state has three months within which to present its reply. Art. 47. Either state may submit the matter to the Commission within three months from the date on which the original communication is received by the respondent state, provided that "the issue is not settled to the satisfaction of the two States involved through bilateral negotiations or by any other peaceful procedure." Art. 48; revised Rules 87–88. The Commission plays no active role in these proceedings and, if the states decide not to take their dispute to it, the negotiations could go on for years without producing any solution.

The second option open to a state is set out in Article 49 of the Charter. It permits a State Party to file an interstate complaint directly with the Commission without going through the procedure outlined above.

Once an interstate complaint has been formally referred to the Commission under Article 48 or 49, it is treated in an identical fashion and the procedures applicable to it are the same. Here the complaint is subject to the requirement that "all local remedies, if they exist, have been exhausted, unless it is obvious to the Commission that the procedure of achieving these remedies would be unduly prolonged." Art. 50.

Once the admissibility requirement has been met, the Commission embarks on a fact-finding process, designed to obtain all relevant information bearing on the case. The Commission is not limited to the information provided by the parties and is free to draw on "other sources." Art. 52. It may also hold hearings at which the states concerned have the right to present written and oral submissions. If an amicable solution "based on the respect of human and peoples' rights" has not been reached, the Commission must prepare a report, "stating the facts and its findings." Art. 52. This report is transmitted to the states concerned and the AU Assembly. In it the Commission may also address to the Assembly whatever recommendations it "deems useful." Art. 53. The Charter contains no provisions requiring any further action by the Assembly on the Commission's report, although presumably any state represented in the Assembly is free to raise the matter at its annual meetings.

The only inter-state complaint to date was submitted in February 1999 by the Democratic Republic of the Congo, alleging that military forces from Burundi, Rwanda and Uganda had committed serious human rights abuses on Congolese territory. In 2006, the Commission found the respondent states in violation of the African Charter. Democratic Republic of Congo v. Burundi, Rwanda, Uganda, Comm. 227/1999, 20th Ann. Act. Rep. Annex IV, 14 IHRR 867 (2007). Although the troops had withdrawn from DRC territory by the time of the decision, the Commission recommended payment of adequate compensation and reparation to the victims of human rights violations committed while those forces were in effective control of the provinces in question.

§ 5–9. INDIVIDUAL COMPLAINTS

The individual communications mechanism set forth in the Charter bears a striking textual resemblance to the relatively limited procedure established by the UN under ECOSOC Resolution 1503. *See* § 2–25, *supra.* As interpreted and applied by the Commission in practice, however, it has increasingly come to approximate the individual petition systems of the European and American Conventions. *See* Ouguergouz, *The African Charter, supra,* at 570–663.

The African Charter outlines a limited role for the Commission in regard to individual communications. Article 55 simply requires the Secretariat of the Commission to compile "a list of communications other than those [from] States Parties to the present Charter and transmit them to the members of the Commission." While this language does not specify that the communications may originate with private individuals, non-governmental organizations, and various other entities, the Commission has accepted and considered several hundred such communications to date, whether or not submitted by victims or their representatives, including some whose authors were not nationals of a State Party to the Charter. No communications may be received, however, concerning a State that is not a party to the Charter. *See* Rule 93 of the Rules of Procedure.

Article 58(1) permits the Commission to act only in relation to "special cases which reveal the existence of a series of serious or massive violations of human and peoples' rights." Like the so-called 1503 procedure, this system was intended to allow the Commission to consider communications alerting it to situations involving large-scale and wide-spread abuses. The concept of a series of serious violations was probably introduced to ensure that the Commission would not deal with isolated violations of the Charter. Conversely, even if a State Party is not engaging in massive violations of human or peoples' rights, a showing that it regularly commits or tolerates serious individual violations, whether related or not, might nonetheless bring the matter within the jurisdiction of the Commission. Rule 84 of the Rules of Procedure now provides that situations of serious or massive violation of human rights may either be brought to the AU Assembly of Heads of State or referred to the African Court.

None of the provisions relating to serious or massive violations has been used frequently, but in December 2015, acting on the request from the Peace and Security Council of the African Union, a delegation of the Commission undertook a fact-finding mission to the Republic of Burundi to investigate human rights violations that had taken place since April of that year. Earlier, the Commission undertook a similar investigation of human rights violations on site in Mali. *See* Report of the Fact-Finding Mission to the Republic of Mali, Afr. Comm'n HPR, June 2013, available at http://www.achpr.org/files/sessions/53rd/mission-reports/mali-fact-finding-2013/misrep_factfinding_mali_2013_eng.pdf.

The Commission has expanded its role considerably by interpreting Article 55 to allow it to consider communications that do not meet the "special case" criteria of Article 58. Instead of considering such communications only to inform it about situations of large-scale and wide-spread abuses, the Commission considers them individually on their own merits. Communications are subject to the admissibility requirements of Article 56, including the obligation to exhaust domestic remedies, the requirement that the claim must not be "based exclusively on news disseminated through the mass media," and the requirement that they be submitted "within a reasonable time" either following exhaustion of local remedies or "the date when the Commission is seized of the matter." Art. 56(4), (5) and (6). Admissibility is determined separately from the merits, and if the concerned State Party fails to respond within three months of the date of notification, the Commission may decide the merits of the issue presented. *See* revised Rules 107–110. The Commission also has the general authority to recommend provisional measures in appropriate cases "to avoid irreparable damage being caused to the victim of the alleged violation." Revised Rule 111(1). *See generally* Viljoen, "Communications under the African Charter: Procedure and Admissibility," in Evans and Murray, *The African Charter, supra.*

The Commission has to date considered several hundred such cases and taken decisions on the merits in many of them; to put this quantity in context, it is roughly equivalent to the number of judgments rendered by the European Court in a single year. The jurisprudence is however much less extensive than that issuing from many UN bodies and special procedures. The relatively small number of cases thus far means each decision of the Commission usually contains new elements of law and for that reason carries substantial weight. In addition to raising questions about the scope of rights and duties, many cases have involved procedural issues, including in particular the requirements for admissibility. Several have addressed the issue of exhaustion of domestic remedies. *See, e.g.,* Zimbabwe Lawyers for Human Rights and the Institute for

Human Rights and Development v. Republic of Zimbabwe, Comm. 293/2002, 24th Ann. Act. Rep. Annex II, 16 IHRR 253 (2009) (unduly prolonged domestic remedies do not require exhaustion).

Other decisions concern alleged violations of fundamental civil and political rights. For instance, the Commission has held that annulment of free and fair elections violates the right of citizens to participate in the government of their country, as well as their right freely to determine their political status, guaranteed by Article 13 of the Charter. Constitutional Rights Project and Civil Liberties Organization v. Nigeria, Comm. 102/93, 12th Ann. Act. Rep. Annex V (1999). With the adoption of the African Charter on Democracy, Elections and Governance by the Assembly in January 2007, it can be expected that the Commission will receive more cases involving fundamental civil and political rights. At its 42nd Ordinary Session in November 2007, the Commission called on AU Member States to ratify the new instrument, recalling that Article 13(1) of the African Charter on Human Rights provides that "every citizen shall have the right to participate freely in the government of his country, either directly or through freely chosen representatives in accordance with the provisions of the law." Res. 115 (XXXXII) 07. Promotion of "democratic principles and institutions, popular participation and good governance" is also among the specified goals of the AU under Article 3(g) of the Constitutive Act. By mid-2017, the new Democracy Charter had been signed by 28 Member States but ratified by only ten of them.

A particular focus of the Commission's attention has been the conditions necessary for a fair trial. A series of decisions has condemned the trial of civilians as well as military personnel by special military courts martial without possibility of appeal (for example, pursuant to "ouster" clauses depriving the ordinary courts of jurisdiction). *See, e.g.,* Constitutional Rights Project (in respect of Wahab Akamu, G. Adeaga and others) v. Nigeria, Comm. 60/91, 8th Ann. Act. Rep. (1995), 18 Hum. Rts. L.J. 28 (1997); International Pen, Constitutional Rights Project, Interights on behalf of Ken Saro-Wiwa Jr. and Civil Liberties Organization v. Nigeria, Comms. 137/94, 139/94, 154/96 and 161/97, 12th Ann. Act. Rep. Annex V (1998), 7 IHRR 274 (2000); Forum of Conscience v. Sierra Leone, Comm. 223/98, 14th Ann. Act. Rep. Annex V (2000); Law Office of Ghazi Suleiman v. Sudan, Comms. 222/98 and 229/99 (2003), 16th Ann. Act. Rep. Annex VII, 11 IHRR 237 (2004) (military courts should not try civilians or deal with offenses under the purview of ordinary courts). More generally, in Malawi African Association v. Mauritania, Comm. 54/91, 13th Ann. Act. Rep. Addendum (2000), the Commission stated that for an appeal to be effective the appellate jurisdiction must objectively and impartially consider both the elements of fact and law that are brought before it and whether failure to do so will constitute a violation of Article 7 of the Charter.

In Article 19 v. Eritrea, Comm. 275/2003, 22nd Ann. Act. Rept. Annex II (2007), 15 IHRR 880 (2008), the Commission held that the incommunicado detention of prisoners for over three years constituted a prima facie violation of due process and arbitrary deprivation of liberty. The decision builds on the Commission's earlier finding in Liesbeth Zegveld and Mussic Ephremr v. Eritrea, Comm. 250/2002, 17th Ann. Act Rep. Annex VII (2003), 12 IHRR 863 (2005), that "incommunicado detention is a gross human rights violation that can lead to other violations such as torture or ill-treatment or interrogation without due process safeguards. . . . The African Commission is of the view that all detentions must be subject to basic human rights standards."

The Commission has also considered cases involving allegations of physical and mental torture and inhuman or degrading treatment, indefinite detention and arbitrary arrest. *See, e.g.,* Free Legal Assistance Group et al. v. Zaire, Comm. 25/89 et al., 9th Ann. Act. Rep. (1996), 4 IHRR 89 (1997), 18 Hum. Rts. L. J. 32 (1997). It has held that detention without charge or possibility of bail violates Article 6 of the Charter, as does deprivation of liberty under a retroactive law and detention beyond the expiration of one's criminal sentence. Constitutional Rights Project and Civil Liberties Organization v. Nigeria, Comm. 102/93, 12th Ann. Act. Rep. (1998), 7 IHRR 259 (2000); Alhassan Abubakar v. Ghana, Comm. 103/93, 10th Ann. Act. Rep. (1996), 6 IHRR 823 (1999). *See also* the Commission's Resolution on Guidelines and Measures for the Prohibition and Prevention of Torture, Cruel, Inhuman or Degrading Treatment or Punishment in Africa, 16 Ann. Act. Rep. Annex VI (2002). It has also held that the politically motivated, summary deportation of long-term residents and long-term refugees violates Article 7. Amnesty International (on behalf of Banda and Chinula) v. Zambia, Comm. 212/98, 12th Ann. Act. Rep. (1999), 7 IHRR 286 (2000). More recently, the Commission condemned the mass expulsion of non-nationals in Institute for Human Rights Development in Africa v. Republic of Angola, Comm. 292/2004, 43rd Ord. Sess., 15 IHRR 180 (2008).

In several cases, the Commission has considered the procedural aspects of cases involving capital punishment. In its decision in Civil Liberties Organisation, Legal Defence Centre, Legal Defence and Assistance Project v. Nigeria, Comm. 218/98, 14th Ann. Act. Rep. (Annex V) (2001), it had stated that "the foreclosure of any avenue of appeal to competent national organs in a criminal case attracting punishment as severe as the death penalty clearly violates" Article 7 of the African Charter. In Interights et al. (on behalf of Mariette Sonjaleen Bosch) v. Botswana, Comm. 240/2001, 17th Ann. Act. Rep. Annex VII (2003), 12 IHRR 856 (2005), it held that the death penalty should only be imposed after full consideration of all the circumstances, including those related to the offense as well as the offender. Nonetheless, it observed, no rule of international law prescribes the circumstances under which the death penalty may be imposed, although it pointedly referred to the "the evolution of international law and the trend towards abolition of the death penalty." In November 2008, the Commission adopted Resolution 136, urging States Parties that still retain the death penalty to observe a moratorium on the execution of death sentences with a view to abolishing the death penalty (in conformity with its earlier Resolution 42 (XXVI) (1999)). It exhorted States Parties to the African Charter on Human and Peoples' Rights that still retain the death penalty to guarantee that every person accused of capital crimes benefits from all the guarantees of a fair trial included in the African Charter and in other relevant regional and international norms and treaties.

The Commission has also had occasion to address the question of self-determination under Article 20(1) of the Charter. The context involved a request by the Katangese Peoples' Congress for recognition as a liberation movement entitled to support and independence, and for an order requiring Zaire (as it was then known) to evacuate Katanga Province. The Commission concluded that the "case holds no evidence of violations of any rights under the African Charter." While recognizing that "all peoples have a right to self-determination," the Commission noted that there may be "controversy as to the definition of peoples and the content of the right" and acknowledged the relevance of the principles of sovereignty and territorial integrity.

> [S]elf-determination may be exercised in any of the following ways: independence, self-government, local government, federalism, confederalism, unitarism, or any other form of relations that accords with the wishes of the people but fully cognizant of other recognized principles such as sovereignty and territorial integrity.

Katangese Peoples' Congress v. Zaire, Comm. 75/92, 8th Ann. Activities Rep. (1995), at para. 4. Later, in the Gunme v. Cameroon case, *supra*, the Commission provided a lengthy discussion of self-determination, including the distinction between internal and external sovereignty.

The Commission has addressed the important question of permissible limitations on rights. As indicated above, the African Charter contains a number of provisions that permit rights to be limited or circumscribed by national law. Such "clawback clauses" have the clear potential for allowing governments to undermine the rights in question. In the eyes of the Commission, however, a narrow interpretation must be given to the clawback provisions. As stated in Media Rights Agenda, Constitutional Rights Project, et al. v. Nigeria, Comm. 105/93 et al., 12th Ann. Act. Rep. (1998), 7 IHRR at 271:

> International human rights standards must always prevail over contradictory national law. Any limitation on the rights of the Charter must be in conformity with the provisions of the Charter.

> In contrast to other international human rights instruments, the African Charter does not contain a derogation clause. Therefore limitations on the rights and freedoms enshrined in the Charter cannot be justified by emergencies or special circumstances.

The only legitimate reasons for limitations to the rights and freedoms of the African Charter are found in Article 27.2, that is that the rights of the Charter 'shall be exercised with due regard to the rights of others, collective security, morality and common interest.'

The reasons for possible limitations must be founded in a legitimate state interest and the evils of limitations of rights must be strictly proportionate with and absolutely necessary for the advantages which are to be obtained.

Even more important, a limitation may never have as a consequence that the right itself becomes illusory.

Id. at paras. 66–70.

More generally with respect to the relationship between the Charter and domestic law, the Commission stated that its jurisdiction does not extend to the adjudication of the legality or constitutionality of national laws. Rather, its function is to examine the compatibility of domestic law and practice with the Charter. "Where the Commission finds a legislative measure to be incompatible with the Charter, this obliges the State to restore conformity in accordance with the provisions of Article 1." Legal Resources Foundation v. Zambia, Comm. 211/98, 14th Ann. Act. Rep. Annex V (2001).

In Lawyers for Human Rights v. Swaziland, Comm. 251/02, 18th Act. Rep. Annex III, 13 IHRR 887 (2006), it emphasized the obligation of States to bring their domestic laws into conformity with the Charter. The Commission has also held that the failure of a State Party to ensure respect for the rights contained in the Charter constitutes a violation even if neither the State nor its agents were the perpetrators of the acts that resulted in the violation. Mouvement Burkinabé des Droits de L'Homme v. Burkina Faso, Comm. 204/97, 14th Ann. Act. Rep. Annex V (2001). To the same effect is Zimbabwe Human Rights NGO Forum v. Zimbabwe, Comm. 245/2002, 21st Ann. Act. Rep. Annex III (2006), 15 IHRR 832 (2008), where the Commission underscored that States have a "positive obligation" to prevent human rights obligations and to protect all persons within their jurisdiction from harmful actions even by private (non-state) actors.

Few of the Commission's decisions to date have addressed substantive issues concerning economic, social and cultural rights. In Free Legal Assistance Group et al. v. Zaire, *supra,* the Commission noted simply that the "failure of the Government to provide basic services such as safe drinking water and electricity and the shortage of medicines" constitutes a violation of Article 16, which guarantees every individual the best attainable states of physical and mental health. The same decision concluded that the government's closure of secondary schools and universities violated the right to education under Article 17. *Id.* Property rights were briefly addressed in Constitutional Rights Project et al. v. Nigeria, Comm. 105/93 et al., 12th Ann. Act. Rep. (1998) ("The right to property necessarily includes a right to have access to property of one's own and the right that one's property not be removed."). *See generally* A. Sisay, *The Justiciability Of Economic, Social And Cultural Rights In The African Regional Human Rights System: Theory, Practice And Prospect* (2013).

On linking civil and political rights with economic, social and cultural rights, *see* Ssenyonjo, "The Protection of Economic, Social and Cultural Rights under the African Charter," in *The Protection of Economic, Social and Cultural Rights in Africa* (Chirwa & Chenwi eds. 2016); Udombana, "Social Rights Are Human Rights: Actualizing the Rights to Work and Social Security in Africa," 39 Cornell Int'l L.J. 181 (2006); Mbazira, "Enforcing the Economic, Social and Cultural Rights in the African Charter on Human and Peoples' Rights: Twenty Years of Redundancy, Progression and Significant Strides," 6 Afr. Hum. Rts. L.J. 333 (2006); Odinkalu, "Analysis of Paralysis or Paralysis of Analysis? Implementing Economic, Social, and Cultural Rights Under the African Charter on Human and Peoples' Rights," 23 Hum. Rts. Q. 327 (2001).

Neither the Charter nor the Rules set forth specific procedures to implement the Commission's recommendations, and no formal mechanisms exist to compel States to abide by them. Still, the Commission's decisions and resolutions are included in its annual activity reports to the AU Assembly of Heads of State and Government, providing a measure of publicity and approbation. Unfortunately, due to objections of a few states which have objected to African Commission decisions taken against them, there have been no activity reports published since 2011. The issue of compliance with Commission decisions is garnering increased attention. *See* Murray & Long, *The Implementation of the Findings of the African Commission on Human and Peoples' Rights* (2015); Viljoen and Louw, "State Compliance with the Recommendations of the African Commission on Human and Peoples' Rights," 101 Am. J. Int'l L. 1 (2007).

§ 5–10. THE AFRICAN COURT OF HUMAN RIGHTS

The African Charter does not provide for a human rights court or any other judicial mechanism. In 1998, the Member States of the OAU agreed on a protocol to the Charter establishing an African Court of Human and Peoples' Rights to hear cases and resolve disputes concerning the interpretation and application of the Charter. *See* OAU/LEG/AFCHPR/ Prot.III, *reprinted at* 12 Afr. J. Int'l & Comp. L. 187 (2000). That protocol entered into force in January 2004 and the first set of eleven judges were elected in 2006. In 2003, the Member States of the African Union also agreed on the establishment of an African Court of Justice to be the main judicial organ of the organization, as provided in the Constitutive Act. *See* Protocol on the Court of Justice of the African Union, adopted July 9, 2003, available at https://au.int/web/en/ treaties/protocol-court-justice-african-union and http:// www.pict-pcti.org/courts/ACHPR_basic_doc.html.   In July 2004, the AU Assembly decided to integrate the two courts, and in January 2005, recommended a new protocol for the merged court. Protocol on the Statute of the African Court of Justice and Human

Rights, adopted in July 2008 at the 11th Ordinary Session of the AU Assembly, text available at http://www.african-court.org/en/. The Protocol will enter into force after approval by 15 Member States. To date only five have ratified it, leaving the Human Rights Court to function independently for the present.

The judges of the Court are elected, after nomination by their respective States, in their individual capacities and are expected to be African jurists of proven integrity and of recognized practical, judicial or academic competence and experience in the field of human rights. In practice, the parties to the African Court have opted for diversity and have elected the eleven members based on equitable representation of gender, the five major African regions, and the major legal systems.

The judges are elected for a six-year or four-year term renewable once. The judges of the Court elect a President and Vice-President of the Court among themselves who serve a two-year term. They can be re-elected only once. The President of the Court resides and works on a full time basis at the seat of the Court, while the other ten judges work on a part-time basis. The African Court has complained that its part-time basis is a challenge to the effective discharge of its mandate. Its quarterly sessions are said to be the only time when effective judicial work can be done and this has resulted in delays in processing cases. *See* Afr. Ct., Annual Report 2012, AU Doc. EX.CL/825(XXIV).

The African Court is unique thus far among regional courts in electing a majority of judges with prior domestic judicial experience, a factor that could affect both the procedures and the outcome of cases, as well as compliance over time. Judges with judicial experience may be better equipped to decide issues of evidence, procedure, and case management. In addition, if domestic courts are held in high regard this could enhance the reputation of the regional court. The prior judicial experience of African judges could also facilitate their relations with other judges in the national systems and encourage incorporation and application of the regional norms and court decisions. It is difficult to evaluate the impact at present, however, given the relatively short period in which the African Court has been operating.

The Human Rights Court has broad jurisdiction, encompassing "all cases and disputes submitted to it concerning the interpretation and application of the Charter, this Protocol and any other relevant Human Rights instrument ratified by the States concerned" (1998 Protocol Art. 3), which will certainly include the Charter on the Rights and Welfare of the Child, the Protocol on the Rights of Women in Africa, and any other human right instruments. Thus far, Article 3 has allowed the Court to find a state in violation of its human rights obligations set forth in the International Covenant on Civil and Political Rights and the 1993 Revised Treaty of the Economic Community of West African States (ECOWAS). *See* Konate v. Burkina Faso, Afr. Court HPR, App. 4/2013, judgment of Dec. 5, 2014.

The African system uniquely allows the possibility of either filing a communication at the African Commission or by-passing the Commission to file a case directly with the African Court. The latter is optional with State Parties, however, and by 2016, only seven of the thirty States Parties to the Protocol had made the declaration recognizing the competence of the Court to receive cases from NGOs and individuals. The seven states are Burkina Faso, Cote d'Ivoire, Ghana, Mali, Malawi, Rwanda and Tanzania. The thirty States that have ratified the Protocol establishing the Court are Algeria, Benin, Burkina Faso, Burundi, Cameroon, Chad, Cote d'Ivoire, Comoros, Congo, Gabon, Gambia, Ghana, Kenya, Libya, Lesotho, Mali, Malawi, Mozambique, Mauritania, Mauritius, Nigeria, Niger, Rwanda, Sahrawi Arab Democratic Republic, South Africa, Senegal, Tanzania, Togo, Tunisia and Uganda. The seat of the court is in Arusha, Tanzania.

The Court delivered its first judgment in 2009 following an application dated August 11, 2008 by Mr. Michelot Yogogombaye against the Republic of Senegal. As of January 2016, the Court had received 74 applications and finalized 25 cases. Many of the applicants represented themselves and most of the petitions were declared outside the jurisdiction of the Court because the States in question had not filed the requisite declaration accepting the right of individuals to sue. Other applicants had not exhausted local remedies and the matter was deemed inadmissible.

The Court issued its first judgment on the merits of a case in June 2013, a highly important case concerning political parties and elections in Tanzania. Mtikila v. Tanzania, *supra*. This is a sensitive issue in a region where States are still heavily committed to the doctrine of non-intervention in domestic matters. In the Mtikila case the government argued that the entire matter should be considered to raise political questions outside the Court's competence. The Court disagreed and gave little deference to Tanzania's arguments about the need to afford it broad discretion in organizing its political system, given its history and social values. The Court's ability and willingness to engage in this scrutiny may have been strengthened by the African Union's recent concern with building African democratic institutions, but the Court also invoked decisions of the African Commission and judgments of the other regional courts to support its reasoning. The second merits determination, Konate v. Burkina Faso, *supra*, concerned criminal defamation statutes and press freedoms, also a topic of concern throughout the region.

In its judgments, the African Court generally cites favorably and as persuasive decisions of the African Commission, invoking them before referring to judgments of other regional courts or to UN practice. *See* Case of Alex Thomas v. Tanzania, Afr. Court HPR, App. No. 005/2013, Judgment of Nov. 20, 2015. The African Court's unique practice in this respect may enhance the legitimacy and credibility of the African Commission, an important element in this system given the paucity of States that have accepted the Court's optional jurisdiction to receive individual communications. For most States in the region, the African Commission is the only regional venue available to victims alleging violations of their rights.

The African Court has perhaps the broadest remedial powers, being given the authority to "order any appropriate measures" to remedy a violation found. The African Court has issued only a few reparations judgments, but has shown concern to provide redress and enhance compliance. *See* Mtikila v. Tanzania (Reparations), App. No. 011/2011, judgment of June 13, 2014; Zongo et al v. Burkina Faso, App. No. 013/2011 (Reparations) judgment of June 5, 2015.

Like other human rights bodies, the African Court has suffered from a lack of resources. It began operating with no registry, offices, equipment, resources, budget or rules of Court. By 2014, the operational budget from Member States was US$6,607,632 with an additional US$2,362,315 for programs coming from external sources, including the European Union. The Court noted, however, that many staff members and judges continue to lack basic furniture and working equipment, necessitating a manual case management system. African Court HPR, Annual Report 2013, *supra.*

The Court has commented on the lack of action by the political bodies to promote compliance or to take action when there is non-compliance with its judgments by States Parties. Article 31 of the Protocol provides that the Court's annual report "shall specify, in particular, the cases in which a

State has not complied with the Court's judgment." Invoking "the spirit" of this provision, the Court decided not to wait for its annual report, but to notify the Executive Council of Libya's non-compliance with a March 15, 2013, order of provisional measures within two months of issuing the order. The Interim Report sent on May 17, 2013, noted the binding nature of provisional measures, extensions of time granted Libya to comply, and Libya's failure to do so. The Report went on to recommend action by the Assembly, including adoption of a decision calling upon all Member States to comply with and implement judgments and orders of the Court. The Court followed up by letter to the Executive Council on October 8, 2013, but no action was taken. In its Annual Report for 2013, the Court was outspoken in seeing non-compliance as a threat to its future. (Annual Report 2013, para. 110).

§ 5–11.   ECOWAS COURT OF JUSTICE

Human rights claims can now also be presented to the Court of Justice of the Economic Community of West African States. Fifteen nations are currently members of ECOWAS: Benin, Burkina Faso, Cape Verde, Côte d'Ivoire, The Gambia, Ghana, Guinea, Guinea-Bissau, Liberia, Mali, Nigeria, Senegal, Sierra Leone, and Togo. Under the 2005 Protocol to the revised treaty which provides the constitutive basis for ECOWAS, individuals can initiate proceedings before the Court. In addition, the ECOWAS Council empowered the Court to hear claims based on human rights principles. One of the first such cases was brought by Nigerian politicians complaining of violations of their human rights in the determination of election outcomes. In 2008, the Court issued a judgment ordering the release from unlawful detention of a journalist in The Gambia, based on articles 6 and 7 of the Banjul Charter. ECW/CCJ/JUD03/08 (June 5, 2008). *See generally* the Court's homepage at the African International Courts and Tribunals website at http://www.aict-ctia. org/courts_subreg/ecowas/ecowas_home.html; Alter, Helfer & McAllister, "A New International Human Rights Court for West Africa: The ECOWAS Community Court of Justice," 107 Am.J.In'tl L. 737 (2013).

IV. ARAB AND ASEAN DEVELOPMENTS

§ 5–12. THE ARAB CHARTER ON HUMAN RIGHTS

The founding Charter of the League of Arab States, adopted on March 22, 1945 does not mention human rights. There were six original members: Egypt, Iraq, Jordan, Lebanon, Saudi Arabia, and Syria. Yemen joined two months later. The Arab League currently has twenty-two members and four observers. On September 12, 1966, the Council of the League of Arab States adopted its first resolution on human rights, calling for the establishment of a steering committee to elaborate a program for the celebration of Human Rights Year in 1968. The Committee recommended the establishment of a permanent Arab Committee on Human Rights and the convening of an Arab Conference on Human Rights. The latter was held in December 1968 in Beirut. *See*

Galal, "The Arab Draft Charter for Human Rights," in Human Rights: Egypt and the Arab World 37 (17 Cairo Papers in Social Science, 1994).

A larger organization of all Islamic states, the Islamic Conference, endorsed human rights in its 1972 Charter, reaffirming the commitment of Islamic states to the UN Charter and fundamental human rights. On August 5, 1990, a meeting of foreign ministers of the Conference Member States adopted the Cairo Declaration on Human Rights in Islam. For an English translation of the Declaration, *see* UN GAOR, Fourth World Conference on Human Rights, 4th Sess., Agenda item 5, U.N. Doc. A/CONF. 157/PC/62/Add.18 (1993), available at http://www1. umn.edu/humanrts/instree/cairodeclaration.html. For a critique of the Declaration, *see* Mayer, "Universal Versus Islamic Human Rights: A Clash of Cultures or a Clash with a Construct?," 15 Mich. J. Int'l L. 307 (1994). For background on the Islamic Conference, *see* Hassan Moinuddin, *The Charter of the Islamic Conference and Legal Framework of Economic Cooperation among Its Member States* (1987). For early background on the League and its human rights activities, *see* Marks, "La commission permanente arabe des droits de l'homme," 3 Rev. Droit De L'Homme [Hum.Rts.J.] 101 (1970).

The League of Arab States initially approved an Arab Charter on Human Rights on September 15, 1994, building on earlier texts adopted by regional non-governmental and inter-governmental organizations. The text is reprinted in 18 Hum. Rts. L.J. 151 (1997). In 2001, by Resolution 6089 (March

12), the Council of the Arab League recommended that Arab states accelerate the process of signing and ratifying the 1994 Charter. Many Arab and international NGOs objected, however, complaining that the 1994 Charter did not correspond to international standards for human rights.

On March 24, 2003, the Council of the Arab League by Resolution 6032–129, encouraged the Permanent Arab Commission on Human Rights to "modernize" the Arab Charter on Human Rights. Amr Musa, Secretary General of the League, explained that the term "modernization" should be understood as the process to bring Charter provisions into compliance with international standards for human rights. The League adopted the revised Charter in May 2004, and it entered into force on March 15, 2008. The text is reprinted in 12 Int'l Hum. Rts. Rep. 893 (2005). *See also* Al-Midani, Cabanettes, Akram, "Arab Charter on Human Rights 2004," 24 B.U. Int'l L.J. 147 (2006); Mervat Rishmawi, "The Revised Arab Charter on Human Rights: A Step Forward?" 5 Hum. Rts. L. Rev. 361–62 (2005). However, the consistency of some provisions in the revised Charter with other human rights instruments has been questioned. *See, e.g.*, the January 30, 2008 statement by former UN High Commissioner for Human Rights Louise Arbour, available at http://www.cartercenter.org/resources/pdfs/peace/democracy/des/revised_Arab_charter_human_rights.pdf.

The text of the revised 2004 Arab Charter is an improvement over the 1994 version, although it retains its condemnation of "Zionism" in Article 2 on the right of self-determination. In addition, Article 3 on equality and non-discrimination adds that "[m]en and women have equal human dignity and equal rights and obligations in the framework of the positive discrimination established in favor of women by the Islamic Shariah and other divine laws and by applicable laws and international instruments." Nonetheless, its Preamble refers directly to international standards including those in the UN Charter, the UDHR, the ICCPR and the ICESCR, and its first stated objective is "to place human rights at the centre of the key national concerns of the Arab States."

The Arab Charter has a relatively lengthy list of non-derogable rights and protects the core rights of physical integrity, including the right to life, although it permits imposition of the death penalty for serious offenses. It contains prohibitions of torture and cruel, inhuman and degrading treatment, slavery and forced labor, non-consensual medical and scientific experimentation, and trafficking in human beings. The guarantees of civil and political rights include the rights of access to justice and to due process, freedom from ex post facto laws, prohibition of imprisonment for debt, freedom from double jeopardy, rights to privacy, family and home life, the right to a remedy, the right to political participation, freedom of association and assembly, freedom of movement, freedom of thought conscience and religion, freedom of information and opinion, and rights to property, nationality, and cultural manifestations. Economic and social rights are also protected by the Charter, including the right to work and form trade unions, the rights to social security, health, an adequate standard of living, education, and the right to development. The Charter is the only regional instrument to contain an article specifically on the rights of persons with disabilities.

States Parties are obligated to implement the rights contained in the Charter. An Arab Human Rights Committee, consisting of seven members serving in their personal capacities for a four-year term, is given the mandate to review periodic state reports on the measures taken to give effect to the rights contained in the Charter. The Arab Human Rights Committee may request from a State Party "additional information relating to the implementation of the Charter" (Article 48(2)), but neither inter-state nor individual complaints are provided for. For additional background, *see* M. Baderin, *International Human Rights and Islamic Law* (2003) and Al-Midani, "Human Rights Bodies in the League of Arab States," 3 Jinan Hum. Rts. J. 109–34 (2012). Information on the non-governmental Arab Organization for Human Rights (AOHR) is available at http://aohr.org.

The political changes and conflicts that have swept many countries in North Africa and the Eastern Mediterranean since 2010 have led the League of Arab States to take several new and stronger actions concerning human rights. On November 16, 2011, the League condemned the human rights violations of Syria's government. The League gave Syria three days to withdraw military forces from occupied cities, start talks between the government and opposition, and pave the way for an observer team of military peacekeepers and human rights experts. The government rejected the demand. Members then voted to suspend the state from participating in the League and overwhelmingly approved sanctions on November 28, 2011. The sanctions included freezing the assets of senior officials in the Syrian government, banning visits by those officials to other Arab nations, and ending transactions with the Syrian central bank.

The second major development was the decision of the League's Council in 2014 to adopt a Statute for an Arab Court of Human Rights, providing for the first time an institution to hear claims of human rights violations. *See* Decision of the Council of the League of Arab States, July 9, 2014, at https://www. acihl.org/article.htm?article_id=44. The Statute confirms "that Arab Conventions on human rights to which relevant States are party, including the Arab Charter on Human Rights, constitute the legal framework for the human being in the Arab States to enjoy and practice his/her rights," and that "the setting up of an Arab Court of Human Rights will help to achieve the purposes and objectives of the Arab Charter on Human Rights."

The Statute will enter into force after seven of the Member States have ratified it and deposited the instruments of ratification; the Statute will then be operative one year after it has entered into force. The headquarters of the Court will be in Bahrain, which has long promoted creation of the Court. An unofficial translation of the Statute by the Arab Centre for

International Humanitarian Law and Human Rights
Education is available at http://www.acihl.org/texts.
htm?article_id=44.

The Court is to have seven Judges, citizens of and
elected by the States Parties for a four-year term
renewable once. The Assembly of States Parties to
the Statute can increase the number of judges to
eleven if necessary. Perhaps for this reason, the
Statute contains the unusual provision that the
Assembly shall establish a list of reserve judges from
among the candidates that were not elected as
primary judges according to the number of votes that
they received. The qualifications for the candidates
nominated by the States Parties include integrity
and commitment to high moral values, competence
and experience in legal or judicial office, and having
the qualifications required for appointment in the
highest judicial or legal offices in their countries.
Experience in the field of human rights is "preferred."
The Court's president is to serve full time and
appoint the registrar and other members of the
registry.

The Court's jurisdiction is to extend to all "suits
and conflicts" resulting from the implementation and
interpretation of the Arab Charter of Human Rights,
or any other Arab convention in the field of human
rights involving a Member State (Statute, art. 16).
There will be no right of individual petition, however.
The Statute provides that cases may be brought on
the basis of diplomatic protection by the state of
nationality of the victim of an alleged violation. In
addition, State Parties can accept, when ratifying or

acceding to the Statute or at any time later, that one or more NGOs that are accredited and working in the field of human rights in the state whose subject claims to be a victim of a human rights violation has access to the Court (Statute art. 19). Admissibility of cases will require exhaustion of local remedies, filing within six months of the alleged violation, and the absence of complaint to any other "regional human rights court" (Statute art. 18). The last-mentioned criterion clearly includes the African Court of Human and Peoples' Rights, and might also be interpreted to include Africa's ECOWAS court. No other regional court has jurisdiction over Member States of the League.

Non-party states can accept jurisdiction for a particular case (Statute art. 20). The Court will also have the power to issue advisory opinions regarding any legal issue related to the Charter or to any other Arab convention on human rights, but only upon request of the League of the Arab State's Assembly or any of its subsidiary organizations or authorities.

Several unique provisions are included in the Statute. First, the Court will be required to hold public hearings in every case, unless the parties request or the Court decides it is in the interest of justice to do otherwise. Second, the Court will have a mandatory sixty days in which to enter a judgment after the end of its deliberations. Third, article 27 of the Statute provides a lengthy list of grounds to ask the Court to reconsideration a decision. Finally, and most problematic for the independence of the Court, its Rules of Court must be submitted to the Assembly of States Parties for approval.

§ 5–13.   ASEAN

For the Asia-Pacific region as a whole, no human rights system exists, perhaps because of the lack of geographic, political and cultural proximity of the many countries that are located from the Caucasus Mountains to the eastern Pacific Ocean. Most efforts have been mounted, therefore, in organizations existing at the sub-regional level. One early non-governmental effort resulted in a 1983 document entitled "The Declaration of Basic Duties of ASEAN Peoples and Governments." The United Nations Center for Human Rights held annual government workshops during the 1990s for officials from countries in the Asia-Pacific region. *See, e.g.,* United Nations, *Fourth Workshop on Regional Human Rights Arrangements in the Asian and Pacific Region*, HR/PUB/96/3 (1996). The workshops produced National Action Plans and programs for human rights education.

The Association of South-East Asian Nations (ASEAN) was established on August 8, 1967. The 10 current Member States are Brunei Darussalam, Cambodia, Indonesia, Laos, Malaysia, Myanmar, Philippines, Singapore, Thailand, and Vietnam. The secretariat is based in Jakarta, Indonesia. For most of its history the organization lacked a constituting treaty. On the 40th Anniversary of the founding of ASEAN, July 30, 2007, a Charter was completed, establishing a legal and institutional framework for

ASEAN. The Charter was ratified by all ten Member States and entered into force on November 19, 2008. *See* http://asean.org/asean/asean-charter/.

The Charter provides the basis for human rights activities in this region. The Charter's Preamble specifies the States Parties' adherence "to the principles of democracy, the rule of law and good governance, respect for and protection of human rights and fundamental freedoms." Among the purposes of ASEAN, set forth in Article 1, are "to strengthen democracy, enhance good governance and the rule of law, and to promote and protect human rights and fundamental freedoms, with due regard to the rights and responsibilities of the Member States of ASEAN." Art. 1(7). Article 2's principles include respect for fundamental freedoms, the promotion and protection of human rights, and the promotion of social justice" (Art. 2(i)) as well as upholding the UN Charter and international law, including international humanitarian law, "subscribed to by ASEAN Member States." Art. 2(j). Respect for the different cultures, languages and religions is called for, while emphasizing common values in the spirit of unity in diversity. Art. 2(*l*).

ASEAN Charter Article 14, which calls for establishing an ASEAN human rights body, was implemented through the creation of the ASEAN Inter-Governmental Human Rights Commission (AICHR) whose Terms of Reference (TOR) were approved by the ASEAN Foreign Ministers. Terms of Reference of the ASEAN Intergovernmental Human Rights Commission, July 20, 2009, http://www.ref

world.org/docid/4a6d87f22.html. Unlike individuals elected to other regional bodies, the AICHR members are not appointed in their personal capacities; instead, each serves at the pleasure of his or her government. AICHR, TOR, Article 5(2),(6). Member States are obliged to pay "due consideration to gender equality, integrity and competence in the field of human rights," but in practice most Commissioners have been current or former government officials. They must act by consensus and have limited powers conferred by the TOR. *See* http://www.aseansec.org.

The TOR lists the purpose of AICHR as follows: "To promote and protect human rights and fundamental freedoms of the peoples of ASEAN." Another purpose is to uphold specific international standards contained in "international human rights instruments to which ASEAN Member States are parties." The promotion work is to be done "within the regional context, bearing in mind national and regional particularities and mutual respect for different historical, cultural and religious backgrounds, and taking into account the balance between rights and responsibilities." The 'promotional' mandate and functions include enhancing public awareness of human rights, promoting capacity building, encouraging Member States "to consider acceding to and ratifying international human rights instruments" and promoting implementation of "ASEAN instruments related to human rights." Although protection is mentioned, that mandate has not been spelled out through the grant of specific functions and powers. Notably, in late March 2010, during the AICHR's first formal session in Jakarta, efforts by families of journalists massacred in Maguindanao, Philippines, to have the Commission receive a formal complaint and investigate the incident were rejected, the Commission being unwilling to imply a power not formally granted in the TOR.

ASEAN also created a Commission on the Promotion and Protection of the Rights of Women and Children (ACWC) and a Committee on the Implementation of the Declaration on the Protection and Promotion of the Rights of Migrant Workers (ACMW). *See* http://www.asean.org/wp-content/uploads/images/2012/Social_cultural/ACW/TOR-ACWC.pdf and http://www.asean.org/wp-content/uploads/images/archive/23062.pdf. Like the AICHR, these human rights bodies are composed of governmental representatives.

On November 18, 2012, the Heads of State of ASEAN adopted the ASEAN Human Rights Declaration clarifying the AICHR's mandate. *See* http://www.asean.org/storage/images/ASEAN_RTK_2014/6_AHRD_Booklet.pdf. Although the AICHR was responsible for drafting the ASEAN Declaration, the actual drafting was done by a group of human rights experts appointed by the AICHR. The Working Group's terms of reference were not made public and drafts of the Declaration remained confidential, although some versions were leaked. AICHR held two regional consultations with civil society organizations late in the drafting process and some individual members of AICHR organized national consultations. Civil society organizations and the UN

High Commissioner for Human Rights criticized the process for its lack of openness.

The 2012 ASEAN Declaration revived the question of regional diversity in part because of the methodology used for its drafting and in part because of critics' claims that some of its provisions fell below global standards. Nonetheless, the Preamble reaffirms adherence to the ASEAN Charter, in particular respect for and promotion and protection of human rights and fundamental freedoms "as well as in the principles of democracy, the rule of law and good governance," and a "commitment to the Universal Declaration of Human Rights, the Charter of the United Nations, the Vienna Declaration and Programme of Action, and other international human rights instruments to which ASEAN Member States are parties."

ASEAN Declaration Articles 10 and 26 affirm all of the civil and political rights and all of the economic, social and cultural rights in the UDHR, as well as the specific rights contained in the ASEAN Declaration itself. Several provisions are quoted verbatim from the UDHR, including Articles 3, 5 and 14, which mirror UDHR Articles 5, 6 and 8, concerning the right to recognition before the law, the right to an enforceable remedy and the prohibition of torture and cruel, inhuman and degrading treatment.

Other provisions are expressed in slightly different terms, but with no change in the scope or meaning, while a few add new dimensions to UDHR rights, including the reference to human trafficking in the Article 13 provision banning slavery and servitude, and the specific mention of the problem of child labor in Article 27, which concerns the right to work. The Declaration also mentions the rights of the elderly, persons with disabilities, and migrant workers. Other new elements include explicit mention of the rights of those suffering from communicable diseases, including HIV/AIDS, and the right to reproductive health within the provision on the right to health (Article 29). Article 28 provides that the right to an adequate standard of living includes the right to safe drinking water and sanitation. More generally, Article 7 echoes the language of the 1993 Vienna Declaration in proclaiming all human rights to be universal, indivisible, interdependent and interrelated, to be treated in a fair and equal manner, on the same footing and with the same emphasis. At the same time, the Declaration notes that the regional and national context must be considered in the realization of human rights, also reflecting the outcome of the Vienna Conference. Among the omissions, the ASEAN Declaration is notable in not mentioning freedom of association.

Importantly, the ASEAN Declaration is seen as a precursor to a formal treaty for the region, as has happened with human rights declarations at the UN and in other regional systems. On the drafting and contents of the Declaration, *see* Catherine Shanahan Renshaw, The ASEAN Human Rights Declaration 2012, 11 Hum. Rts L. Rev. 3 (2013); V. Muntarbhorn, *Unity In Connectivity?: Evolving Human Rights Mechanisms In The ASEAN Region* (2013).

Another sub-regional organization, the South Asian Association for Regional Cooperation (SAARC), was established in 1985 to promote regional cooperation between the Member States, but local conflicts have limited its ability to act. The Member States of SAARC are Bangladesh, Bhutan, India, Maldives, Nepal, Pakistan, and Sri Lanka. Its charter makes no mention of human rights and it currently does not have a human rights mechanism, but in 2002, the organization adopted two treaties linked with specific human rights issues: the SAARC Convention on Preventing and Combating Trafficking in Women and Children for Prostitution and the SAARC Convention on Regional Arrangements for the Promotion of Child Welfare in South Asia. Subsequently, in 2004, SAARC adopted the SAARC Social Charter which addresses many economic, social, and cultural rights. Finally, on February 8, 2011, SAARC adopted a Charter of Democracy which expresses, inter alia, a "shared commitment to the rule of law, liberty and equal rights of all citizens" and "reaffirm[s] faith in fundamental human rights and in the dignity of the human person as enunciated in the Universal Declaration of Human Rights and as enshrined in the respective Constitutions of the SAARC Member States." For a commentary written before adoption of the Charter of Democracy, *see* Surya Deuja, Establishing a Robust Regional Human Rights Mechanism in South Asia, 6 Asian Hum.Rts. Defender 4 (2010).

CHAPTER 6

INCORPORATION AND APPLICATION OF HUMAN RIGHTS IN THE UNITED STATES

I. INTRODUCTION

This chapter examines the laws and governmental policies of the United States as they relate to the domestic incorporation and application of international human rights law. It addresses questions relating to U.S. ratification of human rights treaties, congressional legislation designed to promote human rights abroad, and the application of international human rights law by U.S. courts. Unlike many other countries, the United States lacks a single national institution (in either the executive or legislative branches) with responsibility for overseeing the implementing of its human rights obligations, so that the function is more diffuse than in many other countries and has fallen largely to the courts.

Overall, the United States position on respecting international human rights has been marked by contradictions. On the one hand, protection of individual rights and liberties has been a guiding national principle since the nation's founding. The United States was among the strongest proponents of the human rights movement and a leader in the formulation of the essential human rights instruments in the period following World War II, and it has continued to advocate strongly for human rights at the international level. On the other hand, it refused for decades to ratify any major international human rights treaty and, although it has adhered to a number of them in recent years, it still lags behind most Western democracies.

The United States has strongly supported UN efforts to promote human rights, but for some years it declined to participate in the newly-established Human Rights Council (finally standing for election in early 2009 and again in 2012 and 2016). As a matter of policy, it has given short shrift to economic, social and cultural rights while strongly endorsing civil and political rights. It generally does not submit itself to treaty-based mechanisms permitting individual petitions, but it was among the first countries of the world to condition foreign aid on the recipients' compliance with human rights standards. Those laws continue to serve today as the legal foundation of the country's human rights foreign policy. Other nations have also looked to those laws as models for shaping their own legislation on the subject.

Even though the United States emerged from the Second World War as one of the strongest advocates of a treaty-based international system for the protection of human rights, official U.S. policy on the subject soon became one of complete non-participation, largely as the result of the Cold War and fears of an emergent "world government." This policy was formally reversed in the 1960's. *See* Buergenthal, "International Human Rights: U.S. Policy and Priorities," 14 Va. J. Int'l L. 611 (1974).

The years 1973–74 marked the revival of U.S. interest in and commitment to an effective international human rights system. During that period, the U.S. Congress began to address the subject and laid the legislative foundation for America's current human rights policy. *See* Committee on Foreign Affairs, Human Rights in the World Community: A Call for U.S. Leadership (U.S. House of Representatives, 1974).

The Carter administration made human rights the centerpiece of its foreign policy. Although the Reagan administration initially showed little enthusiasm for the subject, it gradually recognized that it was in the national interest to maintain the promotion of human rights as an important item on its foreign policy agenda. Its human rights policy was amplified by President Reagan's Democracy Initiative, which focused on support for democratic institutions and elections. This approach was strengthened in the administration of President George H.W. Bush and pursued by the Clinton administration. The latter expanded the policy to include, in addition to promoting human rights, bolstering the rule of law and democracy, strengthening the rights of labor, and emphasizing the protection of religious freedom.

The two administrations of President George W. Bush exhibited considerably less enthusiasm for participating in human rights institutions (as well as for international law and organizations as a whole). While vigorously promoting certain goals (such as religious freedom) as a matter of policy, the United States was widely criticized for having engaged in practices as part of its "war on terror" that were manifestly contrary to basic human rights principles, for example by conducting "extraordinary renditions," unlawful detentions, and treatment of detainees in violation of the proscriptions against torture and cruel, inhuman and degrading treatment or punishment.

After taking office in January 2009, the new Obama administration proclaimed a renewed commitment to international human rights and succeeded in claiming a seat on the UN Human Rights Council. It took a number of steps to reverse the policies and practices of its predecessor, including trying to close the detention camp at Guantanamo Bay, and indicated an intent to seek the Senate's advice and consent to pending human rights treaties, in particular the Convention on the Elimination of All Forms of Discrimination Against Women. However, neither goal had been achieved by the end of the administration's second term.

More generally, the Obama administration gave special emphasis to advancing the rights of specific groups (including women, the LGBT community, persons with disabilities, and ethnic minorities), preventing mass atrocities, opposing gender-based violence and human trafficking, and promoting the freedom of religion, assembly and the press. *See, e.g.,* "Obama Administration Leadership on International Human Rights" at https://www.whitehouse.gov/the-press-office/2013/12/04/fact-sheet-obama-administra tion-leadership-international-human-rights and "Promoting and Protecting Religious Freedom Around the Globe" at https://www.whitehouse.gov/the-press-office/2016/08/10/fact-sheet-promoting-and-protecting-religious-freedom-around-globe. Although the Obama administration often criticized human rights abuses committed by other governments, domestic critics frequently took issue with its emphasis on "soft power" and its failure to achieve concrete results. *See generally* Fellmeth, "Leading (A Bit) From Behind: The United States and International Human Rights Law," 40 N.C. J. Int'l L. & Com. Reg. 977 (2015).

Despite the fact that these administrations all acknowledged (to varying degrees) the need to infuse human rights concerns into the foreign policy agenda of the United States and in fact did just that, none of them escaped justified criticism for the manner in which they at times implemented or failed to implement that policy.

Current statements and documents related to administration policy can be found on the website of the U.S. State Department at http://www.state.gov/g/drl/hr. *See also* D. Shelton, ed., *International Law and Domestic Legal Systems: Incorporation, Transformation, and Persuasion* (2011).

II. THE UNITED STATES AND HUMAN RIGHTS TREATIES

§ 6–1. INTRODUCTION

Until 1988, the United States had not ratified any major international human rights treaty. That year the Senate gave its advice and consent to the ratification of the Genocide Convention; President

Reagan ratified it shortly thereafter. The Genocide Convention had been submitted to the U.S. Senate by President Truman in 1949 and was resubmitted by President Nixon more than two decades later. President Carter also signed and submitted to the Senate five human rights treaties but failed to obtain its consent to their ratification. *See* § 6–3 *infra.*

The Senate's 1988 action on the Genocide Convention marked a turning point in U.S. policy towards human rights treaties. In 1992, the United States ratified the International Covenant on Civil and Political Rights. *See* Stewart, "U.S. Ratification of the Covenant on Civil and Political Rights: The Significance of the Reservations, Understandings and Declarations," 14 Hum. Rts. L.J. 77 (1993). Two years later it ratified the International Convention on the Elimination of All Forms of Racial Discrimination and the Convention Against Torture and Other Cruel, Inhuman or Degrading Treatment or Punishment. *See* Stewart, "The Torture Convention and the Reception of International Criminal Law Within the United States," 15 Nova L. Rev. 449 (1991).

Of course, as a member of the United Nations and the Organization of American States, the United States had earlier assumed various treaty-based human rights obligations enunciated in the respective Charters of those organizations. It is also a party to the 1949 Geneva Conventions on international humanitarian law (but not to the two 1977 Protocols Additional). In 1999, the United States signed and ratified ILO Convention 182 on the

Worst Forms of Child Labor, and in 2002 it adhered to the two protocols to the Convention on the Rights of the Child, one on the involvement of children in armed conflict and the other the sale of children, child prostitution and child pornography. In 2005, it also ratified the third CRC Protocol to Prevent, Suppress and Punish Trafficking in Persons, Especially Women and Children.

Some of the treaties the United States has signed but thus far not ratified include the International Covenant on Economic, Social and Cultural Rights, the Convention on the Elimination of All Forms of Discrimination Against Women, the American Convention on Human Rights, the Optional Protocols to the Covenant on Civil and Political Rights, the Convention on the Rights of the Child, and the Convention on the Rights of Persons with Disabilities.

Recent efforts to obtain the Senate's advice and consent to ratification of the Women's Convention and the Disabilities Convention proved unsuccessful. At the beginning of 2017, it is unclear whether renewed efforts will be undertaken to ratify either in the foreseeable future. The Trump administration's human rights policy remains to be articulated. Nonetheless, it is worth examining the U.S. position regarding domestic implementation of the human rights treaties which the U.S. has ratified and its practice of attaching a variety of reservations. The following sections put the main issues in their historical, constitutional and political contexts.

§ 6–2. TREATIES AND THE
U.S. CONSTITUTION

Article VI clause 2 of the U.S. Constitution provides, inter alia, that "this Constitution, and the Laws of the United States which shall be made in Pursuance thereof; and all Treaties made, or which shall be made, under the Authority of the United States, shall be the supreme Law of the Land. . . ." This provision has been interpreted to mean that federal statutes and the treaties which have been duly ratified have the same normative rank under the Constitution. In the case of conflict between a federal statute and a ratified treaty provision (at least a treaty provision that is "self-executing" and therefore does not require additional implementing legislation), the later in time prevails as far as domestic law is concerned. Whitney v. Robertson, 124 U.S. 190 (1888); Bond v. United States, ___ U.S. ___, 134 S.Ct. 2077 at 2098 n.6 (2014); Restatement (Third) Foreign Relations Law § 115. These issues are discussed in more detail in §§ 6–11 and 6–12 *infra*.

It is also no longer disputed that a treaty provision may not be given effect as U.S. domestic law if it conflicts with the Constitution. Reid v. Covert, 354 U.S. 1 (1957); Restatement (Third) Foreign Relations Law § 302. As federal law, self-executing treaties supersede all inconsistent state laws and, unless they contain provisions to the contrary, they may also federalize a subject that heretofore has been governed by state law. Missouri v. Holland, 252 U.S. 416 (1920); United States v. Pink, 315 U.S. 203

(1942). Whether legislation implementing non-self-executing treaties has that effect is a matter of legislative intent, at least in the first instance. *See* Bond v. United States, ___ U.S. ___, 134 S.Ct. 2077 (2014).

As discussed in the following section, the place treaties have in U.S. law and the consequences flowing from it have in the past played a major role in determining the willingness of the U.S. Senate to approve the ratification of human rights treaties.

§ 6–3. THE U.S. SENATE AND HUMAN RIGHTS TREATIES

Some historical background is helpful for understanding implementation of human rights treaties in the United States. When World War II ended in 1945 and the United Nations was established, racial segregation and a variety of other forms of discrimination were either legally mandated or not unlawful in the United States. Much of the law codifying *de jure* racial discrimination was state law, most of it in the South. Segregation was practiced and enforced though a variety of means, including racially segregated schools, anti-miscegenation statutes, poll taxes, and segregated public services and accommodations. A coalition of Southern Democrats and Conservative Republicans in the U.S. Congress made changing this situation by federal legislation extremely difficult.

The political groups dedicated to doing away with *de jure* racial segregation and other forms of discrimination recognized that the human rights provisions of the UN Charter and the UN treaties then being drafted might be used to strike down the laws that Congress was unwilling to repeal or nullify. Among the first judicial suggestions that the UN Charter, as a duly ratified treaty of the United States, was a federal law that outlawed racial discrimination, were the concurring opinions of Justices Black and Murphy in the U.S. Supreme Court case Oyama v. California, 332 U.S. 633, at 649–50 and 673 (1948). They relied on Articles 55 and 56 of the UN Charter, which impose on the Organization and its Member States the obligation to "promote . . . universal respect for, and observance of, human rights and fundamental freedoms for all without distinction as to race, sex, language or religion."

The domestic legal effect of this obligation was faced squarely in Sei Fujii v. California, 38 Cal.2d 718, 242 P.2d 617 (1952). Here, an intermediate California state court held that California's Alien Land Law, by discriminating against aliens of Asian origin, was unenforceable because it violated the human rights provisions of the UN Charter. The court reasoned that the Charter, being a treaty of the United States, was equal in rank to a federal statute and thus superseded any inconsistent state legislation. The Supreme Court of California rejected this view. It ruled that the human rights provisions of the UN Charter were non-self-executing (by which it meant that the provisions did not "create rights and duties in individuals," see 38 Cal. at 722) and, as such, could not supersede state law unless and until they were implemented by Congressional legislation.

(The Court went on to hold, however, that the challenged state law violated the Fourteenth Amendment of the U.S. Constitution.) Since no appeal was taken from this ruling, the holding on the applicability of the Charter's human rights provisions was not presented to the U.S. Supreme Court. For further discussion of *Sei Fujii, see* L. Sohn & T. Buergenthal, *International Protection of Human Rights* 944 (1973); David Sloss, *The Death of Treaty Supremacy: An Invisible Constitutional* Change (2016).

The Sei Fujii decision did not allay the fears of those who saw UN human rights treaty provisions as a threat to discriminatory state legislation, which had thus far withstood constitutional challenge. The clearest warning was sounded by Senator John W. Bricker of Ohio, who spelled out the danger to his conservative colleagues in the following terms: "if the [intermediate court opinion in the] Fujii case should eventually be affirmed by the United States Supreme Court, or if the principle announced therein should be sustained, literally thousands of Federal and State laws will automatically become invalid." To avert this danger, "something must be done to prevent treaties from having such far-reaching and unintended consequences." 98 Cong. Rec. 911 (1952). What needed to be done, according to Senator Bricker, was the adoption of an amendment to the U.S. Constitution that would limit the treaty-making power. *See* D. Tananbaum, *The Bricker Amendment Controversy: A Test of Eisenhower's Political Leadership* (1988); Kaufman & Whiteman, "Opposition to Human Rights Treaties in the United

States Senate: The Legacy of the Bricker Amendment," 10 Hum. Rts. Q. 309 (1988); Richards, "The Bricker Amendment and Congress' Failure to Check the Inflation of the Executive's Foreign Affairs Powers, 1951–1954," 94 Cal. L. Rev. 175 (2006).

Although different versions of the so-called "Bricker Amendment" were introduced in the U.S. Senate between 1952 and 1957, all had three basic aims. The different versions are reproduced in "Report on the 1957 Bricker Amendment," 12 Rec. Bar Assoc. N.Y. 320, at 343–46 (1957). The three aims were: first, to make all international agreements non-self-executing under U.S. law, which means that they would require implementing legislation before they could be enforced in U.S. courts; second, to reverse Missouri v. Holland, 252 U.S. 416 (1920), which recognized that treaties could federalize subjects otherwise within the jurisdiction of the states; and third, to provide expressly what had always been implicit, namely, that under U.S. law, international agreements are subject to those restraints of the Constitution that limit all powers of the federal government. *Compare* De Geofroy v. Riggs, 133 U.S. 258 (1890) *with* Reid v. Covert, 354 U.S. 1 (1957). *See generally* L. Henkin, *Foreign Affairs and the United States Constitution* 170–230 (2d ed. 1996).

The major targets of Senator Bricker's attack were the human rights treaties the United Nations had already adopted and the proposed human rights covenants, which seemed to be nearing completion at the time. *See* Senator Bricker's testimony, Hearings on S.J. Res. 1 and S.J. Res. 43 Before a Subcomm. of the Senate Comm. on the Judiciary, 83d Cong., 1st Sess. 10–11 (1953). In the negotiations that eventually resulted in the defeat of the Bricker Amendment, Secretary of State John Foster Dulles had to make a policy commitment on behalf of the Eisenhower Administration that the U.S. Government did "not intend to become a party to any such covenant [on human rights] or present it as a treaty for consideration by the Senate." *Id.* at 825. This policy statement was officially communicated to the United Nations. 13 M. Whiteman, Digest of International Law 667–69 (1968). As a result, the proposed constitutional amendment failed of adoption by one vote.

The United States adhered to this policy until 1963. In that year, President John F. Kennedy transmitted three human rights treaties to the Senate for its advice and consent—the Supplementary Convention on the Abolition of Slavery and the Slave Trade, ILO Convention 105 on the Abolition of Forced Labor, and the Convention on the Political Rights of Women. *See* 49 Dept. State Bull. 23 (1963). It took four years for the Senate to schedule hearings on the treaties. Hearings on Executive J, K, and L, 88 Cong., 1st Sess., 90th Cong., 1st Sess. (Feb. 23 and March 8, 1967); *id.*, Part 2 (Sept. 13, 1967). These hearings produced consent to the ratification of only the Supplementary Slavery Convention. Later, the United States did ratify the Convention on the Political Rights of Women (1976) and the Forced Labor Convention (1991). U.S. adherence to the Protocol Relating to the Status of

Refugees was easily authorized by the Senate in 1968, but it was not presented as a human rights treaty.

To demonstrate his Administration's strong commitment to human rights, President Jimmy Carter, in an unusual act for a head of state, personally signed three major human rights treaties during his first year in office. He signed the two International Covenants of Human Rights at UN Headquarters in New York and the American Convention on Human Rights at the seat of the Organization of American States in Washington, D.C. A year later, in 1978, President Carter transmitted these instruments, together with the International Convention on the Elimination of All Forms of Racial Discrimination, to the Senate for its advice and consent to ratification. Message from the President of the United States Transmitting Four Treaties Pertaining to Human Rights, Senate Ex. C, D, E, and F, 95th Congress, 2d Sess. (Feb. 23, 1978). In 1979, the Senate Foreign Relations Committee held extensive hearings on this request. Hearings before the [Senate] Committee on Foreign Relations on Ex. C, D, E, and F, 95–2—Four Treaties Relating to Human Rights, Nov. 14–16 and 19, 1979 (1980). Subsequently, at the end of his Administration, President Carter transmitted the Convention on the Elimination of All Forms of Discrimination Against Women. Message from the President of the United States Transmitting the Convention on the Elimination of All Forms of Discrimination Against Women, Senate Ex. R, 95th Congress, 2d Sess. (July 17, 1980).

As previously noted, the Senate took no further action on these treaties until 1992, when advice and consent was given to the ratification of the Covenant on Civil and Political Rights (ICCPR), and again in 1994, when it approved the Convention on the Elimination of All Forms of Racial Discrimination (as well as the Torture Convention). The big breakthrough, however, had come earlier, in 1988, with the U.S. ratification of the Genocide Convention, which after forty years was finally approved with the strong support of President Reagan.

§ 6–4. LEGAL AND POLICY CONSIDERATIONS AFFECTING RATIFICATION

In analyzing the views of those who have opposed U.S. ratification of human rights treaties, or insisted on imposing conditions on ratification, it is not always easy to distinguish the legal from the policy arguments. *See, e.g.,* Hearing before the Subcommittee on the Constitution of the Senate Committee on the Judiciary on the Constitutional Implications of the Proposed Genocide Convention, 99th Cong., 1st Sess., Feb. 26, 1985 (1985); L. J. Le Blanc, *The United States and the Genocide Convention* (1991). Basically, three legal arguments have been advanced at different times by opponents of U.S. adherence to these treaties.

The first argument is that human rights are a matter of domestic jurisdiction and that the U.S. Constitution does not permit the use of the treaty-making power to regulate a matter that is not a proper subject of international negotiations. Whatever force this contention might have had during the era of the Bricker Amendment has long since disappeared. Even assuming that the treaty-making power applies only to matters that are of international concern, it cannot be seriously contended today that human rights fail to meet this test. The huge number of international human rights agreements agreed to and in force today, some of which have been ratified by virtually the entire international community of states, attests to the internationalization of the human rights concern. *See also* United Nations, Human Rights: A Compilation of International Instruments, UN Doc. ST/HR/1/ Rev.6, Vol. 1 (First Part) (2002); *cf.* Kadić v. Karadšzić, 70 F.3d 232 (2d Cir.1995); Filártiga v. Peña-Irala, 630 F.2d 876 (2d Cir.1980); Restatement (Third) Foreign Relations Law § 302, Comment (c). In short, the constitutional standard about what is or is not a matter of international concern for purposes of the treaty power, assuming there is in fact such a requirement, cannot be divorced from contemporary international realities and diplomatic practice.

The second argument against U.S. adherence to human rights treaties is that many of the rights these instruments protect are regulated domestically by state rather than federal law. Ratification of these treaties, it is contended, would improperly federalize these subjects. It is not all that clear, given the manner in which this argument is often put, whether its proponents believe that this federalization would be unconstitutional or merely unwise. For example, in testifying in 1981 against U.S. ratification of the Genocide Convention, Senator Strom Thurmond, then Chairman of the Senate Judiciary Committee, declared:

> Matters concerning fundamental criminal conduct involving murder or conspiracy to commit murder should be primarily a matter of State domestic jurisdiction—I repeat, State domestic jurisdiction. The use of the treaty-making power in this area is inappropriate. In effect, the [Genocide] Convention would continue the policy made possible by the Supreme Court in its decision in Missouri v. Holland, 252 U.S. 416 [1920], in which the Court held that State powers could be transferred to the Federal Government through the treatymaking process as a de facto method of amending the Constitution.

Hearing before the [Senate] Committee on Foreign Relations on the Genocide Convention, 97 Cong., 1st Sess., Dec. 3, 1981, at 9 (1982).

In Missouri v. Holland, 252 U.S. 416 (1920), the Supreme Court held that the Tenth Amendment, which provides that "the powers not delegated to the United States by the Constitution, nor prohibited by it to the States, are reserved to the States respectively, or to the people," does not limit the treaty-making power of the federal government since that power was expressly delegated to the federal government. At the same time, the Court has also made clear that the treaty-making power is not without some constitutional limits. *See, e.g.,* De

Geofroy v. Riggs, 133 U.S. 258 (1890); Reid v. Covert, 354 U.S. 1 (1957). Moreover, a number of recent Supreme Court decisions circumscribing federal authority have re-invigorated the concerns about "federalizing" issues or areas. *See, e.g.,* New York v. United States, 505 U.S. 144 (1992); Printz v. United States, 521 U.S. 898 (1997); United States v. Lopez, 514 U.S. 549 (1995); *cf.* United States v. Morrison, 529 U.S. 598 (2000).

These issues are the subject of a continuing and lively scholarly debate. *See, e.g.,* Bradley, "The Treaty Power and American Federalism," 97 Mich. L. Rev. 390 (1998); Golove, "Treaty-Making and the Nation: The Historical Foundation of the Nationalist Conception of the Treaty Power," 98 Mich. L. Rev. 1075 (2000); Rosenkranz, "Executing the Treaty Power," 118 Harv. L. Rev. 1867 (2005); Spiro, "Resurrecting Missouri v. Holland," 73 Mo. L. Rev. 1029 (2008); Stephan, "What Story Got Wrong: Federalism, Localist Opportunism and International Law," 73 Mo. L. Rev. 1041 (2008); Vázquez, Missouri v. Holland's Second Holding, 73 Mo. L. Rev. 939 (2008); Swaine, "Taking Care of Treaties," 108 Colum. L. Rev. 331 (2008); Hathaway, Amdur, Choy, Deger-Sen, Paredes, Pei and Proctor, "The Treaty Power: Its History, Scope, and Limits," 98 Cornell L. Rev. 239 (2013); Gerkin, "Slipping the Bonds of Federalism," 128 Harv. L. Rev. 85 (2014); Bradley, "Federalism, Treaty Implementation, and Political Process: Bond v. United States," 108 Am. J. Int'l L. 486 (2014); Galbraith, "Congress's Treaty Implementation Power in Historical Practice," 50 Wm. & Mary L. Rev. 9 (2014); Hollis, "An Inter-

Subjective Treaty Power," 90 Notre Dame L. Rev. 1415 (2015); Ramsey, "Congress' Limited Power to Enforce Treaties," 90 Notre Dame L. Rev. 1583 (2015); Baasch and Prakash, "Congress and the Reconstruction of Foreign Affairs Federalism," 115 Mich. L. Rev. 47 (2016); Glennon and Sloane, "The Sad, Quiet Death of Missouri v. Holland: How Bond Hobbled the Treaty Power," 41 Yale J. Int'l L. 51 (2016).

Nevertheless, in Bond v. United States, *supra*, a majority of the Court declined to reconsider the holding in Missouri v. Holland. *But cf.* dissenting opinion of Justice Scalia; *see also* Restatement (Fourth) § 112 (setting forth the holding of Missouri v. Holland as black letter law).

Finally, it has been argued that some human rights treaties contain provisions that conflict with the U.S. Constitution. This is true of a very small number of these provisions. One such clause, for example, is Article 20(1) of the Covenant on Civil and Political Rights, which requires that "[a]ny propaganda for war shall be prohibited by law." Another is Article 20(2), which provides that "[a]ny advocacy of national, racial or religious hatred that constitutes incitement to discrimination . . . shall be prohibited by law." These prohibitions, if enacted into U.S. law, would run afoul of the First Amendment to the Constitution. Here and in similar cases appropriate reservations must be made upon ratification to ensure that the United States does not assume international obligations which it would be unable to discharge on the domestic plane because they violate the Constitution. *See generally* R. Lillich (ed.), U.S. Ratification of the Human Rights Treaties: With or Without Reservations? (1981); Stewart, "U.S. Ratification of the Covenant on Civil and Political Rights: The Significance of the Reservations, Understanding and Declarations," 14 Hum. Rts. L.J. 77, 79–81 (1993); Bradley and Goldsmith, "Treaties, Human Rights, and Conditional Consent," 149 U. Penn. L. Rev. 399 (2000); Swaine, "Reserving," 31 Yale L. J. Int'l L. 307 (2006).

Some opponents of U.S. adherence to human rights treaties have argued that the Supreme Court might at some future time hold that treaties in general were not subject to any of the limitations the Constitution imposes on the exercise of all governmental power. However, the Supreme Court expressly rejected this interpretation in Reid v. Covert, *supra. See also* Restatement (Third) § 302(2), which declares that "no provision of an [international] agreement may contravene any of the prohibitions or limitations of the Constitution applicable to any exercise of authority by the United States." Moreover, various human rights treaties contain a clause similar to that of Article 5(2) of the Covenant on Civil and Political Rights, which declares that:

There shall be no restriction upon or derogation from any of the fundamental human rights recognized or existing in any States Party to the present Covenant pursuant to law, conventions, regulations or custom on the pretext that the present Covenant does not recognize such rights or that it recognizes them to a lesser extent.

See also American Convention on Human Rights, art. 29(b).

Still, concern that treaties should not impinge on the constitutional rights and protections of American citizens continues to resonate in the Congress. In giving its advice and consent to the ratification of the Genocide Convention, the Senate attached a reservation providing "that nothing in the Convention requires or authorizes legislation or other action by the United States of America prohibited by the Constitution of the United States as interpreted by the United States." For the full text of the resolution of ratification, *see* 132 Cong. Rec. S1377–78 (daily ed., Feb. 19, 1986). The Senate Foreign Relations Committee explained this reservation by pointing out that it had no doubt whatsoever that "no treaty can override or conflict with the Constitution. The Constitution is paramount. Reid v. Covert, 354 U.S. 1 (1957)." Report of the [Senate] Committee on Foreign Relations on the International Convention on the Prevention and Punishment of the Crime of Genocide, Exec. O, 81st Cong., 1st Sess., Exec. Rep. 99–2, 99th Cong., 1st Sess., at 20 (1985).

The Committee emphasized instead that the purpose of the reservation was to anticipate the possibility that the International Court of Justice might at some future time interpret the Genocide Convention to require the United States to adopt measures that would be unconstitutional. *Id.* at 20–21. Some members of the Senate Foreign Relations Committee opposed this reservation and argued that it was both unnecessary and unwise. They were unsuccessful in urging the full Senate to vote against it. *Id.* at 30–31. Similar language was adopted by the Senate in giving its advice and consent to other treaties ratified by the United States, but no longer in the form of a reservation. Instead, it is now formulated as a "proviso, which shall not be included in the instrument of ratification deposited by the President. . . ." *See, e.g.,* Report of the Senate Foreign Relations Committee on the International Covenant on Civil and Political Rights, Exec. Rep. 102–23, at 24 (March 24, 1992), approved by full Senate, 102 Cong. Rec. S4781–4784 (daily ed. April 2, 1992).

For background, *see* Katz, "A New American Dilemma: U.S. Constitutionalism vs. International Human Rights," 58 U. Miami L. Rev. 323 (2003).

§ 6–5. THE CONDITIONAL APPROACH: RATIFICATION WITH RESERVATIONS, UNDERSTANDINGS AND DECLARATIONS

Over the past decades, the attitude of the United States to human rights treaties has changed fundamentally from a policy of total non-participation to one that proceeds on a treaty-by-treaty basis in deciding whether to ratify (and how to implement) a particular instrument. This decision is made by taking account of various factors, including the national interest in U.S. participation, consistency with U.S. law and practice, and the likelihood that the Senate will give its advice and consent to ratification. Recent administrations have gradually reached the conclusion that, in general, it is in the U.S. national interest to join such treaties and that, in principle, there are no compelling constitutional objections to their ratification. There is general agreement, moreover, that almost all such treaties present some constitutional issues, but that these can be addressed by appropriate reservations.

To obtain the requisite political support of the Senate, which under Article II of the Constitution must give its advice and consent to the ratification of these treaties by a two-thirds majority, the Executive Branch has evolved a practice of addressing all real and potential objections relating to a particular treaty provision by proposing a number of reservations, understandings and declarations—so-called RUDs—designed to overcome these objections. The practice began in the Carter Administration and has continued since then. Driven by a combination of constitutional imperatives, legal considerations and political expediency, the practice is now insisted upon by the Senate and supported by the Executive Branch regardless of its political affiliation.

Before addressing the implementation of this practice, it is worth distinguishing the nature and legal effect of RUDs as a matter of international treaty law. A reservation modifies the terms of the treaty as between the reserving State and the States accepting the reservation to the extent of the reservation. As such, a reservation changes the international obligation of these States *inter se*. Understandings and declarations are traditionally thought of as unilateral statements by a State regarding its interpretation or position with regard to a given provision of a treaty. As a rule such statements will not modify a State's international obligations, but it is not always clear whether they will or will not have legal consequences because the label a State attaches to these statements is not determinative under the law of treaties. *See* Vienna Convention on the Law of Treaties, art. 2(1)(d); Belilos v. Switzerland, European Court of Human Rights, Series A, No. 132 (Judgment of April 29, 1988).

Hence, a statement denominated as an "understanding" might be treated as a reservation if it appears that it modifies the obligations assumed by a state. Under U.S. constitutional law, however, when the Senate conditions its consent to ratification on certain reservations, understandings or declarations, and the President ratifies the treaty subject to them, they are binding (and have been treated as such by U.S. courts as a matter of domestic law, provided they are within the Constitutional power of the treaty makers (i.e., the President and the Senate) to adopt. *See generally* Restatement (Third) Foreign Relations Law §§ 313 and 314.

Certain categories of RUDs are now attached to all human rights treaties ratified by the United States. First, there are the reservations to any treaty provisions that might be deemed to conflict with the U.S. Constitution. This problem arises most often in the context of First Amendment rights. Typical is the following reservation the taken when the United States ratified the Racial Convention:

The Constitution and laws of the United States contain extensive protections of individual freedom of speech, expression and association. Accordingly, the United States does not accept any obligations under this Convention, in particular under Articles 4 and 7, to restrict those rights, through the adoption of legislation or any other measures, to the extent that they are protected by the Constitution and laws of the United States.

A similar reservation was taken in respect of Article 20 the Covenant on Civil and Political Rights, which deals with war propaganda and advocacy of national, racial, religious hatred. That reservation provides "that Article 20 does not authorize or require legislation or any other action by the United States that would restrict the right of free speech and association protected by the Constitution and laws of the United States." Note that the reservation applies not only to the Constitution but also to U.S. laws according or protecting individual rights. The evident purpose was to reassure skeptics who were concerned that the Covenant provisions might restrict the broad freedoms of speech and expression currently protected under domestic law beyond the requirements of the First Amendment.

Second, as a rule, reservations (or understandings) will be attached to any provision of a human rights treaty to which the United States is unwilling to conform existing domestic law. Thus, the following reservation was taken with regard to the Torture Convention:

The United States considers itself bound by the obligation under Article 16 to prevent "cruel, inhuman or degrading treatment or punishment," only insofar as the term "cruel, inhuman or degrading treatment or punishment" means the cruel, unusual, and inhuman treatment or punishment prohibited by the Fifth, Eighth and/or Fourteenth Amendments to the Constitution of the United States.

A similar reservation was attached to ratification of the ICCPR, relating to the undertaking concerning "degrading treatment."

A reservation was also taken relating to the application of the death penalty to persons under the age of 18. This type of reservation is designed to ensure that the treaty will not be deemed to have superseded existing domestic law in conflict with it, and reflects a strong preference that changes to the law should be made through the ordinary legislative process.

Third, it has now become U.S. practice to attach an understanding containing a so-called "federalism" clause to any human rights treaty to be ratified by this country. Here, the principal concern has been to indicate that ratification is not intended to alter the existing allocation of authority and responsibility between the federal government, on the one hand, and the states and other constituent governmental entities, on the other, with regard to subjects that are dealt with in the treaty. The language of these understandings has been refined over the past few years.

One of the most recent, attached to the Racial Discrimination Convention, reads as follows:

That the United States understands that this Convention shall be implemented by the Federal Government to the extent that it exercises jurisdiction over the matters covered therein, and otherwise by the state and local governments. To the extent that state and local governments exercise jurisdiction over such matters, the Federal Government shall, as necessary, take appropriate measures to ensure the fulfillment of this Convention.

Specifically, the purpose of this understanding is to emphasize, for legal as well as policy reasons, that U.S. ratification will not have the effect of federalizing those subjects regulated by the treaty over which the states and local governments have heretofore exercised jurisdiction. In other words, this understanding seeks to prevent the application of the rule enunciated in Missouri v. Holland, *supra*, which would empower the federal government to legislate on the matters covered by the treaty that would otherwise be within the exclusive legislative power of the states. Unlike traditional federal-state clauses, however, this understanding is not designed to limit the international obligations of the United States. It is intended instead to make clear that the ratification of the treaty does not extend federal legislative power to all matters to which the treaty applies, while recognizing the international obligation of the United

States to "take appropriate measures to ensure the fulfillment of this Convention."

Fourth, it has now also become the practice of the United States to ratify human rights treaties with a declaration to the effect that the United States considers their substantive provisions to be "non-self-executing." The doctrine of non-self-execution is shrouded in technical controversy and confusion, and is discussed in greater detail below at § 6–12. For present purposes, it is sufficient to say that the evident purpose of this declaration has been to ensure that the particular treaty will not be deemed, in and of itself, to create rights directly enforceable in U.S. courts. *See, e.g.*, Medellín v. Texas, 552 U.S. 491, 527 (2008) ("A non-self-executing treaty, by definition, is one that was ratified with the understanding that it is not to [be domestically enforceable] of its own force."). The stated concern of the Administration and the Senate was to avoid generating new "causes of action" for private litigants in U.S. courts based solely on the provisions of the treaties.

Finally, as indicated above in § 6–4, the Senate now also attaches a statement or "proviso" to its resolution giving advice and consent to the ratification of a human rights treaty, which provides that "[n]othing in this Convention requires or authorizes legislation, or other action, by the United States of America prohibited by the Constitution of the United States as interpreted by the United States." The proviso is not generally included in the U.S. instrument of ratification.

It is thus readily apparent that when the United States ratifies a human rights treaty today, it attempts to ensure that it has assumed no international obligations not effectively guaranteed by (or in conflict with) relevant U.S. law. To put it differently, the underlying policy is one of compliance with treaty commitments, either by making sure that the relevant law is in fact adequate to satisfy the obligations which will become binding when the treaty is ratified, or by enacting the necessary implementing legislation.

This practice does not imply categorical opposition to changing domestic law in order to comport with the treaty in question. It does, however, signal opposition to changing the law directly through the treaty itself. In that sense, it reflects a long-standing view, particularly on the part of the U.S. Congress, that any amendments to existing U.S. law necessary to implement human rights treaty obligations should be made through the normal legislative process. That is the reason the United States defers ratification of non-self-executing treaties until any necessary implementing legislation has been enacted.

By making the treaty non-self-executing, the practice seeks to prevent individuals from instituting legal actions in U.S. courts based solely on provisions of the treaty (i.e., making clear the treaty does not by itself provide a federal "cause of action"). By including the federalism understanding, the Executive and the Congress together make clear their intent to avoid federalization of matters that would otherwise be within the exclusive legislative power of the states. It is ironic that this approach for all practical purposes accomplishes some of the goals that the proponents of the Bricker Amendment sought to achieve with respect to human rights treaties. *See* § 6–3, *supra. See also* Henkin, "U.S. Ratification of Human Rights Treaties: The Ghost of Senator Bricker," 89 Am. J. Int'l L. 341 (1995); Kaufman & Whiteman, "Opposition to Human Rights in the United States Senate: The Legacy of the Bricker Amendment," 10 Hum. Rts. Q. 309 (1988). For a contrary view, *see* Morris, "Few Reservations about Reservations," 1 Chi. J. Int'l L. 341 (2000).

It is important to emphasize that none of this excuses the federal government from the obligation of complying with the treaties as ratified. On the contrary, the position of the various Administrations has been that existing U.S. law amply recognizes and protects most of the rights guaranteed by the treaties, so that no new implementing legislation is necessary. In fact, by Exec. Order No. 13107, 63 FR 68991 (Dec. 10, 1998), President Clinton proclaimed that "it shall be the policy and practice of the Government of the United States . . . fully to respect and implement its obligations under the international human rights treaties to which it is a party, including the ICCPR, the CAT, and the CERD." *Id.* at § 1(a). The order established an Interagency Working Group on Human Rights Treaties to provide guidance, oversight and coordination with respect to "questions concerning the adherence to and implementation of human rights obligations and related matters." *Id.* at § 4(b). The duties of that Working Group were later transferred to a Policy Coordination Committee of the National Security Council. *See* National Security Presidential Directive, Organization of the National Security Council System, available at https://fas.org/irp/offdocs/nspd/nspd-1.htm (Feb. 13, 2001), revised by Presidential Policy Directive 1; (Fb. 13, 2009), available at https://www.hsdl.org/?abstract&did=345 60.

The debate over federal versus state implementation must be understood against the background of the continuing legal and political debate over the contours of the U.S. federal system. *See, e.g.,* Exec. Order No. 13132 on Federalism, 64 FR 43255 (August 4, 1999). Where existing U.S. law is inconsistent with, or falls short of the treaty's requirements, then the RUDs reflect that new legislation should be adopted in the ordinary course, either prior to ratification (so that no RUDs would be needed) or following ratification, at which time any relevant reservations could be withdrawn. (The latter situation might arise, for instance, in regard to such controversial issues as capital punishment, the juvenile death penalty or abortion). Some implementing legislation has been adopted. *See, e.g.,* the Genocide Convention Implementation Act, 18 U.S.C. §§ 1091–93 (2008), amended by the Genocide Accountability Act of 2007, Pub. L. 110–151, codified at § 1091(d) and the criminal statute implementing part of the Torture Convention, 18 U.S.C. § 2340A; *cf.* the Torture Convention Implementation Act, Pub. L. No. 102–256, 106 Stat. 73 (1992), codified at 28 U.S.C. § 1350 note (2008) (providing a civil remedy for actions of torture under color of foreign law).

It is clear, of course, that the United States cannot ratify a treaty the provisions of which, without an appropriate reservation, would violate the U.S. Constitution. It does have the constitutional power, however, to ratify a human rights treaty that conflicts with other domestic laws. Under the later-in-time rule, the treaty (or its implementing legislation, if any) would then supersede the incompatible domestic law. The decision of the Senate to insist on reservations so that the treaty itself will effect no changes whatsoever in the relevant domestic law is a policy decision not compelled by any constitutional mandate. The Constitution authorizes the President with the consent of the Senate to ratify treaties that become law and, if they are self-executing, that will supersede conflicting provisions of prior domestic law. The argument of the proponents of the Bricker Amendment and their contemporary disciples that this result should only be achieved by legislation passed by both Houses of Congress is in no way required by the Constitution when applied to human rights treaties. The same can be said about the need for the non-self-executing declaration and the federal-state clause. These are all policy decisions with which one may or may not agree, but they certainly are not compelled by the Constitution.

For arguments for and against these policies, *see* Hearing before the Senate Foreign Relations Committee on the International Covenant on Civil and Political Rights, November 21, 1991, S.Hrg. 102–478 (1992); Hearing before the Senate Foreign Relations Committee on the International

Convention on the Elimination of All Forms of Racial Discrimination, May 11, 1994, S.Hrg. 103–659 (1994). *See* also Stewart, "U.S. Ratification of the Covenant on Civil and Political Rights: The Significance of the Reservations, Understandings and Declarations," 14 Hum. Rts. L. J. 77 (1993); Lawyers Committee for Human Rights, "Statements on U.S. Ratification of the CCPR," *id.*, at 125; "Symposium: The Ratification of the International Covenant on Civil and Political Rights," 42 De Paul L. Rev. 1167–1412 (1993); Stewart, "Ratification of the Convention on the Rights of the Child," 5 Geo. J. Fighting Poverty 161 (1998); Goldsmith, "Should International Human Rights Law Trump U.S. Domestic Law?", 1 Chi. J. Int'l L. 327 (2000); Chung, "The Judicial Enforceability and Legal Effects of Treaty Reservations, Understandings, and Declarations," 126 Yale L.J. 170 (2016).

It should also be noted that a number of western European States, including The Netherlands, Germany, France, Italy, Belgium, and various Scandinavian countries, formally objected to some U.S. reservations to the Covenant on Civil and Political Rights as being incompatible with the object and purpose of the treaty and therefore invalid. These objections were addressed in particular to U.S. reservations relating to the death penalty and to cruel and usual treatment and punishment. The views of these states are echoed by a General Comment of the UN Human Rights Committee with regard to reservations in general. *See* General Comment No. 24 (52) on Issues Relating to Reservations, U.N. Doc. CCPR/C/21/Rev.1/Add.6

(1994). For the U.S. response to that General Comment, rejecting much of its legal analysis, *see* 16 Hum. Rts. L. J. 422 (1995).

III. HUMAN RIGHTS LEGISLATION

§ 6–6. INTRODUCTION

In the early 1970's, the U.S. Congress began a thorough assessment of international human rights issues and their foreign policy implications. The person principally responsible for initiating this process was Congressman Donald M. Fraser of Minnesota, who at that time chaired the Subcommittee on International Organizations and Movements of the House Committee on Foreign Affairs. In 1973, Congressman Fraser's subcommittee held extensive hearings on the subject. Subcommittee on International Organizations and Movements of the House Committee on Foreign Affairs, Hearings on International Protection of Human Rights, 93d Cong., 1st Sess., Aug. 1–Dec. 7, 1973. A year later, the subcommittee presented a comprehensive set of recommendations calling for legislation and other action to ensure that human rights considerations would receive serious consideration in the formulation and execution of U.S. foreign policy. Subcommittee on International Organizations and Movements of the House Committee on Foreign Affairs, Human Rights in the World Community: A Call for Leadership, 93d Cong., 2d Sess., 1974.

The legislative and bureaucratic underpinnings of contemporary U.S. human rights foreign policy have their origin in the efforts of the Fraser committee and the policies of President Jimmy Carter, who was elected in 1976. The latter enthusiastically espoused many of Congressman Fraser's recommendations and made the promotion of human rights the cornerstone of his administration's foreign policy. *See* Weissbrodt, "Human Rights Legislation and U.S. Foreign Policy," 7 Ga. J. Int'l & Comp. L. 231 (1977); Schneider, "A New Administration's New Policy: The Rise to Power of Human Rights," in P. Brown & D. MacLean (eds.), *Human Rights and U.S. Foreign Policy* 3 (1979). *See also* Subcommittee on International Organization of the House Committee on International Relations, Human Rights in the International Community and in U.S. Foreign Policy, 1945–76 (Congressional Research Service, 1977).

The legislation and other measures that the initial Fraser committee hearings produced have been significantly transformed and amplified since then. Today there exists a substantial, indeed expanding, body of law on the subject. The subsequent sections examine the major provisions of that law.

§ 6–7. TERMINATING MILITARY AND ECONOMIC AID: LAWS OF GENERAL APPLICABILITY

The cornerstone of U.S. human rights legislation consists of two laws of general applicability. The relevant laws are § 502B of the Foreign Assistance Act of 1961, as amended (22 U.S.C.A. § 2304), and

§ 116 of the same Act (22 U.S.C.A. § 2151n). These laws tie the grant of military and economic assistance to the human rights policies of the recipient governments. Their underlying policy is well articulated in § 502B(a)(1), which reads as follows:

> The United States shall, in accordance with its international obligations as set forth in the Charter of the United Nations and in keeping with the constitutional heritage and traditions of the United States, promote and encourage increased respect for human rights and fundamental freedoms throughout the world without distinction as to race, sex, language, or religion. Accordingly, a principal goal of the foreign policy of the United States shall be to promote the increased observance of internationally recognized human rights by all countries.

Although § 502B deals with military or security assistance and § 116 applies to economic aid and development assistance, both laws have the same purpose: to deny such assistance to countries the governments of which engage in activities that reveal "a consistent pattern of gross violations of internationally recognized human rights." The concept of "gross violation of internationally recognized human rights" is defined in § 502B(d)(1) as "including" violations such as:

> torture or cruel, inhuman, or degrading treatment or punishment, prolonged detention without charges and trial, causing the disappearance of persons by the abduction and

clandestine detention of those persons, and other flagrant denial of the right to life, liberty, or the security of person.

22 U.S.C.A. § 2304(d)(1). Section 116(a) uses almost identical language. 22 U.S.C.A. § 2151n(a). The use of the word "including" indicates that Congress recognized that other human rights may also qualify as being "internationally recognized." Although one commentator, Cohen, "Conditioning U.S. Security Assistance on Human Rights Practices," 76 Am. J. Int'l L. 246, 267 (1982), found no support for this view in the legislative history of the act, the language used speaks for itself. *See also* D. Forsythe, "Human Rights and U.S. Foreign Policy: Congress Reconsidered," 82 Am. J. Int'l L. 972 (1989).

In looking at the language of this legislation, it is important to note that the phrase "consistent pattern of gross violations," mirrors the language of UN Economic and Social Council Resolution 1503 of 1970. That resolution is at the heart of the UN Charter-based system for dealing with human rights complaints and reflects the view that a state guilty of such violations is in breach of its obligations under the Charter. *See* § 2–25, *supra*. Resort by the U.S. Congress to the UN language is no accident and indicates a desire to ensure that these laws not be considered as constituting illegal intervention in the domestic affairs of other countries. The language also suggests that the Congress wished to reach only governments which systematically engaged in or tolerated massive violations of human rights. Isolated instances of even serious violations presumably would not be covered by the statute, particularly if they revealed that these acts were not the result of a governmental policy. For an analysis of the manner in which the U.S. State Department has applied this test, *see* Cohen, *supra*, at 267–68. *See also* Forsythe, "Congress and Human Rights in U.S. Foreign Policy: The Fate of General Legislation," 9 Hum. Rts. Q. 382 (1987). For a critical analysis of the application of these laws, *see* Lawyers Committee for Human Rights, *Human Rights and U.S. Foreign Policy* 6 (1992).

Over time, the Congress has adopted additional restrictions on assistance to other countries, using the "consistent pattern of gross violations" standard or very similar language. *See, e.g.*, § 403(j)(1) of the Agricultural Trade and Development Act of 1954, 7 U.S.C. § 1733(j)(1) (providing and financing of agricultural commodities); bilateral debt relief under the enhanced HIPC legislation, 22 U.S.C.A. § 262p–8(c)(4); § 104 (a) of the Africa Growth and Opportunity Act, 19 U.S.C. § 3703(a)(3); § 2(b)(6) and (14) of the Export-Import Bank Act of 1945, as amended, 12 U.S.C. § 635(b)(6) and 635i–8(c) (certain functions of the Ex-Im Bank); § 498A of the Foreign Assistance Act of 1961 as amended, 22 U.S.C. § 2295a(b)(1) (assistance to the governments of the independent states of the former Soviet Union); and benefits under the Americas Initiative, 22 U.S.C. § 2430b(a)(4).

Section 116 also establishes an elaborate reporting requirement under which the Department of State must provide an annual human rights status report for all states receiving aid. This requirement has in the meantime been extended to all UN Member States. Similar obligations are imposed by § 502B. These annual "country conditions" reports have become a valuable source of information about world-wide human rights conditions and violations. In compiling the reports, the State Department relies on information provided by U.S. embassies as well as on findings of inter-governmental and non-governmental human rights organizations. *See, e.g.,* Department of State, Country Reports on Human Rights Practices 2015, submitted on April 13, 2016, to the Congress in compliance with §§ 116(d) and 502(b) of the Foreign Assistance Act of 1961 (FAA), as amended, and section 504 of the Trade Act of 1974, as amended. The annual reports are available on-line at https://www.state.gov/j/drl/rls/hrrpt.

Here it is important to note that the legislation requires the State Department, in determining whether a state is a gross violator of human rights, to take into account, among other considerations, "the relevant findings of appropriate international organizations, including nongovernmental organizations, such as the International Committee of the Red Cross. . . ." Section 502B(b)(1). Similar language is found in § 116(c)(1). Both laws also attach considerable weight to the extent to which the particular country cooperates with and permits such organizations "an unimpeded investigation of alleged violations of internationally recognized human rights." *See* § 116(c)(1) and § 502B(b)(2). These requirements strengthen the effectiveness of public and private human rights institutions that investigate and judge violations. Hence, findings—for example, by the UN Human Rights Council or a regional human rights body such as the Inter-American Court or Commission on Human Rights—that a government has engaged in large-scale violations of human rights, should be taken into account by the State Department in preparing its reports and in deciding on the action to be taken in application of §§ 116 or 502B.

Each law contains exceptions. Thus, economic aid does not have to be terminated if "such assistance will directly benefit the needy people in such country." § 116(a). Moreover, the President may continue security assistance to a gross violator if he certifies to the Congress "that extraordinary circumstances exist warranting provision of such assistance." § 502B(a)(2). These and other provisions give the Executive Branch considerable latitude in administering the law with more or less vigor. Ultimately, of course, the question of whether a government is a human rights violator within the meaning of this legislation is a matter of judgment. For one thing, it is not always easy to determine whether conditions have improved in a country to justify resumption of aid. Much also depends upon the political will of the Executive Branch in implementing a strong or weak human rights policy.

Efforts to force the Executive's hand by resort to the courts have not been successful due to the application of the political question doctrine. Crockett v. Reagan, 720 F.2d 1355 (D.C.Cir.1983), cert. denied, 467 U.S. 1251 (1984); Clark v. United

States, 609 F.Supp. 1249 (D.Md.1985). *See* Gibney, "Judicial Failure to Enforce Human Rights Legislation: An Alternative Analysis of Crockett v. Reagan," 4 N.Y. L. Sch. Hum. Rts. Ann. 115 (1985); Griffin, "Constitutional Impediment to Enforcing Human Rights Legislation: The Case of El Salvador," 33 Am. U. L. Rev. 163 (1983).

Additional reporting requirements were imposed by the 1998 International Religious Freedom Act, recently amended by Pub. L. 114–281, 130 Stat 1426 (2016), codified at 22 U.S.C. § 6401 et seq. (2016). This Act mandated the establishment of an Office of International Religious Freedom within the Department of State, headed by an Ambassador-at-Large who acts as the principal advisor to the President and Secretary of State in matters concerning religious freedom abroad. The law also created an independent, bipartisan United States Commission on International Religious Freedom. The Act makes it U.S. policy "to seek to channel United States security and development assistance to governments other than those found to be engaged in gross violations of the right to freedom of religion, as set forth in the Foreign Assistance Act of 1961, in the International Financial Institutions Act of 1977, and in other formulations of United States human rights policy." 22 U.S.C. § 6401(b)(2). The President must annually designate every country "the government of which has engaged in or tolerated violations described in this subparagraph as a country of particular concern for religious freedom." 22 U.S.C. § 6442(b)(1)(A). A report covering every foreign country, coupled with an identification of severe violators, is submitted each year. The 2015 Religious Freedom Report may be found at https:// www.state.gov/j/drl/rls/irf/2015/.

§ 6–8. COUNTRY-SPECIFIC LEGISLATION

In addition to the legislation of general applicability described in the preceding section, the Congress has from time to time enacted so-called country-specific human rights laws. One purpose of such legislation is to force the Executive Branch to cut off aid to a particular country to which the laws of general applicability, in the Congress's view, are not being applied as strictly as they should be. Another purpose is to focus attention on especially serious human rights violations in a given country. Among the states thus singled out at one time or another have been Argentina, Burma, Cambodia, Chile, Cuba, Guatemala, Haiti, Iran, Iraq, Libya, Salvador, South Africa, Sudan and Yugoslavia. This legislation usually has a one year duration, and may be renewed or extended depending upon the actions of the target government.

Country-specific legislation can be very useful in complementing the laws of general applicability by providing the Congress with a more powerful instrument to compel action by an uncooperative or timid Executive Branch. Sometimes the Congress will also simply refuse the Administration's request for security assistance to a country it considers to be a gross violator of human rights.

Another provision of country-specific application is the prohibition against the obligation or expenditure of funds to finance directly any assistance to any country whose duly elected head of state is deposed by decree or military coup. *See, e.g.,* § 7008 of the 2014 Consolidated and Further Continuing Appropriations Act, 2015, Pub. L.113–235 (Dec. 16, 2014), 128 Stat. 2130.

§ 6–9. INTERNATIONAL FINANCIAL INSTITUTIONS

The United States channels substantial amounts of economic aid to developing countries through international financial institutions, the so-called IFIs. These include the World Bank, the International Finance Corporation, the International Development Association, and various regional development banks. Although in most of these institutions the United States lacks the power to veto loans or grants to a specific country, it is a major contributor and as such has substantial influence on the decision-making process of the IFIs. This fact explains why, once Congress began to use economic and technical aid as a lever in seeking to reduce human rights violations, it also started to look at the role the U.S. Government could play in the IFIs in promoting that same policy. *See* Harkin, "Human Rights and Foreign Aid: Forging an Unbreakable Link," in Brown & MacLean, *supra*, at 15. (Congressman, later Senator, Tom Harkin was the leading advocate of the policy that introduced human rights considerations into the decision-making process of the IFIs and the principal sponsor of the legislation on the subject.)

Section 701 of the International Financial Institutions Act of 1977 requires the U.S. Government and U.S. representatives to the IFIs to advance the cause of human rights by using their "voice and vote" to prevent development aid from going to countries whose governments engage in gross violations of human rights. *See* 22 U.S.C. § 262d(a) (2014). The test for determining what types of violations of human rights are covered by this law and how they are to be assessed mirrors the "pattern of gross violations of internationally recognized human rights" criteria contained in the legislation that has been described in § 6–7, *supra*. The same is true, as a general proposition, of the certification requirements and escape clauses.

For a report on how the Executive Branch complies with these provisions of the law, *see* Oversight of State Department Country Reports on Human Rights Practices for 1992 and U.S. Human Rights Policy (Hearing before the Subcommittee on International Security, International Organizations, and Human Rights, 103rd Cong., 1st Sess., March 4, 1993), which also contains testimony by various human rights organizations criticizing the Executive Branch's performance in specific cases.

§ 6–10.   THE BUREAU OF DEMOCRACY, HUMAN RIGHTS AND LABOR

The principal spokesperson and policy adviser on international human rights issues within the United States Government is found in the U.S. Department of State. The U.S. Department of State is divided into so-called functional and geographic bureaus through which it carries on its work. Each of these bureaus is headed by an assistant secretary of state (or the equivalent). Until the mid-1970's, human rights subjects were handled by relatively low-level State Department officials working in different bureaus. As a result, human rights policy questions were poorly coordinated and rarely received high-level attention within the Department. For examples, *see* Buergenthal, "International Human Rights: U.S. Policy and Priorities," 14 Va. J. Int'l L. 611, 614–17 (1974).

In 1976, the Congress took the first steps to deal with this problem. It mandated the establishment of an office of Coordinator for Human Rights and Humanitarian Affairs. A year later, the Congress adopted legislation changing the Coordinator's rank to that of an Assistant Secretary of State, who would head the Bureau of Human Rights and Humanitarian Affairs. *See* Pub. L. 95–105, 91 Stat. 846 (1977). By taking this action, the Congress wished to demonstrate that human rights concerns should have a bureaucratic status within the Department of State comparable to that enjoyed by other major foreign policy subjects. In the Clinton Administration this office was renamed the Bureau for Democracy, Human Rights and Labor (DRL). Pub. L. 103–236, § 161, 108 Stat. 402 (April 30, 1994). The powers and functions of the Assistant Secretary of State for Democracy, Human Rights and Labor are now set out at 22 U.S.C. § 2651a(c)(2) (2016).

This legislation requires the Assistant Secretary to report through the Under Secretary for Global Affairs to the Secretary of State on matters relating to the formulation and implementation of U.S. human rights foreign policy. The Assistant Secretary is also responsible for the preparation of the human rights country reports, prescribed by § 116 and § 502B, as well as the reports mandated by other applicable legislation. The Bureau for Democracy, Human Rights and Labor has a sizeable specialized staff, which plays an important role in administering and coordinating U.S. laws and policies relating to the promotion of human rights, democracy and labor rights. Information about the Bureau's activities is available at http://www.state.gov/g/drl.

The effectiveness of the Bureau depends on the Assistant Secretary's commitment to human rights, bureaucratic skill and clout and, above all, the political will of the President and Secretary of State to have a strong U.S. human rights foreign policy. The attitude of the Executive Branch towards international human rights in general also influences the manner in which U.S. legislation on that subject is applied as well as the foreign policy initiatives the United States is likely to take.

While DRL coordinates U.S. human rights policy at the international level, the Bureau does not perform any oversight functions with respect to domestic U.S. compliance with international human rights norms or otherwise function as a "national human rights institution." Within the federal government, the various departments and agencies (such as Education, Interior, and Health and Human Services) each have some responsibility for domestic implementation of human rights law and obligations within their respective domains, with overall guidance provided by the NSC's Policy Coordination Committee discussed in § 6–5 *supra*. Many states, counties and cities within the United States have independent human rights commissions or councils. Some (such as the State of California and the City of Berkeley) have opted to prepare their own reports under certain human rights treaties. In 2016, the State of Hawaii called upon its departments and counties to affirm the principles of the Convention on the Elimination of All Forms of Discrimination Against Women and to work with the State Commission on the Status of Women to develop gender analysis guidelines, including the examination of race, disability, immigration status, sexual orientation, and other demographic characteristics linked to gender. *See* 2015 Hawaii Senate Resolution No. 97–16, Hawaii Twenty-Eighth Legislature (April 7, 2016).

IV. INTERNATIONAL HUMAN RIGHTS LAW IN U.S. COURTS

§ 6–11.   INTRODUCTION

As a general proposition, treaties and customary international law are the principal sources of international human rights law. States incorporate these principles and provisions into their domestic law in different ways. To understand how American courts deal with international human rights law, it is necessary to review the place given to treaties and customary international law in U.S. law.

In general, U.S. constitutional law accords treaties the same normative rank as federal statutes. *See* Edye v. Robertson, 112 U.S. 580 (1884); Diggs v. Shultz, 470 F.2d 461 (D.C.Cir.1972), cert. denied, 411 U.S. 931 (1973), It also generally equates customary international law to federal common law. *See* Banco Nacional de Cuba v. Sabbatino, 376 U.S. 398, 425 (1964). Restatement (Third) Foreign Relations Law § 131. *But cf.* Bradley & Goldsmith, "Customary International Law as Federal Common Law: A Critique of the Modern Position," 110 Harv. L. Rev. 815 (1997); Vázquez, "Customary International Law as U.S. Law: A Critique of the Revisionist and Intermediate Positions and a Defense of the Modern Position," 86 Notre Dame L. Rev. 1495 (2011). A treaty provision will supersede an earlier federal statute in conflict with it or any inconsistent state legislation only if it is self-executing. Foster v. Neilson, 27 U.S. (2 Pet.) 253 (1829); Restatement (Third) § 111(3).

A federal statute will take precedence over an earlier treaty provision and any customary international law rule in conflict with it. Whitney v. Robertson, 124 U.S. 190, 194 (1888); Cook v. United States, 288 U.S. 102 (1933). Wherever possible, however, U.S. courts will attempt to reconcile U.S. law with the country's international obligations to avoid unintended conflicts. Restatement (Third) Foreign Relations Law § 114 and 115; *cf.* Murray v. The Schooner Charming Betsy, 6 U.S. (2 Cranch) 64,

118 (1804). *See generally* Steinhardt, "The Role of International Law as a Canon of Domestic Constitutional Construction," 43 Vand. L. Rev. 1103 (1990).

In sum, when an international human rights norm has become binding on the United States either as a result of a treaty obligation or, according to the modern position, as customary international law, it has the status of U.S. law. How that law will be applied by domestic courts and what legal effect it will be accorded depends on whether it has been superseded (displaced) by a federal statute and whether, in the case of a treaty, it can be applied without implementing legislation—that is, whether it is "self-executing." The sections that follow will look at the manner in which U.S. courts have applied international human rights law.

§ 6–12. HUMAN RIGHTS TREATIES

The human rights provisions of the UN Charter have been invoked in U.S. courts on a number of occasions. The most important case on the subject is Sei Fujii v. California, 38 Cal.2d 718, 242 P.2d 617 (1952), discussed *supra* in § 6–3. Although the California Supreme Court struck down the law in question as being in violation of the Fourteenth Amendment of the U.S. Constitution, it declared that the human rights provisions of the UN Charter were non-self-executing and that, consequently, they lacked the necessary domestic legal force to invalidate the challenged California law.

Although that decision might also have been challenged on the ground that the treaty provision (even though "non-self-executing") reflected a "pre-emptive" federal policy on the subject, so that a state law in conflict with that policy must yield to it, *see* Zschernig v. Miller, 389 U.S. 429 (1968), U.S. courts have generally followed the Sei Fujii view, holding the human rights provisions of the Charter to be "non-self-executing." *See, e.g.,* Hitai v. Immigration and Naturalization Service, 343 F.2d 466 (2d Cir.1965); Spiess v. C. Itoh & Co., Inc., 643 F.2d 353 (5th Cir.1981); Frolova v. Union of Soviet Socialist Republics, 761 F.2d 370 (7th Cir.1985); Al-Bihani v. Obama, 619 F.3d 1 (D.C. Cir. 2010), 393 U.S. App. D.C. 57 (2010); United States v. Khatallah, 160 F.Supp.3d 144 at 153 (D.D.C. 2016).

The distinction between a "self-executing" and "non-self-executing" treaty concerns the domestic effect of the treaty in question. Doctrinally, a "self-executing" treaty has the force of federal law in the United States without the need for implementing legislation, while a "non-self-executing" treaty is not domestically enforceable by U.S. courts in the absence of implementing legislation, even while it remains binding on the United States under international law.

The exact meaning of the distinction has been controversial ever since the Supreme Court first spoke to the issue in Foster v. Neilson, 27 U.S. (2 Pet.) 253 (1829):

A treaty is in its nature a contract between two nations, not a legislative act. It does not generally effect, of itself, the object to be accomplished, especially so far as its operation is infra-territorial; but is carried into execution by the sovereign power of the respective parties to the instrument.

In the United States a different principle is established. Our constitution declares a treaty to be the law of the land. It is, consequently, to be regarded in courts of justice as equivalent to an act of the legislature, whenever it operates of itself without the aid of any legislative provision. But when the terms of the stipulation import a contract, when either of the parties engages to perform a particular act, the treaty addresses itself to the political, not the judicial department; and the legislature must execute the contract before it can become a rule for the Court.

Id. at 314.

The "self-executing" terminology was first used by the Court in Whitney v. Robertson, 124 U.S. 190, 194 (1888):

When the stipulations [of a treaty] are not self-executing, they can only be enforced pursuant to legislation to carry them into effect. . . . If the treaty contains stipulations which are self-executing, that is, require no legislation to make them operative, to that extent they have the force and effect of a legislative enactment.

Over the years, this distinction has become accepted doctrine. *See, e.g.,* Restatement (Third)

Foreign Relations Law § 111(3) ("a non-self-executing agreement will not be given effect as [U.S.] law in the absence of implementing legislation.) and § 111(4) ("[a]n international agreement of the United States is 'non-self-executing' (a) if the agreement manifests an intention that it shall not become effective as domestic law without the enactment of implementing legislation, (b) if the Senate in giving consent to a treaty, or Congress by resolution, requires implementing legislation, or (c) if implementing legislation is constitutionally required.").

The distinction has long been a matter of scholarly debate. The literature is extensive. *See, e.g.,* Buergenthal, "Self-Executing and Non-Self-Executing Treaties in National and International Law," 235 Recueil des Cours 303 (1992 IV); Buergenthal, "Modern Constitutions and Human Rights Treaties," 36 Colum. J. Trans'l L. 211, 221–23 (1997); Vázquez, "The Four Doctrines of Self-Executing Treaties," 89 Am. J. Int'l L. 695 (1995); Ku and Yoo "Bond, The Treaty Power, and the Overlooked Value of Non-Self-Executing Treaties," 90 Notre Dame L. Rev. 1607 (2015); Ramsey, "A Textual Approach to Treaty Non-Self-Execution," 2015 B.Y.U. L. Rev. 1639 (2015); D. Sloss, *The Death of Treaty Supremacy: An Invisible Constitutional Change* (2016).

In 2008, the Supreme Court addressed the issues again Medellín v. Texas, 552 U.S. 491 (2008). The case arose from the failure of U.S. officials to advise José Ernesto Medellín, a Mexican national, of his right under Article 36 of the Vienna Convention on Consular Relations to report his detention to the Mexican consulate. Medellín had been found guilty of murder by the Texas courts and sentenced to death. His petitions for habeas corpus were deemed barred by the "procedural default" doctrine because he had not raised his claims under the Convention at trial or on appeal.

Before his appeals were exhausted, the International Court of Justice held that because the United States had violated its obligations under the Vienna Convention, Medellín and other Mexican nationals with similar claims were entitled under the treaty to review of their state court convictions. The ICJ did not specify a particular procedure for this review but held that the United States was obligated "to provide, by means of its own choosing, review and reconsideration of the convictions and sentences" to determine whether the failure to provide the notice required by the treaty prejudiced the petitioners. Avena and Other Mexican Nationals (Mex. v. U.S.), 2004 I.C.J. 12 at 72 (Mar. 31).

In response, President Bush issued a memorandum purporting to instruct the Texas courts to give effect to the ICJ's judgment. It said: "I have determined, pursuant to the authority vested in me as President by the Constitution and the laws of the United States of America, that the United States will discharge its international obligations under the decision of the International Court of Justice in [Avena], by having State courts give effect to the decision in accordance with general principles of comity in cases filed by the 51 Mexican nationals addressed in that decision." The Texas Court of Criminal Appeals rejected that instruction, however, on the ground that the President's memorandum was not "binding federal law" and thus could not displace the relevant state law.

Writing for a majority of the Court, Chief Justice Roberts concluded that neither the Avena decision nor the President's memorandum entitled Medellín to the review and reconsideration he sought. As to the first, the Chief Justice focused primarily on Article 94 of the UN Charter, under which the United States "under[took] to comply with the decision of the International Court of Justice in any case to which it is a party." Because Article 94 did not say that the States Parties 'shall' or 'must' comply, 552 U.S. 491, 508 (2008), and for a variety of other reasons, the Court concluded that the ICJ's judgment in Avena did not of its own force constitute binding federal law that pre-empts state restrictions on the filing of successive habeas petitions.

On the second issue, the majority noted that while treaties may comprise international commitments "they are not domestic law unless Congress has either enacted implementing statutes or the treaty itself conveys an intention that it be 'self-executing' and is ratified on these terms [citing to Igartua-De La Rosa v. United States, 417 F.3d 145, 150 (C.A.1 2005)]." *Id.* At 505. In a footnote, it said that a "non-self-executing" treaty is one that "does not by itself give rise to domestically enforceable federal law." 552 U.S. at 505 n. 2. Because the treaty in question (i.e., the UN Charter) was not self-executing, the President therefore lacked constitutional authority bind the state courts to follow the Avena decision. The Court noted that "[t]he President may comply with the treaty's obligations by some other means, so long as they are consistent with the Constitution. But he may not rely upon a non-self-executing treaty to 'establish binding rules of decision that preempt contrary state law.'" *Id.* at 530.

Several aspects of this decision give rise to concern from the human rights perspective. Perhaps the most important is that the executive branch was found, in the circumstances of this case, to lack the constitutional ability to require one of the constituent states of the Union to comply with a national obligation under international law. For many, this result illustrates the difficulties posed by the federal system when it comes to human rights treaty obligations.

Second, some commentators have worried that some of the Court's language might be read to establish a presumption against self-execution. *But see* Vázquez, "Treaties as the Law of the Land: The Supremacy Clause and the Judicial Enforcement of Treaties," 122 Harv. L. Rev. 599 (2008); Bradley, "Intent, Presumption, and Non-Self-Executing Treaties," 102 Am. J. Int'l L. 540 (2008). Commentators have also questioned the Court's suggestion that the domestic effect of the treaty turns on the intent of the political branches ("[o]ur cases simply require courts to decide whether a treaty's terms reflect a determination by the President who negotiated it and the Senate that confirmed it that the treaty has domestic effect.") *Id.* at 521.

Third, concern has been expressed about the Court's dictum that "[e]ven when treaties are self-executing in the sense that they create federal law, the background presumption is that '[i]nternational agreements, even those directly benefiting private persons, generally do not create private rights or provide for a private cause of action in domestic courts.' " *Id.* at 505 n.3. This statement seems to signal a restrictive approach to the status of even self-executing treaties in U.S. law.

Finally, some worry that the Court's statement that a non-self-executing treaty is not "domestically enforceable federal law" and lacks "any domestic effect of its own force" will effectively deprive such treaties of any normative influence whatsoever. Even if they do not provide the basis for bringing a lawsuit, for example, might they nonetheless be invoked by litigants or relied on by courts as providing evidence of customary international law or otherwise relevant standards? Do they still fall within the President's constitutional obligations to 'take care' to enforce the law? These and other questions continue to be vigorously debated in the wake of the Medellín decision. *See, e.g.,* Stephan, "Private Rights for Treaty Violations After Sanchez-Llamas," 11 Lewis & Clark L. Rev. 65 (2007); Swaine, "Taking Care of Treaties," 108 Colum. L. Rev. 331 (2008); Vázquez, "Less Than Zero?," 102 Am. J. Int'l L. 563 (2008); Bederman, "Medellín's New Paradigm for Treaty Interpretation," 102 Am. J. Int'l L. 529 (2008);

Quigley, "A Tragi-Comedy of Errors Erodes Self-Execution of Treaties: Medellín v. Texas and Beyond," 45 Case W. Res. J. Int'l L. 403 (2012); Spiro, "Sovereigntism's Twilight," 31 Berkeley J. Int'l L. 307 (2013); Galbraith, "International Law and the Domestic Separation of Powers," 99 Va. L. Rev. 987 (2013); Ramsey, "Evading the Treaty Power?: The Constitutionality of Nonbinding Agreements," 11 FIU L. Rev. 371 (2016).

§ 6–13.   CUSTOMARY INTERNATIONAL LAW

The place of customary international law in the U.S. legal system has similarly been the subject of differing conclusions. At the Founding, it appears that the "law of nations" was considered part of general common law and thus applicable in federal as well as state courts. In The Paquete Habana, 175 U.S. 677 at 700 (1900), the U.S. Supreme Court appeared to endorse this view when it famously said that "[i]nternational law is part of our law, and must be ascertained and administered by the courts of appropriate jurisdiction as often as questions of right depending on it are duly presented for their determination." The Court continued:

> For this purpose, where there is no treaty and no controlling executive or legislative ac or judicial decision, resort must be had to the customs and usages of civilized nations, and, as evidence of these, to the works of jurists and commentators who by years of labor, research, and experience have made themselves particularly well acquainted with the subjects of which they treat.

175 U.S. at 700. However, the import of this statement can be debated. Not only did the Court ascribe a secondary or "gap-filling" role to customary international law, but the context of the case suggests to some a limited application. The case involved a claim that two Spanish-flagged coastal fishing vessels had been wrongly seized by the U.S. Navy during its blockade of Cuba, and thus arose under the Court's admiralty and maritime jurisdiction (which traditionally relied on customary international law and still does today). Moreover, the concept of general common law applicable in federal courts is no longer accepted. *See generally* Dodge, "The Paquete Habana: Customary International Law as Part of Our Law" in J. Noyes et al., eds., *International Law Stories* (2007); Scoville, "Finding Customary International Law," 101 Iowa L. Rev. 1893 (2016).

Still, the question remains whether, and to what extent, customary international law may play a role in domestic litigation in the absence of an applicable human rights treaty provision. A growing list of international human rights can be characterized as customary international law (*e.g.,* genocide, torture, and prolonged arbitrary detention). Restatement (Third) Foreign Relations Law § 702. Much of that law has evolved from rights and principles proclaimed in international human rights instruments that have their basis in the Charter of the UN and other treaties of a universal character. *See* Chapter 2, *supra.* In fact, U.S. courts have from time to time relied on this law to grant judicial relief.

An important vehicle for bringing these issues into U.S. courts has been the Alien Tort Statute (ATS), codified at 28 U.S.C. § 1350 (2014) (sometimes wrongly referred to as the "Alien Tort Claims Act"). This unique provision, which was adopted as part of the Judiciary Act of 1789, gives federal district courts original jurisdiction over civil actions brought by aliens (non-U.S. citizens) "for a tort only, committed in violation of the law of nations or a treaty of the United States." Exactly why the first Congress enacted this law remains in dispute. *See generally* Burley, "The Alien Tort Statute and the Judiciary Act of 1789: A Badge of Honor," 83 Am. J. Int'l L. 461 (1989); Sweeney, "A Tort Only in Violation of the Law of Nations," 18 Hastings Int'l & Comp. L. Rev. 445 (1995); Dodge, "The Historical Origins of the Alien Tort Statute: A Response to the 'Originalists'," 19 Hastings Int'l & Com. L. Rev. 221 (1996); Lee, "The Three Lives of the Alien Tort Statute: The Evolving Role of the Judiciary in U.S. Foreign Relations," 89 Notre Dame L. Rev. 1645 (2014); Stephens, "The Curious History of the Alien Tort Statute," 89 Notre Dame L. Rev. 1467 (2014); Moon, The Original Meaning of the Law of Nations," 56 Va. J. Int'l L. 51 (2016).

Two things are significant about the ATS. First, it expressly incorporated the "law of nations" (or customary international law) directly into U.S. domestic law. Second, it appeared (and was interpreted by the judiciary) to permit U.S. courts to adjudicate claims of human rights abuses even when the alleged abuses took place in foreign countries and involved no U.S. persons or entities or other

connections to the United States. In this sense, the
statute uniquely provided a kind of "universal civil
jurisdiction" allowing foreigners to sue foreigners in
U.S. courts on the basis of non-codified customary
international law for human rights abuses occurring
outside the United States.

The first modern case to discuss these issues was
Filártiga v. Peña-Irala, 630 F.2d 876 (2d Cir.1980),
which held that the right to be free from torture "has
become part of customary international law, as
evidenced and defined by the Universal Declaration
of Human Rights." *Id.* at 882. That case was brought
by a Paraguayan family against a former Paraguayan
police official for the death of their son in Paraguay.
The court was required to determine whether torture
was a "tort . . . in violation of the law of nations." To
substantiate its conclusion, the court traced the
evolution of the prohibition against torture from the
UN Charter, the Universal Declaration and other
major international human rights instruments. *See*
Blum & Steinhardt, "Federal Jurisdiction Over
International Human Rights Claims: The Alien Tort
Claims Act after Filártiga v. Peña-Irala," 22 Harv.
Int'l L.J. 53 (1981); Lillich, "Damages for Gross
Violations of International Human Rights Awarded
by U.S. Courts," 15 Hum. Rts. Q. 207 (1993).

In the wake of the Filártiga decision, litigants
brought hundreds of § 1350 cases concerning a broad
range of human rights violations in various parts of
the world. In the majority of cases, however, the
respondents did not appear in court to defend
themselves, so that most of the cases resulted in

default judgments. Moreover, the defendants seldom had assets in the United States, meaning plaintiffs were typically unable to recover on the resulting judgments. Given the statute's unique jurisdictional reach, the judgments are highly unlikely to be enforced by foreign courts. Nonetheless, ATS litigation has been frequently used by human rights advocates as a means of giving public voice to complaints about violations of international law occurring in foreign countries.

The Supreme Court considered the question of the scope of the ATS in Sosa v. Alvarez-Machain, 542 U.S. 692 (2004). The central question before the Court was whether an alien could bring a private claim under the ATS as a matter of federal common law or only pursuant to a supplementary congressional statute authorizing such claims. The Court, in an opinion by Justice Souter, held that by its terms the ATS is merely a jurisdictional grant and does not itself create a cause of action. However, it said, the First Congress could not have meant the statute to be "stillborn," an empty vessel to be filled by subsequent legislation (none was enacted), but must have been intended to allow the federal courts to adjudicate claims in violation of "the law of nations" under their common law power. Although the general federal common law no longer exists today (given the effect of Erie Railroad v. Tompkins, 304 U.S. 64 (1938)), the Court said that the law of nations continues to be one of the "limited enclaves in which federal courts may derive some substantive law in a common law way." *Id.* at 729.

The Court considered the criteria to be applied in determining which of the "limited enclaves" provides a cause of action falling within the ATS. When the ATS was originally enacted in 1789, it observed, a tort remedy was available for violation of safe conducts, infringement of the rights of ambassadors, and piracy. "It was this narrow set of violations of the law of nations, admitting of a judicial remedy and at the same time threatening serious consequences in international affairs, that was probably on minds of the men who drafted the ATS with its reference to tort." 542 U.S. at 715. Accordingly, U.S. courts "should require any claim based on the present-day law of nations to rest on a norm of international character accepted by the civilized world and defined with a specificity comparable to the features of the 18th-century paradigms we have recognized." *Id.* at 725.

The Court took care to emphasize the limited scope of this authority. "The door to further independent judicial recognition of actionable international norms," the Court said, "is still ajar subject to vigilant doorkeeping, and thus open to a narrow class of international norms today." *Id.* at 729. Since the "decision to create a private right of action is one better left to legislative judgment," the Court stressed, "courts should not recognize private claims under federal common law for violations of any international law norm with less definite content and acceptance among civilized nations than the historical paradigms familiar when § 1350 was enacted." *Id.* at 727 and 732. Concerning Sosa's specific claim, the Court found that "a single illegal detention of less than a day, followed by the transfer of custody to lawful authorities and a prompt arraignment, violates no norm of customary international law so well defined as to support the creation of a federal remedy." _Id._ at 738.

In emphasizing the need in ATS cases for "great caution in adapting the law of nations to private rights," the Court noted concern over the possible "collateral consequences" of a given decision.

> [T]he potential implications for the foreign relations of the United States of recognizing such causes should make courts particularly wary of impinging on the discretion of the Legislative and Executive Branches in managing foreign affairs. It is one thing for American courts to enforce constitutional limits on our own State and Federal Governments' power, but quite another to consider suits under rules that would go so far as to claim a limit on the power of foreign governments over their own citizens, and to hold that a foreign government or its agent has transgressed those limits.

_Id._ at 728. Accordingly, "there is a strong argument that federal courts should give serious weight to the Executive Branch's view of the case's impact on foreign policy 'a policy of case-specific deference to the political branches'." _Id._ at 733, n.21. The Court also suggested that lower courts should look to international law to determine whether each particular norm extends the scope of liability to private actors such as corporations or individuals. _Id._ at 733 n.20.

The Sosa decision also appeared to indicate the Court's receptivity to an "exhaustion of domestic remedies" requirement in ATS cases. 542 U.S. 693 at 733, n.21. After initially rejecting such a condition, the Ninth Circuit said, in Sarei v. Rio Tinto, PLC, 550 F.3d 822 at 824 (9th Cir. 2008) that "[w]here the 'nexus' to the United States is weak, courts should carefully consider the question of exhaustion, particularly—but not exclusively—with respect to claims that do not involve matters of 'universal concern.' "

In Kiobel v. Royal Dutch Petroleum Co, ___ U.S. ___, 133 S.Ct. 1659 (2013), the Supreme Court considered and largely rejected the extraterritorial application of the judicially-inferred cause of action recognized in Sosa, holding that the cause of action does not extend to cases in which "all the relevant conduct took place outside the United States." In that case, Nigerian nationals residing in the United States had sued Dutch, British, and Nigerian corporations claiming that through their joint subsidiary which was engaged in oil exploration and production in Ogoniland, they had aided and abetted the Nigerian Government in committing violations of the law of nations in Nigeria. The Second Circuit had dismissed the complaint, reasoning that the law of nations does not recognize corporate liability. After initially granting certiorari on that question, the Court ordered supplemental briefing on the question whether U.S. courts can consider claims for violations of the law of nations occurring in another country.

The Court answered that question in the negative, relying on a canon of statutory interpretation known as "the presumption against extraterritorial application." Under that canon, the Court noted, "[w]hen a statute gives no clear indication of an extraterritorial application, it has none" (citing to Morrison v. National Australia Bank Ltd., 561 U.S. 247 (2010)), and it reflects the "presumption that United States law governs domestically but does not rule the world" (citing to Microsoft Corp. v. AT&T Corp., 550 U.S. 437, 454 (2007)). The presumption "serves to protect against unintended clashes between our laws and those of other nations which could result in international discord" (citing to EEOC v. Arabian American Oil Co., 499 U.S. 244 at 248). *See* 122 S.Ct. at 1664.

The Court recalled its caution in Sosa that "the danger of unwarranted judicial interference in the conduct of foreign policy is magnified in the context of the ATS, because the question is not what Congress has done but instead what courts may do." It noted that in Sosa it had "repeatedly stressed the need for judicial caution in considering which claims could be brought under the ATS, in light of foreign policy concerns." Further, it said, "[t]hese concerns, which are implicated in any case arising under the ATS, are all the more pressing when the question is whether a cause of action under the ATS reaches conduct within the territory of another sovereign." *Id.* at 1665.

Nothing in the text of the statute, the Court continued, suggested that Congress intended causes of action recognized under it to have extraterritorial reach. *Id.* at 1665. Neither could "the historical background against which the ATS was enacted overcome the presumption against application to conduct in the territory of another sovereign." *Id.* at 1666. Finally, the Court found "no indication that the ATS was passed to make the United States a uniquely hospitable forum for the enforcement of international norms." *Id.* at 1668. In consequence, it concluded that "the presumption against extraterritoriality applies to claims under the ATS, and that nothing in the statute rebuts that presumption." *Id.* at 1669. Nevertheless, it phrased its ultimate holding in narrow terms:

> On these facts, all the relevant conduct took place outside the United States. And even where the claims touch and concern the territory of the United States, they must do so with sufficient force to displace the presumption against extraterritorial application. *See Morrison,* 561 U.S. 247, 130 S.Ct., at 2883–2888. Corporations are often present in many countries, and it would reach too far to say that mere corporate presence suffices. If Congress were to determine otherwise, a statute more specific than the ATS would be required.

Id. at 1669.

Precisely how claims might "touch and concern the territory of the United States" sufficiently to overcome the presumption against extraterritoriality was not further explained. Justice Kennedy's concurrence noted that the majority was "careful to leave open a number of significant questions regarding the reach and interpretation of the Alien Tort Statute." *Id.* In his concurrence, Justice Breyer (joined by Justices Ginsburg, Sotomayor and Kagan) said that jurisdiction under the ATS could be proper where "(1) the alleged tort occurs on American soil, (2) the defendant is an American national, or (3) the defendant's conduct substantially and adversely affects an important American national interest, and that includes a distinct interest in preventing the United States from becoming a safe harbor (free of civil as well as criminal liability) for a torturer or other common enemy of mankind." *Id.* at 1671.

The lower courts will undoubtedly continue to address this issue over time. Several courts of appeal have already done so, with varying results. *See* Al Shimari v. CACI Premier Tech., Inc., 758 F.3d 516 (4th Cir. 2014); Mustafa v. Chevron Corp.,770 F.3d 170 (2d Cir. 2014); Doe v. Drummond 782 F.3d 576 (11th Cir. 2015); Doe I v. Nestlé USA, Inc., 788 F.3d 946 (9th Cir. 2015); Adhikari v. Kellogg Brown & Root, Inc., 845 F.3d. 184 (5th Cir. 2017). *See also* Cooper, "Aliens Among Us: Factors to Determine Whether Corporations Should Face Prosecution in U.S. Courts for Their Actions Overseas, 77 La. L. Rev. 513 (2016).

Another important aspect of the ATS—whether it can be applied to corporate entities—also remains unresolved. This issue is discussed at § 7–9 *infra.*

There continues to be a spirited debate over the role of customary law in U.S. courts and the legitimacy and propriety of ATS suits. For a sampling, *see* Bradley & Goldsmith, "Customary International Law as Federal Common Law: A Critique of the Modern Position," 110 Harv. L. Rev. 815 (1997); Koh, "Is International Law Really State Law?", 111 Harv. L. Rev. 1824 (1998); Stephens, "Human Rights Accountability, Congress, Federalism, and International Law," 6 ILSA J. Int'l & Comp. L. 277 (2000); Bradley, "Customary International Law and Private Rights of Action," 1 Chi. J. Int'l L. 421 (2000); Bradley, The Alien Tort Statute and Article III," 42 Va. J. Int'l L. 587 (2002); Dodge, "The Constitutionality of the Alien Tort Statute: Some Observations on Text and Context," 42 Va. J. Int'l L. 687, 689 (2002); Van Alstine, "Federal Common Law in an Age of Treaties," 89 Cornell L. Rev. 892 (2004); Casto, "The New Federal Common Law of Tort Remedies for Violations of International Law," 37 Rutgers L. J. 635 (2006); Bradley, Goldsmith and Moore, "Sosa, Customary International Law, and the Continuing Relevance of Erie," 120 Harv. L. Rev. 869 (2007); Bellia and Clark, "The Federal Common Law of Nations," 109 Colum. L. Rev. 1 (2009); Bellinger, "Enforcing Human Rights in U.S. Courts and Abroad: The Alien Tort Statute and Other Approaches," 42 Vand. J. Transnat'l L. 1 (2009); Vázquez, "Customary International Law as U.S. Law: A Critique of the Revisionist and Intermediate Positions and a Defense of the Modern Position," 86 Notre Dame L. Rev. 1495 (2011); Vázquez, "Things We Do With Presumptions: Reflections on Kiobel v. Royal Dutch Shell," 89 Notre Dame L. Rev. 1719 (2014); Tawfik, "To Touch and Concern the United States with Sufficient Force:

How American Due Process and Choice of Law Cases Inform the Reach of the Alien Tort Statute After Kiobel," 37 Mich. J. Int'l L. 539 (2016).

Congress has explicitly provided federal causes of action for torture and extrajudicial killing under the Torture Victims Protection Act, Pub. L. No. 102–256, 106 Stat. 73 (1992), codified at 22 U.S.C. § 1350 (note) (2008). Note that the somewhat related issue of universal criminal jurisdiction to prosecute and punish individuals for human rights violations that constitute international crimes has not yet been raised in U.S. courts.

CHAPTER 7
NON-STATE ACTORS

I. INTRODUCTION

At its origins, international human rights law addressed the relationship between governments and their citizens, and in consequence it focused primarily on the duties and responsibilities of states and state entities. Over time, however, the development of international norms, institutions and procedures for the promotion and protection of human rights has gone hand in hand with an expansion in the scope of application of human rights principles. As a result, the field of international human rights law today encompasses a wide variety of non-state actors.

Even in 1948, the Universal Declaration of Human Rights recognized that governments and individual citizens are not the only human rights stakeholders. It describes human rights as

> a common standard of achievement for all peoples and nations, to the end that every individual and every organ of society, keeping this Declaration constantly in mind, shall strive by teaching and education to promote respect for these rights and freedoms and by progressive measures, national and international, to secure their universal and effective recognition and observance, both among the peoples of

Member States themselves and among the
peoples of territories under their jurisdiction.

UDHR, preambular para. 8. The notion that entities
other than states and individuals are both rights-
holders and bearers of obligations has gained
increasing acceptance during the intervening
decades.

This chapter describes the relevant roles and
responsibilities of several categories of non-state
actors. The term "non-state actor" is wide-reaching,
encompassing entities such as non-governmental
organizations   (NGOs),   inter-governmental
organizations (IGOs), and private bodies as diverse
as voluntary groups and multinational corporations.
Although these groups fall collectively under the
"non-state actors" umbrella, they are quite different
and play varying roles. No specific treaty obligation
or rule of customary international law explicitly
holds all actors liable for committing human rights
violations or provides a forum for redress. However,
the international community has increasingly viewed
non-state actors as being implicitly covered by the
various international human rights instruments.

Moreover, non-state actors have the capacity to
contribute to the protection and promotion of human
rights around the world. Some NGOs have in fact
been established precisely for that purpose and
typically play a dynamic role in advancing human
rights, both domestically and globally. Increasingly,
multinational corporations and financial institutions
(both domestic and international) are in a position to
either be heroes or villains in upholding human

rights, depending on their governing rules and practices. Intergovernmental organizations can also play an influential role in determining how each of those groups operates. This chapter offers an overview of the evolving role of non-state actors in the international human rights field.

II. NON-GOVERNMENTAL ORGANIZATIONS

§ 7–1. NON-GOVERNMENTAL ORGANIZATIONS

Some 1200 NGOs attended the San Francisco Conference during the drafting of the UN Charter and many played an important role. They lobbied for the inclusion of human rights provisions in the Charter and for a system that would give NGOs formal institutional affiliation with and standing before UN organs.

The result was Article 71 of the UN Charter, which provides that "the Economic and Social Council may make suitable arrangements for consultation with non-governmental organizations which are concerned with matters within its competence." Article 71 was implemented in due course by ECOSOC and over time it has come to be interpreted broadly to allow NGOs to involve themselves in UN human rights activities. The subject was first regulated by ECOSOC Resolution 1296 (XLIV) of May 23, 1968, revised and expanded in 1996 by ECOSOC Resolution 1996/31. It established a formal system that enables qualified NGOs to obtain one of three types of consultative status (general, special and roster) with the Organization.

The existence of this system has encouraged the creation of more NGOs and the adoption of similar consultative systems by other international and regional organizations, such as the Council of Europe, the Organization for the Security and Cooperation for Europe, the African Union (including the African Commission for Human Rights), and the Organization of American States. As a result, a myriad of these groups exists around the world: by some estimates, there may be as many as 10 million of them. *See* http://www.cid.org.nz/news-old/25-facts-and-stats-about-ngos-worldwide/. While most are domestically-oriented, many are internationally active.

The term "NGO" is generally understood to exclude entities established by governments or through intergovernmental agreements, as well as private for-profit enterprises. Nevertheless, human rights NGOs come in all sizes and varieties. They can be classified in several categories. On the one hand, generalist NGOs have broad mandates and agendas, covering all categories of human rights, i.e., civil and political, economic, social and cultural rights (*e.g.,* Human Rights Watch or the International Federation for Human Rights (FIDH)). They may act domestically or internationally. By contrast, specialized NGOs have specific mandates, for example covering a particular human rights treaty (the Covenant on Civil and Political Rights) or a specific right (the right to health or water or housing or a clean environment) or the rights of a specific category of persons (such as women, children, persons with disabilities, minorities, indigenous peoples (*e.g.,* the Minority Rights Group International). Some NGOs concentrate only on local or domestic situations, while others have a regional focus and still others work on global issues.

In order to increase their capacity for action and their ability to collect information and speak for various groups, some human rights NGOs have organized themselves into federations. Some have created affiliations in foreign countries that can give them first-hand, reliable information to provide to international bodies. However, such affiliations are generally governed by the domestic legislation of the States where they are established or registered.

The activities of human rights NGOs typically focus on the overall promotion and protection of human rights. Some aim at changing the domestic or international policies of their own (or foreign) governments, and others engage exclusively in education and training, building domestic constituencies, or carrying out international relief efforts. They may conduct inquiries, fact-finding missions, monitoring and investigations into human rights abuses, or visit detention facilities in order to monitor detainees' rights and detention conditions, or assist asylum-seekers and refugees. Some exclusively litigate human rights issues in national courts, including by offering free legal assistance to alleged victims. Others mount grass-roots campaigns against specific types of violations (such as torture, police abuse, or racial or gender discrimination) while still others engage in standard-setting efforts (for example, aimed at improving corporate social responsibility). NGOs may advocate for the ratification of international human rights instruments or become involved in drafting national reports to be submitted to international bodies. They may also assist states in implementing recommendations made by international bodies. Some governments consult with NGOs during the drafting of domestic legislation with human rights dimensions.

The NGO field is diverse, constantly adapting and evolving. As the range of human rights concerns has expanded, NGOs have similarly diversified their work and enlarged their interests. Deregulation and privatization have also had an impact, with non-state groups taking on many humanitarian assistance and aid distribution efforts previously handled by governments or inter-governmental organizations. With their increasing numbers and functions, networks of international and national NGOs have emerged. In recent years, this expanding web of transnational NGOs, other groups, and individuals has frequently been referred to as the "global civil society," and the nature and merits of its increasing role have been debated.

Many NGOs work closely with international bodies such as the United Nations and its specialized agencies (*see* § 7–3 *infra*) as well as regional bodies. Whether or not they have a formal affiliation with an intergovernmental organization, human rights

NGOs have increasingly played an important role in the evolution of the international system for the protection of human rights and in efforts to make it work. Because governments that do not respect human rights are often disposed to undermine international human rights norms, institutions, and procedures, human rights NGOs frequently provide a needed and effective counterweight by highlighting the issues and bringing public pressure to bear (for example, by "naming and shaming" abusers). To a significant extent, NGOs deserve credit for the progress in international human rights compliance that has been made in recent decades.

Consider, for example, the disparate nature and activities of the following human rights organizations. The list is far from exhaustive and includes only a small fraction of the NGOs in the international human rights field. It is included here simply to illustrate the varied nature of NGOs involved in human rights work.

Amnesty International describes itself as a "global movement of people fighting injustice and promoting human rights" through "high-level legislative work, media outreach and grassroots mobilization to shape and promote legislation and policies to advance human rights, protect individuals and free prisoners of conscience." It is active in the areas of arms control, corporate accountability, freedom of expression, the rights of the indigenous and international justice, to name a few. *See* https://www.amnesty.org/en/what-we-do.

The Worldwide Movement for Human Rights (FIDH) is a federation of some 184 national human rights organizations from 112 countries. It works at the national, regional and international levels to defend "all civil, political, economic, social and cultural rights as set out in the Universal Declaration of Human Rights" and to "consolidate democratic processes." *See* https://www.fidh.org/en.

The European Roma Rights Centre works to combat anti-Romani racism and human rights abuse of Roma through strategic litigation, research and policy development, advocacy and human rights education. *See* http://www.errc.org/.

The Association of Women's Rights in Development is an international feminist membership organization committed to achieving gender equality, sustainable development and women's human rights, *inter alia* by providing comprehensive information and analysis on women's human rights and global issues. *See* https://www.awid.org.

The International Commission of Jurists aims at promoting and protecting human rights through the Rule of Law by using the legal expertize of its members to "develop and strengthen national and international justice systems" through the progressive development and effective implementation of international human rights and humanitarian law. It comprises up to sixty lawyers from around the world who known for their experience, knowledge and fundamental commitment to human rights. *See* https://www.icj.org.

Human   Rights   Watch   is   a   nonprofit, nongovernmental organization dedicated to fact-finding, impartial reporting, effective use of media, and targeted advocacy for human rights. Each year, HRW publishes more than 100 reports and briefings on human rights conditions in some 90 countries, with governments, the United Nations, regional groups like the African Union and the European Union, financial institutions, and corporations. *See* https://www.hrw.org.

Médecins Sans Frontières, also known as "Doctors Without Borders," works in war-torn regions and developing countries to provide medical care and assistance through medical professionals, logistical experts,   water   and   sanitation   engineers   and administrators, the majority of whom are volunteers. *See* http://www.msf-me.org/en.

Human Rights First is an "advocacy and action organization that challenges America to live up to its ideals." Among other activities, it works to encourage the   U.S.   government   and   private   companies   to respect human rights and the rule of law and to "create the political environment and policy solutions necessary   to   ensure   consistent   respect   for   human rights." *See* http://www.humanrightsfirst.org.

The Global Fund for Human Rights is dedicated to advancing human rights "by providing resources and tools to the people and organizations on the ground who have real potential to generate positive change." It supports a wide range of human rights issues, such as defending indigenous land rights in Guatemala, promoting women's rights in Morocco, pressing for accountability for war crimes in West Africa, and ending the practice of bonded labor (a form of slavery) in India. *See* http://globalhumanrights.org.

Minority Rights Group International works to secure rights for ethnic, religious and linguistic minorities and indigenous people around the world through advocacy publications, litigation and training projects. *See* http://minorityrights.org.

The International Dalit Solidarity Network advocates for Dalit human rights, promotes national Dalit solidarity, and works internationally against caste-based discrimination. *See* http://idsn.org/about -us/.

Freedom House conducts research and advocacy on democracy, political freedom, and human rights to support "frontline activists in their efforts to defend fundamental human rights, including to document abuses, advocate for justice end impunity and fortify the self-protection of human rights defenders." *See* https://freedomhouse.org.

Article 19 focuses on the defense and promotion of freedom of expression and freedom of information worldwide (as reflected in Article 19 of the Universal Declaration of Human Rights) in the belief that these particular human rights are central to freedom and democracy. Its work includes monitoring, research, advocacy, campaigning, setting standards, litigation, and advising on legislative proposals, among other activities. *See* https://www.article19.org.

The Public International Law & Policy Group provides free legal assistance to states and governments in such areas as peace negotiations, drafting post-conflict constitutions, prosecuting war criminals, and promoting democratic governance. *See* http://www.publicinternationallawandpolicygroup.org.

Habitat International Coalition comprises social movements, community-based organizations, support groups and academics (with members in 117 nations in five continents) aimed at ensuring "a sustainable habitat and a livable planet for all." Its work focuses on rights linked to housing and habitat, housing, clean water, sanitation, a healthy environment, access to public goods and services (*e.g.,* health, education, transport and recreation), and the preservation of social, natural, historic and cultural patrimony. *See* http://www.habitat.org.

International Coalition for the International Criminal Court is a partnership of over 2,500 member organizations in 150 countries that together fight for global justice by supporting the International Criminal Court established by the Rome Statute to prosecute genocide, crimes against humanity, war crimes and aggression and through prosecutions in national courts. *See* http://www. coalitionfortheicc.org.

The International Service for Human Rights is dedicated to promoting and protecting human rights by supporting human rights defenders, strengthening human rights systems, and leading and participating in coalitions for human rights change. *See* http://www.ishr.ch.

Most NGOs are formed, established or registered as private non-profit organizations or associations under domestic (national) law. Only a very few, such as the International Committee of the Red Cross, are recognized as having international legal personality in their own right. Once formed or registered, NGOs often work closely with local populations to engage in advocacy and policy work within a state. Some NGOs work thorough local implementing partners to further human rights norms in foreign countries; others comprise networks or federations of affiliated organizations in different countries.

Both international and domestic NGOs engage in advocacy with state actors to further implementation of human rights norms through recommendations for changes in policy as well as legislation. Some focus on foreign governments, while others aim to change the approach and practices of their own governments. Governmental policies are of course made on the national level, and national political considerations necessarily affect decisions about whether to ratify human rights treaties or which methods should be employed to promote respect for human rights abroad. Many NGOs actively engage in lobbying governments in an effort to influence the formulation and execution of relevant policies. Some human rights NGOs also cooperate (or work directly) with UN field activities.

§ 7–2. REFERENCES.

For more information, *see* the list of Intergovernmental and Governmental Organizations

at http://www.humanrights.com/voices-for-human-rights/human-rights-organizations/governmental.
html; the *UN Human Rights Treaty Information Portal*, available *at* http://www.humanrightsinfo.com/links-ngo.html; the Council of Europe's "Compass: Manual for Human Rights Education with Young People," at http://www.coe.int/en/web/compass/human-rights-activism-and-the-role-of-ngos; and UN High Commissioner for Human Rights, "National human rights institutions: history, principles roles and responsibilities" (UN Doc. HR/P/PT/4/Rev.1, 2010), which is available at http://www.ohchr.org/Documents/Publications/PTS-4Rev1-NHRI_en.pdf.

See also Crowley and Ryan, *Navigating Change for International NGOs: A Practical Handbook* (Kumarian 2016); Boulding, *NGOs, Political Protest, and Civil Society* (Cambridge 2016); Cotton-Betteridge, "An Emerging International Norm for Non-Governmental Organizations, 11 B.Y.U. Int'l L. & Mgmt. Rev. 1 (2015); Edwards, "Assessing the Effectiveness of Human Rights Non-Governmental Organizations (NGOs) from the Birth of the United Nations to the 21st Century: Ten Attributes of Highly Successful Human Rights NGOs," 18 Michigan State J. Int'l L. 165 (2010); Dupuy and Vierucci, eds., *NGOs in International Law: Efficiency in Flexibility?* (Elgar 2008); Gilboa, "The New Public Sphere: Global Civil Society, Communication, Networks, and Global Governance" *in* G. Cowan and N.J. Cull (eds.), *Public Diplomacy in a Changing World* (2008); A.-K. Lindblom, *Non-Governmental Organisations in International Law* (Cambridge 2006); A.-K. Lindblom, *Non-Governmental Organizations in*

International Law (2005); C.E. Welch, ed., *NGOs and Human Rights: Promise and Performance* (2002); Gamble & Ku, "International Law—New Actors and New Technologies: Center Stage for NGOs?", 31 Law & Policy in Int'l Bus. 221 (2000); Mertus, "Considering Norm Generation and Norm Application," 32 N.Y.U. J. Int'l L. & Pol. 537 (2000); Korey, *NGOs and the Universal Declaration of Human Rights* (1998).

§ 7–3. NGO ENGAGEMENT WITH INTERNATIONAL BODIES

In order to engage with the UN and its various commissions, committees and specialized agencies, NGOs working in the international human rights field must have some form of consultative status (with the exception of the UN human rights treaty bodies, which do not require such status). This status permits their representatives (subject to certain conditions and restrictions) to attend meetings of these organizations, to present reports, to be heard by their committees and commissions, and, in certain cases, to influence the agendas of these bodies.

According to ECOSOC's NGO Branch, as of December 2016, more than 4660 NGO's had been registered with the United Nations. *See generally* United Nations, *Working with ECOSOC: An NGOs Guide to Consultative Status*, 2011, available at http://csonet.org/content/documents/Brochure.pdf.

Within Europe, NGOs participate in standard-setting at the Council of Europe through the International Non-Governmental Organizations

(INGO) Conference. They can provide comments on state reports under the European Social Charter and have standing to file complaints under the 1995 Additional Protocol to the European Social Charter providing a System of Collective Complaints. NGOs also participate as *amici curiae* in cases before the European Court of Human Rights. Similar arrangements can be made with other international organizations working in the human rights field, such as the Organization of American States (OAS) through its program for the participation of civil society, the Organization for Security and Cooperation in Europe, and the African Commission on Human and Peoples' Rights.

At the UN level, human rights NGOs mostly engage with the UN Human Rights Council and its subsidiary bodies and procedures (including the Universal Periodic Review) as well as with the various human rights treaty bodies. All of the UN human rights treaty bodies have developed procedures for interaction with NGOs in the various phases of their work. For example, in the context of a State Party's report to a treaty body, NGOs may provide an "alternative" or "shadow" report on that state's progress in implementing its treaty obligations. They may brief Committee members on country conditions, either formally during a meeting before the review or informally at the lunchtime. They may also approach Committee members individually to lobby for the consideration of pressing concerns to raise during the dialogue with the delegation during the review.

Often, the NGO reports provide first-hand information to balance or supplement the information states include in their reports. In addition, they may contribute to the elaboration of General Comments or Recommendations by providing analyses, views and position papers. NGOs have the ability to represent individuals who submit "communications" to treaty bodies and may act as amicus curiae. Lastly, they can provide input to the preparation of *in situ* visits by the UN Sub-Committee on the Prevention of Torture. *See generally* S. Farrior, "International Reporting Procedures," *in* Hannum (ed.), *Guide to International Human Rights Practice* 189 (4th ed. 2004); Buergenthal, "The U.N. Human Rights Committee," 5 Max Planck YB U.N. Law 341, 352–53 (2001).

The more recent treaties have expressly provided a role for NGOs in the work of the relevant treaty body, recognizing that NGOs can sometimes be in a better position than individuals to gather reliable information and to prepare the necessary legal documentation. For example, the Committee on the Rights of the Child (CRC) has received reports, documentation, and other information from NGOs since its first session in 1991 based on the Committee's explicit authority to invite expert advice on the implementation of the Convention from "competent bodies" to assist in "the effective implementation of the Convention and to encourage international co-operation in the field covered by the Convention." *See* Article 45(a) of the CRC. The term "competent bodies" has been interpreted to include NGOs. *See generally* Shelton, "The Participation of

Nongovernmental Organizations in International Judicial Proceedings," 88 Am. J. Int'l L. 611 (1994).

All of the treaty bodies that consider periodic country reports invite NGOs to provide reports containing country-specific information on States Parties under review or consideration. The more recent treaties expressly provide for the submission of such information. *See, e.g.,* art. 74(4) of the Convention on the Protection of the Rights of All Migrant Workers and Members of Their Families and Article 38(a) of the Convention on the Rights of Persons with Disabilities. All treaty bodies that examine State Party reports also set aside time (ordinarily a half-day each week) for a briefing by NGOs in public session regarding the countries being examined in that week. Some also set aside time for their pre-sessional working groups to hear statements from NGOs and others. Some also allow NGOs to appear and brief committee members orally in private. Many contemporary human rights instruments can in fact be traced to proposals and/or drafts prepared by NGOs, including the Convention against Torture and the Convention on the Rights of the Child, as well as the regional African and Arab Charters.

Regarding the UN Human Rights Council, NGOs have made contributions to consideration of major human rights violations in the political bodies of the UN, as they did for its predecessor, the UN Commission on Human Rights. In concrete terms, NGOs can intervene at the Human Rights Council's sessions, which provides them a unique opportunity to draw attention to the human rights violations that occur in some countries and to speak on behalf of the victims. Under the Council's complaint mechanism (formerly called the 1503 procedure), NGOs draw the Council's attention to human rights violations in ·specific states. By putting forth written and oral interventions and by lobbying key representatives and delegations, they have on many occasions helped to focus attention on specific human rights violations which might otherwise not have received attention. NGOs also participate in the Universal Periodic Review and in the work of the Advisory Committee and the working groups created by the Council.

See generally Lucia Nader, "The Role of NGOs in the Human Rights Council," 4 Sur. Rev. int. direitos human. (2007, no.7), available at http://dx.doi.org/10.1590/S1806-64452007000200002; Klaus Hufner, "How to File Complaints on Human Rights Violations: A Manual for Individuals and NGOs" (2010), at https://www.unesco.de/c_humanrights; and Mandat International, http://www.welcomedesk.org/en/home.

§ 7–4. UNIVERSAL PERIODIC REVIEW

The newest mechanism for engagement with non-governmental organizations in the UN human rights system is the Universal Periodic Review (UPR). The UPR, which operates under the auspices of the Human Rights Council, was created by UN General Assembly Resolution 60/251 of March 15, 2006. This unique mechanism involves reviewing the human rights records of every UN member state every four and a half years in light of the human rights obligations and commitments expressed in the various human rights instruments to which the state under review is a party. *See* § 2–23, *supra*.

The UPR consists primarily of three stages. First, a working group in the UN Human Rights Council in Geneva undertakes a review of the human rights situation in the state under consideration. That review is based on reports submitted by that state, the Office of the High Commissioner for Human Rights, and NGOs and human rights institutions. The state's representatives present their report and respond to questions and recommendations. Next, a three member panel "troika of rapporteurs" and members of the OHCHR Secretariat prepare a response with recommendations, which is debated and ultimately adopted by the Council. The state under review accepts, in whole or in part, or notes recommendations, and it makes a policy commitment to take action accordingly. In the four and a half years between the two reviews, states are expected to take the necessary action to implement the voluntary pledges they have made, and they report on their progress at their next appearance before the Council.

NGOs are permitted to engage in the UPR process in several ways. They may participate in national consultations held by the state under review (for example, in the United States, through the Department of State's "UPR Town Hall and Civil Society Consultation" process). NGOs may also submit information directly to the Human Rights Council and may make statements at the regular sessions of the Human Rights Council during which the outcomes of the state reviews are considered. NGOs may monitor the UPR working group sessions, lobby members of the UPR working group, and monitor and participate in the states' implementation of UPR recommendations. However, they are not authorized to make statements during the review itself.

For additional information about the UPR process and the role of NGO's, *see* http://www.ohchr.org/EN/HRBodies/UPR/Pages/BasicFacts.aspx and http://www.state.gov/j/drl/upr/process/index.htm. *See also* Levin, "The Reporting Cycle to the United Nations Human Rights Treaty Bodies: Creating a Dialogue between the State and Civil Society—The Israeli Case Study," 48 Geo. Wash. Int'l L. Rev. 315 (2016).

§ 7–5. ENGAGEMENT IN JUDICIAL AND QUASI-JUDICIAL PROCESSES

In addition to participating in the individual petition or communications processes before the UN Human Rights Council and the various treaty bodies, NGOs can file complaints with the Inter-American Commission on Human Rights, both under the American Convention and under the OAS Charter-based petition system (*see* Chapter 4 *supra*). Thus, for example, a decision by the Inter-American Commission holding that the United States had violated the right to life by permitting the execution of minors originated from a complaint filed by the American Civil Liberties Union and the International Human Rights Law Group. Case No.

9647 (United States), Resolution No. 3/87, *Annual Report of the Inter-American Commission on Human Rights 1986–1987,* OEA/Ser.L/V/II.71, doc.9, rev.1, at 147 (1987).

NGOs can also participate in the various matters that reach the Inter-American Court of Human Rights either in the form of requests for advisory opinions or as contentious cases. The Court has permitted NGOs to file *amicus curiae* briefs in advisory proceedings, and a number of them have done so regularly. *See, e.g.,* Advisory Opinion on Restrictions to the Death Penalty, OC–3/83 of Sept. 8, 1983, Inter-American Court of Human Rights, Series A: Judgments and Opinions, No. 3, para. 5 (1983). *See also* Shelton, "The Participation of Nongovernmental Organizations in International Judicial Proceedings," 88 Am. J. Int'l L. 611 at 638–39 (1994). Rules of Court now provide that the victim's representatives have separate standing to participate in cases submitted to the Court; as such they no longer appear as part of the Commission's legal team. *See* Rules of Procedure of the Inter-American Court of Human Rights, art. 25 (2009).

In the first three contentious cases referred to the Inter-American Court by the Inter-American Commission in 1986, the latter invited the lawyers of the NGOs that had originally filed the cases to join its legal team before the Court. *Annual Report of the Inter-American Commission on Human Rights 1986–1987,* OAS/Ser.L/V/II.71, doc.9, rev.1, at 25–26 (1987). *See* Grossman, "Disappearances in Honduras: The Need for Direct Victim Representation in

Human Rights Litigation," 15 Hastings Int'l & Comp. L. Rev. 363, 378–82 (1992). The Commission now routinely resorts to this practice.

Human rights NGOs have also pioneered the practice of using distinguished foreign lawyers or judges as observers at trials of individuals who have been charged with or appear to be tried for political offenses. Amnesty International and the International Commission of Jurists try to make frequent use of trial observers in order to ensure due process of law for the accused. *See, e.g.,* the annual reports of Amnesty International. The mere presence at such trials of foreign lawyers acting as trial observers has tended to prevent some abuses; at times it has even produced acquittals.

A related practice, utilized with considerable success—particularly by the International Committee of the Red Cross—consists of inspections of prisons and detention centers. The ICRC attempts to ensure that those in detention are treated humanely and that they are provided with medical services and other basic necessities. Other NGOs have carried out important *in loco* investigations of human rights violations for use by intergovernmental human rights organizations and international tribunals. *See, e.g.,* International Human Rights Law Group, *No Justice, No Peace: Accountability for Rape and Gender-Based Violence in the Former Yugoslavia* (1993).

These illustrations demonstrate how national and international NGOs can work together towards a

common   goal   in   and   through   the   various
international human rights bodies.

§ 7–6. NGOs AND NATIONAL
POLICIES AND LEGISLATION

A national government's human rights laws,
policies and practices also may be influenced by
domestic   or   international   non-governmental
organizations. National   political   considerations
obviously affect governmental decisions whether to
ratify human rights treaties or what methods,
national or international, should be employed to
promote respect for human rights abroad. The same
is true of the policies that determine the degree to
which a nation is willing to confer authority on
international organizations like the UN to deal with
such violations. All of these and related issues must
be addressed by a country's human rights foreign
policy. *See* Chapter 6, *supra*. Decisions affecting the
formulation and execution of these policies are as
much subject to various forms of lobbying as are
other foreign policy decisions.

NGOs act in many regions, particularly where
countries are in transition from repressive rule or
armed conflicts, in order to foster democracy and
build institutions. *See* Dakolias, "Legal and Judicial
Development: The Role of Civil Society in the Reform
Process," 24 Fordham Int'l L.J. 26 (2000); Ballengee,
"The   Critical   Role   of   Non-Governmental
Organizations in Transitional Justice: A Case Study
of Guatemala," 4 UCLA J. Int'l L. & For. Aff. 477
(1999–2000); Howland, "Learning to Make Proactive

Human Rights Interventions Effective: The Carter Center and Ethiopia's Office of the Special Prosecutor," 18 Wisc. Int'l L. J. 407 (2000); Price, "Restructuring the Media in Post-Conflict Societies: Four Perspectives on the Experience of Intergovernmental and Non-governmental Organizations," 2 Cardozo Online J. Conflict Res. (2000); Lee, "Legal Reform in China: A Role for Nongovernmental Organizations," 25 Yale J. Int'l L. 363 (2000); S. Calnan, *The Effectiveness of Domestic Human Rights NGOs: a Comparative Study* (2008).

III. CORPORATIONS

§ 7–7. CORPORATIONS AND HUMAN RIGHTS

Over half of the 100 largest economies (economic units) of the world are multinational corporations, not states. In fact, the combined sales from the top 200 corporations around the world surpass that of 25% of the economic activity of both state and non-state actors across the globe. As a result, corporations now enjoy unprecedented power and influence on local communities as well as the global economy in general. The rapid pace of "globalization" means that private corporations increasingly operate in multiple countries and thus have greater potential to contribute to human rights progress—and to human rights violations—at the international level.

Accordingly, there has been an increasing realization that corporate activity is a legitimate and important area of human rights consideration. Until fairly recently, however, corporate law and international human rights law rarely intersected. In the few instances in which corporate failure to uphold high standards of conduct was addressed in the past, the focus was on corrupt practices or unfair business dealings. As multinational corporations have gained more power and influence in the international system, an awareness has emerged that it is legitimate to take into account the broader implications of their activities—beyond narrow economic and business goals.

Whether private entities such as corporations are proper "subjects" of international human rights law (and therefore directly bound by its obligations) remains an open question as a matter of law. *See* Vázquez, "Direct vs. Indirect Obligations of Corporations Under International Law," 43 Colum. J. Transnat'l L. 927 (2005). Yet many corporate entities have today recognized that they should act not only in their economic self-interest (focusing on competitiveness, survival and profitability) but also as good citizens, with appropriate attention to broader social goals such as ethical labor practices, concern for the environment, and the well-being of employees, the community and civil society in general. The incentive can come from corporate leadership as well as a corporation's investors, customers, government regulators or "civil society" including NGO advocacy groups.

This approach has come to be characterized as "corporate social responsibility." Broadly considered, the term refers to business practices by which corporations try to conduct themselves in a socially responsible manner. Among companies adopting CSR polices is Google, which until 2015 embraced the motto "Don't Be Evil" and declined to operate in the People's Republic of China because the government refused citizens access to certain categories of information. For its part, Microsoft introduced "Microsoft YouthSpark" (described as a "global initiative to increase access for all youth to learn computer science, empowering them to achieve more for themselves, their families and their communities") as a means to improve access for millions of children around the world to education, employment, and entrepreneurial opportunities. Chiquita established independently verifiable social and environmental standards for its banana production across Latin America, largely in response to consumers' demand for an "ethical banana." Starbucks offers a line of "fair trade" or "ethically sourced" coffees whose production and marketing in no way harmed the workers or the environment.

One method of energizing private entities to take human rights consideration into account is to call upon them to disclose their relevant activities. *See, e.g.,* Laine, "Integrated Reporting: Fostering Human Rights Accountability for Multinational Corporations," 47 Geo. Wash. Int'l L. Rev. 639 (2015). Some companies have been publicly shamed by civil society into changing their practices. Activist groups frequently bring workers from corporations with human rights violations to speak in the United States and other countries. Their discussions are often covered by the media, inspiring consumers and organizations across the United States, Europe, and

Asia to put pressure on the companies. As a result of such efforts, for example, Carlsberg and Heineken backed out of a deal for a new brewery in Myanmar, and Liz Claiborne stopped sourcing from there.

The mining and raw material extractive industries have attracted particular attention in recent years. The extraction sites are often in politically or socially unstable countries facing armed conflicts, so the multinational companies hire local military forces to protect their assets. Not infrequently, these forces are ill-trained and poorly led and therefore prone to committing grave human rights violations. The violators may go unpunished by the host nation either because the government is incapable of taking appropriate steps or because it benefits from (or perhaps even supports) the atrocities in question. Here, CSR efforts directed at the parent company or headquarters may have a positive effect.

Increasingly there has been recognition that compliance by private entities with international human rights (and international law more broadly) can contribute to economic and social well-being. *See, e.g.*, Stewart, Keynote: "What Does International Law Have To Do With International Development," 42 Denv. J. Int'l L. & Pol'y 321 (2014).

§ 7–8. INTERNATIONAL STANDARDS AND CODES OF CONDUCT

On a broader basis, the adoption of international standards and voluntary codes of conduct can be an effective means for encouraging companies to incorporate human rights principles into their business operations. Such instruments can be formulated by the corporations themselves, articulated by NGO's or other entities such as trade associations, or by international bodies. Adherence can help guide a company's activities and provide strong reputational benefits even if no compulsory external monitoring and enforcement mechanisms are established. Some of the most notable examples have come from attempts by coalitions in the apparel, textile, and footwear sectors to govern labor practices. *See generally* Hellen Keller, *Corporate Codes of Conduct and their Implementation: The Question of Legitimacy* (2006).

Sets of relevant principles have been adopted by human rights bodies, trade associations, and economic organizations. In 2011, the UN Human Rights Council endorsed the United Nations Guiding Principles on Business and Human Rights, which were developed by John Ruggie, the Special Representative of the Secretary General on the issue of human rights and transnational corporations. The first formal set of guidelines endorsed by the UN, the Principles speak broadly to the role human rights should play in business. They address the obligations of business entities as well as states, providing for example that "[b]usiness enterprises should respect human rights. This means that they should avoid infringing on the human rights of others and should address adverse human rights impacts with which they are involved." (Principle 11.) They also encourage the establishment of various dispute (grievance) resolution mechanisms. Although nonbinding, the Guiding Principles have made a very useful contribution to the progress of corporate social responsibility.

See generally Guiding Principles on Business and Human Rights: Implementing the United Nations "Protect, Respect, and Remedy" Framework, UNHCR HR/PUB/11/04 (2011) at http://www.ohchr.org/Documents/Publications/GuidingPrinciplesBusiness HR_EN.pdf; Lucy Amis, *A Guide for Business: How to Develop a Human Rights Policy* (2011), at http://www.ohchr.org/Documents/Publications/DevelopHu manRightsPolicy_en.pdf; and *The Corporate Responsibility to Respect Human Rights: An Interpretive Guide*, Office of the United Nations High Commissioner for Human Rights (2012), *at* http://www.ohchr.org/Documents/Publications/HR.PUB.12 .2_En.pdf. *See also* Backer, "Moving Forward the UN Guiding Principles for Business and Human Rights: Between Enterprise Social Norm, State Domestic Legal Orders, and the Treaty Law that Might Bind Them All," 38 Fordham Int'l L.J. 457 (2015).

The Organization for Economic Co-operation and Development (OECD) adopted Guidelines for Multinational Enterprises, amended in 2011, as non-binding recommendations by states to corporations. These guidelines explicitly incorporate the UN Guiding Principles' "protect, respect, and remedy" framework. Specifically they call upon "enterprises" to "contribute to economic, environmental and social progress with a view to achieving sustainable development" and "respect the internationally recognized human rights of those affected by their activities." (II(a)(1) and (2)). While also non-binding, they do provide for non-judicial review of businesses that have failed to abide by the guidelines. Each OECD Member State must appoint a National Contact Point to hear grievances from any interested party, including individuals and NGOs. If the business is found to be in non-compliance, it will not face sanctions or other formal punishment, but it risks damaging its reputation, largely because the cases are made public. *See* http://www.oecd.org/daf/inv/mne/48004323.pdf.

In the same vein, the Ten Principles adopted by the United Nations Global Compact (a voluntary initiative based on corporate commitments to implement the UN's 2015 Sustainable Development Goals) call upon businesses to support and respect internationally proclaimed human rights and to "make sure" that they are not complicit in human rights abuses. (Principles 1 and 2). The Principles are derived from the Universal Declaration on Human Rights, the International Labour Organization's Declaration on Fundamental Principles and Rights at Work, the Rio Declaration on Environment and Development, and the United Nations Convention Against Corruption. If a corporation fails to abide by these ideals and fails to address the violations, it may be removed from the public list of business participants associated with the compact. *See* https://www.unglobalcompact.org and King, "The UN Global Compact: Responsibility for Human Rights, Labor Relations and the Environment in Developing Nations," 34 Cornell Int'l L.J. 481 (2001).

The Voluntary Principles on Security and Human Rights is an initiative begun in 2000 by NGOs, corporations and governments to address the problems that are especially prevalent when companies in the extractive sector employ security forces to protect their assets. The principles are designed to guide companies in maintaining the safety and security of their operations within an operating framework that encourages respect for human rights. Unlike some other multi-stakeholder approaches, these principles put forth concrete guidelines instead of generalized recommendations, although they lack a reliable enforcement mechanism. *See generally* http://www.voluntary principles.org.

In some cases, investors have also become involved in trying to motivate corporations to uphold human rights. For example, Dreyfus' Third Century Fund and Merrill Lynch's Ecological Trust are ethical-investment mutual funds available for consumers interested in only supporting companies with strong human rights records. Moreover, a growing number of ethical consulting firms have been established to counsel companies on how to avoid human rights violations. In some instances, institutional investors have pulled out of countries or companies they felt were non-compliant with human rights principles. *See generally* Weissbrodt, "Human Rights Standards Concerning Transnational Corporations and Other Business Entities," 23 Minn. J. Int'l L. 135 (2014).

§ 7–9. HUMAN RIGHTS LITIGATION AGAINST CORPORATIONS

For a number of years, the Alien Tort Statute [§ 6.13 *supra*] provided one of the main legal paths for challenging corporate activities abroad on human rights grounds. Many suits were brought in an effort to subject private corporate defendants to liability for their own actions or their alleged collusion or complicity in human rights abuses committed by foreign governments and officials. Because the statute does not specify who or what can be a defendant, the question arose whether it could support litigation against corporate entities. A number of decisions answered that question in the affirmative. *See, e.g.,* Doe I v. UNOCAL Corp., 395 F.3d 932 (9th Cir. 2002); Aldana v. Del Monte Fresh Produce, NA, Inc., 416 F3d 1242 (11th Cir. 2005); Romero v. Drummond Co., Inc., 552 F.3d 1301 (11th Cir. 2008); Sinaltrainal v. Coca-Cola Co., 578 F.3d. 125 (11th Cir. 2009). *See also* Doe I v. Nestlé USA, Inc., 766 F.3d 1013 (9th Cir. 2014).

In Kiobel v. Royal Dutch Petroleum Co., 621 F.3d 111 (2d Cir. 2010) ("Kiobel I"), however, the Second Circuit held that the ATS does not provide subject-matter jurisdiction over ATS cases against corporate defendants. Liability under the statute, it said, rests on customary international law, but corporate liability for violations of international law is not an established rule of customary international law. "[T]he principle of individual liability for violations of international law has been limited to natural persons" and international law "has steadfastly rejected the notion of corporate liability for international crimes, and no international tribunal has ever held a corporation liable for a violation of the law of nations." *Id.* at 119, 120. The U.S. Supreme Court granted certiorari on this issue, 565 U.S. 961, 132 S.Ct. 472, 181 L.Ed.2d 292 (2011), but subsequently revised its grant to focus on the issue of extraterritoriality, 565 U.S. 1244, 132 S.Ct. 1738, 182 L.Ed.2d 270 (2012). Its 2013 decision addressed only the latter issue, leaving open the issue of corporate liability. *See* Kiobel v. Royal Dutch Petroleum Co., ___U.S. ___, 133 S.Ct. 1659 (2013) ("Kiobel II").

The Second Circuit's decision in Kiobel I remains the only circuit decision denying corporate liability for the ATS. Given the Supreme Court's decision on the non-extraterritorial application of the statue in Kiobel II, plaintiffs may have a difficult time setting forth an appropriate claim against multinational corporations for human rights violations taking place abroad. *See, e.g.,* Licci by Licci v. Lebanese Canadian Bank, SAL, 834 F.3d 201 (2d Cir. 2016).

However, the U.S. Supreme Court recently granted certiorari in Jesner v. Arab Bank, PLC, 808 F.3d 144 (2d Cir. 2015), which had reaffirmed Kiobel I as the law of the circuit. *See* 137 S.Ct. 1432 (Apr. 3, 2017). The cases poses the question directly: whether the Alien Tort Statute categorically forecloses corporate liability. A decision is unlikely before early 2018.

Both businesses and human rights groups have major qualms about the ATS, for differing reasons. Businesses argue that the ATS imposes unpredictable liability on them that could deter them from investing abroad. Some human rights groups have also argued against ATS because it is not an efficient or effective manner in which to prosecute businesses; courts often dismiss these cases on political question, comity, or act-of-state grounds, never discussing the merits of the claims. Even when a decision on the merits is favorable to the claimants, collecting the judgment can be problematic. Despite its shortcomings, the ATS at least provides an opportunity to bring the corporations into court and gain media attention.

On the ATS liability of corporate actors, *see* Koh, "Separating Myth from Reality About Corporate Responsibility Litigation," 7 J. Int'l Econ. L 263 (2004); Keitner, "Conceptualizing Complicity in Alien Tort Cases," 60 Hastings L. J. 61 (2008); Cassel, "Corporate Aiding and Abetting of Human Rights Violations: Confusion in the Courts," 6 Nw. U. J. Int'l Hum Rts. 304 (2008); Nemeroff, "Untying the Khulumani Knot: Corporate Aiding and Abetting Liability Under The Alien Tort Claims Act after Sosa," 40 Colum. Hum. Rts. L. Rev. 231 (2008); Hutchens, "International Law in the American Courts—Khulumani v. Barclay National Bank LTD, The Decision Heard 'Round the Corporate World," 9 German L. J. 639 (2008); Magraw, "Universally Liable? Corporate Complicity Under the Principle of Universal Jurisdiction," 18 Minn. J. Int'l L. 458 (2009); Paust, "Kiobel, Corporate Liability, and the Extraterritorial Reach of the ATS," 53 Va. J. Int'l L. Dig. 18 (2012); Sung Je Lee, "The History of the Rise of the Alien Tort Statute and the Future Implications of Kiobel v. Royal Dutch Shell," 17 Scholar 305 (2015).

While to date no other country has enacted a statute identical to the ATS, it is nonetheless possible to pursue litigation against corporate human rights violators in foreign courts on other jurisdictional and substantive bases, such as ordinary tort suits. Some countries have enacted legislation aimed at curbing corporate involvement in or liability for human rights abuses, especially within their own territories.

IV. OTHER ENTITIES

§ 7–10. FINANCIAL INSTITUTIONS

Even more recently, attention has focused on the responsibilities of financial institutions for respecting and advancing international human rights. This attention has been manifested in several ways. For example, in 2007, the United Nations Environment Program Finance Initiative released the Human Rights Guidance Tool for the Financial Sector (available at http://unepfi.org/humanrights toolkit/). Last updated in 2014, the Guidance Tool focuses on "human rights issues relevant to the assessment of business relationships and transactions" and aims at helping finance sector professionals to identify potential human rights risk in lending operations, assess the materiality of the human right risk, and identify possible risk-mitigating factors. It is based on the proposition that human rights are important in relation to all financial sector activity. *See also* the Initiative's publication on Banks and Human Rights, A Legal Analysis (2015), at http://www.unepfi.org/fileadmin/documents/BanksandHumanRights.pdf.

The UN's Guiding Principles on Business and Human Rights (§ 7–8 *supra*), also apply to financial institutions. Because of the financial sector's role in projects, many of the human rights violations with which they are associated are not a direct result of their actions but are instead caused by actions of their business partners. The banks typically do not have control over the offending company and thus may be unable to resolve the issue themselves. However, depending on the amount of leverage the bank has in the business relationship, it might be able to persuade the company to change its practices. A lack of leverage or a business partner's refusal to abide by human rights norms does not, however, obviate any of the financial institution's responsibility to identify, prevent, or mitigate any human rights violations.

In 2013, seven European banks comprising the Thun Group of Banks released a paper discussing the impact of the UN Guiding Principles on large banks. The paper emphasized the importance of upholding human rights norms, noting that this responsibility should lie within the banks at all levels and across all disciplines. In order to accomplish that goal, it recommended that banks develop broader risk management models that allow the banks to identify and address their potential human rights issues. *See* "The UN Guiding Principles on Business and Human Rights: Discussion Paper for Banks," at https://www.

credit-suisse.com/media/assets/corporate/docs/about-us
/responsibility/banking/thun-group-discussion-paper.
pdf.

The OECD Guidelines for Multinational
Enterprises (§ 7–8 *supra*) were expanded in 2011 to
cover activities that occur within the bank's "value
chain" must follow the guidelines. The OECD has
also endeavored to address human rights issues
associated with export credit agencies engaged in
both private and public financing through an OECD
Council recommendation. The Common Approaches
put forth a universal method for completing due
diligence sufficient to identify the negative impacts of
supported export credits. In particular, the OECD
called for export credit agencies to pay special
attention to the human rights implications of their
projects or operations.

In 2012, the International Finance Corporation
(IFC), a member of the World Bank Group, updated
its Environmental and Social Performance
Standards, which provide guidance primarily
intended for the institution's project financing,
bridge loans, and advisory services. These standards
are enforceable when they are incorporated into a
loan agreement, thereby giving leverage over an
offending party to improve its human rights impact
or risk violating the legal agreement. They highlight
the responsibility of business to protect individuals'
human rights and the IFC's interest in engaging in
sustainable business. For additional information, *see*
https://www.ifc.org/wps/wcm/connect/c8f524004a73d

aeca09afdf998895a12/IFC_Performance_Standards.
pdf?MOD=AJPERES.

The 2003 Equator Principles provide a risk
management framework, adopted by financial
institutions, for determining, assessing and
managing environmental and social risk in projects.
They were drafted by a group of banks to apply to
project finance, project finance advisory services,
project-related corporate loans, and bridge loans.
Using the IFC Performance Standards as the
minimum benchmark, these Principles require banks
and their clients to perform sufficient human rights
due diligence, especially when the project involves
high-risk circumstances. Some 82 large financial
institutions in over 35 countries (conducting around
70% of the international project finance in emerging
markets) have adopted the Principles. *See* http://
www.equator-principles.com/index.php/about-ep.

Banks and other financial institutions may also be
subject to human rights scrutiny on other bases. For
example, anti-money laundering laws prohibit
financial institutions from processing funds that
have ties to criminal activity, including those from
rogue governments or armed insurgencies. By
depriving the perpetrators of their ability to take
advantage of the banking system, these laws serve to
reduce the ability of human rights abusers used to
store and grow their illicit financial assets.

Sanctions (whether imposed under international
or domestic authority) may provide additional tools
for curbing human rights abuses. Different types of
sanctions exist. The most restrictive forbid all

transactions with an offending country; others may be selectively targeted at individuals or entities. Sanctions may forbid banks from accepting money or engaging in any sort of business transaction with states, companies, or individuals, engaged in human rights violations. As the use of sanctions increases, financial institutions are likely to be held for violations in a variety of contexts. Consider, for instance, the challenge brought against Riggs Bank in Spain for having allegedly transferred over $8,000,000 of former Chilean President Augusto Pinochet's frozen assets, thereby contributing to his reign of terror. The Bank eventually entered into a settlement agreement with the plaintiffs for its role in facilitating Pinochet's abusive regime.

Similarly, a number of cases are currently pending in Argentina against the country's military junta for their alleged complicity in human rights violations that spanned over a decade. Included as defendants are a number of banks that provided the junta with loans that acted as a lifeline throughout the years. In mid-2013, the Administrative Court ruled that non-Argentinian banks could be brought under the courts' jurisdiction if the banks' complicity contributed to human rights violations.

INDEX

References are to Pages

WOMEN'S RIGHTS
Commission on the Status of Women, this index
Elimination of Discrimination Against Women, this index
Trafficking, this index

WORLD HEALTH ORGANIZATION
Human rights work, 173

YUGOSLAVIA
UN creation of *ad hoc* international tribunal, 6, 22